Praise for *One Mighty and Irre*

One of *Time*'s 100 Must-Read Books of 2020

One of *The Washington Post*'s 50 Notable Works of Nonfiction in 2020

One of *Smithsonian* magazine's Ten Best History Books of 2020

—

"[Jia Lynn] Yang sketches lively portraits of the famous and obscure players behind the legislative fights. . . . [Her] voyage across early-20th-century U.S. immigration debates makes palpable how much diplomacy and perseverance are required to win legislative change."   —Laura Wides-Muñoz, *The Washington Post*

"An effort to understand precisely what kind of nation of immigrants we are and how we arrived at this moment in our history. . . . Admirably thorough."   —Philip Terzian, *The Wall Street Journal*

"Powerful, riveting, and beautifully written, this book tells the story of how the most significant immigration laws in the twentieth century came to pass in the United States. From Takao Ozawa's heartbreaking bid to become a citizen to our nation's rejection of Jewish refugees of World War II, Jia Lynn Yang exposes the myth that ours is a nation that has consistently welcomed immigrants. With force and imagination she transports us to the halls of Congress and the White House and shepherds us through four decades of political conflict. This book could not be more timely: In a divisive moment where the place of immigrants in America is bitterly debated, we need this book more than ever. It is essential reading for anyone who wants to understand how politics has shaped, and can shape, the lives of immigrants in the United States."
                        —Michelle Kuo, author of *Reading with Patrick: A Teacher, a Student, and a Life-Changing Friendship*

ONE

MIGHTY

AND

IRRESISTIBLE

TIDE

*The Epic Struggle Over
American Immigration, 1924–1965*

JIA LYNN YANG

W. W. NORTON & COMPANY
Independent Publishers Since 1923

For information about permission to reproduce selections from this book, write to
Permissions, W. W. Norton & Company, Inc., 500 Fifth Avenue, New York, NY 10110

For information about special discounts for bulk purchases, please contact
W. W. Norton Special Sales at specialsales@wwnorton.com or 800-233-4830

Manufacturing by LSC Communications, Harrisonburg
Book design by Marysarah Quinn
Production manager: Anna Oler

Library of Congress Cataloging-in-Publication Data

Names: Yang, Jia Lynn, author.
Title: One mighty and irresistible tide : the epic struggle over American immigration, 1924–1965
/ Jia Lynn Yang.
Description: First edition. | New York, NY : W. W. Norton & Company, [2020] | Includes
bibliographical references and index.
Identifiers: LCCN 2019050475 | ISBN 9780393635843 (hardcover) | ISBN 9780393635850 (epub)
Subjects: LCSH: Emigration and immigration law—United States—History—20th century.
| Immigrants—United States—History—20th century. | United States—Emigration and
immigration—History—20th century.
Classification: LCC JV6455 .Y34 2020 | DDC 325.73—dc23
LC record available at https://lccn.loc.gov/2019050475

ISBN 978-0-393-86752-7 pbk.

W. W. Norton & Company, Inc.
500 Fifth Avenue, New York, N.Y. 10110
www.wwnorton.com

W. W. Norton & Company Ltd.
15 Carlisle Street, London W1D 3BS

1 2 3 4 5 6 7 8 9 0

To my parents,

Ed and Mei-Shin,

for making the journey

We are the heirs of all time, and with all nations we divide our inheritance. On this Western Hemisphere all tribes and people are forming into one federated whole; and there is a future which shall see the estranged children of Adam restored as to the old hearthstone in Eden. . . . The seed is sown, and the harvest must come.

—Herman Melville,
Redburn (1849)

CONTENTS

Prologue 1

ONE: "God's Crucible" 7

TWO: Slamming the Door 33

THREE: A "Tragic Bottleneck" 62

FOUR: "A Land of Great Responsibilities" 90

FIVE: A Son of Nevada 115

SIX: Internal Security 142

SEVEN: An Irish Brahmin 176

EIGHT: A Bold Proposal 203

NINE: A Martyr's Cause 230

Epilogue 261

Acknowledgments 273

Notes 277

Bibliography 301

Index 309

ONE MIGHTY AND IRRESISTIBLE TIDE

PROLOGUE

O N NOVEMBER 12, 1954, Edward J. Shaughnessy took one last
look around the island that had become his home. A diligent,
broad-shouldered man, Shaughnessy had spent decades working his way
up the ranks of the country's federal immigration service, from lowly
stenographer to the man in charge of running the famed Ellis Island.
So dedicated to the job that he had lived on the island for the last three
years, Shaughnessy felt a pang of guilt leaving it all behind and in such
a sorry state.

This dollop of land in New York Harbor had once been a mighty gate-
way to the New World. More than 20 million immigrants had passed
through Ellis Island, each embarking on a new life carrying unknown
promise, joy, and sorrow. But now the site of their baptism into the
American dream was shutting down. At ten-fifteen that morning, officials had processed the last foreigner: Arne Peterssen, a Norwegian sea-
man who had overstayed his shore leave and had been briefly detained on
the island. Next, officials planned to move furniture and equipment to an
immigration office on Columbus Avenue in Manhattan. The rest of the
twenty-seven-acre complex would be abandoned. "Business is closed,"
Shaughnessy declared.

The news hardly registered with the public. Only the *New York Times* editorial board paused to eulogize: "If all the stories of all the people who stopped briefly or for a longer time on Ellis Island could be written down they would be the human story of perhaps the greatest migration in history. . . . Perhaps some day a monument to them will go up on Ellis Island. The memory of this episode in our national history should never be allowed to fade."

The idea of the United States as a nation of immigrants is today so pervasive, and seems so foundational, that it can be hard to believe Americans ever thought otherwise. But deep into the twentieth century, the country's immigrant past had become a hazy memory, widely regarded as a strange blip of history never to be repeated. The year after Ellis Island closed, historian John Higham concluded that the mass immigration "that had formed one of the most fundamental social forces in American history had been brought to an end. The old belief in America as a promised land for all who yearn for freedom had lost its operative significance." The *Atlantic Monthly*, one of the country's premier publications, did not run a single article about immigration between 1925 and 1953. The issue had fallen so far off the radar that when Senator Herbert Lehman of New York told listeners in a 1952 radio address that he wanted to discuss an important subject with them, he prepared them gently: "Some members of this radio audience may be surprised to hear that immigration is an issue. But it is."

The country did not regard immigration as worthy of discussion because, quite simply, there were not many immigrants. A 1924 law passed by Congress had instituted a system of ethnic quotas so stringent that large-scale immigration was choked off for decades. The quotas aimed to limit not only the volume of people entering the country but the type. In order to keep America white, Anglo-Saxon, and Protestant, the laws sharply curtailed immigration from southern and eastern Europe and outright banned people from nearly all of Asia. More immigrants entered the country in the first decade of the twentieth century than between 1931 and 1971. By the time Ellis Island closed, the share of foreign-born immigrants had dropped into the single digits and kept falling for years as older immigrants passed away. This was exactly as the writers of the 1924 law had intended. As David A. Reed, one of the bill's sponsors, crowed just before its passage:

> The new immigration legislation marks a complete reversal of our previous policy—a landmark in our national history. We no longer are to be a haven, a refuge for oppressed the whole world over. We found we could not be, and now we definitely abandon that theory. America will cease to be the "melting pot."

That would have been the end of the story, except that for the next forty years a small number of lawmakers, activists, and presidents worked relentlessly to abolish the 1924 law and its quotas. Their efforts established the new mythology of the United States as "a nation of immigrants" that is so familiar to all of us now. Through a world war, a global refugee crisis, and a McCarthyist fever that swept the country, these Americans never stopped trying to restore the United States as a country that lived up to its vision as a home for the "huddled masses" from Emma Lazarus's famous poem. Their effort culminated in 1965, when President Lyndon Johnson signed into law a bill that abolished the quotas and banned discrimination against immigrants based on race or ethnicity. It also decreed that preference be given to immigrants who were reuniting with family members, as well as those with special skills in the arts and sciences.

Not many Americans today know about the 1965 Immigration and Nationality Act, but it was one of the most transformative laws in our nation's history. By ending a system of racial preferences among immigrants, the law reversed a decades-long decline in immigration levels and opened the door to Asian, Latin American, African, and Middle Eastern immigration at a scale never seen before—changes that are so evident now that they seem to have been inevitable. But while the architects of the 1965 law imagined themselves to be restoring a lapsed ideal, they were in fact doing something unprecedented. For most of this country's past, it had been firmly established that being an American was inextricably tied to European ancestry. The Immigration and Nationality Act obliterated that notion by daring to outline a vision of belonging that transcended race and ethnic origin, in effect saying to the rest of the world, especially the wide world outside Europe, that all peoples were eligible for the American project.

To the extent that the law's significance has been discussed at all in recent years, it is typically treated as a footnote to the landmark civil rights legislation of the same era, and assumed to have been swept into existence by the undertow of the fight for black equality. While the civil rights movement did popularize a moral framework and contribute political momentum for the law, the Immigration and Nationality Act was the culmination of a distinct, decades-long struggle with its own set of players: the descendants of Jewish, Irish Catholic, and Asian immigrants who saw the country's immigration system as a painful symbol of nativist prejudice. Some of the key figures remain household names. John F. Kennedy and his brothers Ted and Bobby became champions for immigration reform as they tried to win over white ethnic voters. Others were once-powerful lawmakers whose names have faded from public consciousness—fierce liberals including Emanuel Celler and Herbert Lehman, who were descended from German Jews. Still others were never well known outside a community of immigration activists, including Japanese-Americans whose families suffered in shameful internment camps during World War II. Together this coalition of the powerful and the powerless battled to codify the idea that a person could become wholly American, no matter where she had been born.

But as with any law of this magnitude, the people who fought for it could hardly have anticipated the changes it would eventually bring about. Because the law capped immigration from other parts of the Western Hemisphere for the first time, border crossings from Mexico that had been routine for decades became illegal overnight. And despite the lofty principles voiced by its enthusiasts, advocates for the 1965 law would hardly believe that their work would set in motion demographic changes that are now expected to result in nonwhite Americans outnumbering white Americans within a few decades.

—

MY FAMILY was among the many beneficiaries of the 1965 Immigration and Nationality Act. To this day, my mother, who was born in Taiwan, still has a letter from the Justice Department, dated September 3, 1976, approving her petition to qualify for "third preference" under section 203(a)—meaning her science background as a microbiologist counted as a special skill that would increase her chances for a permanent residency visa. My father, who was born in Shanghai, was able to stay in the United States after graduate school through the law's family reunification preference. Similar stories abound in the rest of my family, explaining the presence of my aunts, uncles, and cousins.

Led to believe that the United States had always welcomed immigrants like my parents, I lacked the imagination for most of my life to envision a different America in which my family had been turned away. There was no point in pondering alternatives; a great blessing had been granted, and our central task was to fit in.

One way to do so has been to devour stories about this country's past. But immigration has a way of dislocating history. The story from the land left behind seems forever cut off at the point of departure, but the adopted homeland offers no easy path, either, forcing immigrants and their children to graft their dreams onto the lives of others. I often wonder which strands of the past I have inherited—whose history I can claim or am burdened by. What is my connection to the Chinese Communist Party's decades of brutal political suppression, given that all four of my grandparents left China just as Mao Zedong was coming to power? As an American born in Virginia who is neither black nor white, what is my relationship to the legacies of slavery, Jim Crow, and the civil rights movement?

This book is my attempt to fuse my family's history to the history of the country that found a place for us. I have long been told the story of why we left China and Taiwan. Less familiar to me has been why we were allowed to come to the United States at all. I feel duty bound to name and understand those who fought to allow my family into this country in the 1970s, when so many others have been denied, then and now.

I would argue that the story of these political reformers is one of the best ways to understand how the United States tried to establish its national identity in the twentieth century as it wrestled with questions that still dog us today: Is our Americanness based on being a member of a certain race, or does it entail a set of values that transcend our ethnic origins? To what extent is our democracy bound by moral obligations to people beyond U.S. borders? What does it mean to assimilate and become an American citizen?

We tend to describe immigrants' stories as feats of will and strokes of destiny: the Irish who risked it all to escape the potato famine, the Cubans who fled Castro on makeshift rafts. But in the last century, as our government has erected an increasingly elaborate system for weeding out the wanted from the unwanted, the fate of a family often rests on the minutiae of laws written in Washington. It is not destiny that brings a family here but politics.

"GOD'S CRUCIBLE"

I T WAS A MOMENT of crisis in this new land, so they had come to the place that felt most like home. On March 2, 1924, thirty minutes before the appointed hour of three p.m., more than one thousand people were already crammed into the assembly hall of the Brooklyn Jewish Center. The crowd was so large, it flowed through the corridor and out the front doors of the imposing white stone building onto the sidewalks of Eastern Parkway, the grandest boulevard not only in Brooklyn but in all of America.

The center, just one year old, had quickly become the heart of Jewish life in Brooklyn and a draw for Jewish residents from miles around. The neighborhood of Brownsville, just to the east, had grown so Jewish that it was beginning to earn the nickname the "Jerusalem of America." Many had recently moved to Brooklyn from the Lower East Side, crossing the river in search of more space after the construction of the Manhattan and Williamsburg bridges. Others were new arrivals from eastern Europe, people who had landed in Brooklyn straight from Ellis Island as part of the biggest influx of immigrants the country had seen since its founding.

Between 1905 and 1914, nearly 10 million immigrants had entered the country, more than any ten-year stretch before. The deluge had paused during World War I, but then quickly picked up again. By 1921, so many ships were arriving at Ellis Island that officials diverted some to Boston to handle the load. More noticeable than their numbers, though, was the appearance of these "new immigrants," as some called them disdainfully. They looked different from the Germans, Scandinavians, British, and Irish who had come before. These more recent arrivals spoke Italian, Yiddish, Polish, and Russian. And unlike earlier immigrants, they were more likely to settle in cities to find work rather than head to rural parts of the country to tend farms.

In Europe, Jews had become used to being pushed to the margins, often unable to participate in mainstream cultural and political life. In times of upheaval, the simple fact of being Jewish could cost them their lives. But when they arrived in the United States at the turn of the twentieth century, they found a place where they could carve out a more fluid identity. With no church or royal family dictating that they didn't belong, American Jews had embraced their new homeland as a place for reinvention and refuge.

But now all that was in jeopardy.

Word had spread to Brooklyn that lawmakers in Washington were considering a bill that would cut off the flow of immigrants from southern and eastern Europe. The legislation would effectively erect a wall between Europe and America, where none had existed before; and it symbolized the growing power of a dark force spreading across the country.

The Ku Klux Klan, its iconography dormant for more than a quarter century, was again on the rise, this time with a virulent anti-immigrant core and millions of members gathering not in the shadows but in broad daylight, marching down city streets. *The Saturday Evening Post*, one of the most widely circulated publications in the country, ran regular articles warning middle-class American readers that the new immigrants were racially inferior, impossible to assimilate, and a threat to stability and democracy itself. "An ostrich could assimilate a croquet ball or a cobble stone with about the ease that America assimilated her newcomers from Central and Southeastern Europe," warned journalist Kenneth Roberts in his book *Why Europe Leaves Home*, a compilation of his pieces in the *Post*.

It was one thing for these ideas to be discussed in the pages of books and magazines. It was another for policy makers to adopt them and translate them into legislation on a national level. And so a deep fear had moved immigrants and their children to gather in the Brooklyn Jewish Center that chilly Sunday afternoon. What if, after all the trouble of reaching America, finding work, raising families, and trying to fit in, they had adopted a country that did not really want them?

When Fiorello H. La Guardia strode to the front of the room, he was difficult to see. Just five-foot-two, the Republican congressman, nicknamed "Little Flower," was a fearless politician representing East Harlem who would go on to be elected mayor of New York three times in a row. La Guardia identified with immigrants. His own parents were from Italy (his mother was also Jewish), and during law school, he had earned extra money working as a translator at Ellis Island, using his knowledge of Italian, German, Yiddish, French, and several Croatian dialects.

"It is proper that you are here to protest against a measure that if it came up in Congress tomorrow would pass by an overwhelming vote," said La Guardia in his high-pitched voice, gesturing dramatically with his hands. "The mathematics of the bill disclose the intentional discrimination against the Jews and the Italians." La Guardia explained to the crowd that Congress was considering new quotas designed to keep out people who prayed and dressed like them. Up until then, there had been no numerical caps on who could enter the country. The proposed limits would be calculated based on the number of foreign-born Americans in 1890: only 2 percent from each nationality present that year would now be allowed to enter annually. Jewish immigration was projected to drop from about 80,000 per year to less than 4,000, La Guardia warned. Italian immigration would plummet from 45,000 to 3,000. The year 1890 had been chosen carefully, since it predated the recent wave of immigrants from southern and eastern Europe.

After La Guardia finished, another local lawmaker rose to address the crowd. Blue-eyed and already balding rapidly at thirty-five, Emanuel Celler, or Mannie, as he was known, had grown up just north of the Jewish Center in a modest frame house. Being back home in Brooklyn that weekend was a welcome relief from his new life in Washington, where he had spent the last year as a miserable freshman in the House of Representatives. He missed his family. Soon after his election, he and his wife Stella received the painful news that their baby daughter Judy had been diagnosed with cerebral palsy. While Stella stayed in Brooklyn, Celler's new job in Washington gave him little solace. "A freshman congressman is a lost soul. He cannot find his way, literally and metaphorically," Celler remembered years later. "He has to learn his way about on the floor of the House and in committee. He doesn't know the rules and nobody bothers explaining them. Only back home among his friends and his visitors is he flattered by the sound of 'Mr. Congressman.'"

It was a humble beginning for a man who would go on to become one of the most effective and accomplished liberal lawmakers in the history of Congress, serving his district for nearly fifty years, the fifth-longest stretch ever in the House of Representatives. His uncompromising values, his long tenure—which began with President Warren G. Harding and ended with President Richard Nixon—and his position as chairman of the House Judiciary Committee from 1949 to 1973, with only one short break, would produce a stunning portfolio of transformative legislation, including the Civil Rights Act of 1964, the Voting Rights Act of 1965, and the Twenty-Fifth Amendment to the Constitution, which established an orderly succession process should the president die or become ill.

But the issue that Celler held closest to his heart was immigration. At the Brooklyn Jewish Center, he railed against a much more powerful man. Labor Secretary James J. Davis, a Welsh immigrant who had risen from total poverty to serve in three consecutive presidential cabinets, had turned into a prominent opponent of immigration. In response to the

labor secretary's argument that newer immigrants had lower rates of naturalization, Celler pointed out that English immigrants on average took
longer to apply for citizenship. Accusing the labor secretary of promoting
anti-immigrant propaganda, Celler called Davis "the stumbling block in
our path for immigration progress."

As the meeting drew to a close, four hours after it began, those in
the room agreed to a resolution condemning the immigration bill. They
vowed to deliver their message personally to President Coolidge and both
houses of Congress.

It was not until reading the next day's copy of *The Brooklyn Eagle* that
those who attended the protest would realize: while they were inside,
another two thousand people had tried to join them. All were turned
away for lack of space.

—

CELLER AND HIS PARENTS had been born in the United States, but he
never forgot that the same was not true for his grandparents. According
to a favorite family story, his mother's parents met in New York Harbor, just as they were arriving by ship from Germany, part of a wave of
immigrants driven away by the failed revolutions of 1848. As the vessel
approached the city, it sank, sending Celler's grandmother into the water.
Another passenger jumped in to save her. It was the man who would
become her husband, Celler's grandfather.

The Cellers did not rise to nearly the same social heights as some other
German Jewish families in New York—families like the Loebs or the
Lehmans, who within a generation established themselves in the American elite. But they were better off than many of their Jewish neighbors
who had arrived after them from eastern Europe. These Jews were often
looked down upon by their more acculturated German cousins (so much
so that some scholars believe the slur "kikes" was most likely coined by
German Jews mocking the names of the newer immigrants). Growing

up in Brooklyn, Mannie himself never felt superior to the more recent immigrants, who were his neighbors and whose children often looked up to him since he was born in America.

Mannie could not speak the language of his grandparents, though he absorbed the rhythms of their religion. Every Friday the family ate Sabbath dinner together and sang music, with Mannie's father Henry playing the piano and Mannie on the fiddle. During the High Holy Days of Rosh Hashanah and Yom Kippur, the family went to a nearby synagogue. Mannie, his siblings, and his parents occupied two stories above his father's business, purifying whiskey through a process known as rectification. The income was enough that the Cellers owned their house. Still, they were not so wealthy that Mannie's mother Josephine felt comfortable allowing two rooms to sit empty and not collect rent. Henry and Josephine poured their hopes into their third child, Mannie, the most studious of their four children—leading Mannie to later wonder whether his two sisters and his brother ever resented him.

When Mannie was attending college at Columbia University, the family's fortunes turned: Henry lost money in bad investments and loans to friends that were never paid back. Soon after, both his parents died, and Mannie became the head of the Celler household. On Saturdays, he worked for a local haberdashery. On weeknights, he delivered wine in his old neighborhood in Brooklyn, even taking some Italian classes to more easily chat with immigrant customers. Then he would stay up late studying for school. Celler dutifully fulfilled his mother's dream that he become a lawyer, graduating from Columbia Law School in 1912.

He was practicing law and happily married to his high-school sweetheart, Stella, raising a five-year-old daughter, Jane, when he decided to run for Congress almost on a whim. Though his father had dabbled in Democratic Party politics in Brooklyn, making the occasional speech at a club meeting, and Celler even remembered his father once hoisting him on his shoulders to watch the fiery politician William Jennings Bryan speak in a crowded auditorium, politics weren't an obvious venue for Celler's talents. He was shy like his mother, and never made friends as easily as his father. But at thirty-four, with a successful law practice already under his belt, Celler felt it was time for something more—something that would prove his parents' instincts right that their brightest child was meant for bigger things.

In 1922 no one expected a Democrat running for office in Brooklyn to win. The tenth congressional district, where Celler decided to run, had never before elected a Democrat. Indeed, any Democrat would need to get creative to attract voters in Brooklyn. Dr. William L. Love, another Democratic candidate on the ticket in Brooklyn that year, became known as "the minstrel campaigner" because he sang songs rather than giving campaign speeches. Celler's primary pitch to voters was that he opposed the Volstead Act, the 1919 law banning alcohol. This was an especially popular stance with immigrants who not only enjoyed their wine and beer but resented the constant presence of police in their communities cracking down on alcohol sales and consumption. Early in Celler's campaign he showed off a brash banner illustrated with a giant foaming glass of beer, which read, "Eventually, why not now?" *The Brooklyn Daily Eagle* noted that the "daring" signage won him "both praise and condemnation." Celler canvassed his neighborhood for votes, just like his old wine-selling days, traveling around in the back of a pickup truck, occasionally setting off fireworks. When crowds arrived, "you'd get up and harangue them," he recalled. On November 7, 1922, Celler won his race by 3,111 votes. Immigrant voters were the core of Celler's support, and he would never forget it. Soon after the election, when asked by a reporter to identify his district, Celler, sitting in his office, gestured to a colorful map of Europe hanging on the wall behind him and said, "There's my district—all of Europe."

He made a habit of keeping the front door of his house in Brooklyn open every Sunday so that people could walk in and tell him their troubles. Now, a year into his term, the people of that district were asking for his help.

—

TWO WEEKS BEFORE the meeting at the Jewish Center, *The New York Times* had run an extensive survey of the country's last century of immigration penned by Labor Secretary Davis, an enthusiast for fraternal societies and "a most amiable man," remembered Herbert Hoover, the third president who retained him. Hoover commented in his memoir, "If all the members of all the organizations to which he belonged had voted for him, he could have been elected to anything, any time, anywhere."

Like many other Americans, Davis was growing skeptical of immigrants. In the *New York Times* piece, he used dubious data to warn of dire consequences if limits were not imposed. He doubted "whether such vast throngs could be assimilated and Americanized or would eventually submerge and absorb the American people, as the old Roman civilization was completely submerged by the hordes which once migrated into that fair land for peaceful purposes." In response, Celler wrote in a letter to the editor that the figures cited by the labor secretary were "as useless as a candle in a skull."

A certain amount of delusion is demanded for an immigrant to become a leading voice against immigration—a blindness of one's own modest origins. But it can also be born of the grueling experience of arriving in a new country, and a belief that only some can handle the pressure.

A native of Wales, Davis left his hometown when he was eight years old with his mother and five young siblings to join his father, an ironworker, in Pittsburgh. The family was penniless when they arrived. When Davis was eleven, he left school and secured his first regular job, working in a nail factory earning fifty cents a day. His task was to pick out defective nails—work he believed taught him something about human nature. "Men are like nails," he would say later, "some have the hold-fast will in their heads. Others have not. They were marred in the making. They must be thrown aside and not used in building the state, or the state will fall." At twelve, Davis started apprenticing at the local iron mill. He learned to stoke the fires in which the metals were melted down, his palms and fingers scorching from the heat until they became "hardened like goat hoofs" and his skin took on "a coat of tan" that would last his entire life.

"I lusted for labor, I worked and I liked it." Davis took pride in his work ethic, ascribing it to his Welsh roots. He was not as impressed with other immigrants, particularly those who came after him. "I have always been a doer and a builder, it was in my blood and the blood of my tribe, as it is born in the blood of beavers. . . . The people that came to this country in the early days were of the beaver type and they built up America because it was in their nature to build. Then the rat-people began coming here, to house under the roof that others built," Davis would later recall. "A civilization rises when the beaver-men outnumber the rat-men. When the rat-men get the upper hand the civilization falls."

In his twenties, Davis developed a taste for leadership after persuading a group of workers not to strike. Later, he led the Loyal Order of Moose fraternal society as it recruited more than half a million new members and provided a social safety net for its working-class members, supporting widows if their husbands died doing their dangerous jobs, and opening schools for orphans. It was ambitious enough for the newly elected president of the United States to take notice.

Warren G. Harding, who promised in his 1920 campaign a return to "normalcy," wanted a labor secretary who would be more sympathetic to business interests, and in Davis he found one. The Labor Department was still a young institution, having been created in 1913 in the waning hours of William Howard Taft's presidency, just before Woodrow Wilson took office. Organized labor had clamored for decades to have a permanent voice in the government. Under Wilson, the department stayed true to the original vision to improve the welfare of working people, and it played a major role during World War I, mobilizing millions of workers to support the fighting. But under Davis's control, it tamped down its pro-labor zeal, so much so that Calvin Coolidge, who succeeded Harding when he died in 1923, once said that Davis, despite his title, was good at "keeping labor quiet."

As secretary, Davis turned his attention to the lesser-known corners of the department. From the beginning, the Labor Department had been a hodgepodge comprising four bureaus formerly under the short-lived Department of Commerce and Labor: the Bureau of Labor Statistics, which collected economic data; the Children's Bureau, tasked with overseeing the welfare of young people; and the bureaus of Immigration and Naturalization. Immigration was under the department's purview because, historically, the country accepted newcomers primarily to put them to work. With more immigrants pouring into the country after the war, though, Davis felt that more scrutiny should be placed on who was allowed to enter. It was time to separate the "beaver-men" from the "rat-men."

Davis viewed the country's system of immigration as a mess. People were showing up at Ellis Island without passports or visas. Indeed, a worldwide standard for passports was only just emerging as countries tried to regulate their borders more rigorously. "We have let the alien newcomer roam about the country pretty much without guidance," Davis said at an international convention of his beloved Loyal Order of Moose. "We need to know the whereabouts of these people." Davis declared that he wanted the Labor Department to begin registering immigrants wherever they were, every year, a sign that the days of coming and going easily across the border were ending.

To Celler, this kind of proposal sounded dangerously corruptible. At a large formal dinner at the swanky Astor Hotel in Times Square on December 20, 1923, Davis gave a speech asking Congress to pass a bill that would require alien registration. Celler, among the guests, was furious. As the dinner guests began to leave after midnight, Celler jumped up and demanded everyone's attention. "Don't be fooled by the impassioned words of Mr. Davis," he said to the stunned crowd, who had been led to believe the evening's speeches were over. "I am sorry he has left the room so that I could not say it in his presence, but as a member of Congress I want to say right here and now that I will oppose any such registration bill," which he called "an evil espionage system" and would lead to "perjury, chicanery and graft."

—

MANY FOUND IT HARD to trace where things had gone wrong. Not long ago President Teddy Roosevelt had raved about a new play in Washington that celebrated immigrants. The 1908 show, called *The Melting Pot* and written by the British-Jewish playwright Israel Zangwill, told the story of a Russian Jew escaping a pogrom who lands in New York and tries to compose a symphony about America. In a fevered speech, he tells his love interest, another Russian immigrant, what he admires so much about his adopted country:

> America is God's Crucible, the great Melting Pot where all the races of Europe are melting and re-forming! Here you stand, good folk, think I, when I see them at Ellis Island, here you stand in your fifty groups, with your fifty languages and histories, and your fifty blood hatreds and rivalries. But you won't be long like that, brothers, for these are the fires of God you've come to—these are the fires of God. A fig for your feuds and vendettas! Germans and Frenchmen, Irishmen and Englishmen, Jews and Russians—into the crucible with you all! God is making the American.

The maudlin writing caused critics to savage the play. *The New York Times* called it an "appeal to claptrap patriotism," and "insecure as a work of art and unconvincing as a human document." But the public loved it, and the president himself was a fan. At the play's premiere at the Columbia Theatre in downtown Washington, Roosevelt was a noisy member of the audience, leaning forward in his box seat every time he heard a line he enjoyed to say loudly, "That's all right!" At the end of the second act he led the room in applause.

Three years later Roosevelt wrote Zangwill that his play had made a lasting impression:

> That particular play I shall always count among the very strong and real influences upon my thought and my life. It has been

in my mind continuously, and on my lips very often, during
the last three years. It not merely dealt with the "melting pot,"
with the fusing of all foreign nationalities into an American
nationality, but it also dealt with the great ideals which it is just
as essential for the native born as for the foreign born to realize
and uphold if the new nationality is to represent a real addition
to the sum total of human achievement.

Roosevelt, who was always trying to locate the source of America's spirit,
recognized *The Melting Pot* as a powerful work of nationalist mythmak-
ing. The "melting pot" remains a central metaphor for assimilation today,
largely because of the play that popularized it. According to Zangwill's
vision, the country was not just an experiment in democracy. It was creating a new and superior race of people free from the "blood hatreds
and rivalries" of the Old World. The metaphor made perfect sense to
Roosevelt, himself descended from Dutch, Scottish, English, and Irish
immigrants. He envisioned a process of Americanization that would take
generations of intermarriage to play out, with Germans, Scandinavians,
and all the other European races blended together into one.

On October 12, 1915, in a speech that would make front-page news
the next day and become famous, Roosevelt gave a full-throated rendi-
tion of the melting pot to 2,500 members of the New York chapter of the
Knights of Columbus at Carnegie Hall. It was a celebration for Columbus Day, a holiday that held enormous importance for both Italian and
Irish immigrants, who often suffered discrimination for being Catholic
and counted the popular explorer as one of their own. The former president's subject that day was "Americanism":

There is no room in this country for hyphenated Americans.
When I refer to hyphenated Americans, I do not refer to naturalized Americans. Some of the very best Americans I have
ever known were naturalized Americans born abroad. But
a hyphenated American is not an American at all. The one

absolutely certain way of bringing this nation to ruin, of pre-
venting all possibility of continuing to be a nation at all, would
be to permit it to become a tangle of squabbling nationalities,
an intricate knot of German-Americans, Irish-Americans,
English-Americans, French-Americans, Scandinavian-
Americans, or Italian-Americans.

Roosevelt revealed in his speech the darker side of the melting pot analogy.
As long as an immigrant held up certain civic ideals—and a total devotion
to this country—anyone could be part of the American project. But to
prove that loyalty, they must leave behind all traces of their former culture.

Still, the crowd, cheering itself hoarse, loved the speech. Many immi-
grants embraced the rush to assimilate and prove they were good enough
for America. In a florid hit autobiography from 1912 called *The Promised
Land*, immigrant Mary Antin described her conversion—from a young
Jewish girl in the Russian Empire to an American girl in Boston—as
nothing short of a "second birth." Eager to slough off her former life in
Europe, Antin wrote that it was "painful to be consciously of two worlds.
The Wandering Jew in me seeks forgetfulness."

As more immigrants entered the country, there grew a greater urgency
to create programs that would Americanize them. The brilliant industrialist and carmaker Henry Ford offered free English classes to immigrant
employees after it became clear that many of them didn't understand the
language. The first phrase the students learned was "I am a good American." They were encouraged to value thriftiness and cleanliness. At the
end of the Ford English School program, students participated in a graduation ceremony in which they turned into Americans before the audience's
eyes. Dressed in costumes marking their countries of origin, they walked
up a set of stairs and stepped down into a giant cauldron prop labeled
"American Melting Pot." When they emerged, they all wore identical
dark suits and waved American flags. The transformation was complete.

But not everyone believed that the melting pot analogy served immigrants well. The scholar Horace Kallen, a German-born son of an ortho-

dox rabbi who would go on to help found The New School for Social Research in New York, was one of the first to express doubt. Kallen himself was secular and would later marry a gentile. But he also unabashedly embraced his Jewish heritage. In 1906, soon after arriving at Harvard for college and then at graduate school, he founded a Jewish student group called the Menorah Society. Perhaps inspired by his childhood in a polyglot corner of the German empire called Silesia, Kallen believed in the beauty of a pluralist society, one where many cultures could live side by side.

In 1915, alarmed by the Americanization craze and works like Antin's, Kallen wrote articles in two consecutive issues of *The Nation* entitled "Democracy Versus the Melting Pot." He argued that the Americanization campaigns violated the democratic ideal of freedom by forcing people to abandon their cultures and conform to an Anglo-Saxon mold. Rather than imagining a melting pot, Kallen wrote, Americans should think of their country as a symphony, in which "every type of instrument has its specific timbre and tonality," but together they formed a harmonious whole. As Kallen put it, the only question to ask was this: "What do Americans *will* to make of the United States—a unison, singing the old British theme 'America,' the America of the New England School? or a harmony, in which that theme shall be dominant, perhaps, among others, but one among many, not the only one?"

In another essay a year later, entitled "A Meaning of Americanism," Kallen explained why pluralism was so important: "Democracy involves, not the elimination of differences, but the perfection and conservation of differences. It aims, through Union, not at uniformity, but at variety, at a one out of many, as the dollars say in Latin, and a many in one."

Kallen's ideas were unorthodox. When the *Nation* pieces and his other essays were assembled into a 1924 book called *Culture and Democracy in the United States*, in which he coined the term *cultural pluralism*, there was barely a ripple of response. But he perceived correctly that the most dangerous flaw in the melting pot analogy was that it established the hegemony of an elite Protestant culture—one that everyone was under pressure to embrace. Those who refused to accept it risked being considered disloyal and un-American. Even worse, many of the people demanding Americanization were business owners enriching themselves from the work of immigrants, even as they required the newcomers conform to their capitalist values.

A democracy built on cultural submission was not truly tolerant. Nor was it stable. In time, the melting pot would crack.

—

NOT A SINGLE WORLD WAR I BATTLE was fought on American soil, but it would leave a gash in the country's psyche. The United States entered the fray in April 1917 after watching Europe bleed itself out in the trenches of northern France and Belgium for nearly three years. For the first time, the country was voluntarily entangling itself in Europe's affairs, on President Woodrow Wilson's belief that the Allied cause was morally righteous and would bring peace. America's entry into the war proved critical to the Allies' victory, but when European empires entered a new cycle of rivalry and retribution at the war's end, Americans were left wondering what 116,000 countrymen had died for. Even worse for the nation, when the massive industrial effort powering the war ended, the economy sank into a depression. Unemployment began to climb in 1920, reaching nearly 12 percent—a level that has only been matched subsequently during the Great Depression.

Nationalist fervor had powered the country through the war. Now it was curdling into disappointment and rage. Americans looked around and saw growing income inequality, corporate monopolies, and corruption in their cities. Many feared a revolution akin to the 1918 uprising in Russia. Suspicion intensified against political radicals, who law enforcement began rounding up and even deporting. The spirit of the age preceding the war, the Progressive era, had been marked by boundless optimism—a belief that with the right policy solutions, no problem was insurmountable for America. Now hope appeared to be in short supply, and it seemed obvious that among the people to blame were the ones who had arrived most recently. As Kallen observed in 1924, "What this war did was to turn the anxiety about property into one about people."

Henry Ford, who had only a few years earlier been celebrating the power of Americanization, began a virulent anti-Jewish campaign. Just before the economy crashed in 1920, the automaker magnate had taken out a badly timed loan from Wall Street, and sales plummeted. He became increasingly bitter and blamed the country's problems on an international conspiracy of Jewish bankers. In 1918 he had purchased a small weekly publication from his hometown, *The Dearborn Independent*. A year later he began distributing copies at Ford dealerships across the country, making it one of the most-read publications of its time with a peak circulation of 900,000; beginning in the spring of 1920, customers shopping for a new car who idly picked up a copy would have found nonstop invective against Jews. On the front page week after week, under the heading, "The International Jew: The World's Problem," articles in *The Dearborn Independent* argued that Jews operated a global conspiracy to achieve social and economic power. The newspaper derived much of its information from the *Protocols of the Elders of Zion*, a fake document created by the Russian secret service that purportedly showed Jewish leaders planning to sow chaos around the world before stepping in to seize power. Far from being considered a quack, Ford was a widely respected folk hero beloved by rural Americans who saw him as one of their own because of his Michigan farming roots. His name was often floated as a potential presidential candidate. Now Ford was spreading some of the most vile and anti-Semitic propaganda ever produced.

The 1920s are usually remembered for the Jazz Age and women in glittery flapper dresses, dancing the Charleston. But it was also a decade defined by escalating racial paranoia and violence.

On May 31, 1921, a white mob began a two-day rampage through a prosperous black neighborhood in Tulsa, Oklahoma, burning down homes and businesses, and leaving up to three hundred dead. The attack came two years after a "Red Summer" of race riots that engulfed cities across the country, including Chicago and Washington, D.C.

From the Upper East Side of Manhattan, writer Madison Grant warned that the end of whiteness could be near. Grant's best-selling book *The Passing of the Great Race* insisted that differences between races of people must be acknowledged and confronted. "We Americans must realize that the altruistic ideals which have controlled our social development during the past century and the maudlin sentimentalism that has made America 'an asylum for the oppressed,' are sweeping the nation toward a racial abyss," wrote Grant. "If the Melting Pot is allowed to boil without control, and we continue to follow our national motto and deliberately blind ourselves to all 'distinctions of race, creed, or color,' the type of native American of Colonial descent will become as extinct as the Athenian of the age of Pericles, and the Viking of the days of Rollo."

The nervousness around the pollution of the white race extended to the elite halls of higher education, where administrators were growing concerned about how many Jews were being admitted. In 1922 Harvard president A. Lawrence Lowell proposed a 15 percent quota; the current student body was more than 20 percent Jewish. Lowell explained, "The summer hotel that is ruined by admitting Jews meets its fate . . . because they drive away the Gentiles, and then after the Gentiles have left, they leave also."

This was also the decade in which the Ku Klux Klan reemerged as a powerful national force, beginning in the South but eventually enjoying its greatest popularity above the Mason-Dixon line, in the Midwest and the North. In 1923, at the group's peak, there were roughly 200,000 members in New York alone, with strongholds on Long Island and in the state's southern and far western counties.

The Klan, in its original incarnation, was a violent response to the South's loss in the Civil War. Founded by veterans of the Confederacy, the first KKK tried to restore white supremacy in the South by terrorizing freed slaves and white Republicans. The second iteration, in addition to being anti-black, had a much wider array of targets, with a list of villains that included Jews, Catholics, and immigrants, all of whom the Klan accused of undermining the nation and introducing moral rot. These Klansmen acted as vigilantes enforcing social codes, going so far as to conduct antiliquor raids to enforce Prohibition, one of the group's highest priorities. They made common cause with evangelicals worried about the sin they saw seeping into society, from women's bathing suits to dance halls to movies. The Klan believed that Jews, through the power they held over Hollywood, department stores, and the media, were encouraging women to wear too much makeup and clothes that were too sexual. "Jew Movies urging sex vice," went one complaint. Members of the Klan believed that cities were places of moral temptation because they were home to large Jewish and immigrant populations. By 1915, one out of four New Yorkers was Jewish, and cities like Chicago, Philadelphia, and Boston also boasted large Jewish populations.

As for Catholics, the KKK viewed them as potentially disloyal Americans whose primary allegiance was not to their country but to the Vatican. Klan members were especially suspicious of Catholic schools, where they believed children were being indoctrinated into a foreign cult. In this respect the Klan was clearly descended from the late nineteenth-century nativist group, the American Protective Association, which had insisted that Catholics were arriving in the country as part of a plot to take over the government.

The founder of this new KKK, William J. Simmons, was an Atlanta physician who drew his inspiration from two events that captured the nation's attention. The first was the release of D. W. Griffith's 1915 movie, *The Birth of a Nation*, which glorified the original KKK and mesmerized audiences with the director's wildly innovative cinematic techniques. The movie was a hit and famously received a screening at the White House before President Woodrow Wilson.

Simmons's other touchstone was a lurid crime in Atlanta that transfixed the country. Mary Phagan was a thirteen-year-old worker at the National Pencil Company in Atlanta, where she ran a machine that inserted rubber erasers into the tops of pencils. On April 26, 1913,

Phagan went to the factory to pick up her pay. Early the next morning, around three-thirty a.m., a night watchman found her body in the basement, lying beaten and bloody, partially undressed, in a pile of trash. She had been strangled by a cord. Police soon settled on their prime suspect: Leo Frank, the Brooklyn-raised superintendent of the factory and a member of a well-to-do German-Jewish family. Despite flimsy evidence against him, Frank was convicted and sentenced to death. Frantic Jewish supporters in the North raised funds to fight the conviction in court; *New York Times* owner Adolph Ochs even tried to build support for Frank with sympathetic coverage in his newspaper. But this only served to whip up anti-Semitism among Georgians, who viewed interest from the North as unwanted meddling by outsiders in the state's affairs.

The murder especially touched a nerve among the white working class in Atlanta, who counted Phagan, the daughter of a poor farmer, as one of their own. Phagan symbolized the exploitation of child laborers in Atlanta's new booming factories, where the managers and owners seemed to get rich but never the workers. To these local white workers, Frank was not just a murder suspect. He was a wealthy Jewish outsider peddling corrupt northern industrialization and defiling young white women.

The situation exploded when the governor of Georgia, John Slaton, suddenly announced he was reducing Frank's sentence to life imprisonment. The decision set off mayhem in Georgia, as men bearing guns stalked the governor's home, and a group of 150 men who called themselves the "Knights of Mary Phagan" appeared at the girl's grave in Marietta to vow vengeance. Furious about Slaton's decision, some of the most elite members of Marietta society, including a clergyman and a former sheriff, devised an elaborate plot to abduct Frank.

On August 16, 1915, Frank was sitting in a prison in Milledgeville when a mob of roughly twenty-five men arrived. Armed with rifles and pistols, they quickly overpowered the guards on duty and led Frank out of the prison and into the backseat of a car. After driving him more than one hundred miles to Marietta, they lynched him from a large oak tree. A few months later Simmons invited some of the lynchers to convene at the top of Stone Mountain to burn a cross, much as they had seen in *The Birth of a Nation*, to welcome the resurrection of the KKK.

The group started modestly but took off once Simmons hired two public relations professionals, Elizabeth Tyler and Edward Young Clarke, who gave the Klan a more polished, profit-driven ethos. By 1924, the group had reached a membership of roughly 4 million Americans and set up headquarters in Washington, D.C., as money poured in through dues and sales of Klan life insurance and gear, including the group's infamous robes and pointed hats. Some meetings were secret, but many others occurred in the open, during the day, at fairgrounds and public parks, where the Klan put on a family-friendly face. These large, carnival-like events were open to everyone, with rides and raffles that drew people from miles around. Often the meetings would end in parades with bands and floats. And of course, in the evening, there were enormous cross burnings that would wow the crowds.

But the Klan was not interested only in making a spectacle. It had a political agenda that it pushed by electing its own members to office and supporting lawmakers who backed their nativist platform. At its peak, the Klan counted among its members sixteen senators, dozens of congressmen, and eleven governors. Lawmakers were divided evenly between Democrats and Republicans, so the Klan had a foothold regardless of which party was in power in Washington. But in 1919, when Republicans took control of Congress, the Klan scored perhaps its biggest political coup yet, on the issue it cared about most. It had found a perfect partner in the new chair of the House Immigration Committee.

—

ALBERT JOHNSON had been waiting and planning for this moment for years. A representative for the timber-rich corner of southwestern Washington, Johnson entered politics because of two great passions: his hatred of organized labor and his hatred of Japanese immigrants.

Johnson was born in Springfield, Illinois—as a law student, his father had worked at Abraham Lincoln's law firm Lincoln and Herndon—and then raised in Hiawatha, Kansas. Before he entered politics, he was a journalist who moved where the jobs were, wandering up and down the East Coast. When he landed at *The Washington Post*, he worked as a reporter and then as a late-night news editor, who made sure the publication covered developments from the front of the Spanish-American War after all his colleagues had left for the day. In the fall of 1898, the publisher of the *Tacoma News* traveled to Washington in search of an editor to run his publication and asked the *Post*'s managing editor for recommendations. The editor at the *Post* thought of his industrious night editor, and soon Johnson was headed to the Pacific Northwest, a place he had never visited.

He was entering a cauldron of racial and economic resentment, where arguments were frequently settled in the streets with stones, bricks, and clubs. To a journalist coming straight from a desk job in Washington, D.C., it must have resembled anarchy. White residents seethed at immigrant laborers from China, Japan, and India, whom they viewed as cheaper competition for lumber, mining, and railway jobs. On the night of September 4, 1907, in Bellingham, Washington, more than a hundred miles up the Pacific Coast from Tacoma near the border with Canada, hundreds of white men attacked the town's South Asian migrant workers in their homes and at work, shouting "Drive out the Hindus," even though the men were largely Sikh. The immigrant community soon left town.

Living in the Pacific Northwest brought Johnson into closer contact with people from Asia than ever before. In his home, he employed several young Japanese students as servants. When one became ill, Johnson helped him return home to Japan. The student's father, a wealthy banker in Tokyo, sent a letter thanking him for his help. But rather than feeling closer to the family, Johnson was dismissive. He suspected the student "was engaged on a mission for his government when he sought employment in my residence. It is quite possible, that his purpose was to find out how serious I was in my opposition to Asiatic immigration."

In 1909 Johnson moved to the lumber town of Hoquiam to become publisher of the daily newspaper *Grays Harbor Washingtonian*. Johnson soon become known locally as a powerful voice against the local efforts of the Industrial Workers of the World, or IWW, one of the most radical political organizations in American history. Unlike the older, more established American Federation of Labor, which was only interested in organizing better-paid, skilled workers, the IWW sought to organize everyone—in particular immigrants—with the stated goal of overthrowing capitalism. To Johnson's dismay, the IWW was making inroads locally, attracting workers who wanted an eight-hour day, better pay, and safer working conditions. In 1912 they went on strike, effectively shutting down the center of the Pacific Northwest logging industry. Johnson led an armed movement in Hoquiam to fight back and recall the mayor who had released the IWW strikers from prison.

Local businessmen had already encouraged him to run for Congress. Now Johnson's campaign took on a greater urgency as he viewed immigrants as subversive elements in American society bent on sowing labor unrest. It was time to return to Washington, D.C.—this time as a Republican lawmaker—to address problems he viewed as existential threats to the country. As he wrote in *Grays Harbor Washingtonian* on July 5, 1912, "The greatest menace to the republic today is the open door it affords to the ignorant hordes from Eastern and Southern Europe, whose lawlessness flourishes and civilization is ebbing into barbarism."

That fall, he narrowly won a seat in the House, even though his party lost both the White House and Congress. He then secured a spot on the House Immigration Committee, where at first he wielded little power as a member of the minority party. But he studied the subject closely and made friends with Democrats on the committee. Five years later in 1919, when his party swept into power again, he was ready.

As chairman of the House Immigration Committee, Johnson held one of the most powerful jobs for determining who could enter the country. Committee chairs controlled every aspect of legislation in their chosen subjects: which bills received priority, which were blocked, and when and how bills reached the floor for a full vote. Johnson went straight to work, as there did not seem to be any time to waste. Anti-immigrant activists had sounded warnings that the end of World War I would bring a rush of unwanted arrivals from Europe. Now it appeared those fears were coming to pass. For Jews in eastern Europe, Armistice Day on November 11, 1918, did not bring an end to the war. Conflicts over territory broke out in the region between Russian, Ukrainian, and Polish forces, accompanied by a wave of pogroms. Jewish families fled, and during the fiscal year 1920–21, immigration to the United States from central and eastern Europe reached 119,000—not as high as the prewar numbers but high enough that lawmakers demanded "emergency" legislation to suspend all immigration. Johnson, who hardly needed evidence to act, also cited a State Department document claiming that America was receiving "abnormally twisted" and "unassimilable" Jews who were "filthy, un-American and often dangerous in their habits."

But placing limits on immigration had never been easy in Washington, as one man in the Senate could attest better than anyone. Massachusetts senator Henry Cabot Lodge, nearing the twilight of his long political career, had been trying since the 1890s to curb immigration. Born into one of the most prominent families in America, Lodge was counted among the Brahmins, a caste of Bostonians who proudly traced their lineage to the earliest English colonists. One of his closest friends was Teddy Roosevelt, with whom he wrote a book called *Hero Tales from American History*, a celebration of their idols, leaders like George Washington and Daniel Boone who demonstrated that a country was only as good as the character of its individual men. Unlike his charming friend Teddy, Lodge was an argumentative snob, prone to ruining polite dinner conversation by picking fights with other guests at the table and goading them into verbal combat. Lodge was the ultimate Harvard man, having collected three degrees from the university, including the school's first-ever Ph.D. in political science. Lodge was so enamored of his English roots that he wrote his dissertation on Anglo-Saxon law. He subscribed to the idea, popular at the time, that the Saxon tribe members from northern Germany who settled in England during the collapse of the Western Roman Empire had a particular gift for freedom and self-government. And he believed that America's greatness as a nation relied on maintaining its essential Anglo-Saxon racial character.

As a prominent member of the Immigration Restriction League (IRL), Lodge was among a group of Harvard alumni in Boston who lobbied relentlessly to block immigrants. Their primary vehicle—a literacy test—passed both chambers of Congress in 1896, 1913, and 1915, only to be vetoed by a president each time. First Grover Cleveland, then William Howard Taft, and finally Woodrow Wilson felt the law was too extreme. As Wilson, a segregationist who was hardly the most enlightened man in America on race, wrote in his veto message to Congress:

> This bill embodies a radical departure from the traditional and
> long-established policy of this country, a policy in which our
> people have conceived the very character of their Government
> to be expressed, the very mission and spirit of the Nation. . . .
> It seeks to all but close entirely the gates of asylum which have
> always been open to those who could find nowhere else the
> right and opportunity of constitutional agitation for what they
> conceived to be the natural and inalienable rights of men. . . .
>
> Restrictions like these, adopted earlier in our history as
> a Nation, would very materially have altered the course and
> cooled the humane ardors of our politics.

Earlier in his career, Wilson had written unflattering things about immigrants, saying that the men coming from southern and eastern Europe had "neither skill nor energy nor any initiative of quick intelligence." When he campaigned for president in 1912, he had to explain these remarks to win over immigrant voters, who were becoming a larger part of the American electorate. But his decision to veto the literacy bill five years later was not born primarily of political calculation. As the son of a Presbyterian minister, Wilson imagined America as a divine spiritual project with "God sifting the nations of the world to plant the choicest seed in America." When European immigrants sailed across an ocean to reach America's shores, Wilson could see that they were moved by a deep faith in the promise of the New World. To block them would be to abandon the essential spirit of the country.

He also recognized that for more than a hundred years since America's founding, there had been barely any federal restrictions on white immigration. As a young country, America could not afford to turn people away; there was simply too much land to fill, too much work to be done. Until a central port of entry was established at Ellis Island in 1892, immigrants simply arrived at whichever state-run port on the coast they desired. Even after Congress passed a handful of laws in the late nineteenth century to block immigrants who had certain diseases or were deemed morally degenerate (prostitutes, criminals, and polygamists), barely anyone was stopped at Ellis Island. Between 1880 and World War I, roughly 25 million people entered the country, and only 1 percent of the arrivals were turned back.

But in 1917 the nationalism spun up by the war created an opening for action. Banding together with the country's most prominent labor group, the American Federation of Labor, which feared that immigrants were driving down wages, Lodge and the IRL made another pass at enacting a literacy test. The proposed law required any immigrant over the age of sixteen to be able to read English or another language, which could include Hebrew or Yiddish. In addition, the law would expand the government's power to deport unwanted immigrants. Under an 1891 law, Congress allowed the removal of immigrants who within a year of their arrival became hospitalized, imprisoned, or public charges— with the steamship company that transported them bearing the costs of a return. The new proposal would extend the window to five years and empowered officials to remove a larger category of people, including those suspected of supporting anarchism or communism—a nod to fears of Bolshevism spreading.

The lawmakers also turned their attention to Asia. The Chinese Exclusion Act of 1882, the first immigration law in the United States to discriminate based on race and class, blocked Chinese laborers from entering the country, exempting students, teachers, merchants, and diplomats. Now Congress extended those restrictions to an awkwardly shaped area called the Asiatic Barred Zone, demarcated by various latitudes and longitudes to create an area stretching from the Bosporus strait of Istanbul, through the Middle East and the Gulf, Afghanistan, India, and Southeast Asia.

The 1917 Immigration Act was the most stringent general immigration law the country had ever passed, and when it reached Wilson's desk, he once again issued a veto. This time, though, Congress—which was controlled by his own party—overrode him. The Democrats dared to cross Wilson because he had barely won reelection the year before, winning only 49.26 percent of the popular vote, in one of the closest presidential races in American history. "The League is now all powerful in Washington," bragged the IRL. "No bill as to immigration can be passed if we object, while any bill we favor has a good chance of passage."

The celebration was short-lived, however, because the literacy test failed to significantly stem the number of immigrants entering the country, who were more educated than the Harvard graduate Lodge had guessed.

In 1921 Prescott F. Hall, co-founder executive secretary of the IRL, issued a call to arms. He sneered at the "melting pot" as "the falsest of all shibboleths." The war, he claimed, had revealed that "you can not make bad stock into good by changing its meridian, any more than you can . . . make a mongrel into a fine dog by teaching it tricks." Hall warned that America needed "to become and to remain a strong, self-reliant, united country, with the only unity that counts, viz., that of race. What, then, shall we do? Exclude the black, the brown and the yellow altogether; as to the white, favor the immigration of Nordic and Nordicized stocks."

Hall's reference to the "Nordic" signaled the rise of a new racist force, one that would outstrip every anti-immigrant effort that had come before. Johnson's bill to halt all immigration, even for just a year, would fail in the Senate. But he would get something much more elaborate and sinister instead: a new law based not on mere prejudice but on science.

TWO

SLAMMING THE DOOR

T HE LAWMAKERS WERE ENCHANTED by the bald, ghostly pale man sitting before them. Harry Laughlin was a onetime high-school principal with only a few years of formal science education. But to the members of the House Immigration Committee, he might as well have been unlocking the mysteries of the universe.

"The character of a nation is determined primarily by its racial quali-ties," began Laughlin in his testimony on April 16, 1920, "that is, by the hereditary physical, mental, and moral or temperamental traits of its peo-ple." Laughlin had traveled to Washington, D.C., from the prestigious Cold Spring Harbor Laboratory on Long Island's North Shore to share what he had learned from years of research. In the past, the country's immigration policy had been crafted based on economic concerns—the need for more labor—but now Laughlin believed it was time to factor in the "eugenical element."

Prospective immigrants needed to be visited in their hometowns, where officials could examine whether the prospective American "comes from an industrious or a shiftless family." But the process should not end after admission, Laughlin argued. "As good Americans, concerned in the conservation of our country, we must follow up the immigrant's process of naturalization and Americanization. If, because of insanity, feeble-mindedness, moral turpitude, or shiftlessness, the immigrant does not make good, he should be deported." Laughlin then shared with the lawmakers the latest science on "the problem of the moron," laying out three categories of "the feeble-minded."

At the lowest level were "the idiots," men who "have to be clothed in dresses, and wear diapers." Just above them were "the imbeciles," who cannot be trained to do work. Finally came "the morons," who Laughlin conceded were "border-line cases," with "the bodies of adults but the minds of 9 and 10 year old children."

Listening attentively, William N. Vaile, a Republican congressman from Colorado, interrupted Laughlin to ask how *moron* was spelled, so he could take notes. He was unfamiliar with the word, which had yet to enter the mainstream. "M-O-R-O-N," said Laughlin, adding pedantically that it derived from the Greek word for "a foolish person."

"A moron can slip through the immigration sieve, as it exists today, pretty easily," he continued, and concluded later, "Our failure to sort immigrants on the basis of natural worth is a very serious national menace."

By the end of Laughlin's testimony, the lawmakers were breathless in their praise. John C. Box, a Democratic lawmaker from Texas and the ranking minority member on the committee, said he hoped copies of Laughlin's testimony would be "printed in such numbers that we can get as many as we want." Johnson and others on the committee had been trying for years to manage the country's immigration problem, guided by their instinct that something was wrong with allowing so many people who seemed different to arrive all at once. Now their suspicions were being confirmed by science. Johnson immediately appointed Laughlin the committee's own "expert eugenics agent," so that members could ask him to conduct further studies.

They didn't know it yet, but Laughlin's work would provide justification for the key to the long-lasting immigration restrictions they had long sought: race-based quotas.

—

THE RISE OF NAZI GERMANY would later destroy the reputation of eugenics and expose the movement as a dangerous racial ideology dressed in the garb of science. But in the first few decades of the twentieth century, eugenics captured the imagination of many of America's leading intellectuals. In fields as diverse as economics, environmentalism, and social reform, people saw the potential for eugenics to improve the world by perfecting humanity. Among those who promoted the movement were Irving Fisher, the country's leading economist, Margaret Sanger, the birth control crusader, who viewed eugenicists as potential allies in her cause, and Henry Fairfield Osborn, president of the American Museum of Natural History and a noted paleontologist who named both the Tyrannosaurus Rex and Velociraptor.

The roots of the eugenics movement lay in Gregor Mendel's groundbreaking research into different varieties of peas. Working at an Augustinian monastery at Brünn, Austria, in the 1840s, Mendel bred thousands of plants, studying how their characteristics—their length, say, or crinkliness—were transmitted through each generation. Mendel's work helped to launch the study of genetics, leading other scientists to discover how humans inherited their eye and hair color.

In the early twentieth century, Mendel's project had turned into something more utopian. For a certain kind of idealist, the possibilities of eugenics were intoxicating. "The most progressive revolution in history" could be achieved if "human matings could be placed upon the same high plane as that of horse breeding," Charles Davenport, a foremost evolutionary biologist, once told a prospective donor.

Cold Spring Harbor is now known as one of the world's foremost research facilities for biology, but in its early years it was enmeshed with the dark world of eugenics. In 1910 Mary Harriman, the widow of a railroad baron, agreed to finance an ambitious plan by Davenport to establish a world-class eugenics research facility at Cold Spring that would map the entire array of human traits, from diseases like hemophilia and epilepsy to alcoholism, criminality, and what was then called "feeble-mindedness."

Charles Davenport was a driven man, who had been raised in Brooklyn Heights by a demanding, puritanical father who preached temperance and discouraged any indulgence in pleasure. Amzi Davenport was a founder and deacon of Brooklyn's Plymouth Congregational Church, most famous for its fiery abolitionist minister Henry Ward Beecher. As an adult, Charles Davenport would find his own religion in eugenics.

His life's work was to catalogue every distinct race of humanity. In his 1911 book *Heredity in Relation to Eugenics*, Davenport noted that Italians had a "tendency to crimes of personal violence," while Jews coming from eastern Europe were marked by their "intense individualism and ideals of gain at the cost of any interest." These immigrants "represent the opposite extreme from the early English and the more recent Scandinavian immigration with their ideals of community life in the open country, advancement by the sweat of the brow, and the uprearing of families in the fear of God and the love of country." The new "blood" from Italians and Jews, Davenport concluded, would make the American population "darker in pigmentation, smaller in stature, more mercurial . . . more given to crimes of larceny, kidnapping, assault, murder, rape, and sex-immorality."

The terminology of race in the early twentieth century does not line up with contemporary labels and categories, in part because scientists like Davenport were interested in subdividing whiteness into finer categories. The terms *ethnicity*, *ethnic group*, and *white ethnic* did not yet exist; *white ethnic* would not gain currency until around 1970. Instead, the term *race* at the time was closer to, though not entirely the same as, what we call *ethnicity* today: a group of people with a distinct blend of culture, history, and genealogy. The shape of your nose, your temperament, and most critically, your ability to participate in a democracy were all determined by the quality of your racial "stock." All that put together is what made a person English rather than Greek or Hebrew or Chinese. Indeed a 1911 report on immigration produced by a special congressional committee, known as the Dillingham Commission, noted that the federal government recognized "45 races or peoples among immigrants coming to the United States, and of these 36 are indigenous to Europe." This concept of race, like ours today, was fundamentally a fiction, a pernicious, constantly evolving ideology used to enforce existing social hierarchies. According to Davenport, *race* went deeper than nationality. It was in a person's blood.

Considered this way, each new arrival passing through Ellis Island was entering into the American bloodstream, making it stronger or weaker. And so the eugenicists believed that the "national germ plasm," as Davenport and others called it, had to be protected at all costs.

Not content to toil away in his lab, Davenport wanted his work at Cold Spring to change the world. He found a partner in Harry Laughlin, who was teaching agriculture in Kirksville, Missouri, when he wrote Davenport for advice in 1907 on how to breed chickens. Two years later the men met in person at a gathering of the eugenics group American Breeders' Association. They forged an immediate connection. In Davenport, Laughlin found a willing mentor who could launch him overnight into the world of cutting-edge scientific research. Davenport, for his part, felt drawn to Laughlin's humorless intensity. It was no wonder the two men got along: like Davenport, Laughlin had grown up in a household in which indulgences were frowned upon; Laughlin's mother was a suffragist and temperance movement activist who urged him to sign a no-alcohol pledge that he maintained for the rest of his life.

With money secured from his benefactor, Harriman, Davenport placed Laughlin in charge of a new department at Cold Spring called the Eugenics Record Office, which would popularize the scientists' findings. The Eugenics Record Office organized a yearly conference and began publishing the monthly *Eugenical News*, which described the latest research in the United States and Europe and had a regular feature explaining the success of notable Americans by tracing their lineage. (A January 1918 issue profiled Texas pioneer Sam Houston, calling him "a true son of the Scotch-Irish of western Virginia . . . a fighter, like his father . . . and full of courage like his mother.") Each summer the Eugenics Record Office trained young men and women to fan out across the country and collect hereditary information on albinos, juvenile delinquents, the mentally ill, the Amish, and more. These records would then be meticulously filed and catalogued for the scientists at Cold Spring, "a sort of inventory of the blood of the community," as *Scientific American* put it.

Groups devoted to studying eugenics also sprang up in Europe, particularly in England. But it was the United States that would pioneer the writing of laws based on this burgeoning race science, including aggressive sterilization programs.

By 1913, twelve states across the country, including New York, California, Indiana, and New Jersey, had adopted laws requiring sterilization for anyone whose gene pool threatened to degrade the quality of successive generations. The definition for who should be sterilized could be incredibly broad, including anyone deemed an "imbecile," "sexual pervert," or "degenerate." After Laughlin wrote a treatise called *Eugenical Sterilization in the United States* in which he outlined the "model" sterilization law, the state of Virginia used the text to write its own legislation, which would allow the state to forcibly sterilize more than seven thousand people over five decades—including Carrie Buck, a native of Charlottesville who became the center of one of the Supreme Court's most infamous decisions. Supporters of sterilization, needing a test case to shore up the Virginia law, chose Buck, who had been adopted as a child and was later deemed "feeble-minded." Her case reached the Supreme Court, where Justice Oliver Wendell Holmes argued that Buck, her mother, and her daughter were all carrying inferior traits that needed to be stamped out of the population. "Three generations of imbeciles are enough," Holmes wrote for the majority in the 1927 case *Buck v. Bell*.

The eugenicists attained such political power in part due to a growing worship of expertise in policy making. In Wisconsin, Governor Robert La Follette had pioneered the notion that to solve society's problems, lawmakers should turn to researchers and experts in crafting policy, whether it was about taxes, regulation, or public health. La Follette recruited experts, often from the University of Wisconsin, to turn his state into a lab for progressive goals, applying what was referred to as the "Wisconsin idea." The model became widespread in American politics, where it remains a fixture today, in the form of "wonks" and various blue-ribbon commissions.

For Davenport and Laughlin, influencing state governments was only part of the plan. Because immigration was controlled most powerfully on the federal level, gaining a foothold in Congress was critical. And now they had finally done it.

—

EIGHT MONTHS AFTER Laughlin testified, the House Immigration Committee passed a bill barring immigration for two years, with only a few exceptions for close relatives of citizens. When the bill reached the House floor, lawmakers rolled back the time span to fourteen months but passed it overwhelmingly in a 296-to-42 vote.

In the Senate, the prospects for Johnson's bill were less certain. Lobbyists for farming interests and the National Association of Manufacturers balked at cutting off immigration so drastically, though they acknowledged that some limits were probably necessary. Based on a proposal from Senator William Dillingham of Vermont, who a decade earlier had led the influential commission on race, the House and Senate settled on a compromise. Each European country would be allotted a quota limiting immigration to 3 percent of however many people of that nationality were counted in the 1910 census, and there would be an overall cap of 355,000 immigrants. (Data from the 1920 census was not yet available.) The limit would have the effect of freezing in place the country's demographic balance from a decade earlier—a way to allay fears that Nordic-Americans would soon be overrun in their own country. The proposal was easily accepted by both chambers and signed into law by Warren G. Harding, who had recently won election to the White House on a nationalist "America First" platform.

The measure was supposed to last for about a year as an "emergency" measure, while Congress devised a more permanent solution. But agreeing on an immigration formula would not prove to be easy, given that the country had never before placed a cap on the number of immigrants who could enter. In May 1922 the measure was extended for another two years while Johnson's committee worked feverishly to call witnesses to Washington. "There are only two or three committees out of the sixty-odd House committees that hear as much testimony and do as much work as Johnson's immigration committee," observed *The Saturday Evening Post* in 1923. "He hears press agents, steamship owners, merchant tailors, Greek refugees . . . presidents of steel companies, representatives of organized labor, farmers, clergymen, priests, rabbis, consuls. . . . These people come before the committee and talk for hours and sometimes for days."

Among the loudest voices were leaders of the business community. In 1923 the American economy was regaining some strength, and industrial leaders worried that any restriction on immigration would cut off their access to cheap foreign labor. At U.S. Steel's annual shareholders meeting in 1923, Elbert H. Gary, the company chairman, lamented that the emergency quota law was "one of the worst things this country has ever done for itself economically." Gary, who had a history of hostility to labor unions, wanted maximum power for businesses to pick the workers they wanted. "The restrictions upon immigration should be directed to the question of quality rather than numbers," he asserted in the February 1923 issue of *American Industries*, the magazine published by the National Association of Manufacturers, the country's most powerful business group, which also opposed the quota law.

Johnson had little patience for Gary's argument, countering that companies were behaving selfishly. After spending a week in New York City observing immigrant families, Johnson pointed out that every immigrant laborer who arrives inevitably brings relatives with him. And the country could hardly afford to support so many newcomers. "New York spends millions of dollars a year on the support and care of defective aliens," he claimed. "The country needs and wants restrictive immigration and a still stricter law. The United States will never go back to unrestricted immigration. That is a thing of the past."

While Johnson kept bringing in witnesses, Laughlin was wrapping up research that the committee had asked him to conduct. In the two years since he first appeared before Congress, Laughlin had been busy measuring the "degeneracy" of different races by determining whether certain ethnicities were overrepresented in the country's prisons and mental institutions. On November 21, 1922, he returned to Washington and unveiled his findings in a report he called "Analysis of America's Modern Melting Pot." The research, he claimed, was "not meant to report any preconceived idea" and instead reflected "simply measures of the facts secured at first hand." Johnson, who had no scientific training, affirmed the research, saying he had reviewed Laughlin's data and charts and found "they are both biologically and statistically thorough, and apparently sound." Then Laughlin revealed his findings to the full House Immigration Committee: in terms of deafness or blindness, recent immigrants were superior to the older "stock." But when it came to "feeble-mindedness," insanity, criminality, epilepsy, tuberculosis, and "deformity," "the older immigrant stocks are vastly sounder than the recent." Laughlin declared, "The outstanding conclusion is that . . . the recent immigrants, as a whole, present a higher percentage of inborn socially inadequate qualities than do the older stocks."

Johnson hailed the report as "one of the most valuable documents ever put out by a committee of Congress." The walls of the committee's room were left plastered for months with Laughlin's charts. Excerpts and summaries of "Analysis of America's Modern Melting Pot" were published across the country. *The Saturday Evening Post*, in a lead story, proclaimed, "If the farmer doesn't keep out the weeds by his own toil, his crops will be choked and stunted. If America doesn't keep out the queer, alien, mongrelized people of Southeastern Europe, her crop of citizens will eventually be dwarfed and mongrelized in turn."

As a man of middling intellect, Johnson was thrilled with how his work in Washington was placing him in the company of Americans regarded as among the country's smartest and most elite. In 1923 he was invited to join the American Eugenics Society, a new group that included the movement's leading lights—men such as Madison Grant, author of *The Passing of the Great Race*, and Irving Fisher, the economist.

Under the tutelage of these new acquaintances, Johnson's arguments against immigration grew more sophisticated, especially compared to what they had been in his days of writing screeds for the local newspaper. And he was beginning to settle on a formula for restricting immigration that was even tougher than the emergency measures passed in 1921. The rule now in place limited immigration to 3 percent of the population of each foreign-born group from the 1910 census. Johnson proposed pulling back the percentage to 2 percent and, more significantly, shifting the yardstick to the 1890 census—before the largest wave of immigrants from southern and eastern Europe had arrived, so their quotas would be even smaller. The number of immigrants allowed from countries such as Italy and Poland would be slashed even further: from 42,000 to 4,000 Italians and from 31,000 to 6,000 Poles.

This infuriated Jewish, Italian, and Polish organizations, which argued that the bill blatantly discriminated against newer immigrants and would breed disunity in the country. Opposition was largely concentrated in big cities like New York, Boston, and Chicago, with their huge immigrant populations. Adolph Sabath of Illinois, a Jewish Czech-born Democrat on the House Immigration Committee, said the bill would be "the first instance in our modern legislation for writing into our laws the hateful doctrine of inequality between the various component parts of our population." At gatherings such as the one at the Brooklyn Jewish Center, constituents told their representatives they expected them to fight the bill. Twenty out of the twenty-two Democratic congressmen from the state of New York, including Mannie Celler, signed a letter arguing against the legislation, on the grounds that the bill "fans the flames of racial, religious and national hatreds and brands forever elements already here as of an inferior stock." A host of Jewish leaders testified before the immigration committee to argue against setting limits. Rabbi Stephen S. Wise told the committee that shutting out large groups of potential citizens revealed a "want of faith in America. . . . You are declaring the incapacity of America to Americanize."

Johnson not only rejected the charges of discrimination, he suspected they were ginned up by outsiders, "largely manufactured and built up by special representatives of racial groups, aided by aliens actually living abroad." In its final report embracing the quotas based on the 1890 census, Johnson's committee said it had taken "notice" of a February 8, 1924, article in the *Jewish Tribune* on comments made by Israel Zangwill, the famed author of *The Melting Pot*. "If you create enough fuss against this Nordic nonsense," Zangwill was reported to have said, "you will defeat this legislation. You must make a fight against this bill; tell them they are destroying American ideals. Most fortifications are of cardboard, and if you press against them they give way." The committee seized on these comments as evidence of outsiders meddling with American legislation, and said there was no reason for Jews especially to be offended by the law, since they could enter the United States from any country in which they were born. This ignored the fact that reducing immigration from places like Russia and Poland would disproportionately affect Jews, since at the time large percentages of Jewish immigrants were coming from eastern Europe.

But in the committee's report, Johnson drew a careful distinction that pro-white groups would powerfully employ for years to come. "The use of the 1890 census is not discriminatory," wrote Johnson. "It is used in an effort to preserve, as nearly as possible, the racial status quo in the United States. It is hoped to guarantee, as best we can at this late date, racial homogeneity in the United States." In other words, the committee was not motivated by prejudice. Instead, after being informed by the country's top experts on how different races introduced different qualities into a population, the committee was simply trying to preserve the thing it believed made America unique—its Anglo-Saxon roots, which lay at the heart of the country's ability to sustain a democracy. Maintaining the racial status quo was a matter not of hate but of survival.

In the Senate, lawmakers were largely in agreement with Johnson that immigration needed to be restricted. But the Senate Immigration Committee did not think that Johnson's quota plan could so easily be defended from charges of discrimination. What plausible reason could Congress give for using the 1890 census as the new benchmark, aside from wanting fewer immigrants from southern and eastern Europe? Again, an outside expert pointed the way to a solution. Whereas Laughlin had delivered the cold certainty of science to the House, John B. Trevor, Sr., offered the assuredness of wealth and good breeding to the Senate.

Trevor was an elite New Yorker who proudly traced his ancestry to William Floyd, a signer of the Declaration of Independence, and to Col. Benjamin Tallmadge, a member of George Washington's staff. His father had made a fortune as a pioneering Wall Street stockbroker, putting the family in the company of the very highest society of the Upper East Side. The guests at Trevor's wedding included such luminaries as the young Franklin D. and Eleanor Roosevelt. After fighting in World War I, Trevor came home convinced that a Bolshevik revolution was bound for the United States, and that he needed to do battle in his hometown against a potential insurrection. As head of New York's branch of the U.S. Army's Military Intelligence Division, Trevor began to monitor the city's Jews for radical activity and drew up maps showing what he claimed were ethnic hotbeds of Communism. Based on this work, Trevor came to believe that the only way to root out subversion was to reduce the number of Jews entering the country. Like his associate Madison Grant—with whom he sat on the board of the American Museum of Natural History—Trevor made frequent trips to Washington, D.C., to appear as a witness at hearings on immigration. He lacked scientific expertise, but his wealth lent him legitimacy and time to devote to his political cause, making him a treasured expert for both the House and Senate's immigration committees. In the Senate, he helped lawmakers formulate an alternative to Johnson's formula that would solve the problem of seeming unfair.

Trevor detected a flaw in the way Congress had been constructing its quota bills. In 1921 and again three years later, Johnson had based his quotas on the population of foreign-born. But this left out the people in the country whose ancestors had contributed so much to the founding of America—people like Trevor's family. What if, Trevor proposed, the government calculated the ancestry of the entire country in 1920 and then based quotas on those numbers? According to Trevor's calculations, this would allot 84 percent of total immigration slots to northern and western Europe and leave 16 percent for southern and eastern Europe. (Because his conception of the country included only Europeans, he did not count anyone with ancestry from the Western Hemisphere or Asia, or descendants of slaves or American Indians.) His figures were not so different from what Johnson had calculated based on the 1890 census. But as a response to the attacks from Jewish and Italian groups, the "national origins" plan, as it became known, could be an elegant foil. And it was audacious, because built into its very foundation was the idea that America belonged primarily to its white "native stock."

Trevor found a sponsor in Senator David A. Reed of Pennsylvania, who had also fought in World War I. A tall man who carried himself with great confidence, much of it unearned, Reed had achieved his congressional seat primarily due to his father's position as close friend and legal counsel to the industrialist Andrew W. Mellon. In 1922, when the seat suddenly became vacant, Mellon pushed for his lawyer's forty-one-year-old son to take the job.

The experience of World War I had taught Reed, like Trevor, to fear an onslaught of immigrants from southern and eastern European countries. Reed worried that such nations wanted "to make us the trash basket of all creation by sending us the very worst they have." As a result, Reed argued, "there is only one way in which the question of immigration can be dealt with. We must not legislate for the interests of any country on the globe except the United States." He came to agree with Trevor that the method for calculating the original quotas in the temporary 1921 law was "entirely unfair to the native-born American," since "there was no justice in allowing the unnaturalized alien resident to be represented in calculating the quota of his country while the native-born American was ignored." As part of the Senate bill, Reed proposed launching a committee that would settle on new "national origins" quotas by 1927.

If the idea that one could calculate the exact ancestry of every American in 1920 seems dubious, that's because Reed himself had little idea of how it would be done. The country's first census, in 1790, contained no information about ancestry, and the government did not begin recording the origin of immigrants until 1899. Even then, national boundaries had shifted dramatically after World War I, as empires broke apart and new countries formed overnight. How would the government trace the nationality of a person born in a town in the now-dissolved Austro-Hungarian empire? And how would it deal with someone whose father was German and mother was Scandinavian?

Even though lawmakers had conducted endless hearings on nearly every other aspect of the country's immigration system, they paid scant attention to the details of the "national origins" proposal, which the Senate quickly embraced. This was in part because they were leaving the details to government officials, who would require years to settle on a set of quotas. It was also because a wholly separate issue would soon distract them. Tucked inside Johnson's bill—almost as an afterthought—was a line that threatened to cause a diplomatic crisis on the other side of the world.

—

THE DEBATE OVER IMMIGRATION had thus far focused almost entirely on Europe, the largest source by far of the new arrivals and still the cultural lodestar for much of the country. Immigration from Mexico had surfaced briefly when some hard-liners suggested imposing quotas for the first time on neighboring countries in the Western Hemisphere, since they viewed Mexicans as obvious pollutants to the Anglo-Saxon race. But lawmakers from the Southwest quickly rejected that suggestion, intent on protecting agricultural interests that relied heavily on labor from just over the border.

Immigration from Asia, however, would become a central issue in the final hours of debate over the 1924 law. One gate after another had already come down to block Asian immigrants, starting with the Chinese Exclusion Act of 1882, and then again in 1917, when the Asiatic Barred Zone almost entirely eliminated arrivals from South and Southeast Asia.

But these restrictions had not stopped immigrants from Japan, who were arriving in greater numbers. In 1890 there were only 2,000 Japanese in the continental United States. A decade later there were almost 25,000, many of them coming after making stops in Hawaii. With Chinese laborers cut off, Japanese men stepped into the vacuum, taking up jobs on the railroads and in mines and lumber mills. Many more were poor farmers who had heard there was money to be made in America, after which, as one Japanese saying went, they could "return home in golden brocades." Implicit in that expression was the intention to eventually go back to Japan. But many Japanese immigrants began to settle in Hawaii and on the American West Coast, where they were becoming a conspicuous presence. Local immigrant leaders encouraged them to blend in as much as possible by wearing only Western-style clothing and making sure their children spoke English.

Among those striving to fit in was a man named Takao Ozawa. On the morning of October 16, 1914, Ozawa walked into the clerks' office at the U.S. district court in Honolulu to file a petition for citizenship. To everyone's astonishment, it was accepted. There were a number of reasons to be surprised. Weeks earlier, the forty-year-old father had tried to do the exact same thing and failed. Moreover, Ozawa had been born in Japan and had come to the United States as a young man to find work. No one in Honolulu could think of another time when a Japanese immigrant had been allowed to take even this first step toward citizenship. The country's 1790 naturalization law mandated that only "free" whites were eligible for citizenship; later, the law was extended, but only to those of African descent.

The clerk was so befuddled the first time Ozawa entered his office that he contacted officials all the way in Washington, D.C., who told him to go ahead and accept the petition. They instructed him that the ultimate decision over what to do with Ozawa would be left to federal court. There was more at stake here than one man's citizenship.

Relations between the United States and Japan at the beginning of the twentieth century were cordial, if growing increasingly complicated. Beginning in the mid-1800s, Japan's Meiji government had embarked on a campaign to modernize and industrialize that was quickly bearing fruit. In 1904 Japan shocked the world when it went to war against Russia and defeated its Baltic Fleet. Around the same time, the United States was taking its first steps toward expansion across the Pacific. In 1898, following the Spanish-American War, President William McKinley annexed the Philippines and Hawaii. Suddenly the United States and Japan were face to face in the Pacific, eyeing each other as potential rivals.

They were also encountering each other through the boom in Japanese immigration. An anti-Japanese movement sprouted, particularly in San Francisco, where a group called the Japanese-Korean Exclusion League was formed in May 1905 with the motto "Absolute Exclusion of the Asiatics." Through propaganda, boycotts, and intense lobbying campaigns, the group spread fear that the Asian immigrants threatened the survival of the white race.

Resentment against Asian migrants exploded into all-out hatred after an earthquake hit San Francisco on April 18, 1906, in one of the worst urban disasters in American history. Fires burned for days and destroyed huge swaths of the city. Federal troops were sent into the city's streets to maintain order, and the mayor, Eugene Schmitz, instituted a shoot-to-kill policy against looters. The recovery effort exacerbated inequalities as the city's business elite prioritized its own relief and rebuilding needs over those of ordinary San Francisco residents. On May 26, 1907, more than a year after the quake, a *New York Times* reporter described a city in disarray: "Anarchy is a harsh word; it has an ugly sound, and it is not well to use it recklessly, but the conditions existing in San Francisco would almost excuse the application of the word."

Amid the disorder, mobs of white men regularly attacked Japanese immigrants. In the summer and fall following the earthquake, local police noted nearly three hundred attacks on Japanese residents. When a delegation of Japanese scientists, among the foremost experts on seismology in the world, arrived to help the city determine whether more earthquakes were to come, they were stoned and beaten. White unions encouraged boycotts of Japanese businesses. On October 11, 1906, following intense lobbying by the Japanese-Korean Exclusion League, the San Francisco school board ordered the segregation of all Asian students from white students. Japanese and Korean children would now join the Chinese in the city's Oriental School.

Local school board decisions are rarely worthy of attention on the world stage, but in this case the school board of the city of San Francisco set off a full-blown diplomatic crisis. The Meiji government had spent years cultivating an intense feeling of patriotism and honor among ordinary Japanese, who believed their country was superior to their Asian neighbors and on par with the great Western powers. The idea that Japanese children were being removed from classes with white Americans and lumped together with children from China and Korea, now colonized by Japan, was unthinkable. The American ambassador telegraphed the State Department that the segregation decision caused "the deepest offense" in Japan.

President Theodore Roosevelt immediately discerned the gravity of the situation and realized that if handled poorly, the San Francisco school board's blunder could lead to war. Roosevelt was partial to Japan and believed the Japanese, unlike the Chinese, were "a wonderful and civilized people . . . entitled to stand on an absolute equality with all the other peoples of the civilized world." He had earned Japan's trust when he helped negotiate the end of the Russo-Japanese War in 1905, work for which he was awarded the Nobel Peace Prize. As the school board situation inflamed Japan, Roosevelt told a Japanese envoy and fellow Harvard alumnus, Baron Kentaro Kaneko, that the San Francisco decision was "purely local," and that he had not gotten wind of it until the Japanese reacted. Given Japan's growing naval presence in Asia and the U.S. government's own designs on imperialism in the region, Roosevelt could not afford to anger the Japanese government. He wrote his son Kermit that he was "horribly bothered" by the situation. "The infernal fools in California, and especially in San Francisco, insult the Japanese recklessly, and in the event of war it will be the Nation as a whole which will pay the consequences." In his annual message to Congress in December, Roosevelt called the segregation a "wicked absurdity" and asked Congress to grant citizenship to Japanese immigrants who applied. This only inflamed Californians, including lawmakers on Capitol Hill who told Roosevelt they would never support naturalization for Japanese immigrants. Even southern lawmakers, who scarcely ever had contact with Asian immigrants, came to the defense of the Californians and their own states' rights to separate white from non-white children in schools.

Caught between domestic and diplomatic demands, Roosevelt arranged for a meeting with a delegation from San Francisco, including Mayor Schmitz. They arrived at a solution. The school board would back down: only Chinese and Korean students would be segregated, and the Japanese children could go back to attending school with white children. In return, Roosevelt moved to ban immigration of Japanese laborers from Hawaii, Canada, and Mexico to the mainland. The Japanese government also promised it would not issue passports to Japanese laborers who intended to work on the mainland, with the exception of those who had already been in America and the immediate family of those who were already residents. The deal, which came to be known as the Gentlemen's Agreement, seemed to calm everyone for the time being.

But by the time Takao Ozawa petitioned to become a citizen, it was clear that the Gentlemen's Agreement had not appreciably diminished the presence of Japanese people on the West Coast. The number of Japanese-Americans in fact grew, as single Japanese men brought over "picture brides" they had never met and these couples began having children. And most alarming to the anti-Japanese activists, these immigrants were clamoring to become citizens.

Ozawa made for a sympathetic case. Born just south of Tokyo in

1875, Ozawa arrived in San Francisco when he was about nineteen years old, attended a high school in Berkeley, and studied at the University of California for three years, until the 1906 earthquake and its aftermath forced him to leave for Hawaii. He sent his children to American schools, attended American churches, and spoke English in his home. After living in the United States for more than twenty years, Ozawa had developed a higher opinion of the United States than of his native Japan. If the two countries ever went to war, Ozawa knew he wanted to fight as an American.

But his bid for citizenship in America's courts faced the longest of odds. He was a salesman for one of Hawaii's biggest sugar companies, Theo H. Davies & Co., and not a trained lawyer. Still, he insisted on representing himself in court. In January 1915 he appeared before Judge Sanford B. Dole, one of the most prominent figures in Hawaii. Before becoming a judge, Dole had been the first governor of the Republic of Hawaii and had played a major role overthrowing the Hawaiian queen Liliuokalani so that the islands could be annexed by the United States. Dole quizzed Ozawa extensively on the workings of the American government. He asked if he was a samurai; Ozawa said he was not, but that his brother was. Dole was impressed—to a degree. "He is all right, the only question being that he is a Japanese," he announced at the end of the day's proceedings. Another hearing was scheduled but then delayed when Ozawa requested more time to study naturalization law.

Months later Ozawa appeared again before Dole and said that because he was not a lawyer, "I do not know how to speak in the courts." Instead, Ozawa would submit two remarkable briefings laying out his case for citizenship.

"In name, General Benedict Arnold was an American, but at heart he was a traitor. In name, I am not an American, but at heart I am a true American," wrote Ozawa on twenty typewritten pages to the court. "I have steadily prepared to return the kindness which our Uncle Sam has extended me . . . so it is my honest hope to do something good to the United States before I bid farewell to this world."

Ozawa also attested to his own moral bearing. "I neither drink liquor of any kind, nor smoke, nor play cards, nor gamble, nor associate with any improper persons. My honesty and industriousness are well known among my Japanese and American acquaintances and friends; and I am always trying my best to conduct myself according to the Golden Rule. So I have all [the] confidence in myself that as far as my character is concerned, I am second to none."

He went on to explain how much distance he had put between his family and his native country and culture. He had never registered himself, his marriage, or his children with the Japanese consulate in Hawaii, standard procedure for Japanese citizens. Instead, he submitted his personal information to the U.S. government. His wife had been educated in American schools. Most of the time he spoke English at home, "so that my children cannot speak the Japanese language."

A government attorney assigned to argue in court against Ozawa said he had no case. "None of Ozawa's arguments are based on law," said J. Wesley Thompson. "All of them are based on equity," adding that Ozawa had not shown any precedent for a Japanese citizen being allowed to naturalize in the United States.

By the beginning of the next year, as the case dragged on, Dole stepped down from the court. In his place, Judge Charles F. Clemons heard arguments from both sides and on March 25, 1916, ruled against Ozawa. The immigrant was "in every way eminently qualified under the statutes to become an American citizen," except he was not white and thus not eligible for citizenship.

Still, Ozawa kept up his fight. In September he filed an appeal, pushing the case to the Ninth Circuit Court of Appeals in San Francisco. And now that his case was rising in the courts, Japanese advocacy groups took notice. This was no longer one man's lonely, long-shot crusade. The question of whether Japanese immigrants could naturalize affected the entire community and had taken on new urgency. In 1913 the state of California had passed a law that prohibited "aliens ineligible for citizenship" from owning farmland. The phrasing cleverly did not name Japanese immigrants, though they were clearly the targets. One organization of Japanese leaders, the Pacific Coast Japanese Association Deliberative Council, felt that the Ozawa case was their best hope for securing greater rights. The group lobbied the Japanese government to support the litigation, but a special ambassador temporarily in the country, Ishii Kikujiro, declined, arguing that public opinion in the United States was not ready for such a change. Ishii so strongly opposed the case that on a trip back to Japan, he stopped in Honolulu to personally urge Ozawa to drop it. Ozawa refused and told the council that he would not withdraw his case, even in the "face of death."

The council proceeded and added as chief counsel a man with unimpeachable legal credentials. In a case that was putting whiteness to the test, the Japanese groups wanted someone from the highest levels of social and political power. George W. Wickersham had recently served as attorney general in the Taft administration. Before joining the government, Wickersham had worked at one of the country's most prestigious law firms, Strong & Cadwalader in New York, where he became acquainted with Henry Taft, brother of the president.

Wickersham set to work on the case, which was about to move to a much bigger stage. In June 1917 the Ninth Circuit declined to make a judgment and sent the case to the Supreme Court, which proceeded to delay hearing it. Some suspected that with the United States just having entered World War I and Japan on the side of the Allies, the Court feared inflaming the Japanese government with a negative decision. Finally in 1922 the court moved ahead, just in time for Wickersham to argue before William Taft, the former president who had just been named chief justice. Wickersham tried to argue the case a number of ways: He put forward Ozawa's defense that the content of his character was good enough to be an American citizen, and he also tried to prove that technically, there was a racial connection between Japanese people and Caucasians, and so according to the science, Ozawa should be considered white.

None of it worked. On November 13, 1922, the Supreme Court rejected Ozawa's bid for citizenship. In the majority opinion, Justice George Sutherland conceded that Ozawa was "well qualified by character and education for citizenship." But there was no getting around the fact that he was not white. When the founders specified "free" whites in the country's earliest naturalization law, they clearly did not have Asians like Ozawa in mind.

The Japanese-language press was devastated, if not entirely shocked. "The slim hope that we had entertained . . . had been shattered completely," commented *Shin Sekai*. "We are not too surprised for we have been treated for a long time as if we did not have the right in fact."

—

WELL BEYOND CALIFORNIA, the Supreme Court decision immediately emboldened those who opposed Japanese immigration.

In December 1923 Albert Johnson, whose hatred of Japanese people had inspired him to enter politics, added to his immigration bill a provision banning the admission of any "alien ineligible to citizenship." At first no one moved to stop him. Even the loudest opponents of Johnson's immigration quotas had made clear that they were focused on winning equal treatment for Europeans only. Congressman Adolph Sabath, who had been leading the charge against quotas, said he favored excluding the Japanese. William Edlin, editor of the *Yiddish Day*, testified before the House Immigration Committee that he believed "every worthy man, woman, or child is entitled to be admitted into this country." But when pressed by a lawmaker on whether this included Japanese and Chinese immigrants, Edlin said such people should be banned and that he was speaking only "on behalf of the Caucasian race." He added, "The Chinese, Hindus, and other races do not have those things that we call civilization, and I look upon those people as too far from us for assimilation purposes. . . . We are pleading only for the white population and for no other."

In the Senate, however, lawmakers were nervous that any language effectively banning Japanese immigration would violate the long-standing Gentlemen's Agreement. Reed, the sponsor of the Senate bill, saw no point in enraging Japan and favored a small quota of 146 immigrants per year for Japan.

A powerful delegation from California, led by the newspaper publisher V. S. McClatchy, rushed to Washington to convince the senators a ban was needed. McClatchy called Japanese immigrants "less assimilable and more dangerous" than any other group of non-European immigrants in the country. "They do not come here with any desire or any intent to lose their racial or national identity," McClatchy argued before the Senate Immigration Committee. "They come here specifically and professedly for the purpose of colonizing and establishing here permanently the proud Yamato race. They never cease being Japanese."

But the Californians faced formidable opposition. Ozawa's eminent lawyer Wickersham, the former attorney general and now the chairman of a group called the National Committee on American-Japanese Relations, sent a letter to Congress warning that the bill would be "resented by Japan as a gratuitous act of unfriendly character." Secretary of State Charles Evans Hughes also sent a letter to Johnson expressing his grave concern: "I am unable to perceive that the exclusion provision is necessary, and I must strongly urge upon you the advisability, in the interests of our international relations, of eliminating it."

Hughes, a former Supreme Court justice whose narrow face was marked by a substantial moustache and beard, feared an outbreak of violence after working mightily to establish peace after the last war. In 1916, when the United States had been on the brink of entering World War I, Hughes had run against Woodrow Wilson in a presidential race so close that days before the election, Wilson typed a secret letter saying that should he lose reelection, he would ask his vice president and secretary of state to resign and appoint Hughes the country's new secretary of state. Then if Wilson resigned, under the line of succession, Hughes would immediately become president, so that Hughes could begin work even before his inauguration. The instructions never came to pass, but Hughes got the Secretary of State job eventually under Wilson's successor, Warren G. Harding. After the U.S. Senate failed to ratify the Treaty of Versailles, it fell to Hughes to negotiate a separate peace treaty with Germany. He also brokered one of the most significant disarmament deals the United States ever entered by gathering the world's biggest naval powers in Washington, D.C., to convince them it was better to freeze the size of their respective fleets than to risk another war. Britain and Japan agreed so readily that one historian later remarked that with the Washington Naval Treaty, Hughes had managed to sink more ships "than all the admirals of the world have sunk in centuries."

Hughes was not about to walk away from such hard-won accomplishments, and in the fight over the Japanese ban, he appeared to have the upper hand. Hiram Johnson, the senior senator from California who had been building support for the ban alongside his friend McClatchy, was not in Washington for the debate; he was in the Midwest campaigning for the Republican presidential nomination. His far less charismatic junior colleague, Samuel Shortridge, was left to gather support, and his efforts stalled.

There was one recurring complaint, though, that Hughes felt compelled to address. Johnson and others questioned whether the Gentlemen's Agreement was legally binding, given that it had been negotiated in secret between the two governments rather than passed through Congress. To settle any confusion about the terms, Hughes contacted Japanese ambassador Masanao Hanihara, with whom he had worked closely during the disarmament conference. Hughes proposed that if the ambassador wrote a note summarizing the deal, he could share it with Congress.

Hanihara phrased the letter carefully. He delicately pointed out the lengths to which Japan had gone to clarify the terms of the Gentlemen's Agreement during its negotiations with the United States, defended his country's implementation of the deal, and argued that banning a small number of Japanese immigrants did not seem worth damaging Japan's relationship with the United States.

> It is indeed difficult to believe that it can be the intention of the people of your great country, who always stand for principles of justice and fair play in the intercourse of nations, to resort, in

order to secure the annual exclusion of 146 Japanese, to a measure
which would not only seriously offend the just pride of a friendly
nation, that has always been earnest and diligent in its efforts to
preserve the friendship of your people, but would also seem to
involve the question of the good faith and therefore of the honor
of their Government, or at least of its executive branch.

In closing, Hanihara wrote, "I realize, as I believe you do, the grave consequences which the enactment of the measure retaining that particular
provision would inevitably bring." On April 11, 1924, Hughes delivered
Hanihara's letter.

The next day, as the House prepared to vote on Johnson's bill, Celler
rose to propose an amendment that would clarify that nothing in the legislation should "affect the validity" of the Gentlemen's Agreement with
Japan. Johnson, pretending he did not understand the bill's implication
for Japanese immigration, replied that Celler's amendment did not seem
relevant to the bill. When Celler tried to explain further, the chairman
presiding over the debate, Republican Everett Sanders, cut him off. "The
amendment offered by the gentleman from New York is an amendment
dealing with diplomatic relations. It is not germane at this point of the
bill if germane at all."

In the Senate, Henry Cabot Lodge had remained largely quiet on
the Japan question. But three days after the Hanihara letter arrived, as
debate on the ban continued on the Senate floor, Lodge suddenly moved
that the Senate go into an executive session, a special meeting reserved
for considering treaties and nominations from the president. When the
senators emerged after fifty minutes, Lodge dramatically took to the
Senate floor to restate "what I had said behind closed doors." The letter
from Hanihara seemed "improper to be addressed by the representative of one great country to another friendly country." Referencing the
phrase "grave consequences" out of context, Lodge claimed that the letter "contains, I regret much to say, a veiled threat. . . . The United States
can not legislate by the exercise by any other country of veiled threats."

The speech was a shocking maneuver, Lodge's last grand act in the Senate before dying that November of a stroke. Five years earlier he had delivered a similar knife to Wilson's beloved League of Nations, which he feared would weaken America's sovereignty. Either Lodge detected another such threat, in which his country risked being pushed around by a foreign power, or he was simply being his impulsive, aggressive self. Lodge's speech caused his colleagues to abandon any appearance of solidarity with Japan. Reed withdrew his support for a Japanese quota and said he now favored exclusion. Days later the Senate passed the bill with only six lawmakers dissenting.

President Coolidge made a last-minute plea for the exclusion clause to go into effect in a year or two so that he could try to negotiate with Japan and mitigate some of the diplomatic damage. But his request was rejected. On May 26, 1924, Coolidge, who had promised in his first annual message to Congress that "America must be kept American," signed the Johnson-Reed Act into law.

The lawmakers behind the bill understood the significance of what they had just done. Reed wrote in an April 27 essay for *The New York Times*, entitled "America of the Melting Pot Comes to End":

> In my opinion, no law passed by Congress within the last half
> century compares with this one in its importance upon the
> future development of our nation. . . . It will mean a more
> homogeneous nation, more self-reliant, more independent and
> more closely knit by common purpose and common ideas.

In a speech delivered to the Daughters of the American Revolution in Washington, Johnson said that the new legislation was "America's second Declaration of Independence."

The Japanese were in shock. The Tokyo press declared July 1, the date the law was set to go into effect, a day of national mourning. American movies were boycotted at movie theaters. On May 31 the body of an unidentified forty-year-old Japanese man was found near the former

American embassy in Tokyo: He had disemboweled himself with a six-inch dagger, committing hara-kiri in protest. He left a letter addressed to American ambassador Cyrus E. Woods: "I request by my death the withdrawal of the Japanese exclusion clause. . . . We are now humiliated by your country in the eyes of the world without any justification." Newspapers suggested a national funeral for the man since so many Japanese citizens felt he had captured their feeling of total humiliation by the United States. "I was never more profoundly impressed by a suicide," said the chief of Tokyo's police bureau. "He will probably be shown honors due to a soldier who died on the battlefield."

Other aspects of the immigration law touched off an immediate response overseas. It not only banned Asian immigration and sharply curtailed arrivals from southern and eastern Europe; it created a brand-new process for entering the country. Rather than simply showing up at a U.S. port in hopes of being admitted, prospective immigrants would now need to obtain visas at American consulates overseas before their arrival.

On July 1 thousands descended on consulate offices in Paris and Havana seeking visas. In Paris, the scene was so chaotic that police feared a riot and heavily guarded the consulate. Soon Ellis Island was the calmest it had been in years. A year after the law was signed, a *New York Times* reporter found Henry H. Curran, the island's immigration commissioner, sitting "quietly at his desk overlooking New York harbor with not a worry on his mind." Curran told him that in past years, there would have been twenty ships, "a veritable madhouse." On this day there were just two.

In 1927 Representative Johnson told *The New York Times* that things were going according to plan. The law, he boasted, had raised the bar for the type of person who could be accepted into the United States. "You can see the difference at Ellis Island," he said. "Officials there say that the immigrants who come through look like our own people coming home from a vacation." The effect on the overall numbers was immediate. For the year 1925, total arrivals plummeted 58 percent, from more than 700,000 a year earlier to fewer than 300,000.

On the other side of the Atlantic, a political prisoner in Germany observed these developments with envy. He worried that citizenship in his country was becoming too easy to attain. "Today the right of citizenship is acquired primarily through birth *inside* the borders of the state. Race or membership in the *Volk* [the superior German race] plays no role whatsoever," wrote Adolf Hitler in volume 2 of his autobiography, *Mein Kampf.* "The entire process of the acquisition of citizenship is hardly different from joining an automobile club." But there was a country, in Hitler's eyes, that could serve as a model for Germany:

> There is currently one state in which one can observe at least weak beginnings of a better conception. This is of course not our exemplary German Republic, but the American Union, in which an effort is being made to consider the dictates of reason to at least some extent. The American Union categorically refuses the immigration of physically unhealthy elements and simply excludes the immigration of certain races.

In these ways, Hitler wrote, America "already pays obeisance" to a race-based conception of the state.

Relations between the United States and Japan would continue to deteriorate for years, with some pointing to the law as one of the factors putting the two countries on course for the 1941 attack on Pearl Harbor. As Kikuichi Fujita, commander of the Eighth Squadron heading to Pearl Harbor, wrote in his diary in December 1941, the purpose of the attack was to teach the Americans a lesson after they had mistreated Japan for so long, including the exclusion of Japanese immigrants. The American diplomat George F. Kennan would later observe that relations between the United States and Japan made for a "long and unhappy story" because "we would repeatedly irritate and offend the sensitive Japanese by our immigration policies and the treatment of people of Japanese lineage."

Takao Ozawa continued to live in Honolulu. In 1926 he and his wife, Masako, started a general goods store in a little wooden building in Honolulu's Kaimuki neighborhood. On the night of November 16, 1936, almost exactly fourteen years after the Supreme Court decision that had denied Ozawa U.S. citizenship, he died in a hospital in downtown Honolulu, still a Japanese citizen. Six months before Pearl Harbor, his only son, George, enlisted in the U.S. Army. On October 21, 1943, George Ozawa died on the Italian front. He was twenty-six years old and a U.S. sergeant.

THREE

A "TRAGIC BOTTLENECK"

T HE POSSIBILITY OF WAR could not have felt more distant to Lyndon Johnson and Claudia Taylor in September 1934 as they drove for hours on the roads outside Austin, Texas. They were on their first date. A day earlier a mutual friend had introduced them, and Johnson had insisted on meeting at eight a.m. the next morning. As they cruised past limestone outcroppings and clear blue streams, he spoke about his dreams for his future in Washington, D.C., where, at twenty-six, he was already a powerful legislative secretary for Texan heir and congressman Richard Kleberg. He revealed his salary and how much insurance he carried. He told her about his family and how his mother and father, who had toggled between local politics and small-time farming, had struggled to put their five children through school.

As Johnson drove, Lady Bird, as Taylor had been called since she was a small child, guided them around the outskirts of Austin, a city she knew well. Months earlier she had received a second degree from the University of Texas. After graduating with a bachelor of arts degree in history, she had stayed on an extra year to study journalism because, as she'd later tell biographer Marie D. Smith, "I thought that people in the press went more places and met more interesting people, and had more exciting things happen to them." She confided to Johnson that she wasn't sure what she wanted to do next. She was currently living with her wealthy father in Karnack, a small Texas town near the Louisiana border, and helping him fix up the family's antebellum mansion, known to locals as the Brick House. But the work bored her. Lady Bird, whose mother had died when she was five and whose father had always been consumed by work, preferred reading books to picking out curtains.

By the end of their date, Johnson asked her to marry him. "I just sat there with my mouth open, kind of," Lady Bird recalled years later. He was clearly her opposite: whereas she was careful in her decisions and comfortable with solitude, he barged headlong through life and craved human contact. But something about this tall, eager, forward man excited her. He had ambition. She could not bring herself to accept his proposal—but she wasn't ready to reject it, either.

Johnson returned to Washington, and the breakneck pace of their courtship continued by mail. Because her notes took days to reach him, Johnson complained to the federal postal service that the speed of delivery between Washington and Karnack was unacceptable. He pressed Lady Bird for an answer to his marriage proposal, cajoling her with the same tactics he would later perfect on Capitol Hill. "Tomorrow I plan to call you. Tomorrow I plan to tell you again what you have already heard so many times and probably it will be tomorrow that I learn definitely just how and where you stand," he wrote. "Write me that long letter. Tell me just how you feel—give me some reassurance if you can and if you can't let's understand each other now."

On days when she didn't hear from him, she said she had "had no idea how peculiarly empty a day would be without a letter from you." Her drive for self-improvement, which would surface again in their marriage when she frequently changed her style in order to please him, was plainly evident in her letters. "Lyndon, when I get up to Washington my brain will have reverted to the idiot stage!" she wrote. "'Cause I never use it for anything more exacting than the design I want for my garden seat and the best material to upholster the wicker chairs in et cetera ad infinitum. . . . So I'm going to buy me two or three up-to-the-minute books on economics and government or what's-the-world-coming-to. . . . Do you ever have time to read, lamb, and do you ever read this kind—I mean have you any suggestions?"

Johnson, who had briefly been a schoolteacher before the world of politics beckoned, sent her books on the U.S. Capitol building and his idol, Franklin Delano Roosevelt. He asked before sending her a book on Nazism, perhaps sensing it would be a particularly intense choice for wooing a young woman. She assured him she would be "thrilled" to get the book, as Nazism was "such a controversial subject and I know nothing at all about it."

Many Americans were also in the dark. If they lived in a big city, they had probably seen, on the front pages of *The New York Times*, the *Chicago Tribune*, or *The Washington Star*, stories about Adolf Hitler's startling ascent and the Nazi Party's persecution of political enemies and Jews. But few understood that Nazi ideology posed an existential threat to Jews and liberal, tolerant societies everywhere. Johnson sent Lady Bird *Nazism, an Assault on Civilization*, a collection of essays on the unique horrors of Nazi Germany. They were written by prominent American writers including Dorothy Thompson, a journalist who had been deported from Germany following her negative coverage of Hitler, and who at the time was one of the most famous women in America.

Lady Bird might well have been terrified by what she read. It was a book of shocking prescience and moral clarity, published seven years before the United States entered World War II. As James Waterman Wise, son of noted Rabbi Stephen S. Wise, wrote in the book's introduction:

> Hitler has made clear in word and deed that what he has
> enforced at home he will seek to impose abroad. Nor may
> refuge be taken in the facile assumption that what has been
> perpetrated in Germany is inconceivable in the United States.
> Nazism appeals to the worst in men and peoples, to the latent
> bigotries, to the suppressed hatreds, to the primitive fears which
> still burn beneath the surface of modern life.

Johnson inscribed in the copy he sent, "To Bird in the hope within these pages, she may realize some little entertainment and find reiterated here some of the principles in which she believes and which she has been taught to revere and respect." Within weeks they were married.

Johnson proved to Lady Bird that he could take her far away from Karnack. His gift of a book on Nazism revealed a worldliness that belied his small-town Texas roots—and an indication that he perhaps understood the threats to Jews better than most Americans.

Over the next two decades, as the United States was drawn deeper into a battle against the horrors of Nazi Germany, Johnson and America's leaders would face firsthand the tragic limits of the U.S. immigration system. The racial quotas instituted so urgently in the 1920s to assuage domestic fears of foreigners—shutting the door on much of Europe—would make it nearly impossible for Jews seeking safe harbor to find it in the United States.

Activists and representatives in Congress who sought to change the quota system, even on the margins, faced a brick wall as the public remained instinctively anti-immigrant. Johnson, with his genius for bending systems to his will, would find ways to save a handful of refugees with whom he had a personal connection. But it was a time when one man could only do so much.

—

EVEN THOUGH JOHNSON was born in Texas Hill Country, far from the urban centers that were flourishing with Jewish life, he would grow to hold a special place in his heart for the Jewish people.

His grandfather and his aunt, Jessie Hatcher, were members of the Christadelphian religious sect, which believed that upon the return of Jesus Christ, a kingdom of God would be established in Jerusalem in which Jews would have a place of honor. Hatcher frequently visited her brother—Lyndon's father, Sam Johnson—in Texas. When asked in a 1968 interview what advice she gave to Johnson when he became a politician, Hatcher said she told her nephew to never "go against" Israel and that the Jews are "God's people, and they are always going to be."

Sam Johnson opposed the Ku Klux Klan's religious and racial intolerance during his on-and-off career as a state legislator. He used the phrase "Kukluxsonofabitch" so often that Lyndon's brother, Sam Houston Johnson, later said he didn't realize "son of a bitch" was a separate phrase until he was in high school.

More than these other factors, though, it was Lyndon Johnson's steep climb out of Texas Hill Country that led him to side with underdogs throughout his political career. Johnson took a peripatetic route to Washington, of the kind required of a young man without much in family money or connections. In 1924, instead of going straight to college after high school, he drove to California in a Model T with some friends in search of a more exciting life beyond the borders of Texas. For two years, he worked odd jobs as a field hand, diner cook, mechanic, then legal clerk for a cousin of his mother's. When he returned home, he borrowed seventy-five dollars to attend Southwest Texas State Teachers College in San Marcos. To pay for his costs, he spent nine months earning credits and money teaching Mexican-American children.

In Washington, D.C., where he would spend more than half his life, he never stopped seeing himself as a southern outsider who didn't fit in among East Coast elites. He was crude and loud in social settings where others had been taught to be calm and quiet. He hadn't attended the right schools, and he never forgot it. "My daddy always told me that if I brushed up against the grindstone of life, I'd come away with far more polish than I could ever get at Harvard or Yale," he told Doris Kearns Goodwin after he had left the White House. "I wanted to believe him, but somehow I never could."

When Johnson arrived in Washington in the winter of 1931, the country had entered its third year of the Great Depression, with no sign of the massive economic hardship abating. But for a hungry and willing Democrat like Johnson, it was the perfect time to land in the nation's capital. Within two years, President Herbert Hoover was out, and Franklin Delano Roosevelt had swept into town promising to bring relief to millions of unemployed Americans. Johnson, weaned on his father's populist instincts, embraced FDR's New Deal vision and its emerging coalition of Catholics, Jews, and union members. Roosevelt, having come up through the politics of New York, home to about half of all American Jews, forged a particularly strong and lasting bond between Democrats and Jewish voters. In 1930, as governor of the state, he denounced anti-Semitism. After he was elected president, his lieutenant governor, Herbert Lehman, became New York's first Jewish governor. At the White House, Roosevelt tapped a number of Jewish advisers. This did not escape the notice of bigots, who called Roosevelt's ambitious economic program the "Jew Deal" and claimed that Roosevelt, an Episcopalian, was in fact Jewish.

For his first several years on the Hill, Johnson immersed himself in the network of ambitious young New Deal Democrats working the levers of the largest economic stimulus program the country had ever seen. In 1935 he became the country's youngest state director of the National Youth Administration, a program created by Roosevelt to generate jobs for young Americans. Johnson built important friendships with up-and-comers like general counsel of the Public Works Administration Abe Fortas, a son of Jewish immigrants who would become one of Johnson's closest advisers in the White House and a Supreme Court justice. Johnson felt a sense of kinship with his new friends. In the 1930s Jews were still marked as "new immigrants," part of the wave of people who had arrived from southern and eastern Europe in the thirty-year period beginning in the 1890s. Since the passage of the immigration quotas, they were even more eager to prove that they could fit in the Anglo-Saxon elite.

Johnson also made Jewish friends back in Texas, while he worked for Congressman Kleberg. He frequently traveled on behalf of his boss, who preferred playing polo to mixing with constituents and who was content to let Johnson shake hands and kiss babies in his stead, which allowed the young staffer to quickly build a formidable network of supporters. Jim Novy, a Polish-Jewish immigrant who had settled in Austin and made money in the scrap metal business, became one of Johnson's earliest patrons and oldest friends. When Johnson decided to run for Congress in 1937, Novy gathered local Jewish activists at his lake house to help raise funds. It made sense for Johnson to cultivate support in the Jewish community. The tenth district of Texas, where he was running, was particularly diverse, with immigrants from Mexico, Germany, and eastern Europe entering from the port in Galveston. Johnson remarked years later that at the time he was elected to the House, newspapers in Austin were published in "six or eight languages" and that "from many lands, from many cultures, men brought their families here to escape oppression, to escape war, to search and seek for peace."

—

DURING THE 1930S Johnson made powerful friends in Washington who would help with his extraordinary political rise. But while the prominence of Jewish advisers in the Roosevelt administration was a breakthrough for this particular class of "new immigrants," they still could not turn the political establishment in their favor on the most pressing moral issue of their era.

A guarded man who hid the pain of his polio-induced disability behind a winning smile, Franklin Roosevelt projected tremendous empathy to ordinary Americans during the depths of the Great Depression. But he struggled with how to aid Jewish refugees in Europe. Hindered by the country's strict immigration laws and by anti-Semitism that ran deep both in the country and within some corners of his own administration, Roosevelt often found the obstacles overwhelming, or concluded the political costs of overcoming them were too high. In his second term, he used the powers of the presidency to circumvent some limits imposed by the quotas, and just before his death he established a special agency to save Jewish lives. Still, Roosevelt and Jewish-American leaders understood that many in the country would be less receptive to the war effort if it appeared to be primarily an operation to rescue Jews. Even more damaging, State Department officials who controlled the issuance of visas during his time in office routinely thwarted efforts to admit more Jews, citing the country's fragile economy and later, during the war, the threat of espionage. When Nazis began to invade eastern European countries in 1939, the strict U.S. limits on immigration from nations such as Poland and Romania made it nearly impossible for refugees to enter the United States. Quotas from the 1924 law, true to their design, severely restricted immigration. The law had slashed the number of German immigrants who could be admitted to 25,957. The total allotment for eastern European countries—Russia, Poland, Romania, Lithuania, Latvia, and Yugoslavia—all countries the Nazis would invade—was a meager ten thousand. By the most generous accounting, about 250,000 Jewish refugee immigrants came to the United States between 1933 and 1944. An estimated 6 million died under the Nazis. Even before the war ended, the catastrophic moral failure was clear. "If we had behaved like humane and generous people instead of complacent, cowardly ones, the 2 million Jews lying today in the earth of Poland and Hitler's other crowded graveyards would be alive and safe," wrote liberal journalist Freda Kirchwey for *The Nation* in 1943. "We had in our power to rescue this doomed people and we did not lift a hand to do it—or perhaps it would be fairer to say that we lifted just one cautious hand, encased in a tight-fitting glove of quotas and visas and affidavits, and a thick layer of prejudice."

It is impossible, however, to take the full measure of Roosevelt's actions during this time without acknowledging that from the moment he took office, he faced two historic challenges requiring an unprecedented marshaling of American resources and resolve. The Great Depression had wiped out the savings and jobs of millions of Americans and posed the greatest threat to the survival of the country since the Civil War. On January 30, 1933, thirty-three days before Roosevelt was sworn into office, Adolf Hitler, who had already signaled a terrifying willingness to persecute his enemies, became chancellor of Germany. Roosevelt grasped early on that the United States would need to confront Hitler with military power, but the path to war was politically treacherous in ways that

would also challenge America's ability to admit refugees. The U.S. mood
had turned staunchly isolationist after World War I, a conflict that many
Americans felt had been a pointless exercise in saving Europe from itself.
The nation's leaders had written off the possibility of another war overseas
so much that they had reduced the U.S Army to a size smaller than Portugal's. The nativism that had overtaken the country in the 1920s and that
had led to the strict new immigration quotas had only been made worse in
the 1930s by widespread economic ruin. Mexican immigrants and their
children, many American-born, were deported en masse, for fear that
they were taking jobs from Americans. Anti-Semitism was rampant.

One of the best-known men in America during the 1930s was Father
Charles Coughlin, a Catholic priest whose weekly radio broadcast
attracted millions of listeners. Coughlin won over his fans with a potent
mix of Christian sermonizing and economic populism, layered with a
casual hatred of Jews. In a 1930 sermon, he referred to Wall Street bankers as "modern Shylocks . . . grown fat and wealthy." Coughlin's radio
program reflected the broad anti-Semitism in American society that
remained intact even as conditions for Jews deteriorated in Europe. In
the spring of 1938 the American Jewish Committee commissioned two
polls by the Gallup organization to gauge public opinion: 45 percent of
those polled said that Jews had too much power in the United States,
while 26 percent said Germany would be better off if it drove out its Jewish population.

This was a delicate time to be advocating for Jewish interests, however great the need. Jewish activists were split on how frequently to stage
protests in the United States. On March 20, 1933, the American Jewish
Committee and the Jewish community service organization B'nai B'rith
issued a joint statement expressing "horror at the anti-Jewish action in
Germany," but they condemned any boycotts, parades, or mass meetings
protesting the Nazi Party, citing Jewish contacts in Germany who had
warned them that such displays would only backfire. Many in the Jewish
activist community feared that if they or Roosevelt made too much noise
about persecutions in Nazi Germany, it would only feed the ugliest anti-

Semitic myths about Jews controlling powerful governments. Indeed, Jews had already been accused of starting World War I and ruining Europe in order to enrich themselves and gain more power.

The risks for Roosevelt were also profound. Only after several years of delicate political maneuvering did he succeed in convincing Americans that it was worth sending their sons to die fighting the Nazis. That task would have been even harder had there been even a hint that the war's purpose was to save an unpopular religious minority. Many Jewish leaders, including Brooklyn congressman Mannie Celler, understood the president's situation and were careful not to pressure him too much. But those leaders would sometimes slip, claiming to speak for Roosevelt when desperate advocates wanted to understand how the president viewed the growing crisis.

On July 30, 1935, Celler spoke at a protest meeting at the Pythian Temple on West 70th Street in Manhattan. The building, a 150-foot Egyptian-style Art Deco high-rise built to look like something from a D. W. Griffith movie set, usually housed the headquarters for the secret society the Knights of Pythias, but on this evening it was filled with seven hundred Jewish and sympathetic Christian activists eager to boycott the 1936 Summer Olympics in Berlin. Because the president had said barely anything publicly about protecting German Jews, it fell to Celler to assure the crowd of Roosevelt's private feelings. "I visited the White House this morning," he told them. "I visited the President, and I am happy to tell you he is in sympathy with meetings such as this. He wants you to protest. He is in accord with the aims and purposes of the meeting." He continued: "I know for a fact that President Roosevelt has protested in the past, both to [Hjalmar] Schacht, head of the German Reichsbank, when he was in this country, and to the German ambassador in Washington. He has summoned the German Ambassador to the White House and told him that Hitler had better beware."

Roosevelt had indeed met privately with Schacht, the Nazi Party's brilliant financial architect, two years earlier, and had afterward written to Judge Irving Lehman, a leader of the American Jewish Committee, that "at last the German Government now knows how I feel about things. . . . It is probably better to do it this way rather than to send formal notes of protest, because, frankly, I fear that the latter might result in reprisals in Germany."

The meeting with Schacht typified Roosevelt's approach to diplomacy: back channels were paramount. He and Churchill would later lay the groundwork for the United States to formally join the war, saving Great Britain from falling to the Nazis, via secret meetings aboard ships. At a moment when tensions with Germany were already high, Celler had potentially upset the balance by revealing the content of Roosevelt's meetings with senior Nazi officials.

The next day, at the president's press conference, reporters first asked Roosevelt about a diplomatic impasse over an American mob that had torn down a Nazi swastika flag from a German shipping liner, the *Bremen*, docked in New York. The German government was protesting the act, and Roosevelt declined to comment about the incident. He was then asked about Celler's remarks, which had appeared in *The New York Times*. Roosevelt didn't deny the Brooklyn congressman's account, but neither did he elaborate on what he'd told Celler. Celler was concerned enough about the situation that he immediately dispatched a letter to Roosevelt expressing "regret" for any embarrassment he may have caused:

> I want to assure you that I was most careful in my remarks at this meeting. I clearly indicated the required limitations of the Presidential office in matters of this sort, and that it would be most impolitic for any President to accede to the extreme wishes of many of those who deplore the Nazi atrocities. . . . I urged [the protesters] to have the greatest confidence in you and that I felt you would leave no stone unturned within the limitations of your office to assuage these Hitler wrongdoings. . . . I hope that you were not in any way rendered uncomfortable at the aforesaid press conference.

Roosevelt responded breezily to his loyal New Deal ally, addressing him as "Dear Mannie": "It was good of you to write me in explanation of the statements you made in your New York address last Tuesday. Everything is all right. It is another case of water over the dam—a closed incident as far as I am concerned." One can almost hear the sigh of relief from Celler. But Roosevelt had merely forgiven his friend a political trespass. He did not say whether Celler's statement had been correct.

—

THE ONLY THING more politically explosive than speaking out against the Nazi threat was advocating for more German Jews to be admitted to the country, and on this front there was little progress. At first, the 1924 immigration quotas were not the problem: the issue lay instead in the State Department's criteria for permanent residency visas. In 1930, as the U.S. economy was unraveling, President Herbert Hoover ordered the State Department to more rigorously enforce a measure from an 1882 immigration law barring any foreigners likely to become "a public charge." The term had originally applied to those with physical or mental disabilities, but now in the context of the Great Depression, when jobs were scarce, Hoover wanted to apply it widely to any immigrants the government suspected would wind up on the welfare rolls. This was hardly a time when foreigners wanted to come to the country or stay if they were already residents; in 1931, for the first time in the nation's history, more people left the United States than entered it.

Soon after Roosevelt's inauguration, Jewish leaders and advisers, including Irving Lehman and Felix Frankfurter, encouraged him to loosen Hoover's interpretation of the law to allow more German Jews to immigrate to the United States. The rule seemed especially cruel when applied to those who were newly barred from holding many jobs in Germany, including in the country's civil service. Frankfurter, who later became a Supreme Court justice, went so far as to draft executive orders for the president to undo Hoover's rule. But the State Department officials who oversaw the American visa system were dead set against aiding persecuted Jews, believing the threat of the Nazi Party was overstated. A few of them also harbored anti-Semitic prejudices. Undersecretary of State William Phillips once wrote in his diary, in reference to a trip to Atlantic City, that the place was "infested with Jews. In fact the whole beach scene on Saturday and Sunday afternoon was an extraordinary sight—very little sand to be seen, the whole beach covered by slightly clothed Jews and Jewesses."

In the spring of 1933, Labor Secretary Frances Perkins, who had become the first female cabinet secretary, appealed to Roosevelt to relax the Hoover rule. But the president, who often preferred to stay out of conflicts within his administration, declined to take a side in the fight between State and Labor. For five crucial years, during which the situation for Jews under Nazi rule steadily turned nightmarish, America's German immigration quota of roughly 25,000 went unmet.

In September 1935, Hitler established the Nuremberg Laws, which stripped Jews of the basic rights afforded by citizenship. In fiscal 1936 only about 6,300 Germans, mostly Jews, came to the United States. More than 97,000 had intended to immigrate by the end of that year, according to State Department data.

In January 1937, after Roosevelt decisively won reelection, his administration finally tweaked the Hoover rule so that consuls were instructed to reject applicants who were "probable public charges" rather than just "possible public charges." That fiscal year the number of German immigrants surpassed 10,000—though that was still well below the quota limit.

The next year the quota was quickly filled, yet American-Jewish activists and lawmakers continued to disagree about how hard to press the issue. On March 24, 1938, Celler introduced a bill that would allow the president to lift the immigration quotas to admit victims of religious, racial, and political persecution. But when news emerged that he had introduced his bill, Jewish leaders were furious. The bill was controversial on its own, but having a Jewish congressman propose it made it seem self-interested.

Rabbi Stephen S. Wise wrote to Frankfurter, "Celler, to our amazement and horror, is introducing a resolution into Congress . . . which is very bad, so bad that it almost seems the work of an agent provocateur." Wise criticized Celler as being "not a particularly . . . scrupulous person. Even if it were all true and he really were thinking of nothing but November 8, 1938 [the date of the upcoming elections], he should have had a non-Jew introduce the measure." Celler's proposal went nowhere. The following month Jewish lawmakers in the House agreed with one another not to introduce any more bills aimed at loosening immigration laws.

In November of that year most Americans reacted in horror to the infamous *Kristallnacht*, in which Nazi rioters attacked Jewish residents and destroyed hundreds of synagogues over the course of a single night. On November 15 Roosevelt read from a statement at a press conference, "The news of the past few days from Germany has deeply shocked public opinion in the United States. . . . I myself could scarcely believe that such things could occur in a twentieth century civilization." But when questioned by reporters whether the president would now relax the country's immigration restrictions to admit Jewish refugees, Roosevelt replied, "That is not in contemplation. We have the quota system."

Roosevelt could sense that while Americans were disturbed by the actions of Nazi Germany, they were not ready to abandon, or even revisit, the 1924 immigration law. Two months after *Kristallnacht*, a national poll asked Americans, if they were part of the incoming Congress, whether they would support a hypothetical bill "to open the doors of the United States to a larger number of European refugees than are now admitted under our immigration quota." Eighty-three percent said no.

Back-channel attempts to adjust the quotas also failed. In late 1938 British ambassador Ronald Lindsay asked Undersecretary of State Sumner Welles if the quota for German immigrants to the United States could be increased if Britain gave up the bulk of its unused 65,000 slots. This way the Americans could save more Jews from what looked now to be certain violence. Welles dismissed the idea, saying that the quotas were the quotas and could not be transferred between countries.

Faced with a nearly impenetrable wall of bureaucracy, some refugees took to relying on powerful connections to escape. One of those tapped for help was none other than Lyndon Johnson, who in 1937 had won a special election to Congress after Texas legislator James Buchanan died.

—

JOHNSON FAMOUSLY WORKED HIMSELF and his staff to exhaustion. One Austin journalist reported that Johnson signed 258 letters to his constituents a day. Every newly married couple in his district received a personal letter of congratulation from Johnson; every new mother was sent a copy of the book *Infant and Child Care*. And letters were the least of it. Johnson's hardest work went into making sure the fruits of the New Deal reached his district. The Rural Electrification Administration had brought electric power to his childhood community. He had obtained millions of dollars in WPA grants for the counties in his district, including $112,000 for an Austin City Hall project and $27,000 for a sewing-room project in Bastrop County. He had improved mail service for Austin and secured federal loans for farmers. "When I thought about the kind of Congressman I wanted to be," he later reflected, "I thought about my Populist grandfather and promised myself that I'd always be the people's Congressman, representing all the people, not just the ones with money and power."

Johnson surely believed this—the same impulse would animate his Great Society agenda decades later—but from the earliest days of his political career, he also carefully tended to a handful of wealthy benefactors, whom he enriched by directing contracts to their businesses and cultivated by flattering their egos.

One of those benefactors was Charles Marsh, a millionaire and a savvy newspaper publisher who had begun his career as an editor in his home state of Ohio before hopping across the country turning small, family-owned publications into profit machines. Throughout the 1920s and 1930s, he built an empire of newspapers, including the *Austin*

American-Statesman, the *Waco News-Tribune*, and the *Orlando Sentinel*. He parlayed his money into other business interests, particularly in Austin, where he also owned a streetcar franchise and significant real estate. Lady Bird described him as one of the most interesting people she ever met and noted that he had a "head like a Roman emperor ought to look." He had the temperament to match: Marsh was a domineering man. "His lifestyle was on purpose different from other people, and I think he did it in a way, perhaps, to irritate some people," Lady Bird recalled. At his eight-hundred-acre estate near the edge of the Blue Ridge Mountains in Virginia, named Longlea after the English manor on which it was modeled, Marsh gathered politicians, journalists, musicians, academics, and businessmen—whoever he needed in order to generate scintillating conversation over elaborate dinners. Always by his side at Longlea was his partner, Alice Glass, a statuesque blonde described by one colleague as "a Viking princess." Glass matched Marsh's appetite for politics, arts, and interesting people. "Alice had a great presence," said Frank Oltorf, a lobbyist who was a regular at Longlea. "When she walked in a room, everyone looked at her." She was celebrated for her impeccable, effortless style and could command a conversation on any topic with other intelligent, charming people. Men raved about the soothing sound of her voice. When Marsh met Glass, twenty-four years his junior, in 1931, he became so taken with her that he soon left his wife and children for her.

Lady Bird had briefly crossed paths with Glass in Austin, when the future first lady was still a student at the University of Texas and Glass was working as a secretary for a Texas legislator. The diffident Lady Bird, who preferred wearing shoes with low, thick heels, felt intimidated by Glass, the kind of woman who seemed designed to make other women feel insecure.

Johnson, on the other hand, fit easily into the world of Longlea, where he made other guests feel like political insiders by regaling them with stories from Washington. Marsh immediately liked Johnson and wanted to play a role in elevating the congressman to a greater office. Glass, too, was smitten. A few years into their marriage, Lady Bird learned she wasn't the only woman who could be quickly seduced by Lyndon Johnson. The fine print in their unspoken marital contract was beginning to emerge: She would indeed gain entrée into intellectual circles like the one cultivated by Marsh and Glass, but in exchange, she—a woman who had grown up with servants in her father's home—was expected to be the consummate politician's wife, entertaining guests in their small Kalorama apartment on short notice, accompanying constituents on endless tours of Mount Vernon, and filling her husband's ink pens and laying out his clothes for him at the start of each day. She would also have to swallow her pride when he didn't come home at night. Johnson made no secret of his philandering. An interviewer years later confronted Lady Bird about her late husband's womanizing, and she responded, "You have to understand, my husband loved people. All people. And half the people in the world were women. You don't think I could have kept my husband away from half the people?"

At some point after meeting each other, Johnson and Glass began a series of trysts that some historians believe lasted for years. The affair was reckless for both parties; Johnson risked crossing Marsh, one of his earliest and most important backers, and Glass, who also depended on Marsh for his money and later bore two of his children, could lose everything. It is not clear if Marsh ever discovered the affair, though there were certainly some close calls. Johnson's congressional secretary John Connally unwittingly revealed his boss's whereabouts once when Marsh was trying to find Johnson at his office. Marsh called Johnson at the St. Regis in New York—where he was meeting Glass for a tryst. Johnson berated his aide for sharing a contact that was to be used only in case of emergencies: "Do you have a brain in your head? The next time I tell you not to let anyone know where I am, I mean exactly that."

—

REGARDLESS OF THIS ENTANGLEMENT, Johnson had every motivation to help his benefactor when Marsh asked him in the spring of 1938 to intervene on behalf of a twenty-six-year-old Jewish-Austrian named

Erich Leinsdorf. Marsh had met Leinsdorf only once, in Salzburg, where the Austrian had built a career as an orchestra conductor. Leinsdorf was the product of the illustrious musical scene of his native city, Vienna, where he had studied piano, cello, musical theory, and composition. When he was twenty, he had hiked 150 miles to Salzburg, the birthplace of Mozart and home to an annual summer opera festival helmed by two of the greatest conductors of the twentieth century, Arturo Toscanini and Bruno Walter. Both were impressed by Leinsdorf's talent and took him on as an assistant for the following few summers, to prepare operas that the world's most ardent music lovers—people like Charles Marsh and Alice Glass—traveled thousands of miles to attend.

But by 1937 the rise of the Nazis was casting an increasingly ominous shadow over the three musicians. Walter, a German Jew, had already been threatened by the Nazi Party and essentially banned from performing in Germany. Toscanini, an avowed antifascist, made sure the Salzburg festival continued to feature Beethoven's *Fidelio*, an opera written during Napoleon's sweep across Europe, about a political prisoner who triumphs over tyranny. In the summer of 1937, when Marsh and Glass met Leinsdorf at the festival, political controversy nearly engulfed the event. Toscanini was planning a performance of Wagner's *Die Meistersinger*, an opera that in recent years had been co-opted by the Nazi Party, which frequently played the music at its events. Toscanini's plan to perform the famous opera in Salzburg was his way to reclaim the work. He refused to allow German radio to broadcast the performance, and in retaliation the Nazi government threatened to block any German singers planning to leave for Salzburg. The performance was still a success (a *New York Times* reviewer called it "glorious"), but that year's festival ultimately became a valedictory performance for Toscanini, Walter, and Leinsdorf.

On March 12, 1938, German troops stormed into Austria, and the Nazi blueprint followed: Jews were attacked on the streets and purged from all corners of Austria's political and cultural life. Leinsdorf was at this time in the United States, four months into a six-month visa, working as an assistant conductor at the Metropolitan Opera. With two months left on his visa, Leinsdorf felt sure he would find a way to stay in the United States, because he had just secured another conducting contract, which would allow him to meet the government's standard of not becoming "a public charge." When he finished his engagement at the Metropolitan Opera, he filed an immigration application and then headed south to Longlea, where Marsh and Glass had invited him to stay. Even for Leinsdorf, a man who loved wearing beautiful clothing and drinking the finest French clarets, the decadence on display at Marsh's estate was shocking. "There was a constant stream of guests. . . . The accents were new, the lavish and easy life with martinis served at eleven in the morning was new . . . the eighteen black servants were new—I just sat goggle-eyed," he would later recall.

As a conductor, Leinsdorf developed a reputation for coaxing performances out of his orchestras that were so controlled and meticulous that some listeners found his style too cold. A 1962 *New York Times* profile noted that he was so "careful" that "he always wears a seat belt when riding in an automobile." "You know, what is considered great emotionalism can be, to me, just wild thrashing about," he once told a reporter in a characteristically blunt interview. Yet in the spring of 1938 he became so lost in the comforts of Longlea that he forgot about his perilous visa situation. He remembered "with a terrific shock," only eight days before his visa was set to expire, that he had never heard back from the U.S. government about his application. Marsh, "a man of quick decisions," sprang into action. That night he phoned his friend Johnson.

Marsh asked Johnson to meet him and Leinsdorf the next day, a Sunday, in downtown Washington, at the Mayflower Hotel, where Marsh maintained an apartment. Leinsdorf remembered that "a lanky young man appeared. He treated Charles with the informal courtesy behooving a youngster toward an older man to whom he is in debt." As Marsh and Leinsdorf relayed the problem, Johnson listened "impassively," not because he was indifferent but because Johnson had likely handled immigration cases for his former boss, Richard Kleberg, and knew the bureau-cratic system better than most young congressmen.

The first step was to determine whether Leinsdorf's bid for staying in the country had gone through. On Monday, Johnson phoned with the answer. He told Leinsdorf that authorities had rejected the application but a clerical oversight had prevented the notice from being mailed. Using that as leverage, Johnson explained he had "exerted his pressure to have the customary phrase 'You have seven days to leave the United States' changed to, 'You have six months.'" The next step was getting Leins-dorf assigned an immigration quota number associated with Austria, the country of his birth, so that he could receive a permanent visa. That spring, following the political union of Austria and Germany known as *Anschluss,* Roosevelt had combined the quota numbers for the two coun-tries for a total of 27,370 slots, to alleviate some of the pressure. The problem was figuring out who would be willing to issue the conductor a visa, given that hundreds of thousands were clamoring unsuccessfully for the same slots. That same year Anne Frank's father, Otto, applied for a visa for his family; at the time they were hiding in the Netherlands but would be counted under the German quota. The waiting list was so long that the family was never interviewed; their application was lost in a 1940 Nazi air raid of Rotterdam that destroyed the U.S. consulate and all the records inside.

For Jews desperately trying to enter the country, U.S. consuls held all the power. Many were anti-Semitic, but not all. Coert Du Bois, the American consul in Cuba, was known to be extraordinarily sympathetic to the plight of Jewish refugees. To expedite the admission process, Du Bois would sometimes delegate immigration paperwork directly to Jew-ish advocacy groups. Johnson asked Du Bois to assist Leinsdorf, who went to Cuba and immediately received a visa under the Germany-Austria quota. Seven days later the conductor was in the United States. In 1942 he became a U.S. citizen. When Leinsdorf tried to bring his mother and her sister to join him, Johnson successfully inquired on their behalf with the State Department. In 1944 Leinsdorf wanted to sponsor two refugees he had met in Cuba and asked Johnson for a letter of reference. Johnson wrote: "In short, Erich Leinsdorf always has a blank check with my name signed to it because he is possessed with the qualities that justify his being called a great American." Later, after Johnson became a senator, Leinsdorf sent him a note disapproving of a particular vote he had cast. As Leinsdorf recalled, Johnson wrote back, "I did not know what a marvelous citizen I was going to help in making when I was fortunate enough to be able to be of service." The way Leinsdorf had expressed his opinion, Johnson declared, was "just what this country's made of and about."

Johnson would use the same method to help other Jewish refugees, including Gela Nowodworski, the widow of Austin-based Johnson supporter Jim Novy's brother, Sam, and two of her sons. Nowodworski and her sons had escaped from Poland to Mexico, but now they wanted to reach the United States to be reunited with the rest of the Novy family. Jim Novy booked a ship for them to New Orleans and awaited their arrival on the appointed day, but they were not allowed into the country: U.S. officials had blocked their passage. Novy reached out to Johnson, who, weeks after helping Leinsdorf, turned again to the consul in Havana. Johnson told Novy to put his family on a boat to Cuba. There the family's papers were immediately processed. A few weeks later they arrived in the United States. Johnson would later also help Nowodworski's third son enter the country.

At times Johnson's efforts fell tragically short. In late 1938 Rabbi Abram Vossen Goodman, head of Austin's oldest synagogue, Temple Beth Israel, contacted Johnson in desperation. Soon after *Kristallnacht*, Goodman had received a cable from his German cousin Hermann Winter saying he had been arrested and sent to Dachau. Winter was going to be released, but only on the condition that he would leave Germany. Johnson turned to his usual solution, Cuba, but the political situation there had changed in a matter of months. Like the United States, Cuba was now suffering from an economic downturn, and its government was becoming less willing to host, even temporarily, more refugees. Johnson suggested Mexico to Goodman as an alternative, writing to the assistant secretary of state for assistance. He also called on State Department staff. No help materialized. In April 1939 Johnson wrote to the American ambassador to Mexico, Josephus Daniels, asking him to request that Mexican officials expedite a temporary entry permit for Winter. By way of reference, Johnson wrote of Goodman, "He is one of our finest and most esteemed citizens in Austin." Daniels in turn wrote to his bosses in Washington to ask if he could assure Mexican authorities that Winter would stay in their country only for a short while and that the United States would admit him once his quota number came up. But assistant secretary of state George Messersmith was not interested in bending the rules one iota. "While the difficult position of persons in Central European countries who find it necessary to emigrate to other countries and who desire to come to the United States eventually is appreciated," he wrote, "there is no way under the law by which an American consular officer may give an assurance that any applicant on the waiting list will be found at some future date to qualify for a visa, since the qualification of an alien for a visa can only be determined when his turn is reached for final consideration."

This was not a surprising response from Messersmith. Months earlier he had written a memo opposing Roosevelt's desire, spurred by *Kristall-nacht*, to extend indefinitely the visitors' visas of any Germans currently in the United States. Messersmith said the decision was illegal and risked inflaming the public and Congress, both of which were still hostile to any loosening of immigration laws. Roosevelt had ultimately overruled him.

Rejected by Messersmith, Johnson told Goodman to continue pressing Winter's case through other channels, including the Mexican ministry of the interior. Months later Johnson told Goodman that he could finally get Winter into Mexico, if not the United States. Johnson booked him passage on a steamer from Hamburg to Tampico, Mexico, scheduled to depart on September 1, 1939. That day Germany invaded Poland. The steamer voyage was canceled, and Winter never left. He would die in a forced labor camp.

The number of such tragedies was about to grow exponentially. Following the takeover of Poland, the Nazis spent the next year invading and occupying Denmark, Norway, Belgium, the Netherlands, Luxembourg, and France, and the moral tests for America turned more discomfiting. In May 1939 the *St. Louis* sailed from Hamburg to Havana, carrying more than nine hundred Jewish refugees. Most of those on board had paid handsomely for tourist permits to land in Cuba, but while they were en route, the Cuban government decided to invalidate the documents. As the ship approached Havana, the passengers were informed that they were no longer permitted in the country. One man, traveling with his wife and two children, slit his wrists and jumped into the bay. Twenty-two refugees were allowed to land because they had immigration visas the government considered legitimate. The rest were stuck. The ship's captain, Gustav Schroeder, feared a "collective suicide pact" among the passengers if they were forced to return to Germany. After being forced to leave Havana, Schroeder diverted the *St. Louis* toward the Florida coast, while the U.S.-based Jewish Joint Distribution Committee negotiated with the Cuban government. The *St. Louis* sailed close enough to the U.S. shore that the passengers on board could see the lights of Miami. By now the story of the ill-fated ship had landed on the front pages of American newspapers. Friends and relatives of the passengers pleaded with the Roosevelt administration to act, but the State Department again refused to change its position, and the president declined to intervene. More than seven hundred on board were waiting for permanent American visas, but the combined German-Austrian immigration quota for that year—27,370— had already been filled. The wait list now stretched for several years, and U.S. officials did not want the refugees on the *St. Louis* cutting in front of others. Weeks later the ship sailed back across the Atlantic. The Joint Distribution Committee helped persuade Belgium, Britain, France, and the Netherlands to take many of the passengers. Still, an estimated 254 died after returning to Europe, most in extermination camps.

—

THAT YEAR CONGRESS would put forth its boldest effort to aid Jewish refugees—one they felt no one would be callous enough to reject. Senator Robert Wagner of New York and Representative Edith Rogers of Massachusetts introduced a bill that would permit the entry of twenty thousand refugee children above the immigration quotas. Prospects for the bill initially looked good. Neither of the legislation's cosponsors was Jewish, inoculating it against charges of tribalism, and it had the support of former president Herbert Hoover, American Catholic bishops, and Eleanor Roosevelt, in the first lady's first public display of support for the Jewish refugee cause. But opponents, including the American Legion and the Daughters of the American Revolution, seized on fears that any loosening of the 1924 quotas—even to aid children—would lead to a breakdown of the country's border control. Anti-Semitic critics also didn't like the idea of young Jews entering the United States when, as Senator Robert Reynolds, a North Carolina Democrat, put it, refugees were already "systematically building a Jewish empire in this country." In the end, the anti-immigration lawmakers prevailed. The immigration committees in the Senate gutted the Wagner-Rogers bill so severely that Wagner ultimately withdrew his support for it. It never reached the floor for a vote, and Roosevelt never commented on it.

As a legislator, Lyndon Johnson followed the lead of the president he admired deeply and trod lightly on immigration, leaving only a few footprints. In May 1937, soon after he took congressional office, he supported an immigration bill that would block the deportation of fifteen immigrants, most of them eastern European Jews. The refugees had arrived in the United States with fake visas sold to them by corrupt consular officials, but they had already established themselves in their new American communities. Two years later pro-restriction congressman Samuel Hobbs of Alabama sponsored a bill allowing the secretary of labor to indefinitely detain any immigrant who violated U.S. law and couldn't be deported. Johnson voted against the legislation.

Like many Americans, Johnson was at first circumspect about the United States entering the war. He understood through his involvement in specific cases that the Nazis posed a particular threat to Jews, but he also had a sizable German-American immigrant population in his district that he didn't want to antagonize. By 1941, though, after Nazi Germany had steamrolled through much of Europe and after the Japanese attack on Pearl Harbor, Johnson joined Roosevelt in a full-throated call to action. When the country entered the war later that year, Johnson was one of the first congressmen to enlist in the armed forces. He had already obtained a commission in the Naval Reserve and was appointed congressional inspector of the war's Pacific front. He came under fire during an aerial combat mission and received a Silver Star for his bravery. The war would redefine his view of America's place in the world, and its obligations. "One thing is clear, whether communist or fascist or simply a pistol-packing racketeer, the one thing a bully understands is force and the one thing he fears is courage," he said in a speech before Congress in 1947. "I want peace. But human experience teaches me that if I let a bully of my community make me travel the back streets to avoid a fight, I merely postpone the evil day. Soon he will chase me out of my house."

Roosevelt had succeeded in making the moral case for war, but he had generally sidestepped any mention of the Nazi persecution of Jews. As a result, Americans felt no more need to admit more European Jews than they had before entering the war. In fact, quite the opposite: the country became gripped by fear of a "fifth column" of foreign spies. Roosevelt relied on FBI director J. Edgar Hoover to use whatever means necessary to hunt down enemies within. Hoover ordered the arrest and detention of more than a thousand "suspected enemy aliens" of German and Italian descent. Later, Roosevelt would authorize the mass incarceration of Japanese Americans for no reason other than their ancestry.

For nations that were allies, however, American immigration laws loosened slightly as lawmakers and the administration realized, perhaps for the first time, that some of the xenophobic restrictions were getting in the way of U.S. foreign policy goals. Since 1882 the United States had banned anyone who was Chinese from establishing permanent residency and had excluded all Chinese immigrants from naturalization. That law was the first to single out a group of people in order to block them from immigrating and obtaining citizenship. But with China now a major ally in the war, the Chinese Exclusion Act was becoming an embarrassment. In late 1943 Congress repealed it. In a speech explaining why the ban should be lifted, Roosevelt said of the faith China had placed in its allies, "We owe it to the Chinese to strengthen that faith. One step in this direction is to wipe from the statute books those anachronisms in our laws which forbid the immigration of Chinese people into this country and which bar Chinese residents from American citizenship. Nations, like individuals, make mistakes. We must be big enough to acknowledge our mistakes of the past and correct them." This profession of generosity, however, did not match the actual change to the law. Following the repeal, only 105 "persons of the Chinese race"—and this included those born anywhere in the world, not just China—were permitted to enter the country each year.

Few others were being admitted to the United States. During the war, the State Department, already notorious for its anti-Semitism and its hostility toward refugees, became even more closefisted in its handling of visas. Beginning in 1940, Breckenridge Long, the scion of a powerful St. Louis family and an old friend of Roosevelt's, oversaw the State Department's visa operations. In a 1940 memo Long wrote, "We can delay and effectively stop for a temporary period of indefinite length the number of immigrants into the United States. We could do this by simply advising our consuls to put every obstacle in the way and to require additional evidence and to resort to various administrative devices which would postpone and postpone and postpone the granting of visas."

Celler and many Jewish advocates immediately distrusted Long. He was "cold and austere, stiff as a poker, highly diplomatic in dress and speech," Celler recalled. "He seemed to be far away as far as humanity is concerned." Celler met Long several times in meetings at the State Department, at funerals, and at receptions, and every time the men crossed paths, Celler would raise the issue of refugees. Long would tell him he was "very sorry about Hitler's action against the Jews," but the State Department did nothing. In November 1943 Long testified before the House Committee on Foreign Affairs that the country had taken in roughly 580,000 refugees over the last ten years, but as Celler pointed out, the majority were not Jews who had the greatest need to escape Europe. Long's statement "drips with sympathy for the persecuted Jews, but the tears he sheds are crocodile," Celler was quoted saying in a *New York Times* article. "I would like to ask him how many Jews were admitted during the last three years in comparison with the number seeking entrance to preserve life and dignity. It is not a proud record. Frankly, Breckenridge Long is least sympathetic to refugees in all the State Department. I attribute to him the tragic bottleneck in the granting of visas."

As the Nazis instituted the mass murder of Jews in each new country they invaded, it was becoming clear that they were no longer interested in merely expelling Jews from Europe; they wanted to exterminate them. Hitler's victims were trapped in a form of hell, the details of which the world is still struggling, today, to comprehend. As information on what became known as the Holocaust reached the White House, Roosevelt felt the best course of action for saving Jews would be to defeat Nazi Germany. But some inside his administration pressed harder than ever for the country to admit more refugees. Treasury officials John Pehle, Randolph Paul, and Josiah DuBois investigated the depth of the State Department's efforts to block Jewish immigrants and in January 1944 gave their results to Treasury secretary Henry Morgenthau, the only Jewish member of Roosevelt's cabinet. "Report to the Secretary on the Acquiescence of This Government in the Murder of the Jews" did not mince words: "Unless remedial steps of a drastic nature are taken, and taken immediately, I am certain that no effective action will be taken by this Government to prevent the complete extermination of the Jews in German controlled Europe, and that this Government will have to share for all time responsibility for this extermination." Then, quoting a withering line from Celler on Long, the memo concluded, "If men of the temperament of Long continue in control of immigration administration, we may as well take down that plaque from the Statue of Liberty and black out the 'lamp beside the golden door.'"

Morgenthau, Paul, and Pehle shared the findings with Roosevelt, and nine days later the president established the War Refugee Board, which would become the most direct and tangible U.S. effort to rescue Jews from the Holocaust. The board delivered relief supplies to concentration camps and helped evacuate refugees from Nazi-occupied countries. The exact number of lives saved cannot be known, but it certainly numbered in the many thousands.

The agency to save Jews was only one symbol of how the war had thrust a reluctant country onto the world stage as an important moral actor—and how this new role conflicted with America's immigration policies. The racial quotas were the product of a society with little regard for events or people outside its borders. But by the time Roosevelt died on April 12, 1945, while sitting for a portrait at his retreat in Warm Springs, Georgia, the United States was irrevocably entangled with the affairs of other nations. One war still needed to end, and another was about to begin. And to fight it, more walls would need to come down.

FOUR

"A LAND OF GREAT RESPONSIBILITIES"

T HE AMERICAN PEOPLE did not at first know what to make of their new president. Roosevelt, even as his health declined, had maintained the shine of his moneyed New York roots, and by the start of his fourth term he had taken on the air of an emperor. Harry S. Truman seemed so plain by contrast that it felt like watching a next-door neighbor suddenly be called upon to fulfill an immense duty. "In the long cabinet room he looked to me like a very little man as he sat waiting in a huge leather chair," said Roosevelt's press secretary Jonathan Daniels. Perhaps no one was more stunned than Truman himself. On the day after he was sworn into office, he asked reporters on Capitol Hill to pray for him. "I don't know whether you fellows ever had a load of hay fall on you. But when they told me yesterday what had happened, I felt like the moon, the stars, and all the planets had fallen on me."

This was the exact scenario Truman had feared. At the 1944 Democratic National Convention in Chicago, he had panicked upon learning that he might be named to Roosevelt's ticket to replace the sitting vice president, Henry A. Wallace. He told his Kansas City friend Tom Evans he was satisfied with being a senator for Missouri and feared the potential responsibility of being Roosevelt's vice president, given that "just a heartbeat, this little"—Truman gestured with his forefinger and thumb—separated him from the presidency. Roosevelt's aides, anticipating that the war would end during Roosevelt's next term, wanted someone like Truman, who had strong relationships on the Hill, to help lobby for the passage of important peace treaties. But at the convention, other men, including Wallace, were jockeying for the ticket and threatening to tear apart the Democrats. When party leaders, ensconced in a hotel room with Truman, informed Roosevelt that the Missouri senator was waffling, the president spoke into the phone so loudly the entire room could hear, "Well, you tell him if he wants to break up the Democratic Party in the middle of a war that's his responsibility," then hung up. Truman accepted, and in his convention speech he promised, "I've never had a job I didn't do with all I have."

Indeed, Truman's life so far had been a series of commitments into which he had thrown every inch of his being. Born in 1884 in a small town 120 miles south of Kansas City, Truman had grown up watching his father struggle to provide financial stability to his family. John Truman was a restless man who liked taking chances. He moved his family frequently as he tried farming on different patches of land, hoping each would be less dismal than the last. Around the time Harry graduated from high school, his father bet all the family's money, including his wife's inheritance, on grain futures. The move was a disaster. He lost everything and moved everyone to Kansas City so he could take a job as a night watchman. For Harry, the bad gamble meant he could not go to college. (Later he would become the only American president in the twentieth century who did not have a college degree.)

Truman had dreamed of living a big life, worthy of being written about in one of his most treasured books as a child, a four-volume set called *Great Men and Famous Women*, purchased by his mother for his tenth birthday. Because he had had unusually poor eyesight from a young age, Truman could not play sports with other children, lest he break the expensive eyeglasses his family could not afford to replace. Instead, he spent countless hours poring over stories about men like Moses and Andrew Jackson and developing a lifelong fascination with outsize figures of history.

Determined to transcend his family's rural roots, Truman went to work as a bank clerk in booming Kansas City, the largest city between San Francisco and St. Louis due to its location at the junction of the Kansas and Missouri rivers. But as soon as he grew accustomed to the rhythms of city life, he was called back home. His aging father had gone to work on his wife's parents' farm and needed help tending to the large property. Truman had so little interest in farming that his friends thought he might stick around for a few weeks—certainly no more than a year. Instead he remained for eleven years. Even if this was not the life he had envisioned, he was determined to do the job well. A perfectionist, Truman carefully studied how to rotate the crops of wheat, clover, corn, and oats to get the maximum harvest each year. He worked the farm daily to the point of exhaustion. "I have been working over an old binder," he wrote of a machine for harvesting wheat and oats in a letter to his future wife, Bess Wallace. "My hands and face and my clothes are as black as the ace of spades—blacker, because the ace has a white background. . . . I hate the job before me."

When Truman finally left the farm in 1917, it was to volunteer to fight in World War I. By then he was thirty-three, two years older than the cutoff for the draft, but he felt obligated to go. It was "a job somebody had to do," Truman told a friend.

Being a soldier finally gave Truman a glimpse of his destiny and exposed him to people and places unlike any he had known before. He led a field artillery unit named Battery D, made up mostly of Irish and German Catholics from Kansas City who were initially skeptical of their captain, a farmer from rural Missouri who wore thick glasses and seemed easy to push around. The group had developed a reputation for being difficult to control, and Truman realized that if he didn't instill some discipline, quickly, the results would be deadly on the battlefield. When it came time for combat, they were ready. Battery D fought in the sprawling Meuse-Argonne campaign, at the time the biggest offensive ever launched by the American military. Truman led his unit on a grueling march, much of it in the rain. They fought until the day of the armistice, November 11, 1918. More than 26,000 Americans died in the Meuse-Argonne offensive, none of them directly under Truman's command.

When Truman came home from the war, the powerful Tom Pendergast, known as the "big boss" of Kansas City, approached him about running for county judge. He won, then did not stop rising. Within ten years, he was in Washington, D.C., representing Missouri in the Senate. Now at the age of sixty, after a wildly circuitous path, he was the U.S. president.

Truman would dedicate himself to the job with the same single-mindedness he had brought to every other challenge in his life. But he quickly learned that among the many problems he had inherited was a catastrophic refugee crisis in Europe—one that had no easy solutions and that would force a reckoning with America's strict immigration system.

—

EVERY NIGHT AT THE WHITE HOUSE, after his staff had gone home, Truman carried his briefcase from the West Wing to his family's private quarters upstairs. He laid out a tall stack of papers and began to read. "I know nothing of foreign affairs," he confessed to Frank Walker, his first postmaster general, "and I must acquaint myself with them at once." As he pored over his documents, he tried to piece together the complex universe of problems he had inherited from Roosevelt, who had left behind few concrete plans. Truman committed to reading thirty thousand words a night, severely straining his already-weak eyes.

On the evening of August 24, 1945, Truman read a report that stopped him cold. The information it contained, he would tell senior aides the next morning, "made him sick."

Two months earlier Truman had authorized a mission in Europe to conduct a survey of Jewish refugees. The idea had come from Henry

Morgenthau, the Treasury secretary who had pressed Roosevelt for a War Refugee Board in order to save Jewish lives, albeit late in the war. Morgenthau, still mourning Roosevelt, had been trying to figure out a suitable role under the new president. (His friendship with Roosevelt had been the "most important thing" in his life, he once told an aide.) The only son of a German-Jewish real estate mogul in New York who dropped out of Cornell to become a gentleman farmer, Morgenthau had a nervous energy that often made people around him feel anxious. The British economist John Maynard Keynes, after just one meeting, found him "a difficult chap to deal with. . . . Everybody agrees that he is jealous and suspicious and subject to moods of depression and irritation." But around Roosevelt and his high-wattage charisma, Morgenthau had felt completely at ease. In 1934 Roosevelt had appointed Morgenthau, whom he lovingly called "Henry the Morgue," to the role of Treasury secretary.

Under Truman, Morgenthau found himself on entirely different— and weaker—footing. Truman, who could be prone to nursing grudges for years, never forgot that when he first joined the Senate in 1935, Morgenthau had seemed to snub him for his ties to the Pendergast Democratic machine. And Truman distrusted Morgenthau for other reasons, believing he was a Roosevelt crony who was unqualified for his job. As Truman pondered his next move in Europe, Morgenthau agitated for a harsh plan to strip Germany of its industrial capacity, in order to prevent the country from ever starting another war. Truman was skeptical of such an approach, believing, "You can't be vindictive after a war." But he kept Morgenthau as Treasury secretary for the time being, promising that when the time came for him to step down, Morgenthau would "hear from me first. Direct." On May 9 Morgenthau wrote in his diary that he believed Truman "likes me and has confidence in me, and I must say that my confidence in him continues to grow."

By the end of July, Morgenthau would be gone, along with several other members of the old Roosevelt cabinet. But before he left, he set in motion an ambitious plan to aid more Jewish refugees. Germany's surrender earlier that spring ended the mandate for the War Refugee Board. But Morgenthau soon heard from Jewish groups that the suffering was far from over. While Americans celebrated, more than 7 million displaced persons remained in occupied territories. Among them were devastated Holocaust survivors—roughly sixty thousand Jews who had walked out of liberated Nazi concentration camps. More than a third had died from malnutrition and disease within a week; the rest were now languishing in Allied-run camps.

Morgenthau lobbied his new boss to help them. In May he proposed to Truman that the War Refugee Board be replaced by a committee of three cabinet members from the departments of State, Interior, and Commerce, who were equipped to tackle the problem of displaced persons. On a memo from his chief administrative assistant Edward D. McKim that outlined Morgenthau's idea, Truman scrawled a handwritten note: "What good would such a board accomplish?" The idea did seem vague—an institution that would supplant the War Refugee Board but without a clear mission. A few days later, Truman decided against it, telling Morgenthau in a short note, "I have about made up my mind not to appoint any committee," and promising to discuss more in person.

Meanwhile Jewish leaders in Europe despaired that with every passing month, even more Jews would die. It was time to pressure the Americans. On June 7 Chaim Weizmann, one of the most influential Zionist activists in Europe, wrote to his American confidant, Meyer Weisgal, "I wonder whether the situation is being made clear to Talboker?" a Hebrew-coded reference to Morgenthau. (*Morgen* meant *boker* and *thau* equaled *tal*.) Weisgal, who served as a power broker for the Zionist cause among American Jewish organizations, contacted Morgenthau immediately and suggested that given the dire situation in Europe, the Truman administration should conduct a survey of the suffering. Morgenthau worked with the State Department to present the idea to Truman, who was more receptive to this approach. Instead of a committee, this would be a focused mission that could aid the president with important information.

Morgenthau recommended that Truman send Earl Harrison, dean of the University of Pennsylvania Law School and a former top-level immigration official, to conduct the survey. Harrison had grown up Presbyterian, so there would be no charge of pro-Jewish bias. On June 22, 1945, Truman authorized the trip. "It is important to the early restoration of peace and order in Europe that plans be developed to meet the needs of those who for justifiable reasons cannot return to their countries of pre-war residence," Truman wrote to Harrison. "I wish you every success in your mission and will be interested to receive your report upon your return."

Harrison was known as a cheerful man, but his trip to Europe brought him low. "Seldom have I been so depressed," he wrote in his diary on a day when he had spent seven hours, what "seemed like a life-time," at Bergen-Belsen, the infamous concentration camp, which had been turned into a makeshift shelter for displaced persons. Officials initially told him there was nothing to see since the site had been burned down and no one was left. But he found fourteen thousand people, more than half of them Jews, trapped behind barbed-wire fencing. In one area he found eighty-five people confined in a space no larger than eighty feet by twenty feet. Over the course of his trip he would visit about thirty camps to examine their conditions.

In August, Harrison's full report arrived at the White House. He wrote that three months after victory in Europe, the Jews had been "'liberated' more in a military sense than actually," and that their so-called liberators were now ignoring their needs. He observed:

> [Many Jews] are living under guard behind barbed-wire fences,
> in camps of several descriptions, (built by the Germans for
> slave-laborers and Jews) including some of the most notorious of
> the concentration camps, amidst crowded, frequently unsanitary
> and generally grim conditions, in complete idleness, with no
> opportunity, except surreptitiously, to communicate with the
> outside world, waiting, hoping for some word of encouragement
> and action in their behalf.

Clothing was scarce, so many still wore the uniforms of their concentration camps, "a rather hideous striped pajama effect," Harrison noted.

Some were even wearing old S.S. uniforms. "It is questionable which clothing they hate the more," said Harrison. Food was in short supply for everyone, but Harrison argued that the Jews, after suffering years of near-starvation in Nazi camps, could not be expected to survive on what they were now being fed: coffee and bread, often "black, wet and extremely unappetizing."

Then came the line that likely shook Truman to his core. "As matters now stand, we appear to be treating the Jews as the Nazis treated them except that we do not exterminate them," wrote Harrison. "They are in concentration camps in large numbers under our military instead of S.S. troops. One is led to wonder whether the German people, seeing this, are not supposing that we are following or at least condoning Nazi policy."

All this seemed inexcusable to Truman, given that the stated reason for the war had been to protect innocent people from the Nazis. In 1943 Truman had given a speech in Chicago in which he spoke eloquently of the moral justification for America's participation in World War II. He had condemned the "systematic slaughter throughout Europe, not only of the Jews but of vast numbers of other innocent peoples." Truman had added, "This is not a Jewish problem. It is an American problem—and we must and will face it squarely and honorably."

There was another reason Truman felt particularly moved by the plight of the displaced survivors of the war. During the Civil War, his mother's family had been harassed and then removed from their home in western Missouri by Union commanders trying to root out Confederate guerilla fighters. In 1863 a ruling that became infamous in Missouri for years—General Order No. 11—required the removal of twenty thousand people from their homes near the border with Kansas. Truman's mother remembered being permitted to take only one wagonload of the family's belongings. "For weeks they wandered along the hot Missouri roads until they found a safe place to stay," Truman remembered his mother telling him. Union soldiers pillaged the abandoned homes and burned what was left. The feeling of bitterness toward the Union Army was so strong that when Truman came home at some point during World War I to show his grandmother his National Guard uniform, she apparently warned him, "Harry, this is the first time since 1863 that a blue uniform has been in this house. Don't bring it here again." Years later Truman connected the suffering faced by his mother's family from Order No. 11 to the plight of the refugees in Europe after the war. "What happened to her and to thousands like her was happening to the Germans in Poland and Czechoslovakia in 1945."

After all his nighttime reading, Truman was beginning to see that one of his primary tasks as president would be to rebuild the continent of Europe, and the plight of Jewish refugees was a problem of the "highest humanitarian importance and urgency." Spurred by Harrison's report, he sprang into action, first turning his attention to the U.S. military, which was ill-equipped for the catastrophe.

After V-E Day, American soldiers suddenly found themselves faced with the task of handling a historic refugee crisis. Driven by a combination of ignorance and anti-Semitism, most did not know how to handle Holocaust survivors and were discouraged from treating Jewish displaced persons any differently from other Europeans. An American War Department pamphlet from 1944 instructed, "As a general rule, military Government should avoid creating the impression that the Jews are to be singled out for special treatment, as such action will tend to perpetuate the distinction of Nazi racial theory." As a result, the army failed to separate concentration camp survivors from non-Jewish refugees, some of them former guards or Nazi collaborators.

In southern Germany, General George S. Patton mandated that every camp be surrounded by barbed wire and overseen by armed guards. He wrote in his diary on September 15, 1945, that some "believe that the Displaced Person is a human being, which he is not, and this applies particularly to the Jews who are lower than animals." He added that if the refugees were not treated as prisoners, "they would not stay in the camps, would spread over the country like locusts, and would eventually have to be rounded up after quite a few of them had been shot and quite a few Germans murdered and pillaged." As one U.S. Army officer told a survivor, "The lowest thing in my country are the Negroes and the next lowest are the Jews. . . . We allow them to live but we don't like them."

On August 31 Truman sent a letter, attaching a copy of Harrison's report, to Dwight D. Eisenhower, commander of the Allied troops in Europe. Truman quoted Harrison's cutting conclusion and asked Eisenhower to "clean up the conditions" in the camps. "I know you will agree with me that we have a particular responsibility toward these victims of persecution and tyranny who are in our zone," Truman said. "We must make clear to the German people that we thoroughly abhor the Nazi policies of hatred and persecution. We have no better opportunity to demonstrate this than by the manner in which we ourselves actually treat the survivors remaining in Germany."

Harrison's report also forced Truman to confront an issue that would frustrate him throughout his presidency. Roosevelt had deftly avoided the question of whether there should be a Jewish state in Palestine, but with so many refugees spilling out of Europe, Truman felt obligated to find a place for them—if not in the United States, where resistance to adjusting the quotas remained strong, then in a slice of land that had been claimed by Britain amid the shards of the Ottoman Empire after World War I.

As Weizmann and Weisgal might have hoped, the Zionism issue surfaced in Harrison's report. Many of the Jews he interviewed said they wanted to leave Germany and Austria immediately and go to Palestine, "because they realized that their opportunity to be admitted into the United States or into other countries in the Western hemisphere is limited, if not impossible."

The Zionist movement had gained steam in the decades before the war. In the nineteenth century, nationalist movements proliferated throughout Europe, resulting in the formation of new states, such as Germany and Italy. As these nations were defined along ethnic lines, many in Europe argued that there was no room for an alien group of people like the Jews. Anti-Semitic persecution and violent assaults spread across the continent, pushing many Jews to flee to America,

Argentina, and the United Kingdom. The idea of establishing a Jewish state gained currency. If Germans were forming their own country, it made a certain sense for Jews to establish a nation in their ancient home of Palestine, if only to ensure their physical safety.

But Palestine was not an empty desert that Jews could simply enter. It was home to a sizable Christian and Muslim Arab population that also viewed the place as "Holy Land." In 1917 Britain made what became known as the Balfour Declaration, a formal endorsement of Palestine as a "national home for the Jewish people," to be established at some unnamed date. But since then, Britain had waffled on making good on its promise, fearing that angering the Arab population would endanger its access to oil in the region.

Truman might have been a neophyte on foreign affairs, but the politics of Zionism were not new to him. As a senator, he had received appeals to support a Jewish state from constituents in Kansas City and St. Louis, and he had occasionally lent his name, as did many other politicians, to support the cause. Truman felt genuine sympathy for the Jewish people. His close friend Eddie Jacobson, with whom he had started a haberdashery business after coming home from the war, was the New York–born son of eastern European Jewish immigrants. Jacobson later became an impassioned proponent within the White House for the United States to recognize Israel. But Truman also understood that supporting a Jewish state was simply good politics. New York, home to nearly 2 million Jews, was a hotly contested battleground in every presidential race, with the winner taking the largest number of Electoral College votes in the country. Although support among Jews for the Zionist cause was not unanimous, in 1944 both political parties included support for unfettered Jewish immigration to Palestine on their official presidential platforms. That year Roosevelt assured Senator Robert Wagner of New York, a leading supporter of Zionism, that if he were reelected, he would "help bring about [the] realization . . . of the establishment of Palestine as a free and democratic Jewish commonwealth." At the same time, however, Roosevelt told the Saudi leader Ibn Saud that he "would do nothing to assist the Jews against the Arabs."

Almost immediately upon taking office, Truman heard conflicting signals about what to do on the question of Palestine. Eight days after being sworn in, he received Rabbi Stephen S. Wise, leader of the American Zionist Emergency Council, who wanted to make sure Truman understood why the Jewish people were so interested in establishing a homeland in Palestine. But the State Department warned Truman to tread carefully. A May 1, 1945, memo from acting secretary of state Joseph Grew cautioned that "although President Roosevelt at times gave expression to views sympathetic to certain Zionist aims, he also gave certain assurances to the Arabs which they regard as definite commitments on our part." Truman also heard from the prime minister of Egypt, Mahmud Fahmy el-Nokrashy, who told him that while he felt sympathy for what the Jews had suffered at the hands of Hitler, the Arabs would resist a Jewish state "at all costs." Truman promised Mahmud he would consult both sides before making any decision.

On the day he wrote the letter to Eisenhower, Truman also wrote a long note to British prime minister Clement Attlee, who had succeeded Winston Churchill, attaching a copy of Harrison's report. As the Zionists who had helped press for the report had hoped, one of Harrison's recommendations was that one hundred thousand of the Jews in Europe be allowed to immigrate immediately to Palestine. Truman endorsed Harrison's proposal, adding, "No single matter is so important for those who have known the horrors of concentration camps for over a decade as is the future of immigration possibilities into Palestine." Truman was so determined to press the issue with the British that he did not even consult his own State Department before writing the letter, perhaps guessing correctly that officials there would try to talk him out of it.

Attlee, who lacked Churchill's warmth and charisma, was dismissive. He disagreed with the notion in Harrison's report that Jews should be treated any differently from other displaced persons. And he argued that any effort to open Palestine up to such levels of Jewish immigration, ignoring Arab interests, would "set aflame the whole Middle East."

Sensing that the British would not be as cooperative as he had hoped,

Truman pressed for Congress to make changes in the U.S. immigration system. He reached out to an old friend from the Senate, Walter George of Georgia, who served on the Senate Foreign Relations Committee:

> I sincerely wish that every member of the Congress could visit the displaced persons camps in Germany and Austria and see just what is happening to five hundred thousand human beings through no fault of their own. . . . There ought to be some place for these people to go—I am trying to find a place for them. There isn't a reason in the world why one hundred thousand Jews couldn't go into Palestine, nor is there any reason why we couldn't allow the unused quotas of northern Europe to be used to allow the entry of some of these displaced persons into our country. . . .
>
> I am not interested in the politics of the situation, or what effect it will have on votes in the United States—I am interested in relieving a half million people of the most distressful situation that has happened in the world since Attila made his invasion of Europe.
>
> Your ancestors and mine, if I remember correctly, came to this country to escape just such conditions. There is no place for people to go now unless we can arrange it.

The Zionist groups favored the establishment of a Jewish state in Palestine over other potential solutions. Some even downplayed the goal of admitting more Jews to the United States, fearing that such a move would hurt the argument that Palestine had to be opened *now* for Jewish entrants or they would have nowhere else to go.

The effort to come to an agreement with the British government, though, continued going nowhere. That fall the British had invited the United States to form a group, the Anglo-American Committee of Inquiry, to settle what to do about Palestine. When Truman announced the formation of the committee, Celler dismissed it as "just another British dodge and stall," adding, "I am surprised that President Truman has fallen into the British trap."

Before the war, Jews like Morgenthau and Celler had more or less ignored Zionism. They were descended from German Jews whose primary ambition had been to assimilate into the country. At fifty-two, Morgenthau had never even attended a Passover seder. But the Holocaust had changed their minds. They believed that the United States, having failed to admit enough Jews during Hitler's massacre, now needed to back a Jewish state in Palestine, in addition to admitting refugees from the war. "The Nazi terrors had brought many Johnny-come-latelies into the Zionist fold," Celler wrote later. "I supposed I could be counted among those."

Celler turned out to be right in his prediction that the Anglo-American Committee would lead nowhere. By December, Truman continued to hold out hope, but he also understood that the plight of the Jewish refugees in Europe could not wait for the Americans and the British to come to a solution on Palestine. Nor did Congress appear as if it would act anytime soon, despite Truman's pleas. Lawmakers, reflecting the opinions of the general American public, did not want to encourage greater immigration. In fact, groups like the Daughters of the American Revolution, the American Legion, and the Veterans of Foreign Wars were still pressing for a complete five-to-ten-year ban, fearing that a flood of World War II survivors would enter the United States bringing Communist beliefs. In January 1946 a poll by the American Institute of Public Opinion, a precursor to the Gallup poll, asked Americans how many people from Europe the country should admit relative to before the war. Only 5 percent said "more." Thirty-two percent said "same," and 37 percent "fewer." Fourteen percent of Americans polled said that "none at all" should be admitted.

———

A WEEK BEFORE CHRISTMAS Truman was eating breakfast alone when he called over Alonzo Fields, the White House's chief butler and the first

African-American to hold the job, to ask a favor. Could Fields find a black family in Washington, D.C., who needed "a real happy Christmas dinner"? Money problems continued to loom over the Trumans, even when they were in the White House, to the point that Bess often mailed her husband ten-dollar bills from Missouri; still, Truman took out his wallet and handed Fields some cash with further instructions. "This is to buy each child in the family a present. If this isn't enough, let me know." The president asked Fields not to tell anyone about his mission (a promise Fields would keep until he wrote his memoir sixteen years later).

Fields found a family in southeast Washington—a woman with nine children whose husband had been murdered three months earlier. But when he went to their home, he discovered that they lacked a working stove, which meant that sending an uncooked turkey would not do. Fields reported his findings to Truman, and they decided that the White House should stuff and cook a turkey dinner and deliver it to the family in a private car, beginning a Christmas tradition: each year, Fields and the chief of the Secret Service would select needy families to receive dinners.

For Truman, the Christmas season evoked special obligations to other people. It was a time to reflect on those with the greatest need, and this December—his first holiday season as president—his thoughts kept turning to the Jewish refugees whom everyone seemed to be letting down. With no potential avenue through Congress, he concluded, like many presidents faced with a legislative roadblock, that it was time for an executive order. Three days before Christmas, Truman issued a directive to speed up assistance to the refugees.

Truman's executive order mandated that displaced persons from the war should receive preferential treatment within U.S. immigration quotas, and that orphans in particular should receive the highest priority. "The immensity of the problem of displaced persons and refugees is almost beyond comprehension," he wrote in his statement announcing the directive. "In this way we may do something to relieve human misery and set an example to the other countries of the world which are able to receive some of these war sufferers. I feel that it is essential that we do this ourselves to show our good faith in requesting other nations to open their doors for this purpose." He ordered the State Department to open up consulate offices near displaced persons camps to expedite the process.

Then he adjusted a longtime requirement in U.S. immigration law that a person could be admitted into the country only if they could support themselves and not become a "public charge." That requirement was preposterous for survivors of the war, so Truman decreed that American social welfare groups could effectively sponsor refugees and guarantee their smooth adjustment by helping them find jobs and housing. To this day, the concept of charitable groups being able to act as guarantors for refugees is central to the U.S. immigration system.

One last part of his announcement was greeted with unabashed joy at a small camp on the shores of Lake Ontario in Oswego, New York, directly across the water from Canada.

After Roosevelt established the War Refugee Board, he had allowed more than nine hundred refugees to be removed from camps in Italy and moved to a military fort in New York for the duration of the war. They were the only group of wartime refugees sheltered in the United States for humanitarian reasons, and in return they were supposed to return to Europe at the war's end. They viewed their arrival in the United States as nothing short of a miracle. As they sailed into New York Harbor, they waved at the Statue of Liberty with tears in their eyes. A rabbi knelt to kiss the iron floor of the ship, then led them in a prayer, "May God bless you and keep you and make His countenance to shine upon you and bring you peace. And may God bless this new land." As one refugee, Walter Greenberg, recalled, that summer he felt as if he were "being born again. . . . Lake Ontario for me was an ocean, separating the Old World, the years of insanity, a time when world amnesia and a bankrupt, amoral society allowed the stench of burning flesh, and with the death of 6 million Jews, the worst chapter in a supposedly organized, cultured, civilized society."

But with the war over—and the War Refugee Board disbanded—the refugees worried they would soon be deported. Jewish advocates went to

Morgenthau and again asked for his help, but he hesitated, recalled Ruth Gruber, an aide to Harold Ickes, the interior secretary. "You're asking that we change the instructions issued by the President," Gruber remembered Morgenthau saying. "I can't go back on my promise to the dead President. I couldn't sleep with my conscience."

Truman had no such qualms: under his executive order, the refugees would be allowed to stay. "In the circumstances it would be inhumane and wasteful to require these people to go all the way back to Europe merely for the purpose of applying there for immigration visas and returning to the United States," he argued.

The refugees of Oswego still technically had to re-enter the country, and so on January 17, 1946, groups of them boarded buses to Canada, where they were greeted, at Niagara Falls, by a U.S. consul who gave each of them a visa decorated with a ribbon. Then they turned around for the three-hour ride home to the United States.

—

TRUMAN'S ORDER, though well intentioned, did not come close to meeting the magnitude of the refugee problem. The overall U.S. immigration framework—the national origins quotas—allowed only about 13,000 immigrants from all of eastern Europe per year, and roughly 26,000 from Germany. In the first nine months of 1946, only 5,000 displaced persons came into the country. There were a million displaced persons in Europe, and that figure was only growing.

In Poland, the end of the war had not ended the persecution of Jews. In July 1946 residents in the town of Kielce, south of Warsaw, attacked and killed dozens of Jews who had survived the Holocaust and tried to return home. The violence began when a nine-year-old Polish boy left home without telling his parents and, upon returning, claimed he had been kidnapped and held in the basement of a building that served as shelter for many Jews. In response, a group of vigilantes descended on the building and attacked their Jewish neighbors, beating them to death and mutilating their bodies. By the end of the day, as many as forty-two Jews had been killed and another forty injured.

The event shocked people around the world and signaled to Jewish survivors that Poland's new Communist government would not protect them, causing more Jews to flee eastern Europe, taking routes that brought them to American displaced persons camps in Germany or to Palestine. That summer more than 100,000 Jews left Poland. Others moved westward from the Soviet Union to escape Stalin's rule. One year after Harrison compiled his devastating report, the U.S. military had improved some of its treatment of refugees, but the exodus from eastern Europe was again straining the camps.

By this time, the British and the Americans were trying to negotiate yet another plan, one allowing 100,000 Jews to immigrate to Palestine, as Truman had insisted, but on condition that separate Jewish and Arab provinces be established. Truman approved of the proposal, seeing it as an effective way to alleviate the Jewish displaced persons crisis, but many Zionists balked at the notion of sharing Palestine. At a cabinet meeting on July 30, 1946, Truman lost his temper, venting, "Jesus Christ couldn't please them when he was here on earth, so how could anyone expect that I would have any luck?" Notwithstanding the anti-Semitic outburst, Truman remained determined to find a solution.

On August 16 he set out on his first extended vacation of his presidency, a cruise trip up the coast to New England. The same day he said he might ask Congress to pass legislation allowing more refugees to enter the country, beyond the limits of the quotas. Truman did not specify a number, but he sent a clear signal. More than two decades after the establishment of the national origins quotas, it was time to revisit the country's immigration laws.

The *New York Times* editorial board praised his pledge, saying that the U.S. "must assume our fair share of responsibility for the whole problem of the refugees." But lawmakers immediately recoiled. Georgia senator Richard Russell, the Democratic chairman of the Senate Immigration Committee, said that any move to lift the nation's immigration quotas would establish a "dangerous precedent." Having recently visited India, Russell said he had witnessed "misery and starvation" and did not think the United States could open its doors to large numbers of hungry people. The idea was also unpopular among some Zionists, who thought the president should stay focused on establishing a Jewish homeland in Palestine.

Still, some leading Jewish groups spotted an opening and formed the Citizens Committee on Displaced Persons (CCDP), which launched a major campaign to change public opinion about immigrants. The organizers took care to recruit Protestant faces to represent their cause, like Eleanor Roosevelt and Edward R. Stettinius, Jr., fresh from a short tenure as secretary of state. For its chairman, the group selected Earl Harrison, whose report on displaced persons had stirred Truman's sympathies so deeply. The group launched extensive letter-writing campaigns to lawmakers and pushed its message out to radio stations, magazines, and newspapers. In its messaging, the group went out of its way to emphasize that most of the displaced persons in Europe were Christians, and some were political exiles from Communist governments. One of its flyers claimed that before the war many had worked in agriculture and construction—jobs that the average American did not associate with Jews.

The activists moved with a sense of urgency, especially as talks to allow Jewish immigration to Palestine kept falling apart. Non-Zionist groups in particular supported settlement in Palestine but felt that establishing a new country could not resolve the refugee issue. In a letter dated October 7, 1946, Joseph Proskauer, president of the American Jewish Committee (AJC)—one of these groups—warned that with winter coming, and thousands of Jews still in camps in the American zones in Germany and Austria, any further delay in removing refugees would likely "result in catastrophe." "It is perfectly clear that only if the United States takes the initiative in making immigration opportunities available will other countries do the same," he wrote, and he vowed that the AJC would "undertake to devote its utmost efforts to the promotion of a liberalized policy of immigration into this country."

Two days later fifteen national Jewish groups launched a drive to admit 100,000 Jews into the United States. Mannie Celler, now on the House Judiciary Committee, which oversaw all immigration issues, spotted a chance to reach out to Proskauer to tell him he had an ally. Looking to the midterm elections only one month away, Celler explained to Proskauer that he would become either the ranking member or the chairman of the committee. "These circumstances will place me in a rather advantageous position when considering [immigration] legislation."

But, he warned, "the task ahead will be arduous," adding that Proskauer should expect lawmakers to introduce bills that would restrict immigration, not loosen it. "It will be essential to bear down hard on the opposition to dissipate it. We shall need all the strength we can possibly muster."

But Celler's power would be limited. The midterm elections were devastating to Democrats—control of the House and Senate swung to the Republicans for the first time since 1928. It was a direct repudiation of Truman, who, more than a year into the presidency, faced growing skepticism that he was the right man for the office. His critics picked on him relentlessly, still believing that he was an unworthy successor to Roosevelt. When Truman visited a county fair in Caruthersville, Missouri, people mocked him for attending such a local event. Even his closeness with his mother became the butt of jokes. Seizing on the public's lack of enthusiasm for Truman, the Republican Party had campaigned on a slogan of "Had enough?"

But Truman remained unfazed, declaring that "all good citizens accept the results of any fair election." In his annual state of the union message to Congress two months later, Truman said he still did not feel that the United States had done its part to admit refugees from the war. Within "the limitation of the existing law and existing quotas," agencies were doing "all that is reasonably possible." But congressional legislation was needed "to find ways whereby we can fulfill our world responsibilities to these thousands of homeless and suffering refugees of all faiths." Even more striking, decades after American leaders had concluded that admitting immigrants presented a threat to democracy, Truman suggested the opposite—that in a global fight against Communism for ideological supremacy, the admission of refugees was a powerful weapon: "If we share our great bounty with war-stricken people over the world, then the faith of our citizens in freedom and democracy will be spread over the whole earth and free men everywhere will share our devotion to those ideals."

While Truman did not provide a draft bill, the CCDP outlined specifics for Congress to consider. "We are completing our plans for quite a fight," Harrison wrote to Celler on February 15, 1947, after receiving from the lawmaker a list of all the members on the immigration subcommittee within the House Judiciary Committee. The group's goal, backed by a million-dollar budget, much of it from Jewish supporters, was to pass legislation that would admit 400,000 refugees over a four-year period. In early 1947, it found a willing bill sponsor in William G. Stratton, a soft-spoken Republican representative from Illinois. Stratton had served as a navy lieutenant in the South Pacific during the war, and while he was conservative on many domestic issues—he had opposed much of Roosevelt's New Deal agenda—he felt it was important to help solve the refugee problem. For the CCDP, his key qualification, aside from his support for the cause, was that he was not Jewish.

On April 1, 1947, Stratton introduced a bill to admit 400,000 displaced persons into the United States. Truman thought the figure was unrealistic, writing to an aide, "The idea of getting 400,000 immigrants into this country is, of course, beyond our wildest dreams. If we could get 100,000 we would be doing remarkably well." This assessment likely led Truman to remain silent on the bill, while aides like David Niles, the White House's point person on Jewish issues, supported it behind the scenes.

And indeed, the bill at first seemed doomed to fail. The Republican assigned to head the Senate Judiciary Committee's immigration subcommittee was William Chapman Revercomb of West Virginia, who had no appetite for allowing Jewish refugees into the country; he had once remarked to colleagues, "We could solve this DP problem all right if we could work out some bill that would keep out the Jews." After a trip to Europe to investigate the refugee situation, Revercomb concluded that the immigrants who would be coming in weren't suitable. "Many of those who seek entrance into this country have little concept of our form of government," he reported. "Many of them come from lands where communism has had its first growth and dominates the political thought and philosophy of the people. Certainly it would be a tragic blunder to bring into our midst those imbued with a communistic line of thought when one of the most important tasks of this Government today is to combat and eradicate communism from this country."

Revercomb's attitude reflected a growing fear among Americans that Communists were infiltrating the country. Such fears had first emerged after World War I and the Bolshevik Revolution, but they were increasing in intensity with America's budding rivalry with the Soviet Union. New Mexico senator Carl Hatch, a Democrat, admitted that on the subject of immigrants, "I have heard it said—and I am ashamed to say that frequently it is said in the Halls of Congress: They are nothing but Communists, nothing but Jews—hated, despised, unwanted spawn from the Old World."

Adding to the fears, a growing housing shortage was sweeping the country. New housing development had all but stopped during the war as the country mobilized to fight, and soldiers returning home were having trouble finding places to live. Frank J. Quin, who fought in the air force, complained in a letter to Celler that he was "now trying to find a place to live." Celler had proposed his own bill in the House to admit 250,000 refugees, and Quin asked, "Just where do you propose to put these people?? Will they create jobs for themselves, or take over the decreasing number open to veterans and citizens?? My parents' grandparents were immigrants, too. But the America of those years provided plenty of housing and jobs." Celler responded that most of the refugees would stay with family or friends when they arrived. And he insisted that new immigrants would only help the country. "Just as the human frame can deteriorate as the result of no food, so the Nation's frame can likewise wither if there is no new blood."

Two months after Stratton's bill was proposed, the House Judiciary

Committee held public hearings. A number of Truman's top officials testified in support. Secretary of State George Marshall, architect of an ambitious plan for rebuilding Europe, stressed the country's continued obligations to the continent. Admitting refugees was a way for the United States to demonstrate leadership, he argued. "The tasks that are imposed by a declaration of war are not completed when the guns ceased [*sic*] fire. This is one of the tasks which we have not completed."

But opponents dusted off arguments that had been used twenty years earlier. John Trevor, the influential lobbyist for the American Coalition of Patriotic Societies who had helped argue for the national origins quotas in 1924, returned to trot out a similar line of reasoning, arguing that "our political institutions could not survive further dilution of the basic strain of our population." Trevor declared, with no evidence, that the people "for whose benefit [the Stratton bill] was devised [are] peculiarly susceptible to the absorption of socialistic propaganda."

Other anti-immigrant forces that had gone dormant reemerged. On May 22, at the annual meeting of the Daughters of the American Revolution in Washington, Paul H. Griffith, the head of the nation's largest veterans group, the American Legion, gave a fiery speech denouncing immigrants. Immigration, Griffith said, "has become a lawless torrent that is undermining the very foundations of our American way of life." Immigrants, he claimed, were not only robbing veterans of opportunities but also "building up a fifth column in this country that may well be the margin by which we may meet with disaster in the next war." He dismissed the arguments from pro-immigrant groups as "sob stuff with which we are being beguiled." And he urged that all immigration be suspended for at least a year.

But this time, compared to the debate of the 1920s, pro-immigrant groups were far more organized. The CCDP flooded Capitol Hill with letters supporting the Stratton bill. Activists also won over mass media, which began to present audiences with sympathetic portrayals of European refugees. In 1947 millions of Americans saw the RKO film *Passport to Nowhere* in movie theaters; it depicted the plight of refugees, with an introductory narrative encouraging viewers to support the Stratton bill. Editorial boards at *The New York Times*, *The Washington Post*, and *The Louisville Courier-Journal* all supported the cause. *Life* magazine ran an editorial in a September 1946 issue called "Send Them Here!" arguing that the United States should accept refugees and that "it is about time for the U.S. to review its whole attitude, not just toward [displaced persons] but toward immigration policy in general. We have not really debated it since 1924 and there are several new arguments." Frank Fellows, the Republican chair of the House subcommittee on immigration, complained that he and others on the subcommittee had been targeted by "a very definite propaganda movement from all over the country," backed by "a very strong, well-paid lobby." "They're putting on tremendous pressure of the type I don't like," he said. "We've been receiving armfuls of telegrams, letters, postcards; many of them alike."

With pressure from the public mounting, Senator Revercomb of West Virginia realized that he had to act. But what he proposed—and what eventually passed through House and Senate—was a far cry from what advocates wanted.

The bill allowed for the admittance of 100,000 refugees over two years, one-fourth the number proposed by Stratton and the advocates. Even worse, the bill seemed designed to discriminate against Jews. Only those who had been in a displaced persons camp in the American, British, and French zones of Germany, Austria, and Italy on December 22, 1945, were eligible, which meant that many of the Jewish refugees who had fled Poland and the Soviet Union would not qualify. In addition, many of the new visas granted would be reserved for agricultural workers, which appeared to be another snub aimed at Jews who were statistically less likely to work in farming. Priority would also be given to people from areas annexed by Russia—eastern Poland and the Baltic states— where some Jewish groups claimed there were an especially large number of Nazi collaborators.

Even the State Department said it was displeased with the bill, saying the cutoff date would be impossible to enforce. It recommended doubling the number of refugees admitted, which the Senate agreed to do in an amendment.

Still, the rest of the bill largely stood, and those who had pushed for Stratton's original measure were aghast. Harrison blasted the legislation, calling it a "booby trap," and said its "racist character makes all decent Americans hang their heads in shame." Celler wrote that the bill "wasn't 'half a loaf'; it wasn't even half a slice.'" And William Haber, who was aiding refugees as a Jewish adviser to the army, called it "the most anti-Semitic bill in US history."

The Stratton bill's advocates were now in an uncomfortable position: Should they support this bill since it allowed at least some refugees to enter? Or was it too offensive? Irving Engel, one leader, had already concluded that he "would rather have no bill than see this measure pass." But with time running out in the congressional session, and the refugee crisis worsening by the day, there were no good options.

On June 25, 1948, Truman signed "with very great reluctance" the country's first-ever law aimed squarely at assisting refugees. "In its present form," Truman said, "this bill is flagrantly discriminatory." The cut-off date "discriminates in callous fashion against displaced persons of the Jewish faith." He explained that he was signing the bill "in spite of its many defects, in order not to delay further the beginning of a resettlement program and in the expectation that the necessary remedial action will follow when the Congress reconvenes."

True reform would have to wait.

FIVE

A SON OF NEVADA

T HE CONVENTION HALL in Philadelphia was stiflingly hot. More than ten thousand Democrats had gathered in July 1948 to nominate Harry Truman for another term in the White House, and they were sweating, without air conditioning, under the heat of enormous lights set up by television networks experimenting with live broadcasting a national political convention for millions of Americans to watch. It should have been a triumphant moment for Truman. Instead, it appeared that his star-crossed political career might be ending.

After the drubbing the Democrats took in 1946, party leaders feared a repeat. Weeks earlier they had been so nervous about Truman's prospects that they approached war hero and famed general Dwight D. Eisenhower and urged him to step up and run for president as a Democrat. Eisenhower gave the offer some thought and then declined. American voters remained skeptical of Truman, who was still viewed as an accidental president. Meanwhile, the Democratic Party appeared to be on the verge of splitting wide open over the issue of civil rights.

With the end of the war, efforts to address American racism had taken on a new urgency. Hundreds of thousands of black veterans were returning home, only to find racial violence and discrimination in their hometowns.

For liberals in the Democratic Party, racial discrimination was not merely wrong in and of itself: it damaged U.S. prestige abroad, and in the burgeoning Cold War, the United States needed to establish its moral superiority. Hubert Humphrey, a liberal mayor of Minneapolis who was running for a U.S. Senate seat that fall, gave a stirring speech at the convention, pressing his fellow Democrats to approve a strong pro-civil-rights platform. "Every citizen in this country has a stake in the emergence of the United States as the leader in the free world. . . . For us to play our part effectively, we must be in a morally sound position."

Truman watched the beginning of the convention from the White House. When he arrived in Philadelphia to give his acceptance speech, he remained holed up in a room within the convention hall that was so bleak and hot that his aide, Clark Clifford, dubbed it the "Black Hole of Calcutta." Celler, who was on the party's platform committee, found Truman in the room and encountered "a lonely figure": "He was there alone. Nobody was in his room at all and I started to cheer him up, not that he needed much cheering up, but it was rather ironic: Here was the great Democratic party and here was their presidential candidate forlorn."

The scene in the hall was not much better. After the party followed Humphrey's lead and approved a pro–civil rights platform, the entire Mississippi delegation and half of Alabama's walked out of the convention. The growing pressure from Democrats to racially integrate threatened the dominion of white southerners, and as one delegate from Alabama put it, the South "is no longer going to be the whipping boy of the Democratic Party." The Dixiecrats would later nominate Strom Thurmond of South Carolina as their presidential candidate on a separate ticket.

When it was finally Truman's turn to talk, the convention was running almost four hours behind schedule. It was nearly two in the morning, and few Americans were likely to still be watching on television. Inside the hall, perspiring attendees tried to keep themselves awake. "Never have I seen so much smoke without a fire as I saw that humid night in Philadelphia. I thought sure I was going to expire. Oxygen was my only thought," remembered Truman's daughter Margaret. As the band played "Hail to the Chief" to announce Truman's entrance, a delegate from Pennsylvania released dozens of white pigeons from a six-foot-tall replica of the Liberty Bell made of red and white carnations. But the attempt to add majesty to the occasion resulted in pure chaos. The pigeons, desperate for air, swooped all around the hall, narrowly avoiding people's heads and landing on the platform where Truman was supposed to speak. The birds, Clifford noted, "began, not surprisingly, to drop the inevitable product of their imprisonment on any delegate who had the bad luck to be underneath them." Sam Rayburn, the convention chairman who was supposed to introduce Truman, swatted them away and yelled, well within earshot of the television microphones, "Get those damned pigeons out of here."

In this atmosphere of faction and frustration, Truman delivered the most important address of his career. Seemingly unconcerned in his double-breasted white suit and dark tie, the president strolled to the lectern and waited for the crowd to settle down. Then he uncorked a scathing speech.

He blasted the Republican-led Congress for failing to act on health care, the housing crisis, education, and civil rights, accusing them of "misrule and inaction." Then he attacked them for the just-passed displaced persons bill, promising that if elected, he would "ask for adequate and decent laws for displaced persons in place of this anti-Semitic, anti-Catholic law which this 80th Congress passed." American voters had long found Truman's manner of speaking, with his choppy hand motions and unusual midwestern-crossed-with-southern drawl, uninspired. But on this night, Truman's energy electrified the crowd and "lifted the delegates out of their doldrums," reported the *Time* correspondent.

In the months that followed, Truman revealed a flair for retail politics, taking a train out west and ditching prepared scripts for extemporaneous remarks that showed voters his plain-speaking charm. Rather than seeming too small for the job, his directness made him seem like exactly the kind of person who could be trusted with weighty decisions. Still, by late September, Truman was polling well behind his Republican opponent, Thomas Dewey, and the press was convinced he could not win. *The*

New York Times declared Dewey's victory "a foregone conclusion." Even his wife Bess asked White House aide Tom Evans, "Does he really think he can win?"

The day of the election, Truman seemed to be the only one confident of his chances. He spent the evening at a hotel in Excelsior Springs, Missouri, and relaxed with a Turkish bath and, for dinner, a ham sandwich and a glass of milk. He went to bed after hearing some of the election results over the radio. But deep into the night, around four a.m., when it became clear that he might pull off the impossible, his Secret Service detail stirred him awake and drove him to his campaign headquarters in Kansas City. The good news for Truman was not confirmed until returns from Ohio landed around eight-thirty a.m. The popular vote was not close: Truman had beat Dewey by more than 2 million votes. The next day, on his way to Washington, he stopped in St. Louis, where someone handed him a copy of the *Chicago Tribune* with the infamous headline, "Dewey Defeats Truman," which he held up for an iconic photo.

The *Washington Post* editorial board, which had also dismissed Truman's chances, sent him a telegram to invite him to a "Crow Banquet," in which political writers, editors, and columnists from around the country would be served "Breast of Tough Old Crow En Glace," while Truman could eat turkey. Truman demurred. He was used to being underestimated and didn't need to lord his win over anyone. "As I said en route to Washington, I have no desire to crow over anybody or to see anybody eating crow, figuratively or otherwise. We should all get together now and make a country in which everybody can eat turkey whenever he pleases."

High on Truman's agenda was fixing the flawed displaced persons bill that had passed months earlier. And this time he was poised to have much more help on Capitol Hill. American voters, in addition to keeping Truman in the White House for a second term, had returned control of the House and the Senate to the Democrats.

In the House, this meant that Celler would ascend to chair of the House Judiciary Committee, a job he would maintain, with only one brief interruption, for the next twenty-four years. The young man from

Brooklyn who had entered the House unsure of its ways and its rules had secured one of the chamber's most powerful positions. He would now play a major role overseeing the country's federal courts and its law enforcement agencies, and more important for him personally, his portfolio now included national immigration policy. His loud advocacy for more liberal immigration laws had already made him a powerful force on the Judiciary Committee. Now, he could lead the charge to fix an unjust law and help displaced persons still suffering in Europe.

In January 1949 Celler introduced a bill that greatly resembled the original Stratton proposal, allowing 400,000 refugees to enter the United States. Crucially, the bill extended the cutoff date for entrants to April 21, 1947, to include Jews who had escaped the postwar pogroms in Poland. The debate in the House moved quickly, accelerated by support in the other chamber by Senator Alexander Wiley, who had formerly chaired the Senate Judiciary Committee and championed the 1948 law. Now Wiley announced that he regretted lending his support. "If we revise this law speedily and equitably," he said, "it will be a real inspiration to all free people. It will be a weapon in our ideological war against the forces of darkness, the forces of Communist tyranny." Just three hours after Celler's bill was put to the House floor for debate, it was passed by a voice vote. With Democrats controlling the Senate as well, and with the president's support, change seemed at hand. But there was one person they had failed to take into account.

—

SENATOR PAT MCCARRAN was not a man who deferred to the bidding of others. Standing five-foot-seven and weighing more than 230 pounds, with a head full of wavy white hair, the Nevada senator alternately cowed and infuriated his Democratic colleagues from his perch as chair of the Senate Judiciary Committee. Though he was obsessed with rooting out Communism, he was never as well known as Joseph McCarthy of Wisconsin, the Republican senator who hogged the spotlight with his splashy accusations that the government was full of Soviet sympathizers. But because McCarran was a senior member of the party in power, he would do more damage to innocent Americans, hauling dedicated civil servants to the witness stand and advancing bills that curbed civil liberties. In the annals of the Senate, few lawmakers have matched McCarran's talent for amassing and then abusing power. Lyndon Johnson, who understood well how to build influence in the Senate, once called McCarran "an earth-shaking force" who "impressed his personality deeply and indelibly upon the institution of the Senate and upon the history of the nation."

McCarran, a lifelong Catholic, saw himself as a fearless protector of American values—principles that felt especially vulnerable to infiltration and destruction in the earliest years of the Cold War. "There is nothing in the world today so great or so grand or so much deserving of the love and esteem of the people of this country as the United States of America," he said in a televised talk in 1952. Staunchly isolationist, he believed the presence of the United Nations Headquarters in New York was "an open door for foreign spies and Communists." Regarding refugees, he thought that too many were entering as "active subversives . . . who have no other purpose than to undermine our American way of life." McCarran was especially loathed by his liberal colleagues in the Senate. "There goes an evil man," Paul Douglas, a Democratic senator from Illinois, once said, pointing to McCarran.

From childhood, McCarran learned to not care what anyone thought of him. Born in 1876, he grew up an only child on a sheep farm on the Truckee River, tucked into a rocky, barren hillside east of Reno. It was a harsh and beautiful landscape, one in which sheep outnumbered humans in one of the least populous states in the country. (Indeed, when Nevada became a state in 1864, it had only one-fifth the population needed to qualify, but President Lincoln and Republicans in Congress made an exception in order to strengthen a Union-sympathetic ally in the West.) His parents had left Ireland in the mid-1800s; his father did not know how to write his own name.

School in the nearby settlement of Glendale was intermittent and difficult to squeeze in between farm chores. Each day McCarran had to milk twelve cows before class started, then again after coming home from school. When McCarran turned fifteen, his father promised that if he helped with that year's harvest, he could attend school in Reno, the nearest town, located fifteen miles away. When he showed up in late October for seventh grade at fifteen years of age, classes had already been going on for weeks. McCarran wanted to impress his new classmates but did not know what to wear. At his little schoolhouse in Glendale, he was used to wearing overalls, a flannel shirt, and a canvas coat. When he arrived at school in Reno, he wore a new pair of overalls, a chinchilla coat, and a new pair of shoes. "My garb evidently was a matter of much comment, as it should have been, but I knew no different and was content."

McCarran, gifted with his father's sharp memory, graduated from Reno High School as valedictorian of a class of sixteen. He attended the University of Nevada at Reno, but during the spring of his senior year, his father, nearing seventy, hurt himself falling from a wagon. Two months before graduation, McCarran quit school to help with the farm. When his class graduated that June, he rode in from the ranch with his mother to watch his classmates receive their diplomas. He was happy to support them. She cried the entire time.

Unwilling to give up on his ambitions, McCarran studied to become a lawyer while herding sheep, always carrying with him a copy of *Blackstone's*, the foundational legal text, and practicing his oratory skills on his flock. Years later McCarran's copy of the book still bore the markings of his saddle strings. After passing the bar, he quickly became one of Nevada's premier criminal defense and divorce lawyers. "McCarran defended all types: accused murderers, ladies of the night, bank robbers, an abortionist (twice, which was rather surprising for a prominent Roman Catholic layman)," wrote historian Jerome Edwards. He proved a charismatic presence in the courtroom. "McCarran could make you weep. He could completely sway his audience," remembered one observer. His legal career took off just as the city of Reno was earning its reputation as the "divorce capital of the world" because of its lax residency and divorce requirements.

By this time, McCarran had fixated on attaining a major political prize: representing Nevada as a U.S. senator. The quest would consume him for more than fifteen years and require him to wrest power from the state's most entrenched financial and political interests, people who had no interest in ceding authority to a former sheep farmer. In 1915 McCarran decided to challenge Democrat Key Pittman, one of the state's sitting senators, who enjoyed full party backing. By this point McCarran was a justice on the Nevada Supreme Court, and the state's constitution barred sitting judges from running for other political office. The state's Democratic leadership viewed McCarran's run as reckless; McCarran didn't care. His unsuccessful run would establish his tendency to pursue his own interests while paying no heed to those of his party. Indeed, after his loss to Pittman, McCarran was ostracized from Democratic Party politics for more than a decade. He also refused to kiss the ring of the state's most powerful political kingmaker, banker George Wingfield.

When the Great Depression swept the country, Wingfield's banking empire collapsed, and McCarran finally had his opening. In 1932, at fifty-six, he defeated Republican incumbent senator Tasker Oddie and became the first Nevada-born person to ever represent the state in the Senate. "One particular pleasure comes to me on this occasion, and that is that I go into the Senate of the United States independently," he boasted. "I owe my success to no faction and to no power."

Nevada had by far the smallest population of any state in the country, which meant that it was overrepresented in the Senate. But it was also unusually vulnerable to federal intervention, as it remains to this day. Gambling, which the state legalized in 1931, rapidly became Nevada's largest industry, so long as the federal government didn't impose taxes. Nevada also had and still has a greater proportion of its land under federal control than any other state—nearly 85 percent. The result, as Edwards noted, is that Nevada voters "believe they have a special need for protection in the national capital."

McCarran positioned himself perfectly for such a demand. Upon arriving in Washington in 1933, before he was even sworn in, he met with party leaders to secure prestigious committee assignments—the only way to exert power as a freshman senator. He somehow landed positions on two of the Senate's most important committees: Appropriations and Judiciary. As a member of the Appropriations Committee, he could influence the government's discretionary spending. The power of the Judiciary Committee was arguably even greater. Most Senate legislation had to pass through the committee, which controlled the appointment of every federal judge or attorney, giving McCarran enormous power over patronage in his state. McCarran and Pete Petersen, Reno's postmaster, together established a formidable political machine, doling out every last job to expand their influence. Even a janitor position in a post office warranted their attention: Petersen wrote to McCarran that he had picked a person recommended by one of the senator's top aides, Eva Adams.

In Washington, McCarran continued to make enemies out of fellow Democrats, just as he had in Nevada. In 1937, when Roosevelt tried to add more justices to the Supreme Court, McCarran became one of the president's most vocal opponents. In a speech on the Senate floor that drew national attention, he attacked Roosevelt's plan as if he were back in the courtrooms of Reno, transfixing juries once more. McCarran had been in poor health—an illness the year before had nearly killed him. "This is the first time for a year and a half that I have attempted to deliver a speech of any magnitude, and I am delivering it now contrary to a doctor's orders, but I think the cause is worth while. I think the cause is worthy of any man's life," said McCarran, his voice trembling. "I think this cause in which we have enlisted, and in which I say without hesitancy we constitute a battalion of death, to the end that the Constitution of the United States shall prevail, is worthy of the effort." National and local press called his speech sensational.

Within a decade, though, they would all turn on him over an issue that was gaining sympathy among ordinary Americans: the plight of European refugees desperate to immigrate to the United States.

—

SENATE MAJORITY LEADER Scott Lucas was determined to make progress on a new displaced persons bill, as promised by Truman and the party during the previous year's election. But after months of trying to get fellow Democrats to agree on any part of the president's ambitious agenda, he was exhausted.

Truman's agenda was ambitious. He wanted universal health care and an increase in the minimum wage. He sought the most comprehensive civil rights legislation ever proposed by an American president: a federal antilynching law, greater protections for the right to vote, and a ban on poll taxes and racial discrimination against travelers taking buses and trains across state lines. He viewed these matters the way he viewed the situation of refugees in Europe: there was an urgent, moral need for change. "When a mayor and a City Marshal can take a negro Sergeant off a bus in South Carolina, beat him up and put out one of his eyes, and nothing is done about it by the State Authorities, something is radically wrong with the system," he told a friend in a private letter.

But the party remained as fractured as it had been in Philadelphia, with liberals sparring constantly with the Dixiecrats. After Thurmond's defeat in 1948, the southern Democrats realized that even if they lacked power on the national stage, they could at least gum up the works on Capitol Hill. And poor Lucas, in only his second term in office, bore the brunt of it. "The president's control is the stuff of legend and of dreams and in such circumstances it is perhaps not surprising that the Majority Leader of the Senate has become worn and haggard," wrote *The New York Times*. In better times, Lucas had been known as a handsome man with "a taste for snappy double-breasted suits" and an athletic build from his days playing semiprofessional baseball. The son of an Illinois tenant farmer, he had dutifully campaigned for Truman in the Midwest when others had abandoned the president, and he had been rewarded for his loyalty with a plum leadership role. But the work of wrangling unruly Democrats was devastating his health. In the summer of 1949 he spent three weeks hospitalized for a mysterious ailment. Some attributed it to "exhaustion," while others reported a bleeding ulcer; in reality, he may have suffered a heart attack.

When Lucas returned from the hospital, he was ready to pick up Celler's displaced persons bill. But here, too, there was a problem: the Senate's version of the legislation was making no progress. It had disappeared somewhere in the bowels of McCarran's Judiciary Committee. "The award of the week for blocking and tackling and general all-around obstruction must go to that stout citizen from Nevada, Senator Pat McCarran," wrote *The Washington Post*, which would spend the next several years denouncing McCarran's tactics. "His outstanding achievement is in bottling up the proposal to change the Displaced Persons Act."

As chair of the Judiciary Committee, McCarran appointed himself head of a separate subcommittee devoted especially to reviewing Celler's bill, and he picked other senators for the panel who were also skeptical of liberalizing immigration laws. McCarran rejected criticism that the 1948 Displaced Persons Act was discriminatory, calling it "a despicable charge, wholly at variance with the facts." He said he saw "no reason" to rush to change the law and that unemployment in the country was high enough that Congress should be wary of admitting immigrants.

For months, the subcommittee had done nothing to move the bill forward. By the summer, it was clear that if the Democrats wanted to move it forward, they would need to take potentially unorthodox steps. "Senator McCarran happens to be in a position where he can block DP legislation all by himself until hell freezes over the DP camps in Europe," observed the *Post* editorial board. "Or until his colleagues take the matter out of his hands and make good on this country's moral obligation."

During one committee meeting, Celler confronted McCarran, arguing that a "groundswell of public opinion" demanded action on displaced persons. McCarran replied that there had been "$875,000 worth of groundswell, the biggest lobby in history," a reference to the CCDP. Celler wielded a telegram from Earl Harrison asserting that the United States had admitted fewer displaced persons than any other country in the world. McCarran remained unmoved.

The Nevada senator was not motivated solely by his suspicion of Communists infiltrating the country through its immigration system.

For years he had nursed a grudge against Truman, a onetime colleague in the Senate; with Truman now president, McCarran was determined to undermine the leader of his own party.

On paper, McCarran and Truman seemed to have much in common. Both knew firsthand the poverty and boredom of farm life. Both had had dreams of graduating from college, only to fall short because of family obligations. But their political temperaments could not have been further apart, and a bitter rivalry emerged between them that would last for decades.

It began in 1938, when McCarran and Truman clashed over establishing the Civil Aeronautics Authority (CAA), precursor to the modern Federal Aviation Administration. Truman claimed credit for creating the CAA, but the visionary legislation that brought it into being was almost entirely the work of McCarran, whose name now graces the Las Vegas airport. In the mid-1930s, with domestic airlines such as United and TWA just beginning to establish themselves, McCarran astutely saw the need for a central federal agency to oversee the burgeoning commercial aviation industry, especially regarding safety. In 1931 a plane crash killed the popular University of Notre Dame football coach Knute Rockne, triggering an outpouring of grief and demands for higher safety standards. Then in 1935 another crash killed Senator Bronson Cutting of New Mexico. That same year McCarran began to champion a bill that would create a new bipartisan commission to regulate commercial air travel, with five members to be appointed by the president and removable only in the case of "inefficiency, neglect of duty or malfeasance in office." The Roosevelt administration, however, wanted greater control. Truman, ever the loyal party man, introduced an alternative bill exactly the same as McCarran's, except that it allowed the president to remove a board member without having to assign a reason. McCarran bristled: "There is only one difference between the Senator from Missouri and myself, and that is that I want an independent agency that is really independent. . . . I do not want an agency that can be destroyed by the White House either under a Republican administration or a Democratic administration."

When Truman's alteration turned into an amendment to McCarran's bill, the Nevada senator threw a fit. "Not only will I not vote for the bill if the Truman amendment prevails, but I will ask that my name be stricken from the measure and I will fight it as long as I can stand on my feet. It destroys the entire theory of the bill and the entire principle of freedom." Despite his protests, McCarran ended up voting for his brainchild. But the Roosevelt administration still found a way to punish him for his intransigence, over the court packing as well as the CAA. The Roosevelt White House rejected all of McCarran's suggested appointments to the new aviation commission, then selected as the new Nevada U.S. attorney one of McCarran's political enemies, William S. Boyle. The move to appoint Boyle so enraged McCarran that, a year later, he said, "I do not know that I should go into what the feelings were. I think it best to leave that out."

Over the next several years, Truman and McCarran would only grow to loathe each other more. In a diary entry describing a flight over Nevada, Truman dismissed McCarran's home state as "the great gambling and marriage destruction hell" that "never should have been made a State." When Truman became president in 1945, McCarran was skeptical that his former Senate colleague was up to the task, and by 1952 he was convinced that he was not. "Truman will go down in history as the dirtiest as well as the most treacherous of all presidents. This pissant in human form is a disgrace to this country."

—

LUCAS, UNLIKE TRUMAN, was unwilling to give up on McCarran just yet. On the Nevada senator's seventy-third birthday, August 8, 1949, Lucas and other fellow Democrats presented him with a cake, in hopes that it "might produce in the distinguished Senator a mellow mood, and while in that mood he would consider the bill." Lucas remembered: "It was a large cake, too. It was a delicious cake." But it had no effect on McCarran.

Two days after the birthday cake flop, Lucas demonstrated even greater desperation, "invading" a policy meeting of Senate Republican leaders to try to get their cooperation. Winning just enough support to make his strategy worth trying, Lucas, on August 24, introduced a resolution to wrest the bill from McCarran's committee. He explained that "ordinarily" this was not good parliamentary procedure, but "I have tried, by every means within my power, to secure the release of this bill."

McCarran stunned everyone with his next move. He announced that he was headed to Europe—to spend three weeks investigating the conditions of the displaced persons camps for himself. A week earlier the *Washington Post* editorial board, whose views on McCarran were rapidly souring, had already concluded under the headline "Pooh Bah McCarran": "The smallest State in the Union from the standpoint of population has the distinction of having contributed a one-man monkey wrench to the legislative process in Washington."

McCarran, as usual, was unfazed.

—

ON SEPTEMBER 14, 1949, in New York, McCarran and his wife set sail for Europe on the opulent *Queen Mary*, the famed transatlantic ocean liner, which had been retrofitted during the war to move British troops but was now once again accepting paying passengers. The McCarrans were among 1,826 onboard, including twenty-five preparatory school students heading to England for an exchange program, and Herbert Marshall, a Hollywood actor who had appeared in Alfred Hitchcock's *Foreign Correspondent* and William Wyler's *The Little Foxes* with Bette Davis. While most of his fellow passengers were heading out for a holiday, McCarran announced that he intended to work. He would visit England, France, Italy, Germany, Switzerland, and Belgium in order to examine displaced persons camps and see how American dollars were being spent in the rebuilding of Europe. He believed that admitting too many immigrants would damage job prospects for Americans, even though the country's economy had scarcely ever been stronger. "Since I am defending the economy of the country, I want to find out how many of these people should come in and why. I want to find out what they'll do once they get here," McCarran vowed.

When they arrived in Paris about a week later, McCarran and his wife stayed at the Hôtel de Crillon, a palace commissioned by King Louis XV coated with marble, gilded mirrors, and chandeliers. But the Nevada senator was unimpressed. "I wouldn't give one block of Reno for this whole city. Its old houses and ancient palaces and antiquated squares and monuments are all right but they are a century behind the times," McCarran wrote to his daughter Mary.

Even though McCarran was now hundreds of miles away, his power could still be felt in the Senate. He continually sent notes to friendly colleagues to be read aloud on the Senate floor. In one October cable, he told senators that he had discovered fraud in the current displaced persons law, and that any liberalization would be a "serious mistake." He suggested deferring any Senate action and argued that, if anything, the rules should be tightened. Several days later came another missive, read aloud on the Senate floor by Senator Edwin C. Johnson of Colorado, in which McCarran charged that those seeking to change the existing bill wanted "to tear down our immigration barriers to the end that this country will be flooded with aliens."

McCarran had also shrewdly made sure that in his absence, a trusted protégé, Senator James Eastland, would help lead opposition to the bill.

—

NEARLY THIRTY YEARS YOUNGER than McCarran, Eastland was a taciturn racist who shared his mentor's paranoia about Communism and his resistance to expanded immigration, despite the fact that the two men had very different backgrounds. The Mississippi senator came from a prominent, wealthy cotton-planting family in the Delta, the flat stretch of land along the Mississippi River where the rich soil made for plentiful farming and where white landed elites depended on the labor of black sharecroppers. His maternal grandfather, Richmond Austin, had been a cavalry officer under Confederate Army general Nathan Bedford Forrest, who would become the first grand wizard of the Ku Klux Klan during Reconstruction. Eastland was born on his family's cotton plantation in Doddsville, a giant plot of land purchased by his paternal grandfather for just one dollar an acre. His father, Woods Eastland, doubled as a plantation owner and attorney in the central part of the state, known as Hill Country, representing workers who had sustained injuries toiling in large sawmills. The Delta was filled with genteel plantation owners who fancied themselves high-class gentlemen. By contrast, Hill Country was filled with poor white farmers, working on less fertile soil, who resented the wealthy planters.

Less than a year after James was born, Woods Eastland moved his family more than one hundred miles to the southeast to a town called Forest, in Hill Country, and it was in this part of the state that James Eastland grew up, and where his wealth made him stick out. Eastland, an only child, drove a car in high school, a luxury that was unheard of among his classmates. In 1956 a clerk in a general store in Forest, when asked about the senator, told a *Time* correspondent, "I hear folks say what a grand job Jim Eastland is doing and what a fine man he is, but I don't know. I always remember him as an uppity kid."

Eastland, who could come across as cold and arrogant, did not inherit the genial nature of his father, who also served as district attorney for five counties in central Mississippi. Still, his father groomed him for a life in politics: "My father completely controlled me." Eastland studied first at the University of Mississippi, then at Vanderbilt, and then at the University of Alabama, never collecting a degree. Instead he dropped out of school to run for the state legislature. There he became a loyal supporter of Governor Theodore Bilbo, a towering figure in Mississippi politics who paired virulent racism with populist initiatives to fund road improvements, provide child welfare, and build hospitals for white constituents. Bilbo, so powerful that he was known statewide simply as "the Man," championed the poor white farmers who were his core supporters and who loved his racist rhetoric.

In 1932, tired of fighting with Bilbo's rivals, Eastland left the state legislature and moved to his family's plantation in Doddsville in the Delta. It seemed, for several years, that he might be finished with politics. He got married and threw himself into the work of running the plantation. But then in 1941 a U.S. Senate seat suddenly became vacant with the death of Pat Harrison, and Governor Paul Johnson, a close friend of Woods Eastland, asked Woods to take the job. Instead, Woods told Johnson to appoint his son. At thirty-six, Eastland became a U.S. senator.

During these early years, Eastland made little mark. "Colorless, closemouthed and seldom consulted by his colleagues," according to *Time*, "Eastland was just another Southern Senator who supported low tariffs, opposed organized labor, and generally went along with the Administration on foreign policy. His only noticeable personal interest was agriculture—especially cotton." Eastland's heart remained with his plantation in Doddsville. His Washington residence was sparsely decorated, and he and his wife rarely socialized. Eastland preferred to be at home reading detective novels, and in the summer, in Doddsville, he could relax by hunting and riding his two Tennessee walking horses, then having friends over for dinner. He loved tending to plantation business, which was more a factory than a farm, given the volume of cotton, corn, and soybeans it produced. He had dozens of black sharecroppers working under a plantation manager. "Cotton obsessed, Negro obsessed . . . it is the deepest South, the heart of Dixie," remarked sociologist Rupert Vance in 1932, of the corner of the country from which Eastland hailed. "Nowhere are ante bellum conditions so nearly preserved."

Eastland would never sound as crassly racist as Bilbo, who in 1946, while campaigning for reelection in the U.S. Senate, told a group of white supporters, "I call on every red-blooded white man to use any means to keep the niggers away from the polls. If you don't understand what that means you are just plain dumb." But Eastland would likewise make racial segregation a central promise to Mississippians, albeit dressed up in more respectable language. An avowed segregationist who frequently warned against the potential "mongrelization" of races, Eastland promised constituents that he would bar blacks and whites from eating together even in Washington. He once stated from the floor of the Senate that "the Negro race is an inferior race," and that the white people of Mississippi will "maintain control of our own elections and . . . will protect and maintain white supremacy throughout eternity." Like a number of other southern Democrats, he had no interest in his party's new agenda—the push to expand civil rights for black Americans and liberalize the country's immigration laws.

Eastland put immigrants, African-Americans, and Communists in the same category—forces that threatened to undermine white American purity and values. In 1946 southern Democrats fought a pitched battle against a bill that would have established a permanent commission to stop racial discrimination by employers. Eastland said the bill "would rape the Magna Carta itself" because it represented a triumph of the values of newer immigrants from eastern and southern Europe:

> For 50 years that school of thought has grown as immigrants
> have come to this country, and from it there has been a con-
> certed attempt to destroy our Anglo-Saxon system of juris-
> prudence, of justice, and of liberty, a school of thought which
> reaches the high point in this bill, which is part of a campaign
> to destroy the America which we have loved, and which thou-
> sands of men have laid down their lives to create and preserve.

He and McCarran believed that Communists were trying to infiltrate the country, and that it was up to men like them to defend America's best principles. And they were not afraid of infuriating their own Democratic Party, if that was what it took. "I am not a party hack. I will vote my convictions on all measures," Eastland said in 1949.

In fact, Eastland, together with McCarran, could be counted among the most disloyal members of the Democratic Party. During the 1948 presidential race, Eastland had been part of the Dixiecrat rebellion. Early in the party's nomination process, he threatened to block Truman over the president's support for antidiscrimination laws, including a ban on racial segregation in interstate transportation. "All we have to do is to refuse to vote the ticket. Give our electoral votes to some other candidate. We can dictate the party's policies." After the States' Rights Democratic Party nominated Thurmond for the presidency, Eastland abandoned the Truman ticket and campaigned for him. After Truman's reelection, he and other Democrats entered into an alliance with Republicans to combat the southern Democrats. Rather than strip the Dixiecrats of important committee postings, Democratic leaders curbed their ability to take advantage of the patronage system. Truman did not consult Eastland on any federal appointments in Mississippi, making it impossible for him to nominate his own picks.

Eastland was not chastened.

—

McCARRAN WAS SUPPOSED to be gone for only three weeks, but one month into the European trip, no one quite knew when he would return. Meanwhile Democratic leaders were trying to manage another crisis he had left behind just before leaving town, when he appointed Eastland chairman of the civil rights subcommittee. The move, which torpedoed any hope of Senate action on the president's antiracism agenda, was such an obvious slap in the face to Truman that reporters laughed when asking him what he made of McCarran's decision. When Truman said he had no comment, the press corps laughed again.

The appointment seemed to embolden Eastland to dig in even harder on the displaced persons bill. Then in October the stalemate broke. One of Eastland's uncles died, causing him to leave for Mississippi for the funeral. Lucas and the acting Judiciary Committee chair, Harley Kilgore, a Truman loyalist and liberal senator from West Virginia, spotted their opening. The committee voted, 7 to 3, to finally send the bill to the Senate floor.

Opponents of the displaced persons bill were outraged. "It was rough treatment for those fellows and I'm going to have something to say about it," said William E. Jenner of Indiana. Eastland rushed back, determined to block the bill. "The key to the situation appeared to lie in the hands of Senator James O. Eastland, Democrat, of Mississippi, now en route back to Washington by train," *The New York Times* observed. Eastland and Washington Republican Harry P. Cain insisted the bill be sent back to the Judiciary Committee. As they drummed up support, McCarran's allies fiercely defended him with passionate speeches on the Senate floor. "I wish the senior senator from Nevada were here, with his mane of white hair, to fight for himself, as he could do so ably," said Cain, who spoke for almost six hours in an attempt to filibuster the bill. Eastland said the treatment of McCarran was "outrageous," and that the Senate should "uphold his hand, instead of insulting him by taking the bill from his committee." Senator William Langer of North Dakota, another of McCarran's allies, concluded, "What this comes down to is a personal question of whether the Senate will repudiate Pat McCarran." An exasperated Lucas retorted to critics that if the Senate had to wait for McCarran in order to act, all a chairman had to do to stop a bill would be to "take a two-week trip someplace."

With the legislative session approaching its end, time was running out—and many senators had already left town. On the afternoon of October 15, it became clear that the Senate was going to vote on a motion from Eastland and Cain to send the bill back to committee later that evening, at seven p.m. Long-distance phones started ringing to tell lawmakers to come back in time for the vote. Democrats who had campaigned on fixing the Displaced Persons Act were desperate to arrive in time to stop Eastland's maneuver. Robert Taft of Ohio, having received an honorary doctor of civil laws degree at Marietta College in Ohio at four-thirty p.m., flew back to vote against the motion. John Foster Dulles, who had been appointed a senator of New York three months earlier and was running in a special election that fall in order to keep the seat, halted his campaign to rush back to Washington, saying that if the bill were sent back to the committee, it would be "no more than burial" of the legislation. Henry C. Dworshak of Idaho, who had been appointed just a day earlier to replace the late senator Bert H. Miller, hurried to Washington and sped through a swearing-in ritual.

It was not enough. Eastland's measure passed, 36 to 30. McCarran's allies had triumphed, and the bill would have to wait until the next session. In the war between Truman and McCarran, the president had lost. The next day's front-page headline in *The Washington Post* declared the vote a "major defeat for Truman." McCarran had won.

—

WITH CELLER'S BILL safely defeated for the moment, McCarran remained in Europe to meet with one of his personal heroes. The Spanish dictator Francisco Franco had triumphed a decade earlier in the Spanish Civil War by defeating the Republican government and using brutal force to kill civilians, most infamously in Guernica, where he had enlisted Hitler's help to drop bombs on his own people, an atrocity immortalized by the Picasso painting of the same name. During World War II, Spain had technically remained neutral but kept its sympathies with Nazi Germany. After the war, the newly formed United Nations treated Franco as a pariah and refused to allow Spain entry.

To McCarran, Franco was simply a misunderstood man. Where others saw a fascist dictator, McCarran saw someone who, during the Spanish Civil War, had rescued his country from Communism by defeating Spanish leftists. Under Roosevelt, McCarran had opposed the United States entering World War II, believing that Communism was a greater threat than Nazism. McCarran was also among a number of prominent American Catholics, including Cardinal Francis Spellman of New York and Senator Joseph McCarthy, who viewed Franco as an ally of the Vatican, which had been sidelined in the Spanish Republic before Franco's rise but was now empowered. McCarran, despite his limited exposure to the church while growing up, took religion seriously; two of his daughters were nuns, and he was enamored of Franco's vision of Spain as a conservative Catholic state that had successfully defeated Communism.

During McCarran's travels in Europe, the news about the rise of Communism grew increasingly ominous. On October 1, 1949, China officially fell under Communist rule with Mao Zedong's defeat of the Nationalists and the establishment of the People's Republic of China. To American conservatives, it seemed that any country could be next, and McCarran believed that Spain was the only nation in Europe that had beat Communism. "My visit with Franco was exceedingly interesting and I was most agreeably surprised to learn the nature and kind of man that he is," he wrote to his aide Eva Adams. "He has been frightfully slandered and maligned. . . . I found the sentiment of the people in Spain from the lowest in stature to the highest, outspoken in praise of Franco's regime and of Franco himself." When Truman was asked about McCarran's visit with Franco, the president bit his tongue and said simply that the senator was representing only himself and not the U.S. government.

Earlier in the year, McCarran had tried to persuade Secretary of State Dean Acheson to give Spain aid as part of the Marshall Plan, and he was determined to obtain a $50 million U.S. loan to support the Franco regime. Spain was excluded from the Marshall Plan, but McCarran wasn't ready to give up. He told reporters after his meeting with Franco that he had tried to offer the dictator some advice. He had promised that "with a little smart handling at this end, Spain can be right back in the front parlor by this time next year."

On December 7, nearly three months after his departure, McCarran arrived back in New York. He declared that he had found living conditions in displaced persons camps in Europe "far better than living conditions of the average inhabitant of many areas in the United States." And he said he found countless instances of fraud: "Inadequate screening of applicants, with little or no regard for background, political beliefs and predilections of the applicant, has opened the gates to persons who will not become good citizens—persons who do not believe in our form of government and who will become ready recruits in subversive organizations to tear down the democracy of the United States." McCarran promised that all the evidence would be placed before his committee in January and that the resulting bill "will be founded on facts, not on flimsy fiction, misrepresentations, bias or prejudice."

As 1950 began and he rounded out his third term in the Senate, McCarran was at the peak of his power. He had vanquished most of his political enemies in Nevada—no one of stature would dare to challenge him in the primary that year, when he was up for reelection. A survey of Nevada voters showed that 71 percent approved of him. Still, he was seventy-four years old, with his health fragile as ever, and after the previous year's performance blocking the displaced persons bill, he had become extremely unpopular with the press. In March *Time* magazine named him one of the Senate's eight "most expendable" legislators, calling him "pompous, vindictive and power-grabbing." He was also turning into a target of the legendary *Washington Post* editorial cartoonist Herblock, who coined the phrase "McCarthyism." With his immense build and prominent nose, McCarran proved an easy subject for caricature.

In McCarran's paranoid mind, the growing attacks from the media and his political opponents served only to prove that he was right. The Communists would use any means to infiltrate the country, and America needed a fearless legislator like him to protect its values. In particular, he and his supporters resented the work of the CCDP, which continued to lobby for liberalized immigration laws. McCarran frequently alluded to the CCDP as "one pressure group" that he said spent $1 million lobbying to support liberalized immigration. "This money has not, of course, been spent for the relief of displaced persons but solely for the dissemination of propaganda designed to influence legislation to repeal the safeguards of our immigration laws." McCarran's aides echoed this feeling, particularly during the hearings that were starting up again in the immigration subcommittee. Richard Arens, the top aide assigned to immigration, was more powerful than the senators on the committee, so much so that he was nicknamed "super Senator," as the influential newspaper columnist Drew Pearson noted. "That man has created more havoc than dozens of men in Washington in reference to immigration and naturalization," said Celler in 1950. During sessions spent grilling the bureaucrats who administered the 1948 displaced person legislation, Arens would heap praise on his boss, at one point reminding everyone, apropos of nothing, that "every patriotic American in this country ought to get on his knees every night and thank the Good Lord that we have the senior senator from Nevada who has been waging this fight against tremendous odds and against a million dollar lobby [the CCDP], that has been defaming him from one end of the country to the other."

With his reelection campaign coming up, McCarran's supporters dropped hints that all the hubbub over displaced persons legislation was part of a larger plot against him. Eastland said in a statement that "outside pressure groups," which were proof of a "Communist conspiracy" being transplanted in this country, were trying to "get McCarran." Some of the comments carried unmistakable tones of anti-Semitism. The *Nevada State Journal*, a publication friendly to McCarran, accused "a New York invasion, backed by money" of trying "to determine the kind of Senator we want." McCarran, for his part, spotted a political opportunity in talking about these threats. In a letter to an aide, he acknowledged there wasn't much "Jew money" entering Nevada. But he still wanted to make himself look like a victim of outside Jewish meddling, writing, "What we want them to do is to send the money on and get it into the hands of our friends, and we'll use their money for my election. I think we should get the work started on this plan."

During the immigration subcommittee hearings, Arens maintained that Jews in particular were committing fraud to enter the country as displaced persons. In one exchange between Arens and an administrator of the DP laws, Arens asked if there was "any particular element or group among the displaced persons which has a greater percent, proportionately, of the fraud and false documents as compared to other groups." The employee, John Wilson Cutler, Jr., responded, "Yes, those cases I gave you referred completely to all, I would say, over 95 percent to one group." Arens shot back, "What group is that?" Cutler: "That was the Jewish group."

Despite efforts by Arens and McCarran to cast the country's displaced person program in a dubious light, popular support for altering the 1948 law was growing too strong to resist. *The New York Times* and *The Washington Post* both supported a revision. Telegrams from Eleanor Roosevelt and Lucius D. Clay, until recently the commander in chief of U.S. forces in Europe, urged the Senate to act. Finally realizing he could no longer block new legislation from leaving his own committee, McCarran relented, though when the bill reached the Senate floor, he tried to add 130 amendments. His colleagues blocked the effort.

On April 5, 1950, the Senate approved an amended version of Celler's bill that would make the 1948 law more expansive and generous. Whereas the law from two years earlier allowed for the admission of fewer than 250,000 people, the Displaced Persons Act of 1950 made room for more than 400,000, and it extended the cutoff date so that a broader pool of refugees were eligible. It also eliminated the preferences for those with agricultural backgrounds and those from the Baltic states. Like the 1948 law, the added numbers were technically outside the annual quotas but would be made up for by mortgaging from future years.

When the bill landed on Truman's desk, he signed it "with very great pleasure":

> The countrymen of these displaced persons have brought to us
> in the past the best of their labor, their hatred of tyranny and
> their love of freedom. They have helped our country grow in
> strength and moral leadership. I have every confidence that the
> new Americans who will come to our country under the provi-
> sions of the present bill will also make a substantial contribution
> to our national well-being.

The results were immediate. Under the country's first legislative refugee program, roughly 400,000 additional people were admitted to the country. The majority were escaping the USSR and eastern Europe. Contrary to the suspicions spread by McCarran and others, just 16 percent or 63,000 were Jews; many more were Roman Catholic or "of Protestant and Orthodox faith." About half were younger than thirty. Nearly one-third settled in New York, and another 11 percent landed in Illinois.

Among those who came were Zinaida Supe from Latvia, who in December 1950 became the 200,000th person admitted under the new displaced person policy. She and her four children, ages seven to eleven, were greeted by New York mayor Vincent Impellitteri after arriving on a U.S. naval ship; the next day they flew to Colorado Springs, where Supe planned to work as a waitress. Vaclovas Paplonskis, who adopted the American name "Vince," arrived from Germany in the fall of 1948 and settled in Baltimore. A year later he told *Life* magazine that in his spare time he enjoyed studying English and U.S. history and hoped to take his family on an educational trip to Washington as soon as they could afford it. His boss recalled that during Paplonskis's first New Year's Eve in the United States, the new immigrant repeated softly to himself, "God love America on this New Year."

The legislative loss enraged McCarran. On the night of the final vote, while leaving the Senate gallery, he ran into William S. Bernard, executive secretary of the CCDP, on the elevator. They were silent. Then, walking down the Capitol steps, with McCarran ahead of Bernard, McCarran suddenly whipped around and yelled, "You son of a bitch!" To which Bernard replied simply, "Thank you, Senator." McCarran walked away with his head down. Later, he wrote to his daughter, "I met the enemy and he took me on the DP bill. It's tough to beat a million or more dollars and it's something worth while to give the rotten gang a good fight anyway, and they know they have been to a fight for its [*sic*] not over yet."

McCarran understood that while his political enemies had prevailed in allowing more refugees to settle in the country, a far more important battle lay ahead. By invoking a humanitarian crisis, those who had pushed for the Displaced Persons Act were also beginning to challenge the foundation of the American immigration system itself—the national origins quotas passed in 1924. And on this, McCarran had no intention to yield.

SIX

INTERNAL SECURITY

O N DECEMBER 8, 1950, Anna Rosenberg appeared before the
Senate Armed Services Committee accused of being a Communist. Senator Herbert Lehman of New York watched the hearing, tears
rolling down his face. None of it made sense. Just a month earlier, the
country's widely revered defense secretary George C. Marshall had recommended Rosenberg for a senior role that would later make her the
highest-ranking woman ever to serve in the Pentagon. As an assistant
secretary of defense, Rosenberg would be charged with addressing the
U.S. military's manpower shortage—a critical job, as the country had
entered a new war, in Korea, that summer, but still had far-reaching
commitments to maintain stability in Europe and Japan. Rosenberg, a
petite and charming woman with a taste for expensive jewelry and per-
fume, seemed perfect for the job: she had spent years managing big projects during the New Deal and running several wartime agencies in New
York. A Jewish-Hungarian immigrant who had arrived in the United
States as a child, she had also built a lucrative business consulting companies on labor issues. She had a long list of powerful friends, from Nelson
Rockefeller to New York mayor Fiorello H. La Guardia, who once said

of her, "She knows more about labor relations and human relations than any man in the country."

Now she was being denounced as perhaps the worst thing an American could be called in 1950. The entire year had been engulfed by one stunning newspaper headline after another of ordinary citizens facing accusations of working as Communist agents. Lawmakers like McCarran had already employed red scare tactics to block refugee legislation, but what followed was of an entirely different magnitude, as the United States succumbed to an awful fear. In January a jury convicted former State Department official Alger Hiss of perjury for denying he had shared documents with Whittaker Chambers, a confessed Soviet spy. The news shocked Washington because of Hiss's impeccable credentials; he was a Harvard Law School graduate who had clerked for Supreme Court justice Oliver Wendell Homes before taking on a number of senior roles in the Roosevelt administration. Then in April, Klaus Fuchs, a German-born scientist working for the British and American governments to develop an atomic bomb at Los Alamos, confessed he had handed secret details about the project to the Soviet Union. His apprehension led to the arrest of others, including the married couple Julius and Ethel Rosenberg, who would later become the first American civilians to be executed for espionage.

While some of those initially accused were guilty of their crimes, countless innocent Americans soon became the targets of unconscionable smear campaigns that would permanently destroy their reputations. In February 1950 Senator Joseph McCarthy delivered a speech in Wheeling, West Virginia, that vaulted him into the national spotlight, assailing "enemies from within" and claiming that he had a list of about two hundred Communists who were working in the State Department. If people like Hiss and Fuchs were part of the secret Communist underground, McCarthy and his ilk warned, there was no telling how many others had wormed their way into the U.S. government in order to sabotage its foreign policy.

None of this sat well with Lehman. When McCarthy returned to Washington after his February speech, Lehman, Scott Lucas, and Brien McMahon of Connecticut confronted the Wisconsin senator and demanded proof. McCarthy dodged their requests, but his speech had been enough to drive other senators into fearful silence. As Lehman would remember bitterly years later, "Nearly all the senators did not lift a finger for two or three years." What enraged him the most was not McCarthy's gall; it was the timidity of his colleagues. He had expected more out of such an esteemed institution.

At seventy-one, Lehman was a new senator for his home state of New York, but in the twilight of his career. After nearly a decade as governor of New York, and having spent much of his career advancing the causes of his close friend Franklin Roosevelt, Lehman belonged to a small class of Jews who had ascended to the highest echelon of public life—men including Supreme Court justice Felix Frankfurter and financier and presidential adviser Bernard Baruch. When he entered the Senate in January 1950, he had already been better known nationally than most of his colleagues. Still, he had been determined, at least at first, to defer to those more senior than him. "I hope to make a little news, but as little noise as possible," he told reporters.

He had coveted a seat in the Senate for more than a decade, and when he finally arrived, he "felt a very real thrill." But he also found the work exhausting and grindingly slow compared to the pace of executive office. Assigned to a number of committees, he learned that he was expected to rush around the cavernous halls of Capitol Hill constantly attending meetings, some scheduled for the same time. "If I were to compare the actual work load of a governor with that of a senator, I would say that the Senator's job is the more strenuous. In Washington almost every day is a race against the time hand."

He was not a member of the Senate Armed Services Committee when it began to review Anna Rosenberg's nomination; he was too junior. Still, he made time to attend every day of Rosenberg's hearing, so concerned was he about its outcome. Rosenberg was an old friend;

they had connected through Roosevelt's network of ardent New Dealers. When McCarthy and others attacked her, Lehman released a statement that said she was "one of the most capable women I have ever met," adding, he had "always found her completely loyal and deeply devoted to the interests of the country." But his support was drowned out by the right-wing voices gathering against her. One of her biggest detractors was Gerald L. K. Smith, a white supremacist preacher from Arkansas who was behind several organizations—the America First Party, the Christian Nationalist Crusade, and the magazine *The Cross and the Flag*—all united in spreading a message of hate against Jews and minorities. Latching on to the anti-Communist cause as well, Smith and his allies attacked Rosenberg's Jewish identity, no doubt trying to taint her by association with Julius and Ethel Rosenberg, even though there was no relation. Fulton Lewis, Jr., a popular conservative radio host, criticized Rosenberg almost daily, and Reverend Wesley Swift, a KKK supporter, told his congregation that Rosenberg was not just a "Jewess . . . but an alien from Budapest with Socialistic ideas."

Rosenberg's references, from the likes of Eisenhower and Baruch, had been so sterling that the Senate Armed Services Committee at first unanimously approved her nomination. But her conservative critics soon found an audience on Capitol Hill. After being contacted by Smith, Representative John Rankin, a Democrat from Mississippi, voiced concerns about Rosenberg's nomination. "While our boys are dying by the thousands in foreign fields . . . it is no time to put any questionable character, especially a foreign-born character, in a position of this importance," Rankin said in a statement entered into the *Congressional Record*.

Then suddenly a witness emerged—a man who said he would swear under oath that Rosenberg had belonged to Communist groups and had helped put Communists in important government positions.

On that December day of her hearing, as Lehman watched, the star witness was former Communist Ralph De Sola, who insisted he had seen Rosenberg at several meetings of the John Reed Club, a Communist group, during the 1930s. When asked if the woman sitting in the room was the same person he had seen years earlier, De Sola said yes. After listening to his testimony, Rosenberg confronted him—and the committee: "He is a liar. . . . It is inhuman what he has done to me in the past few days. . . . If you don't think I am fit to take this office, say so. I don't care what you charge me with, but not disloyalty, Senator. It is an awful thing to carry around with you."

Then, just as quickly as the case against Rosenberg had materialized, it disintegrated. Two weeks after De Sola's testimony, the FBI announced it had found a second woman named "Anna Rosenberg," who admitted she had been associated with the John Reed Club. The committee moved immediately to approve Rosenberg's nomination. Faced with a case that had collapsed, even McCarthy backed down and said he would vote for her.

—

ALTHOUGH ROSENBERG had survived the attack, Lehman still felt deflated. The McCarthyist crusade sweeping the country was not just aimed at rooting out Communism. It was an attempt to dismantle the social reforms of the New Deal by weakening labor unions and discrediting those who supported an expanded welfare state or corporate regulation. McCarthyists were also exploiting the same fears of Jews and immigrant outsiders that had overtaken the country after World War I. For Herbert Lehman, this was devastating.

Coming from one of the wealthiest and most prominent Jewish families in the country, Lehman did not need to work to sustain himself financially. His father, Mayer, and his uncles, Henry and Emanuel, had arrived from Bavaria in the 1840s in the same wave that had brought Mannie Celler's grandparents—except that rather than settling in New York, the Lehman family made their home in Montgomery, Alabama. The three brothers opened a store that initially sold dry goods and groceries to local farmers—but soon they turned their energy to the biggest business in the state. Growing demand for cotton came from Britain and New England,

and Montgomery was at the center of the trade; the Lehman brothers became one of the principal brokers, buying and selling. The Civil War nearly destroyed the business, but the brothers, who had grown to love their adopted southern home, did everything in their power to support the Confederate cause. Emanuel traveled to London at the behest of the Confederacy to sell bonds and raise money for the South. At one point, Mayer negotiated a large sale of cotton to pay for supplies to support soldiers suffering in northern prisons. Alabama governor T. H. Watts wrote of Mayer Lehman to Jefferson Davis in 1864, "He is a business man of established character and one of the best Southern patriots. He is a foreigner, but has been here fifteen years and is thoroughly identified with us." After the war, the cotton business bounced back, and so did the family business, now officially called Lehman Brothers.

By the time Herbert Lehman joined as a partner in 1908, the business had turned into an investment bank, financing the construction of railroads, textile mills, and timber companies, as well as backing large banks and iconic companies in New York. In 1906 Lehman Brothers and Goldman Sachs sold preferred shares in Sears, Roebuck and Company, as the retail business boomed across the country.

Maintaining the family business could easily have occupied Lehman for the rest of his life, except that he met, through New York politics, a man named Franklin Delano Roosevelt. Lehman had felt called to public service since he was a young man. He had grown up supremely sheltered in Manhattan, socializing mainly with other acculturated German-Jewish families, all of whom attended the same small set of private schools and Reform temples. But he never forgot a visit he had taken to the Lower East Side when he was fourteen and seeing "the poverty and the filth and bleakness." During breaks from college, he volunteered downtown at the Henry Street Settlement House, a social service agency founded by the visionary reformer and nurse Lillian Wald. But it was not until 1928, at the age of fifty, that he seriously entertained the idea of running for office. It was a year in New York politics that would alter the course of the country.

With New York governor Al Smith running for president, the Democratic Party desperately needed a strong candidate to replace him in Albany. But it was unclear if the most obvious person for the job was available: though Roosevelt was a rising star in the Democratic Party, he was also trying to piece his body back together after being diagnosed with polio several years earlier, and he was spending most of his time rehabilitating in Warm Springs, Georgia. Lehman, whose moneyed connections had earned him a spot on the Democratic Party's national committee that year, agreed with Smith and others that Roosevelt should run. The men hounded him over the phone, but Roosevelt rebuffed them, saying he needed at least two more years to recover. Finally, with time running out, Smith made one last plea to Roosevelt, this time sweetening the deal. "You know the job of governor isn't impossibly difficult, and we'll give you Herbert Lehman as lieutenant governor, so that you can go away for as long a time as you like." Roosevelt then asked for Lehman to get on the phone and asked him directly if he would run for lieutenant governor. When Lehman said yes, Roosevelt acceded. "Well, I guess that in view of this very strong appeal that has been made, I'll accept the nomination." With Lehman at his side, Roosevelt won the governor's seat, setting him on a course to the White House.

As Roosevelt frequently returned to Warm Springs to recuperate, Lehman became known as New York's "other governor." When Roosevelt was elected president in 1932, Lehman became the first Jewish person elected governor of the state, eventually serving four terms. He grew to love Roosevelt, though the two men were tremendously different. Roosevelt carefully analyzed every political angle and worked each one to achieve maximum leverage, whereas Lehman approached politics with an unbending earnestness. "He refused to admit the utility of compromise," wrote his biographer Allan Nevins. "Principle was principle and must not be weakened by expediency." The crushing pressure to always do right, though, meant that Lehman could be paralyzed by big decisions. Unlike Roosevelt, who staked his claims and never looked back, Lehman obsessed over details and was prone to second-guessing himself, staying up all night wondering if he had misjudged something. When Roosevelt was once asked if he worried about anything while he was governor of New York, he responded, "I let Herbert do the worrying for me." His wife, Eleanor, had a similar impression of Lehman's decision-making process: "He will think about it all night, and he will worry about it the next day, and will talk to everybody about it, and it will go on being a worry after there is no use worrying." Every time Lehman ran for office, he agonized over the decision until Roosevelt convinced him. Eleanor remembered one time observing a meeting with Roosevelt, Lehman, and Roosevelt's early, devoted political adviser, Louis Howe, to discuss some banking problem. As they talked, with Roosevelt in his wheelchair and Howe sitting still the entire time, Lehman paced the room. Lehman's restlessness annoyed Roosevelt so much that when the phone rang and Howe moved to answer it, Roosevelt snapped, "Louis Howe, can't you sit still?"

Now that he was in the Senate, Lehman would stay up at night fretting over legislation that channeled the worst of McCarthyism. His primary nemesis for the next two years, though, would be not the Wisconsin senator but Pat McCarran, who was intent on protecting the country— especially from foreigners.

———

A QUARTER-CENTURY EARLIER immigration debates had centered on the struggle to control the race and nationality of Americans, guided by the fear that the United States had to maintain a certain ethnic makeup to protect its democracy. Concerns over Communist infiltration by immigrants had played a supporting role in passing the 1924 law. Now they were taking center stage.

On August 10, 1950, McCarran introduced a sprawling bill that would treat Communism as a national emergency—a threat so dire that it required a serious curbing of Americans' civil liberties. The chief feature of the bill, called the Internal Security Act, was to require all Communist and Communist-front organizations to register with the attorney general. If a group was suspected of being Communist, a newly established Subversive Activities Control Board would be able to hold hearings to weigh the evidence. Anyone associated with a Communist group would be banned from working for the government, be unable to use their passport, and if not yet a citizen, would not be allowed to naturalize. But the bill also dealt with immigration, following, as it did, McCarran's bitter fight over the Displaced Persons Act and its subsequent amendment. Reviving his arguments that a lax immigration policy would allow subversive forces to enter the country, McCarran included a provision in the Internal Security Act that would exclude from entrance to the United States anyone who had belonged to a Communist organization in their home country. If an American naturalized after January 1, 1950, engaged in any Communist-related activity within five years, that person's citizenship would be revoked. The law also empowered the president, during a national emergency, to detain anyone if there was "reasonable ground to believe that such person probably will engage in, or probably will conspire with others to engage in, acts of espionage or sabotage."

The vague language raised alarm bells among liberals, but there was little they could do. Lehman was learning, as others had before, how much power McCarran wielded as head of the Judiciary Committee. "He'd come into the chamber and lay down the law," Lehman remembered. "It didn't make any difference who had the floor. He'd just take it and insist on his legislation being taken up at his will, frequently out of turn. He paid no attention to the amenities or to fair play." Still, Lehman fought. In a thirty-three-page speech, he called the Internal Security Act of 1950 "the most dangerous and violent curtailment of our civil liberties of any legislation that has ever been proposed in the American Congress." When Lehman finished speaking, McCarran snarled, "Is the Senator from New York trying to defend Communist front organizations?"

Lehman and others proposed an alternative bill with greater protections for the accused, but the Senate easily rejected it. Elections were coming in the fall, and few dared to expose themselves to accusations of being Communist sympathizers. When the time came to vote on the bill, only seven senators went against it, with Lehman the only one facing an election in November. He declared, "I am going to vote against this tragic, this unfortunate, this ill-conceived legislation. My conscience will be easier, though I realize my political prospects may be more difficult. I shall cast my vote to protect the liberties of our people." Afterward theologian Reinhold Niebuhr wrote in a letter to *The New York Times* that "a special accolade should be awarded to Senator Lehman," the only senator facing reelection who had "dared to brave the dangerous hysteria which is arising in this country." In the House, a separate version of the bill championed by California congressman Richard M. Nixon moved forward with similar speed; Celler was among just twenty who voted against it.

With the bill now headed to Truman's desk to sign, the president faced a difficult choice. The legislation had passed by overwhelming margins, and with Truman's falling poll ratings, Democrats needed ammunition against Republican charges that they were pro-Communist. The notion that Truman could stop a bill marked as "anti-Communist" in the current political climate seemed unrealistic. "Even in administration quarters it was held that a veto did not have a ghost of a show of being sustained," observed *The New York Times*. But like Lehman, the president was deeply unsettled by the anti-Communist hysteria on Capitol Hill, and he was in no mood to cave in to the McCarthy crowd, which had been targeting members of Truman's own administration. His secretary of state, Dean Acheson, had recently been accused of being soft on Communism, after Mao Zedong's victory in China and the Soviet Union's development of an atomic bomb. At one point, McCarthy sent Truman a telegram demanding that the president cooperate with vetting State Department employees, with the threat, "Failure on your part will label the Democratic Party of being the bed-fellow of inter-national Communism." Truman wrote a letter back giving McCarthy a piece of his mind: "Your telegram is not only not true and an insolent approach to a situation that should have been worked out between man and man but it shows conclusively that you are not even fit to have a hand in the operation of the Government of the United States. I am very sure that the people of Wisconsin are extremely sorry that they are represented by a person who has as little sense of responsibility as you have." Truman, as he often did, let off steam by writing the letter—but he never sent it.

Lehman recognized in the president a kindred stubbornness in the face of bullying by McCarthy and his followers, and he and two other senators encouraged Truman to stop the McCarran bill with "a message of such force and clarity" that it "would arouse the nation to a realization of the dangers we confront." The country was in no mood to listen, but years later Truman's statement explaining his decision to veto the Internal Security Act of 1950 stands as a true act of moral courage. No matter the political cost—and he would pay a heavy one—Truman refused to back down on the country's core principles during its worst days of anti-Communist paranoia. The idea of requiring Communist organizations to register, he pointed out, was "about as practical as requiring thieves to register with the sheriff." But more troubling was the bill's lack of clear criteria for what constituted a Communist-front group; as a result, it "would open a Pandora's box of opportunities for official condemnation of organizations and individuals for perfectly honest opinions which happen to be stated also by communists." After exhaustively listing all the flaws he detected in the bill, Truman concluded: "This is a time when we must marshal all our resources and all the moral strength of our free system in self-defense against the threat of communist aggression. We will fail in this, and we will destroy all that we seek to preserve, if we sacrifice the liberties of our citizens in a misguided attempt to achieve national security." Years later Lehman regarded Truman's statement as "one of the great state documents of our time," and asked a White House aide if the president could send him a signed copy. As predicted, though, the political pressures proved too great for Capital Hill Democrats to join their president; the veto was overridden.

The Internal Security Act had an immediate, damaging effect on the country's ability to admit displaced persons from Europe, undercutting the laws that Truman, Celler, and others had fought so hard to enact. Within weeks of the law passing, officials at Ellis Island struggled to make sense of its broad ban on anyone associated with the Communist Party and detained 127 people. The Metropolitan Opera feared it would need to replace at least eight European singers coming to New York for the current season. Between September 1950 and March 1951, more than 100,000 refugees were blocked from entering the United States because of the attorney general's interpretation of the Internal Security Act; these refugees had lived under Communist rule and joined the party before growing disillusioned and migrating to camps in the West. The law also became an impediment to fighting the Cold War. The CIA was especially interested in sowing discord in Soviet bloc countries by finding defectors who could spread anti-Communist propaganda—but when it came time to allow these defectors to enter the United States, the Internal Security Act blocked them, because they had been members of local Communist groups, often out of necessity. As Harry N. Rosenfield, who was appointed by Truman to oversee the resettlement of refugees after the war, put it, the United States was "spending millions of dollars to encourage resistance from behind the Iron Curtain and defection from Communism," then "fail[ing] to make good on its word to the victims of the propaganda war with the Soviet Union."

The Internal Security Act failed on its own terms as well. As Truman predicted, Communist Party organizations in the United States refused to register with the government. A long legal battle ensued, and in 1965 the Supreme Court ruled that the Internal Security Act's registration requirement was unconstitutional, since the Fifth Amendment protected Americans from self-incrimination.

Regardless, the signal from Capitol Hill was clear. Red scare forces were on the march, and they would not be easy to stop.

—

MANNIE CELLER AND PAT McCARRAN were glaring at each other, red in the face.

On March 6, 1952, McCarran had begun joint House and Senate

hearings on new legislation that he boasted would be the most ambitious reworking of the country's immigration system in decades. In his opening remarks, he said the present laws had "many inequities" and "loopholes" and that it was time to fix the country's "piecemeal" rules. Six officials from Japan's Supreme Court were present as visitors, observing American democracy in action. Then, just as McCarran moved to call his first witness, his counterpart in the House, Celler, interrupted the proceedings.

"I asked to be heard," said Celler, to which McCarran responded, "I know you want to be heard. I want to hear you, Mr. Celler. . . . I want to hear you at length." But, annoyed, McCarran instructed Celler that there would be time later to hear his remarks, and it would be "unfair to those who have come here" to deviate from the agenda already set.

Celler insisted that as chairman of the House Judiciary Committee, which oversaw immigration, he had as much right to speak as McCarran.

"You wouldn't get away with it," declared McCarran.

By this point, the two men were engaged in a staring contest. One can hardly imagine what the Japanese visitors made of the scene. Finally, McCarran relented. "You may be heard for three minutes . . . three minutes."

Celler took seven or eight minutes to speak, and then hurried out of the committee room.

McCarran viewed Celler the same way he did Lehman—with suspicion. To the Nevadan, the two men were Jewish lawmakers from New York who relentlessly advocated for minority interests, with no regard for the country at large. The country needed to be vigilant, he thought, because it was not just the future of the United States at stake. "I believe that this Nation is the last hope of western civilization," McCarran once said on the Senate floor, "and if this oasis of the world shall be overrun, perverted, contaminated, or destroyed, then the last flickering light of humanity will be extinguished."

McCarran had a long memory for personal slights and had not forgotten the bitter loss from the displaced persons fight. His triumph with the Internal Security Act had only whetted his appetite to press his anti-immigration crusade even further. For two years his immigration sub-committee, together with his counterparts in the House, had studied the country's immigration laws, in the most ambitious congressional assess-ment carried out in over forty years. They traveled to Europe to inter-view people who processed emigrants headed to the United States. They amassed testimony from the U.S. immigration service and private groups that worked with new arrivals.

The result was a massive, nine-hundred-page report that identified problems with current U.S. immigration policy and laid out recommen-dations for how best to address them. It was the first time in nearly three decades that the country's leaders had revisited the immigration system laid down by the Johnson-Reed Act of 1924. But while the climate for the debate had changed since then, with the science of eugenics now largely discredited, the subcommittee was not prepared to abandon the core system of quotas based on "national origins." The report suggested keeping the quotas "without giving credence to any theory of Nordic supremacy"; still, it contained pointed references to the large number of Jews among the newer immigrants, noting that "the population of the United States has increased three-fold since 1877 while the Jewish pop-ulation has increased twenty-one-fold during the same period." And the report insisted that quotas favoring northwestern Europeans were defen-sible because it was important to preserve "similarity of cultural back-ground." It also warned that the country's current population already exceeded its optimal level, implying that any new immigration would need to be heavily controlled.

In other words, the arguments made by McCarran and his allies in 1952 were not substantially different from those presented in the 1920s. Lawmakers and activists who favored liberalizing the country's immigra-tion laws, however, had also been studying the evidence and marshaling their arguments.

In 1945 the National Committee on Immigration Policy, a pro-reform lobbying group chaired by Earl Harrison, had initiated its own study. The result was a 1950 book, *American Immigration Policy: A Reappraisal*, that painted a very different picture from what McCarran's subcommittee produced around the same time. The book, written by the group's staff director, William S. Bernard, who would go on to become an influential immigration scholar, argued that a more a liberal policy would help rather than hurt the country. The United States needed more immigrants in order to forestall a decline in population growth, Bernard argued. More important, he outlined a foundational political argument that would power the pro-immigration movement for years to come: the national origins quotas were ill suited to modern times. Now, in the midst of the Cold War, the United States was pitching to the world its vision of a superior democratic society, yet it had an immigration system that "implies the doctrine of racialism." Still, supporters of a more liberal immigration policy were not ready to abandon national quotas entirely, likely because they had no replacement in mind, though as Bernard mused, "some more equitable method can surely be devised." In the meantime, he recommended that the country double its annual limit of 154,000 immigrants and allow unused quotas to be pooled for immigrants from countries that had exhausted their numbers already and for political refugees.

In Washington, however, the men with the most power over U.S. immigration law were not listening to such suggestions.

McCarran proposed a bill, to the surprise of no one, that closely followed the recommendations of his own immigration subcommittee's report. His plan retained the national origins quota system based on the 1920 census and raised the overall limit only slightly from 154,000, allotting about 85 percent of the slots to northwestern Europe. Within these slots, there would be new preferences: at least half would go to those with special skills that would substantially benefit the United States. Thirty percent would go to parents of adult U.S. citizens, followed by 20 percent for spouses and children of permanent residents. Only after these preferential slots went unfilled were other immigrants allowed in.

Immigration legislation moved first in the House, which on April 23, 1952, began debating a bill from Francis Walter, the conservative Democrat from Pennsylvania who chaired the House immigration subcommittee and whose proposal was nearly identical to McCarran's. Known widely as "Tad," the Pennsylvania congressman was a mercurial man whose opinions were often difficult to pin down. "He was a rough and hard fighter, sometimes indeed a vindictive one, resentful of criticism, intolerant of opposition, a formidable exponent of his own deeply felt beliefs in a country where conflict of opinion is the essence of the political process," wrote the *Washington Post* editorial board upon his death in 1963. A World War I veteran, he had opposed the country entering another war until the Pearl Harbor attack, at which point he took leave from Congress and briefly joined the navy. In 1944, on the day before D-Day, he presented President Roosevelt with a letter opener made from the forearm of a Japanese soldier killed in the Pacific. Walter apologized to Roosevelt for presenting such a small part of the soldier's anatomy. "There'll be plenty more such gifts," Roosevelt assured him.

Walter's positions on immigration proved equally befuddling. He had supported refugee relief after the war. But he had also staunchly supported anti-Communist efforts to root out supposed foreign subversives as chairman of the House Un-American Activities Committee.

On the day the House began debating Walter's bill, Celler was the first speaker to oppose it. He attacked national origins quotas as un-American and proposed an amendment that would combine unused ones. Walter dismissed the idea, saying that it "would have the effect of destroying entirely our theory of national origins." John Wood, a Republican from Idaho, also rose to oppose Celler's amendment, arguing that entry into the country was not a privilege but a right. "It seems to me that the question of racial origins—though I am not a follower of Hitler—there is something to it. We cannot tie a stone around its neck and drop it into the middle of the Atlantic just because it worked to the contrary in Germany. . . . I believe that possibly statistics would show that the Western European races have made the best citizens in America and are more easily made into Americans." Wood further complained that immigrants would become good American citizens faster if they weren't "penned up among the people of their own kind in the large eastern cities where they do not learn to talk English readily. They read their own newspapers." Even so, he insisted he held no prejudice. "I do not know that I have any opposition to any peoples at all. . . . The only importance with me is whether they are material that will make good American citizens readily; if they are, it is all right with me."

Two days later, on April 25, Walter's bill passed easily, 206 to 68. In the Senate, however, Lehman and his colleague Hubert Humphrey had launched a pitched battle to stop McCarran.

—

ONE IMMEDIATE CHALLENGE the opposition faced was that McCarran's bill was so complex that scarcely any of the lawmakers voting for it understood what they were enacting. In a confidential memo to Truman, respected attorney and former New Dealer Felix S. Cohen scoffed at the notion that the bill would clarify existing law. The section on whether admitting an immigrant was in the public interest, Cohen pointed out, was "sub-clause (b) of clause (ii) of sub-paragraph I of paragraph (28) of sub-section (a) of section 212 of Chapter I of Title II of Chapter 6 of Title VIII." He added, "It is doubtful whether one immigrant in a thousand could read this bill and learn from his reading what rights and liabilities the bill puts upon him," though he noted sardonically that the bill, if enacted, would provide much work for lawyers.

The bill was sprinkled throughout with evidence of McCarran's continued interest in stamping out Communism. Some provisions sounded strikingly similar to those already contained in the Internal Security Act—for instance, authorizing the attorney general to deport any immigrant who, after entering the country, became a member of an organization considered subversive. The bill also decreed that if a naturalized American, within ten years of that person's naturalization, refused to testify before a congressional committee on any alleged "subversive activities," such an act would be grounds for losing citizenship.

On May 13, 1952, from the Senate floor, McCarran explained his bill's underlying philosophy to his colleagues:

> Today . . . as never before, a sound immigration and natural-
> ization system is essential to the preservation of our way of life,
> because that system is the conduit through which a stream of
> humanity flows into the fabric of our society. If that stream is
> healthy, the impact on our society is salutary; but if that stream
> is polluted, our institutions and our way of life become infected.

In response, Lehman blasted the bill and said it reflected a "xenopho-bic" and "racist" attitude, premised "on the assumption that America is under the constant threat of losing her Anglo-Saxon character because of immigration." He argued that especially after World War II, there was no justification for retaining quotas based on such discriminatory ideas. "This racist philosophy, based on belief in blood-stocks and the superiority of the Nordic strain," is "strikingly similar to the basic racial philosophy officially espoused so unfortunately and with such tragic con-sequences in Nazi Germany."

Lehman and Humphrey proposed an alternative that would retain the quotas but move the benchmark census to 1950—which would auto-matically raise the number of immigrants allowed from southern and eastern Europe—and allow flexibility for shifting unused quotas to countries that needed them. But McCarran refused to hold a hearing for the Lehman-Humphrey bill, on the grounds that his subcommittee had been so thorough in its deliberations that to suggest the need for more discussion was "an insult to the integrity of the Senate and committee." And it did not escape his notice that the same senators who had opposed him on the Internal Security Act were now backing the proposal from Lehman and Humphrey. Only "small isolated 'radical' groups" and "a gang of cloak and suiters from New York" opposed his immigration bill, he sneered. The debate on the Senate floor became so ugly that at one point after McCarran finished speaking and Lehman began to respond, McCarran and his allies walked out of the Senate chamber. Lehman, recalled his aide Julius Edelstein, could scarcely believe that such a breakdown in Senate decorum had occurred.

It was not just McCarran who treated Lehman, Humphrey, and other opponents with indifference: the Senate chamber was left almost entirely empty every time they spoke. Most of their colleagues were content to take McCarran at his word that his massive bill was worth passing, especially since there were elections coming that fall, and few incumbents dared to appear to be blocking important anti-Communist legislation. They had all seen what happened two years earlier, after Majority Leader Scott Lucas fought both McCarthy and McCarran. McCarthy had campaigned for Lucas's opponent, calling the majority leader soft on Communism, and Lucas had lost his seat in a landslide.

On the evening of May 22, after Lehman and his allies' last-ditch effort to add more than a hundred amendments failed, the Senate passed the McCarran bill with a voice vote. Only about a dozen senators were on the floor at the time. A *New York Times* headline described the Senate in that moment as an "apathetic chamber."

The opponents of the bill now looked to President Truman to see if he would repeat his performance with the Internal Security Act and veto the bill.

The president was not ending his second presidential term on a political high note. The Korean War had failed to resolve quickly, and Americans were dying in battle every week. The country was growing weary of fighting and tired of Truman. A Gallup poll in November 1951 showed the president at an approval rating of 23 percent, a historic low. A *New Yorker* profile by John Hersey described the president as "making his diurnal way through the thickets of power—the rank, trackless, strangely beautiful tangles of dreadful responsibilities and pompous trivialities through which he was obliged to move." Truman could run for reelection—he was technically eligible for another term. But the sheer weight of his responsibilities was tiring. As early as April 16, 1950, he wrote in his diary that "eight years as President is enough and sometimes too much for any man to serve in that capacity."

Given his acrimonious history with McCarran, it would have surprised no one if Truman had vetoed the immigration bill. When asked the morning after it passed in the Senate what he would do, Truman simply smiled and said he did not like to comment on legislation until it was formally in front of him. The reporters "guffawed" in disbelief.

Telegrams and letters poured into the White House, urging Truman to act one way or another. On June 20, 1952, William J. Hopkins, the White House executive clerk, counted close to eleven thousand pieces of correspondence pressing Truman to veto McCarran's bill. Hopkins noted that most of the opposition originated with Jewish groups. Some notes of support also arrived, though; Hopkins counted roughly five hundred letters telling Truman to sign the law. They were coming from an unusual source.

—

Mike Masaoka was overjoyed. As the brash lobbyist for the Japanese American Citizens League (JACL), he had been working the halls of Congress for years trying to get lawmakers to pay attention to the needs of Japanese-Americans. Walter Besterman, a staff member on the House Judiciary Committee, once lightheartedly accused Masaoka of spending so much time in Besterman's reception area that he wore out the room's green couch. When Masaoka tried to get an audience with Congressman John Robison of Kentucky, a member of the House Judiciary Committee, he followed him into the men's room and kept talking to Robison while the lawmaker used the urinal, until Robison relented and agreed to a more traditional setting for a meeting. Masaoka's assertiveness was all the more remarkable given how rare it was to see an Asian American roaming the halls of the Capitol; one time in the Cannon House Office Building, a guard was so startled by Masaoka's appearance that he stopped him at the entrance, took him into a room, and demanded to know why he was there.

Now, with the House and Senate votes supporting McCarran's bill, Masaoka was within arm's reach of achieving a legislative goal long dear to him: embedded in the thickets of the McCarran bill was a provision that would finally give Asian immigrants the right to naturalize.

After the 1924 bill blocked them from immigrating to the United States at all, Asians had sought and won a handful of narrow exemptions that allowed them to trickle into the country. There was the 1943 allowance made by Roosevelt for Chinese immigrants. In 1946 Celler helped win a hundred-person annual quota for Indians and Filipinos, as well as the right for them to naturalize. The War Brides Act of 1945 allowed mostly Chinese wives of American citizens to enter the country outside the quota system.

But the rules were not uniform. While small numbers of Chinese, Indian, and Filipino immigrants were allowed to enter the country and then eventually naturalize, Japanese and Koreans were not. For these groups, the exclusion clauses from the 1924 law remained in effect, and for Japanese-Americans in particular, the intervening years had only heightened the sting of the racism.

For first- and second-generation Japanese-Americans, known as issei and nisei, the experience of World War II was a traumatic reckoning with their adopted homeland. After the Japanese attack on Pearl Harbor, U.S. military officials who feared that an invasion of the American West Coast could soon follow drew up plans to remove Japanese-Americans from their homes. On February 19, 1942, President Roosevelt signed the infamous Executive Order 9066, which authorized the secretary of war to remove "any or all" persons from certain designated military areas. The news stunned Japanese families, who could scarcely believe that though they had been law-abiding members of their communities for decades, the U.S. Army was now insisting that it could not tell which of them were "loyal" or "disloyal" and that the only solution was to put all of them in camps. Between 1942 and 1945, about 120,000 Japanese-Americans, two-thirds of them American citizens and not one of them charged with a crime to justify their removal, were forced to live in makeshift barracks, surrounded by barbed wire and under armed guard. Given only days or weeks to prepare for their new lives, many sold their businesses and homes in a hurry, at a steep loss.

Masaoka was twenty-six years old when his mother and siblings were forced into an internment camp; he was spared only because he lived outside the zone targeted by the military for removals. It was not the first time the Masaokas had experienced the limitations of their rights as Japanese-Americans. Masaoka's father, Eijiro, had left his native Japan for the United States in 1903 and initially wanted to settle with his growing family in California. But the state's laws banning land ownership by noncitizens caused Eijiro to move his family to Utah, where he purchased a plot of land with borrowed money. When the family arrived, they discovered they had been scammed; the land they had purchased was on the bed of the Great Salt Lake, useless for farming. Then came more tragedy: the night before Mike Masaoka's ninth birthday, his father died in a car accident. His mother was left to support Mike and his seven siblings.

Rather than shrink from the strangeness of being a Japanese-American boy in a largely white Mormon world, Masaoka ingratiated himself with teachers, who recognized his gift for oratory. At the University of Utah, he became a star on the school's debate team. When he dazzled judges at a tournament in Denver, a local newspaper editorial treated him as something of a circus freak, writing, "When an alien of Asian parentage is able to master the intricacies and absurdities of our orthography and to overcome lingual handicaps in pronunciation and articulation, to acquire an ability to think, to arrange his ideas in logical sequence, and to express them clearly and forcefully, there is no excuse for failure among American students." Masaoka, who could barely speak or understand any Japanese, was annoyed but kept his mouth shut.

He would continue to startle white audiences, who were not used to seeing someone with his face speak so fluently and with so much conviction. In early 1942, while the decision to intern Japanese-Americans appeared to still be under review, Masaoka testified before a congressional committee. The white lawmakers were surprised that Masaoka spoke

English without an accent and that he was Mormon rather than Buddhist. They may also have been stunned that Masaoka, who was speaking as a representative for JACL, seemed to barely put up a fight. "If, in the judgment of military and federal authorities, evacuation of Japanese residents from the West Coast is a primary step toward assuring the safety of this nation, we will have no hesitation in complying."

When the U.S. Army proceeded with its plan to put Japanese-Americans into camps, Masaoka insisted that his community show complete fealty to the country that was depriving them of their rights. He encouraged terrified families to cooperate with the evacuation orders, then lobbied the Pentagon to allow nisei to enlist in the U.S. military. Because Masaoka lived in Salt Lake City, an area not covered by the evacuation order, he could move freely around the country and speak to officials in Washington, where he feared the momentum was growing to further curtail the rights of Japanese-Americans. "There are politicians even now who are trying to pass laws in Congress to strip us of citizenship and ship us to Japan when the war is over," he argued. "The most effective weapon against this kind of persecution is a record of having fought valiantly for our country side by side with Americans of other racial extraction."

But many other Japanese-Americans were furious that they could be asked to serve a country that had stripped them of their basic rights. After Masaoka and the JACL leadership voted on a resolution endorsing military service, fights broke out at an internment camp in Manzanar, California. Fred Tayama, a delegate from Manzanar who had attended the JACL gathering in Salt Lake City, was beaten so badly upon his return that he was hospitalized. Among the most bitter at the camp was Joe Kurihara, who had served in the U.S. Army during World War I. Kurihara swore "never to do another day's work to help this country fight this war" and renounced his American citizenship. After the war, he and thousands of other Japanese-Americans felt so betrayed that they left for Japan.

Masaoka ignored these dissidents. "In my lifetime there have been many decisions I agonized over, that kept sleep away for long restless nights. The decision to agree to a segregated combat unit was not one of them," even though "many of us might never come back and, in a way, I would be responsible for their deaths." Masaoka successfully lobbied the Pentagon to allow Japanese-Americans to enlist in a segregated combat team. Importantly for Masaoka, the creation of the regiment forced Roosevelt into an about-face regarding the status of Japanese-Americans. As Roosevelt wrote on the establishment of the 442nd regiment of the U.S. Army, which would be composed entirely of second-generation Japanese-Americans, "The principle on which this country was founded and by which it has always been governed is that Americanism is a matter of the mind and heart. Americanism is not, and never was, a matter of race or ancestry."

The 442nd regiment of the U.S. Army would go on to become one of America's most decorated World War II units. About eighteen thousand men served in the unit, which earned more than three thousand Purple Hearts, three hundred Silver Stars, eight hundred Bronze Stars, and one Congressional Medal of Honor. In a telegram to the war secretary, Henry Stimson, Masaoka was among the first to volunteer, together with his four brothers. He participated in one of the regiment's most famous episodes: the 1944 rescue of the so-called "Lost Battalion" in the Vosges Mountains in eastern France. About two hundred members of a battalion from Texas were trapped on the top of a mountain, surrounded by German forces. The 442nd regiment, whose motto was "go for broke," battled to rescue the Texans and in a week sustained about eight hundred casualties. Among the deaths: Masaoka's older brother Ben, who had been the best man at his wedding.

When the war was over, Masaoka and JACL wasted little time pivoting to the issue of immigration and naturalization rights. Masaoka's strategy again struck some of his fellow Japanese-Americans as pure hubris, given that they had very recently been forced into camps. Yet Masaoka believed that with their sacrifices on the battlefield still fresh, there would never be a better time to demand equal treatment. It was the kind of blind faith that had given him the nickname now being used by both admirers and detractors: "Moses Masaoka," the man who would lead his people to the promised land.

—

AMONG THOSE MASAOKA IMPRESSED in Washington was Walter Judd, a Republican from Minnesota who had taken an unusual path to Congress. While most of his colleagues knew very little about East Asia, Judd had spent several years as a medical missionary in China in the 1920s and '30s, where he had had a front-row seat to the historic events shaping the country as it emerged from thousands of years of imperial rule. He witnessed the Nationalists and Communists fight for control of the country, which was so chaotic in the years Judd lived there that he nearly died twice during confrontations with bandits. He saw the devastation of the Japanese invasion as he treated women and girls who had been raped by Japanese soldiers.

As a boy growing up in the plains of Nebraska, he had daydreamed during Sunday school as he stared at maps that showed Saint Paul's travels around the Mediterranean; he longed to explore the world as a medical missionary and to follow in the footsteps of his idol David Livingstone, the famed doctor and Africa explorer. In China, he found adventure and his life's purpose. Judd grew to believe he was "welded . . . with the heart of the Chinese people." Even when Japanese aerial attacks intensified, Judd refused to leave the hospital in Fenchow that he had been tasked with running. At one point, in the middle of a brutal air campaign, he was so desperate to save his hospital that he went to the roof of the building and unfurled an American flag in an effort to stop the Japanese from destroying the facility. When the Japanese conquered Fenchow in 1938, Judd continued to try to save Chinese lives, smuggling the injured out of town—he knew the Japanese did not take prisoners of war.

Later that year he made the painful decision to return to the United States, where he vowed to warn as many people as possible about Japan's dangerous imperial aims and to win support for sending China more aid. He then embarked on an extraordinary campaign as a private citizen. Over two years and across forty-six states, he delivered fourteen hundred speeches on China's plight, sometimes making six presentations a day, speaking at 250 words a minute. Judd, whose thinning hair was always combed back neatly, exuded an unlikely charisma. He would lift both of his arms during the climactic parts of his speeches, and his passion was contagious, sometimes bringing audiences to their feet. His pace was relentless; in Minneapolis, where he set up a medical practice, he would sometimes deliver a baby, give a speech, then go back to the hospital to deliver another. On the morning of Sunday, December 7, 1941, he spoke at the Mayflower Congregational Church in Minneapolis, warning again about Japan's aggression. As he drove to work afterward, he heard on the radio that the Japanese had attacked Pearl Harbor.

When he entered Congress in 1943, Judd brought the same message, with just as much zeal. He went into the office every Saturday while Congress was in session; the first Saturday he did not work was in 1957, on his daughter Mary Lou's wedding day. At night, before driving home to the old house he and his wife had purchased near National Cathedral in northwest Washington, he would often stop in front of the Lincoln Memorial. In the dark, he would ponder Lincoln's words, carved into the cold white marble, and receive what he called "spiritual inspiration." He imagined Lincoln watching the events in the Capitol from his seat, across the Reflecting Pool and the Mall. In Judd's mind, the challenge before China was even tougher than what his own country had faced during the Civil War. "Abraham Lincoln's task was a little afternoon tea party as compared with the task of Chiang Kai-shek," Judd once said. His first speech before Congress, titled "How Can We Win in the Pacific?," so impressed Eleanor Roosevelt, who read the *Congressional Record* every day, that she invited Judd and his wife to the White House for a Sunday dinner of oysters, roast beef, and Yorkshire pudding.

During his first year in office, Judd played a pivotal role in persuading Congress to pass the bill lifting the ban on Chinese immigrants, given the country's role as an ally. But after the war ended, he knew the United States had to go further. In 1947 Judd introduced a bill that would end the exclusion of Asian immigrants, which, he argued, would "influence greatly the battle for men's minds and hearts that is going on between the two philosophies of life and government that are locked in mortal struggle in our world." He proposed establishing an Asia-Pacific Triangle system, in which every Asian country east of Iran and north of Australia would receive a small quota of 100 to 185 people. Even more significantly, the bill would end all racial restrictions on naturalized citizenship. Judd cited the story of Sadeo Munemori, a member of the 442nd regiment who had died in Italy during the war and whose mother's citizenship application was subsequently turned down. "What then is the measure of citizenship?" he asked. "What further price must Mrs. Munemori pay to prove her worth?" The legislation won the support of the State Department, which liked the idea for the same reasons as Judd. And in the House, not even California lawmakers opposed it.

Judd's bill was not without its flaws, however. The Asian quotas were race-based, not country-based, meaning that a person of Chinese ancestry living anywhere in the world—including Britain or Ireland, countries that enjoyed large quotas—would be counted against China's slots. Even more regressive, a provision in Judd's bill would close a loophole from the 1924 law that allowed black residents of Caribbean colonies to immigrate to the United States within the large quotas of England, the Netherlands, and France, the countries that ruled over them. Each year thousands of black immigrants from the Caribbean had been arriving under this system, and by the end of World War II, more than 250,000 had settled in the United States, most of them in New York City and Chicago. Judd's bill would impose a quota of one hundred immigrants from each of these colonies. New York congressman Adam Clayton Powell, Jr., whose wife was a black immigrant from Jamaica, argued against the so-called "empire quota" and said that while he supported the effort to give equal rights to Asian immigrants, he did not understand why that demanded a limit on black Caribbean migration. When Judd defended the measure by claiming that the quotas, however low, marked a kind of racial equality, Thurgood Marshall, then the NAACP's legal director, retorted that the "House evidently believes that each step forward must be accompanied by a step backward."

Masaoka did not relish watching the interests of Japanese-Americans pitted against black immigrants, but he was determined to move forward. "Certainly, we do not want either rights or privileges taken away from other minority groups," he wrote. "But, at the same time, we do believe that there should be equality in naturalization and immigration law," and "other sections, if necessary, should be sacrificed in order to gain the greater principle."

He continued his lobbying effort to back the bill and ensured that hearings in the summer of 1949 included further references to the war record of the nisei. General Mark W. Clark, who had opposed the internment camps and then later commanded the 442nd regiment, wrote to Congress that the parents of the heroic nisei "should have the privileges of the democracy their sons helped to preserve." Even the editorial board of the *Los Angeles Times*, which had had a long run of racist anti-Asian commentary, came around to the idea. Masaoka found the work exhausting, and he and his wife, Etsu, were paid barely enough by JACL to cover living expenses, but their newfound ability to win audiences with lawmakers was exhilarating. After a long day of lobbying, they would spend humid evenings eating modest dinners of rice balls next to the Potomac, enjoying their novel place in Washington. "I had learned my way around the Hill, and hard work and sheer persistence finally were beginning to pay off."

But while McCarran embarked on his ambitious reworking of the country's immigration laws, Judd's bill stood little chance as a stand-alone measure. Instead, it found its way into the recesses of McCarran's massive 1952 bill—the one that, on June 20, 1952, sat on Truman's desk awaiting his signature.

—

JUDD AND TRUMAN knew each other well. In 1943, when Judd was still a freshman congressman and Truman a senator, the two men had gone on the road together for two weeks to raise support for the creation of a new international organization that would help to preserve peace. Despite belonging to different political parties, Truman and Judd were intent on defeating pro-isolationist forces in the country. They went to nineteen different cities in the Midwest and stopped off in Judd's hometown in Nebraska, where they had a dinner of fried chicken and whipped potatoes with Judd's parents. Truman's direct and honest manner impressed Judd's father, who declared, "Well, I'm a Republican, and I don't know about his politics, but I'd trust that fellow with my pocketbook."

On the question of whether to veto the McCarran bill, though, Truman was not in agreement with Judd—and he faced dissent even within his own administration.

The cabinet secretary whom Truman likely respected most, Secretary of State Dean Acheson, thought the president should sign the bill. The State Department's argument, essentially, was that while the bill had some flaws, its elimination of racial barriers to naturalization was an important step forward. The United States was just ending its occupation of Japan, and relations between the two countries were still delicate. Lifting the immigration and naturalization ban on Japanese would only engender goodwill and show that the United States was eager to bring Japan once more into the international fold. "This is such a tremendous step forward, from the foreign relations point of view, that it should not be jeopardized by any attempt to remove all discrimination in immigration privileges unless there is a practical certainty of favorable action during this session of Congress." Furthermore, the State Department argued, "The achievement of our foreign policy objectives in Asia would be jeopardized if the United States does not soon remove existing barriers. Failure to enact this legislation would give the Kremlin more grounds for propaganda in the Far East than anything it can find in the bill as it stands." The CIA and Department of Justice also saw no reason for Truman to veto the bill.

On the other hand, Secretary of Labor Michael J. Galvin encouraged Truman to veto. Some of Truman's supporters viewed the law as an affront to civil rights. As A. Philip Randolph, international president of the Brotherhood of Sleeping Car Porters, an influential union and civil rights group, wrote to the president on May 29, "This McCarran bill, by striking a sinister blow at civil rights and the doctrine of racial democracy and racial equality, thereby constitutes a grave threat to the vitality and strength of our American democratic system and aids and abets the world-wide drive for universal power of Stalinist Russia."

Truman likely needed little convincing that the bill should not go past his desk. As Harry Rosenfield, who had overseen the admission of displaced persons after the passage of the refugee law in 1948, warned him in a June 12 letter, signing the bill "would be a repudiation of all you have accomplished, over Senator McCarran's bitter opposition, on the Displaced Persons program." Retaining the national origins quota system would make it impossible for the United States to admit Iron Curtain refugees at the level Truman thought suitable. And with only months left in his presidency, Truman wanted to send a powerful message that whoever succeeded him, Democrat or Republican, needed to address the fundamental racism of the U.S. immigration system.

Truman often gave more attention to veto messages than to other pronouncements from the White House. In the case of his veto message for the McCarran-Walter Act, he took great care to outline what he did and did not like about the legislation. He singled out for praise the Judd-created provision to end racial barriers to naturalization and to give Asian countries quotas, but he said the measure was "embedded in a mass of legislation" filled with too many unjust proposals. "The price is too high, and in good conscience I cannot agree to pay it."

He went on to blast other aspects of the law and cemented the notion that U.S. immigration law is a vital instrument in the country's foreign policy:

> The basis of this quota system was false and unworthy in 1924.
> It is even worse now. At the present time, this quota system
> keeps out the very people we want to bring in. It is incredible to
> me that, in this year of 1952, we should again be enacting into

law such a slur on the patriotism, the capacity, and the decency of a large part of our citizenry.

Today, we have entered into an alliance, the North Atlantic Treaty, with Italy, Greece, and Turkey against one of the most terrible threats mankind has ever faced. We are asking them to join with us in protecting the peace of the world. We are helping them to build their defenses, and train their men, in the common cause. But through this bill we say to their people: You are less worthy to come to this country than Englishmen or Irishmen; you Italians, who need to find homes abroad in the hundreds of thousands—you shall have a quota of 5,645; you Greeks, struggling to assist the helpless victims of a Communist civil war—you shall have a quota of 308; and you Turks, you are brave defenders of the Eastern flank, but you shall have a quota of only 225! . . .

In no other realm of our national life are we so hampered and stultified by the dead hand of the past, as we are in this field of immigration. . . . The time to shake off this dead weight of past mistakes is now. The time to develop a decent policy of immigration—a fitting instrument for our foreign policy and a true reflection of the ideals we stand for, at home and abroad— is now.

The veto was remarkable, in that Truman again defied his own party's leadership on the Hill, just as he had done with the Internal Security Act. McCarran denounced Truman's veto as "one of the most un-American acts" he had ever seen during his time in the Senate; Truman had "adopted the doctrine that is promulgated by *The Daily Worker*," a newspaper published by the American Communist Party. One day after the veto, Truman received a letter from an angry citizen writing from the Hotel Roosevelt in New York, Phyllis Craig: "We know that you defeated it to gain votes and fill our once fine country with morons and other unworthies who are here in large numbers through lax immigration laws to get all they can out of America and bring nothing but filth and self interest."

———

ON JUNE 27 MASAOKA and his mother sat in the Senate gallery nervously watching the action below. Debate on whether to override Truman's veto began at noon, and a vote was to begin in two and a half hours. The day after Truman's veto, the House had immediately overridden it with a vote of 278 to 113, seventeen more than needed. The Senate vote, however, would be much closer. McCarran started off with a speech blasting Truman: "In God's name, in the name of the people of America, in the name of the future of America to which we all look, let us have the courage today to override this unfortunate veto message."

In the last forty-eight hours, Masaoka had rallied JACL members for a "now-or-nothing lobbying effort" sending telegrams to their senators urging them to support the bill and override Truman's veto. Masaoka himself rushed to the Capitol to find senators with whom he had spent years cultivating relationships. "If we lost this opportunity to win citizenship for our parents, there was no assurance that a second chance would become available in their lifetimes."

Down on the Senate floor, Lehman made his last stand, arguing that the McCarran bill would make immigration "a myth" by "reducing it to a mere trickle." Senator John O. Pastore of Rhode Island, the first Italian-American to be elected to the senate, accused the bill of seeking "to perpetuate, reestablish, and reaffirm a policy of bigotry."

The JACL's lobbying was clearly having some effect. Senator Harry P. Cain of Washington, who had bravely opposed the internment of Japanese-Americans, waved several telegrams he had just received from JACL delegates. One from Thomas S. Takemura in Puyallup, Washington, called Truman's veto "an insult to our ancestry." Cain vowed to vote for the bill.

Finally, the roll call began. Masaoka and his mother tried to keep tally, not an easy task since note-taking was prohibited in the Senate gallery. Instead, they used their fingers to count. Democrats and Republicans were not voting along party lines, and thirteen were not even present on the floor. Slowly, the full count became clear: eight Republicans and eighteen Democrats voted to sustain the veto. Thirty-two Republicans and twenty-five Democrats voted to override. By just two votes, the bill was law.

For McCarran, the passage of the law, which became known as the Immigration and Nationality Act of 1952, marked the culmination of a years-long battle against liberal forces that had tried, since the war, to weaken the country's national security. He bragged that it was "the consummation of five years of the most intensive and objective effort ever performed under the direction of a committee of the Congress."

Liberal opponents were furious. After the United States' failure to rescue more Jews from the Holocaust, after the collapse of the eugenics movement, Congress still had enthusiastically and indefinitely renewed the system of national origins quotas. Humphrey was dejected; the bill and other recent legislation made him "a lot less enthusiastic" about the Democratic Party. "We have made a serious mistake that will injure this Nation in the eyes of the world. That was a bad, ugly bill." Three days after the Senate overrode his veto, Truman did not mince words. "I am certainly sorry that happened because that Bill is one of the worst that has ever come to my desk," he wrote to Senator Estes Kefauver of Tennessee.

Meanwhile Celler, having witnessed the fight to end quotas rage for nearly three decades, girded himself for another battle. On December 22, 1952, days before the Immigration and Nationality Act went into effect, he suggested to Lehman that they team up on legislation to defeat it. "My ultimate objective is to get a bill that you and I could introduce at the same time and do battle for it."

For those who had opposed the law, one of the bitterest aspects of their defeat was that pro-immigration groups had been unable to stick together. Compared to 1924, their effort had been more aggressive and better coordinated, building on momentum from the fight to assist displaced persons. But it was impossible to ignore that their charges of racial discrimination were severely undercut by the challenge from Masaoka and his Japanese-American group. "It is impossible to compute the amount of harm which the Japanese-American Citizens League and Masaoka caused to effective opposition to this legislation," concluded an analysis conducted by the American Jewish Congress.

Rather than linger in Washington, Masaoka rushed to pack for San Francisco, where the JACL was in the middle of its biennial convention. He wanted to celebrate with the other Japanese-Americans who had fought so hard for this moment. As his plane flew westward, he thought of the last time he had seen his brother Ben before he died in combat. "I blessed the memory of all the other good men who hadn't come home."

SEVEN

AN IRISH BRAHMIN

J ACK KENNEDY had been raised to think of himself as only tangentially Irish. For his domineering father, Joe Kennedy, Sr., proper parenting meant leaving no trace of the family's immigrant past on the next generation. After amassing a fortune on Wall Street and producing movies in Hollywood, Kennedy had been intent on making his large brood of children fit seamlessly into the rarefied White Anglo-Saxon Protestant (WASP) meccas of Bronxville, New York, Cape Cod, and Palm Beach, Florida. In a sign of how little he cultivated his children's connection to their Irish homeland, Joe Sr. served for two years under Roosevelt as ambassador to the United Kingdom—and not once did his son Jack visit Ireland. Upon seeing himself described in a Boston newspaper as an "Irishman," Joe Sr. yelled, "Goddamn it! I was born in this country! My children were born in this country! What the hell does someone have to do to become an American?"

But when Jack Kennedy decided to build a political career in Massachusetts, a state with one of the country's highest proportions of immigrants, he would need to embrace his family's ethnic roots—a makeover that would eventually lead him to champion a radical rethinking of the country's immigration system.

For Jack's first political campaign in 1946, his father settled on Massachusetts's eleventh congressional district as a good place to start. Jack moved into a two-room suite at the Bellevue Hotel to establish residency in a city he barely knew as an adult, apart from his undergraduate days at Harvard. The eleventh district included the East End, where his father had been born, and the North End, with its warren of tight, winding streets, where his grandparents had spent their childhoods surrounded by other working-class Irish Catholic families. For Jack and his siblings, this was alien territory.

An early campaign manager, William DeMarco, remembered initially meeting the candidate in 1946 on a rainy Sunday afternoon on Hanover Street in the North End. Kennedy, who appeared to be visiting his grandparents' old neighborhood for the first time, wore an expensive suit with no raincoat or hat. With the suit "shriveling to bits" in the downpour, DeMarco ushered the young candidate into an Italian-American social club to get him out of the rain and began introducing him to people. The young men at the club, who were playing Italian card games over beer and wine and trying to relax after their recent return from the war, grumbled when DeMarco called a meeting with a politician none of them recognized. But the men softened when they learned who his mother and grandfather were.

Rose Kennedy was the beloved oldest child of John F. Fitzgerald, a charismatic son of Irish immigrants who had risen from ward boss to congressman to mayor of Boston. His remarkably smooth personality had earned him the nickname "Honey Fitz." As one local verse went: "Honey Fitz can talk you blind / on any subject you can find / Fish and fishing, motor boats / Railroads, streetcars, getting votes." By the time his grandson ran for office, Honey Fitz had been retired from politics for years, but he was still a parishioner at St. Stephen's Church in the North End and a widely recognized Boston personality who could vouch for Jack among older voters. Rose, meanwhile, captivated Bostonians who remembered watching her grow up as their mayor's beautiful and charming daughter; her 1911 debut was "one of the most elaborate coming-out parties ever conducted in Boston." Now Rose had risen even higher as the wife of the former ambassador to the Court of St. James's, though the role had marked the end of Joe Kennedy's political career, after he staked his reputation on stopping the United States from entering World War II. To the white ethnic voters of Boston, that didn't matter; it was simply astonishing to imagine that two of their own could end up sitting down for tea with the queen of England.

Compared to his grandfather Honey Fitz, Jack Kennedy was an unimpressive campaigner at first, perhaps because he couldn't quite believe he was running for Congress. His older brother, Joe, was supposed to be carrying the weight of their domineering father's vast political ambitions. But Joe had died in World War II, after his plane exploded during a risky secret mission over the English Channel. Joe Kennedy, Sr., later explained of his two eldest sons, "Joe used to talk about being President some day, and a lot of smart people thought he would make it. He was altogether different from Jack—more dynamic, sociable, and easygoing. Jack in those days . . . was rather shy, withdrawn and quiet. His mother and I couldn't picture him as a politician. We were sure he'd be a teacher or a writer." But Jack understood completely what his father, consumed by grief, needed him to do. "I'm just filling Joe's shoes," he told friends. "If he were alive, I'd never be in this." At the beginning of his political career, he came across like an understudy who hadn't quite memorized his lines.

That fall the Democratic Party suffered its worst showing since 1928, losing control of both the House and the Senate. But buoyed by the goodwill toward his Irish Catholic family and carrying the hopes and dreams once pinned on his older brother, Jack Kennedy won his first political race. Now he just needed to figure out what he believed in.

—

WHEN HE ENTERED CONGRESS at age twenty-nine, Kennedy did not match his surroundings. As he shuffled around the marbled halls with his hands often stuffed into his pockets, he had a casual, college-boy air. In a 1947 photo of several House freshmen, Kennedy stands next to fellow newcomer Richard M. Nixon, who is only a few years older and radiates a suave, serious aura; by contrast, Kennedy's hair sits untamed on top of his head, making his prominent ears seem to stick out even more. During his first week on Capitol Hill, a veteran House member mistook him for a page and was stunned when the Massachusetts Democrat told him he was an elected member of Congress.

There wasn't much glamour in being a freshman congressman. The job clearly bored Kennedy, who preferred his evening life, entertaining a rotating cast of women at the Georgetown townhouse he shared with his friend Billy Sutton, his younger sister Eunice, and a family cook. He once commented about a colleague in the House, "I never felt he did much in the Congress, but I never held that against him because I don't think I did much. I mean you can't do much as a Congressman." A more patient person could accomplish a great deal in the House, working his way up to running powerful committees, as did Mannie Celler over his fifty-year career. But Kennedy was in a hurry. After watching his brother die at twenty-nine, followed two years later by his twenty-eight-year-old sister, Kathleen, in a plane crash, Kennedy was keenly aware of his mortality. As he once said to his friend George Smathers, "The point is that you've got to live every day like it's your last day on earth. That's what I'm doing." Besides, he and his father had always viewed his House seat as a jumping-off point to greater things. "I think from the time he was elected to Congress, he had no thought but to go to the Senate as fast as he could," remembered *New York Times* reporter and columnist Arthur Krock.

By the spring of 1952, Kennedy and his father had decided on their moment. Jack would challenge the popular Massachusetts incumbent senator Henry Cabot Lodge, Jr. The matchup, while tough, contained delicious historic echoes: the candidates' grandfathers had been political rivals five decades earlier. Henry Cabot Lodge, Sr., had represented the peak of Boston high society, while Honey Fitz symbolized the newer Irish leaders who hoped to displace the old guard. In the 1890s Fitzgerald, while in Congress, had fiercely opposed anti-immigration legislation sponsored by Lodge. On the floor of the House on January 27, 1897, Fitzgerald gave a rousing speech against Lodge's bill: "It is fashionable today to cry out against the immigration of the Hungarian, the Italian and the Jew; but I think that the man who comes to this country for the first time—to a strange land without friends and without employment—is born of the stuff that is bound to make good citizens." Fitzgerald claimed that after his speech, he had a confrontation with Lodge in which the senator said to him, "You are an impudent young man. Do you think the Jews or the Italians have any right in this country?" To which Honey Fitz responded, "As much right as your father or mine. It was only a difference of a few ships." Lodge later beat Fitzgerald in a 1916 Senate race, making the prospect of a rematch especially compelling to the budding Kennedy dynasty.

But with the Republican Dwight Eisenhower on the top of the ticket and expected to win the presidency that fall, Democrats running down-ballot were at a disadvantage. Even without such headwinds, Kennedy had picked a challenging race to win. A popular and handsome man with a famous name in Boston, Lodge had carved out a reputation as a reasonable centrist Republican. His closeness to Eisenhower, renowned as a war hero, only cemented his image as a credible leader. By comparison, Kennedy had produced few notable achievements during two and a half listless terms in the House.

But just as appearing comfortable in the North End after a lifetime of summers in Hyannis Port had been a challenge, Jack would have to adjust some of his political stances as well.

To the extent Jack was interested in policy, he had studied foreign affairs. In the spring and summer of 1939, while Joe Kennedy served as ambassador, he had arranged special treatment for his son, still a student at Harvard, as he traveled throughout Europe interviewing businessmen, reporters, and diplomats. The exposure to Europe on the brink of war gave Jack the confidence to write an undergraduate senior thesis, which was later published as a best-selling book called *While England Slept*. On domestic issues, Jack Kennedy's footing was less sure. He was vaguely a deficit hawk, which made him skeptical of programs such as Social Security that were popular among his working-class constituents in Massachusetts.

The only issue on which Kennedy had shown a striking consistency as a House member was on the Communist threat during the Cold War—and in doing so, he consistently sided with those who opposed changing the country's immigration quotas. Kennedy had largely inherited his views from his father, who counted Joseph McCarthy, another ambitious Irish Catholic politician, as a friend, frequently inviting him to the Kennedy home in Hyannis Port. McCarthy even dated two of Jack's sisters, Eunice and Patricia. Later, his wedding present to Eunice and Robert Sargent Shriver was a silver cigarette case with the inscription, "To Eunice and Bob, from one who lost."

For Jack and later Bobby Kennedy, the family's association with McCarthy would haunt their political careers: during one of the nastiest chapters in American political history, the Kennedys had picked the wrong side. For years, Jack felt protective of his father's friend. In early 1952, at an anniversary event for Harvard's Spee Club, one of the speakers said he was relieved that Harvard had never produced an Alger Hiss or a Joe McCarthy. Jack angrily interrupted, "How dare you couple the name of a great American patriot with that of a traitor!" The room went awkwardly quiet. Kennedy later stormed out.

In Congress, during the worst hours of the red scare, Kennedy took easy stands that allowed him to maintain his anti-Communist bona fides. While Herbert Lehman and others risked their careers fighting McCarran's Internal Security Act in 1950, Kennedy supported the law; after Truman vetoed it, Kennedy voted to override the president. He lectured the Truman administration on its foreign policy in China at a time when the State Department was already vulnerable and under attack. "The failure of our foreign policy in the Far East rests squarely with the White House and the Department of State," he said on the House floor, ignoring the considerable deficiencies of Chiang Kai-shek and the Chinese Nationalists. Kennedy even said he was pleased in 1950 when Nixon beat a liberal opponent for a Senate seat, Helen Gahagan Douglas, whom Nixon had smeared as the "Pink Lady."

But by the summer of 1952, with a high-stakes political campaign coming up, the playbook needed some reworking. Winning the statewide office of senator would take more than a dash of Kennedy mystique and loads of money. The family would have to overcome a liability in the form of Joe Kennedy himself.

—

IT IS ONLY from a comfortable distance, in white America, that different immigrant groups can appear to have easy, natural alliances with one another. In reality, there have often been intergroup conflicts, sometimes violent, over jobs, housing, and political representation. This was true for Irish and Jewish Americans at the turn of the twentieth century: as eastern European Jews arrived in American cities in large numbers, some Irish feared that the newer immigrants were skipping ahead in the line for American success.

To the degree that Joe Kennedy was anti-Semitic, his feelings were driven in part by a desire to protect his hard-earned status as an Irish Catholic who had made it to the highest echelons of society. He never forgot the sting of social rejection at Harvard, where being an Irish Catholic from an unfashionable part of Boston had excluded him from the school's most prestigious social clubs; later, several friends would remember him arguing against his alma mater admitting too many Jews. On Wall Street and in Hollywood, he encountered Jewish competitors and claimed that "a bunch of ignorant Jewish furriers" dominated the movie industry "simply because they had unethically pushed their way into a wide-open virgin field."

The public perception of Joe Kennedy as anti-Semitic took hold after his decision, in 1938, to support British prime minister Neville Chamberlain's appeasement of Nazi Germany. Kennedy rightfully feared that Britain entering the war would lead to the United States' involvement, a development that could destroy his family. He worried that a war could undermine the international system of financial markets, wiping out the family fortune and sowing enough chaos to breed Bolshevism. To Kennedy, anything—even perhaps Nazism—seemed preferable to Communism. Contrary to his reputation, he was not completely indifferent to the plight of Jews in Europe. At one point he even tried to broker a plan to resettle German and Austrian Jews to parts of the British Empire. But he also felt that such troubles were ultimately not his business—and certainly not worth going to war over. "Anti-Semitism is their fight—just as anti-Irishism was my fight and the fight of my fathers in this country," said Kennedy in an unpublished interview in May 1944. "I have never discussed anti-Semitism in public, because I could never see how it would be helpful. Whenever I have been asked for a statement condemning anti-Semitism, I have answered: 'What good would it do?' If the Jews themselves would pay less attention to advertising their racial problem, and more attention to solving it, the whole thing would recede into its proper perspective."

But in 1952, as liberal Jewish voters in Massachusetts considered whether to make Jack Kennedy their senator, they looked warily upon the outsized presence of the family patriarch.

"We were in a real bind with respect to the Jewish people," said Phil Fine, who worked on Kennedy's Senate campaign. "At first we didn't have a soul with us." During one speech at the Boston Club, with hundreds of Jews in the audience, Jack Kennedy tried to remind his listeners, "Remember, *I'm* running for the Senate, not my father."

Just then a perfect opportunity presented itself for Jack to show clearly that he was on the side of Jewish voters. The year he ran for the Senate was also the nadir for those who wanted to abolish the country's national origins quotas.

So on October 2, 1952, Jack Kennedy sat on the witness stand of courtroom six in the stunning Art Deco–style Federal Building in downtown Boston. The defendant in this case was not a person but a law: the McCarran-Walter Act that had passed earlier that summer.

Two months after losing his effort to veto the 1952 immigration law, President Truman had issued an executive order creating a commission to study the country's immigration system. It is easy to imagine that a president, rebuked in the waning months of his presidency by his own party in the House and Senate on a major piece of legislation, might let the matter go. But that was not Truman's manner. He viewed immigration reform as a critical part of his legacy in retaining peace after the war. The commission, whose members he would appoint himself, would have four months to produce a comprehensive report, due on Truman's desk no later than January 1, 1953, soon after which it would disband. The findings were to be based on a careful, if quick, study that would be based on hearings taking place around the country. And on this summer day, the commissioners had come to Boston to hear what Kennedy and others there had to say.

The study was billed as an exercise in open inquiry, but its true intent— to undercut the McCarran-Walter Act before it went into effect—was evident the moment Truman named the commissioners. For its chairman, Truman chose Harry Rosenfield, who had helped oversee the resettlement of refugees in the United States after World War II. During the fight over the McCarran-Walter Act, he had gone so far as to visit Truman and personally urge him to veto the law. "Even for the president, it took guts to stand up against McCarran and Walter," Rosenfield remembered admiringly years later. The vice chairman of the commission was Earl Harrison, whose report on the plight of Jewish refugees had moved Truman so deeply. Another member of the commission, Monsignor John O'Grady, secretary of the National Conference of Catholic Charities, had written in June, during the debate, that the legislation "contains more inequities than any immigration bill ever passed by Congress."

In addition to establishing the commission, Truman personally attacked U.S. immigration laws while campaigning for Democratic presidential candidate Adlai Stevenson. Weeks before the election, during a stop in New England, Truman sent a message to be delivered by Howland H. Sargeant, assistant secretary of state for public affairs, to a gathering of Jewish leaders at the Statler Hotel in Washington. In the message, Truman linked the national origins quotas, the discriminatory provisions of the Displaced Persons Act of 1948, and the "second-class citizenship" imposed by the McCarran-Walter Act as all adding up to "the philosophy of racial superiority developed by the Nazis, which we thought we had destroyed when we defeated Nazi Germany and liberated Europe." Truman blamed these laws on the Republican Party, even though Democrats like McCarran had played a leading role in creating them. He then accused Eisenhower of being willing to accept "the very practice that identified the so-called 'master race.'" Given Eisenhower's unimpeachable war record defeating the Nazis, the remarks were so stunning that they landed on the front pages of *The New York Times* and *The Washington Post* the next day; on the front page of the *Post*, the story was even accompanied by a separate headline highlighting a statement from Eugene Meyer, the newspaper's chairman of the board, denouncing Truman's comments. South Dakota senator Karl E. Mundt, a Republican, called the comments a "disgusting exhibition" by the president, especially since Eisenhower had said the night before—apparently before Truman wrote his remarks—that any law implying the inferiority of any European group should be struck down. Truman, relishing his last chance for a good partisan fight before leaving office, never apologized.

Now Kennedy, as another critic of the law, was eager to add his voice, testifying that day in Boston that the law was "un-American and discriminatory. It virtually freezes immigration from eastern and southern Europe and the Mediterranean area, and sets up barriers which did not formerly exist." Even though his voice had been largely absent from the congressional debates against McCarran and McCarthy, Kennedy was now trying to refashion himself as a steadfast liberal.

As soon as the members of the commission had been announced, Kennedy sent a telegram to Philip B. Perlman, a former solicitor general and member of the group, offering to help in any way possible. Perlman thanked him and told him the commission would be holding a hearing in Boston in early October. The note from Perlman was so significant that campaign staffers routed it directly to Bobby Kennedy, Jack's younger brother, who was now running the campaign. The Kennedy brothers spotted an avenue of attack against Lodge. On the day the Senate over-rode Truman's veto, Lodge had been absent from Washington; fearing that the Republican Party was on the verge of nominating the isolationist Ohio senator Robert A. Taft, Lodge had been spending the year of his reelection focused not on his own campaign, or on his work in the Senate, but on getting Eisenhower onto the presidential ticket.

The same day Kennedy testified before the immigration committee, Lodge also made an appearance and made a similar argument against the McCarran-Walter Act. But the evening before at a rally, Kennedy pounced on his opponent, saying that "Massachusetts needs a United States senator who will protect the rights of its minority groups on the floor of the United States Senate, not one who votes by remote control." This was a bold argument from someone who had himself frequently been absent for votes. But perhaps the most striking implication was that Kennedy, more than his opponent, understood the needs of "minorities" because of his own Irish Catholic background.

After spending a lifetime of trying to fit in with WASP culture, Kennedy the Senate candidate was making an especially hard sell of his family's immigrant roots to Jewish and Italian voters. He solicited support from high-profile lawmakers from New York such as Celler, who was flown into Massachusetts by the campaign to charm Jewish audiences. Vincent R. Impellitteri, the Italian-born mayor of New York, also came to Boston to lend support and vouch for Kennedy's record on immigration. The campaign even made use of an April letter from Herbert Lehman thanking Kennedy for his opposition to the McCarran-Walter Act—a precious sign of approval from a figure widely admired by Jewish voters for his humanitarian work with refugees and for being the first Jewish governor of New York. The Kennedy campaign ran a series of ads in English- and Yiddish-language newspapers across Massachusetts that simply showed a copy of the letter next to the words "CHAMPION OF HUMAN RIGHTS."

On the night of the election, Kennedy scored a remarkable victory, narrowly beating Lodge by 70,737 votes, even though Eisenhower won in Massachusetts by a much larger margin. Lodge's decision to turn on Taft had angered Republicans in the state and likely cost him the election. But Kennedy's victory also reflected a shift in the electorate, as Catholic and Jewish voters came out in force for "the first Irish Brahmin," as people were beginning to call him. Among Catholic precincts in Boston, Lodge's support fell from between 41 and 45 percent in 1946 to between 19 and 25 percent; among Jewish districts, it dropped from between 60 and 66 percent to under 40 percent. As Jack's college roommate and close friend Torby Macdonald told him on election night, "I think that you represent the best of the new generation. Not generation in age but minorities, really. The newer arrived people."

The Kennedys and Fitzgeralds, having been in the country for about a century, could hardly be counted as new Americans. But for a man as conscious of his class as Joe Kennedy, Sr., his son's victory over the scion of one of Boston's oldest and most storied families could not have felt sweeter. Only in his eyes could his wealthy, Harvard-educated son have been counted as an underdog, and he complained to a friend that Jack was not receiving enough credit for his achievement. "Sometimes in reading the papers," he wrote, "I wonder whether they are not all mad at Jack for having had the temerity to lick this fair-haired Goliath."

—

THE SHIFTING CONTOURS of race in America are often invisible to the naked eye, moving quietly and slowly like glaciers, even as they carve dramatic changes into the social landscape. By the early 1950s the distinctions that had seemed so clear to Joe Kennedy, Sr., between his own family, the Lodges, and his Jewish competitors in Hollywood were becoming harder for his children's generation to discern.

Since the debate over the 1924 immigration law, the very definition of the word *race* had changed. Where once lawmakers and scientists obsessed over minute traits distinguishing the Nordic, Jewish, Slavic, and Italian races, scholars after World War II abandoned the idea that these groups were biologically distinct, especially as information emerged about the horrors of the Holocaust. Instead, academics focused on the cultural roots of these differences, giving rise to terms like *ethnicity* and *ethnic group* that had scarcely appeared before in the context of race. (The *Oxford English Dictionary* still defines the word *ethnic* as meaning "heathen," since the word's roots in ancient Greek and Hebrew were used to denote "nonbelievers.") Abandoning the smaller groupings, scholars focused on three major branches of race—Negroid, Caucasian, and Mongoloid—defined by skin color rather than by nation.

This rewiring of race in America was perhaps the most lasting legacy of the national origins quotas. The influential white nationalist Lothrop Stoddard portended in 1927 what was to come when he noted that "most of the immigrant stocks are racially not too remote for ultimate assimilation," and that because the "new immigrants" constituted such a small percentage of the white population, thanks to the new quotas, they could "be absorbed into the nation's blood" and would not "endanger the stability and continuity of our national life." (He was of an entirely different opinion about Chinese, Japanese, and Mexican immigrants.) Stoddard, in one respect, was right. Over the first half of the twentieth century, the new European immigrants and their children all came to be considered part of the white race; after Congress cut off immigration, the country's very idea of whiteness had expanded. Invoking race during a discussion of Europeans began to feel outré, even discriminatory, as demonstrated in the 1947 Oscar-winning movie, *Gentleman's Agreement*, in which Gregory Peck plays a WASP journalist posing as a Jew to expose society's anti-Semitism. The premise of the movie, and the book upon which it was based, is that Peck can "pass" as Jewish because there is no actual distinction between Anglo-Saxons and Jews; they are all white.

The most important racial difference in America remained that between white and black. After World War I, with the Great Migration of African Americans from the South to cities in the North, Midwest, and West, the Jim Crow concerns of the South became national issues. In 1945 Truman issued an executive order that created a Committee on Civil Rights, which ultimately recommended sweeping changes to existing civil rights legislation, including guaranteeing African-Americans equal access to public accommodations, the ballot box, and housing. In 1947 he became the first U.S. president to address the NAACP, in a speech delivered at the Lincoln Memorial. A year later he desegregated the military. These efforts changed what it meant to be black in America—but they did not bring black Americans into the white mainstream.

The immigrant experience was not only different from the black experience, it was often defined against it. To climb the social ladder as an immigrant was to increase one's social distance from black America and gain acceptance in a broader swath of white society. And as Jewish-, Italian-, and Irish-Americans increasingly joined the ranks of white Americans, it became more popular to celebrate the country's immigrant past—and a new nationalist myth was born.

—

THE NOTION OF STUDYING IMMIGRATION as a part of the country's history emerged only in the middle of the twentieth century, pioneered by Oscar Handlin, a Harvard historian whose work would help imprint the idea of the United States as "a nation of immigrants." As the country's foremost scholar on immigration, Handlin's views were particularly influential, and as part of the Truman commission's findings, his work would form the framework for immigration reform over the next decade.

Handlin, the son of Russian-Jewish immigrants, was born in New York City in 1915 soon after his parents arrived. A freakishly talented student, he was enrolled in the newly opened Brooklyn College by age fifteen. After graduating in three years, he attended Harvard for a doctoral program, intent on studying medieval history under Charles Homer Haskins, a famed scholar. But when Haskins became ill and retired soon after Handlin began, he turned to a new adviser: Arthur Schlesinger,

Sr., whose son, by the same name, would later become the country's most famous historian when he served as an adviser in the Kennedy White House. Handlin, in search of a dissertation subject, was talking with Schlesinger one day when the professor mentioned a letter he had just received. Another student, Herbert W. Hill, was dropping out of the program, since he had found a job at Dartmouth. Schlesinger suggested that Handlin pick up where Hill left off—on a thesis about immigrants in Boston. "Why don't you do it?" suggested Schlesinger. Years later Handlin characterized his response: "I did. As simple as that. No angst." That work would go on to become *Boston's Immigrants*, a seminal book published in 1941.

A decade later Handlin released another book, the one that would make him famous. *The Uprooted: The Epic Story of the Great Migrations That Made the American People*, which won the Pulitzer Prize, was an unusual work of social history. Written in a lyrical style, it described the immigrant experience as one unified story involving suffering, loneliness, and only limited assimilation. His opening words established immigration history as not only an important area of study but a central strand of the American narrative: "Once I thought to write a history of the immigrants in America. Then I discovered that the immigrants *were* American history." According to James Grossman, a historian and executive director of the American Historical Association, "He reoriented the whole picture of the American story from the view that America was built on the spirit of the Wild West, to the idea that we are a nation of immigrants."

Because Handlin did not limit his work to academia, his conception of American history entered the bloodstream of political debate. In the early 1950s he served as an adviser to Truman's commission on immigration and to Senator Lehman. In a statement to Truman's commission, Handlin argued that the 1920s concern that "new immigrants" and their children were harming the country had been proven wrong. And like the Japanese-American advocates, he pointed to fighting in a war as the ultimate proof of assimilation.

Two wars have tested the American descendants of the new
immigrants; and I know of no evidence that they gave less than
their share in loyalty and in sacrifices. In sum, it seems to me,
the distinction between the "old" and the "new" immigrants
was invalid; the latter have proved themselves as capable of
becoming American as the former.

He also downplayed the possibility that abandoning the quotas would
return the country to the old days of huge numbers of immigrants, a
rationale that would be repeated in 1965:

The framers of the quota system had in mind a world of free
movement; their task, they thought, was to build a dam to hold
back the onrushing tide. The world familiar to the men of 1920
has, however, disappeared; and it is only confusing the issue
to imagine that the alternative to our present restrictions is a
restoration of the kind of immigration we knew before the First
World War. Even had we no regulations, the volume of the flow
would not rise to its old levels, for we no longer live in the old
world of free movement. . . . Whatever the limits we set upon it
the immigration of the future will involve much smaller numbers, and it will consist largely of persons sponsored by families
or by American philanthropic organizations and brought across
under carefully planned conditions.

Released on New Year's Day 1953, the commission's full report, entitled *Whom We Shall Welcome* and numbering more than three hundred
pages, went much further than any legislation previously proposed by
even the most liberal lawmakers, including Lehman. It recommended
that the McCarran-Walter Act, which had gone into effect only a week
earlier, be revised "from beginning to end." Witnesses at the commission's hearings had called the law "an arrogant, brazen instrument of

discrimination based on race, creed, color and national origin." The commission called for abolishing the national origins quota system altogether and allocating visas "without regard to national origin, race, creed, or color," based on the right of asylum, reuniting families, and the needs of the country.

It was a bold statement, after years of defeats in Washington over much less ambitious changes to the immigration system—and the arguments laid out in the report would serve as a road map for years to come. Truman, unsurprisingly, praised the report and said it "ought to receive the most serious consideration." But McCarran was furious, imagining it was another attack from the Communist sympathizers in Washington whom he had already fought off many times before. He insisted that his law "does not contain one iota of racial or religious discrimination" and added, "It is, however, tough, very tough on the Communists, as it is on criminals and other subversives, and that is why they are squealing." Then he all but named his enemies: "It is a tragic fact that the out-and-out Reds have ready colleagues in this fight: the 'pinks' and the well-meaning but misguided 'liberals' and the demagogues who would auction the interests of America for alleged minority bloc votes. In my work with the Senate Internal Security subcommittee I have learned to know them for what they are; and I shall fight them with every last ounce of my energy."

But there was not much strength left in the Nevada senator, who was by now seventy-six years old, with a mind not so sharp as it once had been. Soon after the Truman report came out, a young Reno reporter, Ed Olsen, was surprised to see McCarran at a bar one night in Riverside, Nevada. The senator had not been seen in public in several weeks, and here he was, wearing dark glasses indoors and eating dinner by himself. Olsen boldly walked over to his table to ask him where he had been. McCarran, paranoid as always, asked, "How do I know that you're who you say you are?" Olsen, who didn't have a press card with him, took out his driver's license and a gasoline credit card. McCarran looked at them, shoved them back across the table, and yelled, "You're nothing but a Goddam Communist that's been following me across the country, that's what you are!" The senator shoved the table toward Olsen, sending a plate of steak, dishes, and cups flying into the middle of the dining room. McCarran then stomped away.

The senator's mood had only grown darker with time. In the previous few years he had suffered at least three major heart attacks and become a regular visitor at Bethesda Naval Hospital. His daughter Patricia, a nun, told Harry Rosenfield's wife Leonora that once, when her father was sick, someone from the Truman White House—perhaps the president himself—called McCarran at the hospital to find out how he was doing. As Patricia told Leonora, "You know, they're only interested to see if he is going to croak."

But in the fall of 1954, McCarran was determined to stay in politics. Until the Democrats lost control of the Senate the year before, he had led the Senate Judiciary Committee on and off for eight years, and he wanted a taste of that power again. After sowing so much division within the Democratic Party, McCarran hit the campaign trail to help other Democrats get elected. "Every man on the ticket is my candidate," he said in a campaign message. "It is imperative that a Democratic Congress be elected in order that your Senior Senator may resume his position as head of the Judicial Committee of the Senate and continue his fight against Communism." During a campaign stop in Hawthorne, Nevada, on September 28, 1954, McCarran declared that "at no day in history has the U.S. been in such jeopardy." After stepping down from the podium, he paused to speak with a woman who had walked up to greet him. As he turned away, he fell backward. It was another heart attack, and he died instantly.

J. Edgar Hoover sent his condolences to McCarran's widow via a telegram: "His work will remain a living inspiration to those dedicated to preserving the American way of life." Lyndon Johnson, then the Senate minority leader, said on the floor of the chamber where McCarran had wielded so much power, "He was a giant who plunged fearlessly into the controversies of our day—an elemental force who refused to drift with the currents and tides. . . . There were many people for Pat McCarran and against him. But nobody was indifferent. He loomed too large on the national scene to be ignored."

The day before McCarran died, the anti-Communists had received another blow on Capitol Hill. Ever since Joseph McCarthy began spewing his venom, Lehman had been one of the rare senators to stand up to him. The two men verbally sparred so much on the Senate floor that colleagues feared they would beat each other up. Once, during a particularly ugly debate, "I moved up to protect Herbert," recalled Paul Douglas, a senator from Illinois, who was several inches taller than Lehman. In June 1954 Lehman put forward a resolution to remove McCarthy from his committee chairmanships, but with Democrats and Republicans alike unwilling to cross McCarthy, his effort went nowhere. But McCarthy caused his own downfall that summer when he attacked the army in televised hearings. When everyday Americans saw his demeanor on camera, it was as if a spell had been broken. Finally, on September 27, 1954, a special Senate committee recommended that McCarthy be "condemned" for violating Senate rules. In early December the Senate voted to censure him for conduct that "tended to bring the Senate into dishonor and disrepute." Lehman eagerly joined in the censure, but he was also disappointed. McCarthy had done far worse than break decorum: he had destroyed lives.

Kennedy, meanwhile, was not even present for the debate on the censure; he was recovering from one of his frequent medical procedures for his back, which had never fully healed from his time fighting in the South Pacific during the war. From his hospital bed, he could have instructed aides to record him on a vote. Instead, he was silent. Ultimately he could not bring himself to publicly undermine his father's friend.

—

McCARTHY WAS NOT THE ONLY giant of the Senate suffering from health problems. On Tuesday, July 5, 1955, the chamber fell into hushed silence for one minute and fifteen seconds as every senator bowed his head. One reporter described it as "one of the most poignant occasions in congressional history." A few days earlier Senate Majority Leader Lyndon Johnson had suffered a heart attack and was recovering at Bethesda Naval Hospital. On the Senate floor, Lehman moved that the entire legislative body pray together for Johnson's rapid recovery. After the silence, one senator after another paid tribute to Johnson. Lady Bird, who was sitting by her husband's bedside day and night, printed out the pages of the *Congressional Record* containing the speeches and put them in a scrapbook for Johnson to read. For a man who craved love and attention, the thrill was akin to attending his own funeral. He pored over his colleagues' comments. From Senator Morse: "What I wish to say about this great leader is that too frequently we do not appreciate the qualities of some of our closest friends until some misfortune overtakes them." From Senator Gore of Tennessee: "Seldom in the history of our country has a member of this body attained such proportions and such influence as he has reached and maintained."

Johnson later told Lehman that "one of the most important things that ever happened to me in my life was that minute of silent prayer you led in the Senate." The prayer meant so much that Lady Bird also thanked Lehman and said it "pulled [her husband] through the dark and troubled hours." The timing of the heart attack was devastating to Johnson, who had hoped to run for president the following year and attain his lifelong dream of reaching the White House. Doctors were now requiring him to lie low for months, a tough order for a man used to being in constant motion. To help keep his mind occupied, Lehman gave Johnson a tremendously thoughtful gift: a small transistor radio that Johnson could use to listen to news. Hubert Humphrey recalled that the radio meant so much to Johnson that he would "speak of it a hundred times."

Lehman's generosity was another demonstration of the senator's fundamental decency, because on Capitol Hill Johnson had been treating the New York senator abominably. As Senate majority leader, Johnson had little patience for Lehman and his clique of liberals—men he called "crazies." "Johnson didn't enjoy talking with the liberals," recalled Humphrey.

"He didn't think they had a sense of humor. He thought that most liberals were never so unhappy as when happy, or so happy as when unhappy." Johnson warned Humphrey, who was close with Lehman, to avoid emulating the New York senator. "You'll be ignored, and get nothing accomplished you want." Johnson was not necessarily ideologically opposed to the ideas of Lehman and others; what offended him was their unwillingness to compromise, and so he wanted Humphrey to be a "liberal doer," not just a "liberal talker." There was no point in doing business with such men, thought Johnson. "He wouldn't return Lehman's phone calls for days on end," remembered Lehman's aide Julius Edelstein, and he would toss Lehman's messages straight into a waste bin. When Lehman made a speech on the Senate floor, Johnson would deliberately walk out to the cloakroom; what was the point of listening to a speech, however eloquent, if it was not a preamble to a winning vote? Edelstein remembered that other colleagues would take their cues from Johnson on how to treat his boss. "You'd walk down the hall, and there would be an averting of eyes so that they wouldn't have to say hello."

Lehman ignored the slights. He could be neurotic when it came time to make a big decision, but he was not insecure about his place in the world. Being a senator was possibly the last chapter in his political career, and he had nothing left to lose advocating for principles he believed in. A coalition of Republicans and southern Democrats threatened the ideas he held dear, and so Lehman was determined to stand firm. And he had not given up on changing the country's immigration laws.

The rules were not going to be easy to alter. Lehman, with support from Kennedy in the Senate and Celler in the House, repeatedly introduced legislation to undo or weaken the quota system. But each time the trio's efforts failed.

Finally, on February 8, 1956, they seemed to catch a small break. President Eisenhower, possibly feeling the pressure of a reelection year when he would need to win states such as New York, delivered a special message to Congress on immigration. Among his proposals, Eisenhower wanted to raise the overall quota from 154,657 to 220,000, and to allow unused quota numbers to be pooled together, so that oversubscribed countries in southern and eastern Europe could benefit from the lower numbers of immigrants coming from northern and western Europe. Lehman was disappointed that Eisenhower did not push for abolishing the national origins quotas altogether, but the Republican president's involvement gave him some hope that Congress would now act.

But Johnson would have to work a miracle in the Senate to turn Eisenhower's ideas into a bill that could pass. Up to this point, Johnson had largely sat out the immigration debates that had consumed Capitol Hill since World War II. He had no personal animus against immigrants, having aided people like Erich Leinsdorf, but as a senator from Texas, unlike Kennedy, he had less political impetus to be out in front on liberal immigration policies. And because immigration was wrapped up in red scare politics, Johnson was wary of picking fights with McCarthy and McCarran. During the McCarran-Walter debate of 1952, Johnson sided with McCarran.

But now, with his grander national ambitions to reach the White House, Johnson needed to do more to win over liberals. He coveted Lehman's status as "Mr. Sincerity," so much that he began to drop the word "sincere" into his interviews with the press, hoping the reputation would rub off on him. It didn't work.

More than four months after his heart attack, with his health now mostly restored, Johnson announced that as Senate majority leader, he would make immigration reform part of his "program with a heart," along with eliminating the poll taxes that prevented African-Americans from voting, expanding Social Security, and reducing taxes for the poor.

The barriers to immigration reform were significant. In the House, Francis Walter felt wounded by the attacks on the legislation bearing his name that claimed it was bigoted and discriminatory. Anytime a colleague suggested changing the legislation, Walter would personally intervene. In the Senate, the chances for success had diminished even further. Harley Kilgore of West Virginia, a supporter of civil rights, had replaced McCarran as the chairman of the Judiciary Committee—but just weeks after Eisenhower's statement, Kilgore died suddenly of a cerebral hemorrhage. His successor, James Eastland, McCarran's old protégé, was a renowned racist with no interest in liberalizing immigration policy.

As summer approached, Johnson decided the strongest path to victory would be to build upon a modest bill primarily designed to admit a few hundred Basque sheepherders. The bill had already been approved by the House, and in the Senate, pro-immigration Democrats could propose amendments on the Senate floor, bypassing Eastland and the Senate Judiciary Committee. With Congress on the verge of adjourning, there was little time to waste. Almost no debate took place in the open as Johnson cajoled his colleagues behind the scenes instead. Finally on July 27, the last day of Congress, Johnson and Lehman made their move.

Lehman offered as amendments to the sheepherder bill his usual proposals to replace the national origins quota system. But he also promised to support potential amendments by colleagues, since he welcomed "any progress that can be made on this front, even inches of progress." As expected, Lehman's amendments were defeated easily. But then Senator Everett McKinley Dirksen of Illinois laid out a compromise that had been carefully crafted in talks with Johnson. The proposal would give about 18,500 unused quota slots from England and other countries to nations such as Italy that had much smaller allocations. It also granted permission for about 40,000 refugees to enter the country from Communist-controlled countries, and it addressed a wrinkle from the earlier displaced persons legislation, which had borrowed against some countries' unused quotas to make room for refugees from countries that were oversubscribed. Dirksen's bill would cancel out those "mortgages."

Eastland immediately jumped in: Dirksen's amendment was "something cooked up, and not even printed, and not given committee consideration, but just offered on the last day, here on the floor." Eastland rehashed the same arguments used countless times before to defend the national origins quota system, saying it was "designed not only to assure maximum assimilation of the quota immigrants whom we receive for permanent residence, but more important, it is designed to preserve and protect our American traditions, our American institutions, our American way of life."

Eastland was right about the process at least: an amendment altering the country's immigration laws had received no review in hearings, had not been seen by most members, and now was being voted on. Johnson, who hated Senate debate so much that he sometimes shooed his colleagues away from their podiums when they were speaking, defended the amendment. "I know the bill is not agreeable to every Senator, but I think it represents the best compromise which can be reached." Despite Eastland's opposition—and insistence that the amendment would "emasculate" the McCarran-Walter Act—the Senate passed the amendment.

The House would now need to take the next step. Aware of Walter's sensitivity to attacks on the McCarran-Walter Act, senators had been careful to avoid going after him personally during their brief debate. In fact, the Senate Democratic Policy Committee had consulted Walter throughout their negotiating on the Senate side, and the amendment passed by the Senate matched what had been under discussion with Walter. But the next day Walter waffled, as Eastland and Richard Arens, another McCarran protégé, tried to convince him that the bill would undercut his legacy. From midafternoon until eleven p.m., with whispered entreaties in the Speaker's lobby, Johnson, Celler, and House Speaker Sam Rayburn all tried to intercede. Just before eleven p.m., Representative Kenneth B. Keating of New York tried to bring the immigration bill up for a vote by himself. The effort failed. On the last day Congress was in session, the bill died, never making it to the House floor.

Johnson confided to Lehman that he was "particularly disheartened" by the loss, since he had his "heart set on that one." But the majority leader felt that "the way to handle this issue is to begin nibbling at it," and that "if we nibble long enough, we will break its back."

The results of this last congressional session were particularly devastating to Lehman. While Johnson had been maneuvering to help Lehman's cause on immigration, he had also been outfoxing the New York senator on civil rights legislation that would have strengthened the government's ability to enforce voting rights for African-Americans. In fact, a *Washington Post* article noted that several southern senators offered "only token opposition" to Dirksen's immigration amendment because they were "mindful of Johnson's help in keeping the civil rights bill off the floor."

Johnson ultimately did not want to risk exposing the Democratic Party to a messy debate over civil rights—the most divisive issue in the party—ahead of the fall elections. In March several lawmakers had signed the so-called Southern Manifesto, which attacked the Supreme Court's 1954 *Brown v. Board of Education* ruling that segregated schools were unconstitutional. In the manifesto, the lawmakers, most of them from the South, vowed to use "all lawful means to bring about the reversal" of the Court's decision. Johnson was among only three southern Democrats who did not sign the document. That summer, on the night of July 13, in a sign of how ugly the debate over civil rights had become, a cross was burned in front of the Sheraton-Park Hotel where Lehman stayed when he was in Washington. One of the senator's fellow residents was Earl Warren, the chief justice of the Supreme Court; a note next to the burning cross indicated it was aimed at them both.

Lehman was not easily intimidated, but he was also growing tired. At seventy-eight, he was still in fine health but was wary of signing on for six more years of fighting other Democrats and feeling marginalized by Johnson. On August 21, 1956, Lehman formally declared that he was not running for reelection. The loudest voice in the Senate for abolishing the national origins quotas was leaving Washington. In an interview in December just before the end of his term, Lehman told *The New York Post*, "A fight is worthwhile even if you know you're going to lose it. . . . It's the only way to crystallize attitudes, educate people. And in the end I've seen many hopeless causes win out."

For Lehman, it was time for a new generation to inherit the causes he held dear. Kennedy, who was nearly four decades his junior, was eager to have Lehman's respect. He gave Lehman a copy of his 1956 book *Profiles in Courage* with the inscription, "Senator Lehman, a Senator of courage and integrity," and he cosponsored some of Lehman's failed bills to overhaul the country's immigration laws. But Kennedy had a fundamentally different style, largely ducking the Democratic Party's major fights, choosing instead to boost his national profile by giving speeches around the country as he eyed a run for the White House in 1960. He did not help Lehman and other liberals outmaneuver Eastland on the civil rights bill. And while he voiced his support for Lehman's efforts on immigration, his own achievements on the subject, an issue he had touted in his campaign, were limited.

In August 1957 he cosponsored a bill, later signed by Eisenhower, that broadened the definition of a refugee and made it easier for immigrant parents to be reunited with their children and for orphans adopted by U.S. citizens to enter the country. But the measures were so powerless that nine months later, Kennedy wrote to Secretary of State John Foster Dulles asking why hardly any visas for refugees had been processed. Then in another narrow victory, he was able to help thousands of Portuguese displaced by natural disaster. Beginning on September 27, 1957, and lasting for a number of months, volcanic eruptions near Faial Island, hundreds of miles off the coast of Portugal, sent plumes of ash raining down on villagers; earthquakes damaged buildings, displacing thousands of families. Far away in Washington, the tragedy attracted Senator Kennedy's notice. "Everywhere within a four-mile radius the lava and ash spread fear and destruction," Kennedy said from the Senate floor on June 30, 1958. He and John Pastore of Rhode Island sponsored the Azore Refugee Act, which authorized fifteen hundred visas, counted outside the quotas, for those displaced by the disaster. The measure passed and was later extended, allowing thousands of Azoreans to settle in the United States, many of them in Massachusetts, where a large Azorean community exists to this day. These were all minor reforms.

But soon Kennedy would have a chance to do far more than Lehman, Celler, or anyone else had done to demolish the country's national origins quotas. Regardless of his perpetually thin legislative résumé, he was growing more popular on the national stage. With his glamorous wife Jackie and new baby daughter, Caroline, Kennedy exuded charisma. Gone were his gawky days as a freshman congressman. His father Joe bragged in an interview in the late 1950s, "Jack is the greatest attraction in the country today. I'll tell you how to sell more copies of a book. Put his picture on the cover. . . . That is why the Democratic Party is going to nominate him."

Roughly three decades after Al Smith's ill-fated run to become the country's first Irish Catholic president, a descendant of the ethnic ghettos of Boston was about to enter the White House. And he carried with him the hopes of European immigrant families across the country that their moment of full inclusion in the American project had finally arrived.

EIGHT

A BOLD PROPOSAL

On January 21, 1961, the day after President Kennedy's inauguration, White House aide Myer "Mike" Feldman stood stiffly in the Oval Office. It was his first time inside the room, and looking around, the space was almost completely bare. All the items that would later mark Kennedy's presence—his beautiful model ships; the ornate Resolute Desk that his toddler son, John F. Kennedy, Jr., would famously crawl underneath to play; a watercolor painting of the White House by his wife, Jackie—were not yet in place. There was only one chair, and it was for the president, who was still taking in his surroundings. On his second full day in the White House, as he spun around in his chair, Kennedy asked his brother, Ted, and a friend, Paul Fay, as they looked around the Oval Office, "Do you think it's adequate?" Fay replied, "I feel any minute somebody's going to walk in and say, 'All right, you three guys, out of here.'"

Though the furniture was still being selected, Kennedy had already hand-picked a few men—only men—who would surround him as his closest White House aides. The staff was full of big egos who would go on to write best-selling memoirs and dine out for years on their association with Camelot—men like Pierre Salinger, Kennedy's suave press secretary, and

Arthur Schlesinger, Jr., the Harvard-professor-turned-court-historian. By comparison, Feldman was nearly invisible; a 1964 article in *The New York Post* called him "the White House's anonymous man." But those who were close to Kennedy understood Feldman's importance. When he left the White House in 1965, his old boss, Ted Sorensen, wrote to him, "You were far more indispensable than the public knows to John Kennedy's success as a Senator, candidate and President. He knew it, however; and I know he would want me to express his deep gratitude."

During the presidential race, Feldman had distinguished himself by running a team of researchers who assembled a comprehensive "Nixopedia," a record of Richard Nixon's every word, going back years, aimed to help Kennedy demolish his opponent in debates. By the end of the campaign, Feldman had grown so close to Kennedy that as the election results came in, he was one of the select few gathered with the Kennedy clan in Hyannis Port. The next morning he and Sorensen were among the first to greet Kennedy with the words, "Good morning, Mr. President."

From the beginning of Kennedy's presidency, Feldman's responsibilities were sprawling. His portfolio would grow to contain tariffs and trade, special programs to help the oil, textile, shoe, and lumber industries, aviation policy, relations with Israel, and presidential proclamations and executive orders. In the Oval Office that early winter day, Feldman handed Kennedy his first executive order to sign: tasking the secretary of agriculture with expanding food distribution across the country to fight hunger. Ten days later another White House aide, Frederick G. Dutton, wrote Feldman with an urgent question about giving the new attorney general, Bobby Kennedy, more power over individual immigration cases: "I understand that you are the immigration expert in these offices."

It was true, but only compared to everyone else around him. Feldman had only recently become well versed in immigration policy. Himself the son of Ukrainian immigrants, Feldman grew up in Philadelphia and was orphaned as a young boy when his father died in the 1918 influenza epidemic. After training as a lawyer, Feldman joined the Securities and Exchange Commission, where he worked for about a decade. In 1958 he met with Kennedy at the suggestion of Sorensen, an aide to the senator. Feldman and Kennedy spoke for more than half an hour—longer than any job interview Kennedy had given before, according to Sorensen—and at the end, the senator told Feldman he wanted him to join his office. Feldman wasn't sure he was interested. At forty-three, he was three years older than Kennedy and fourteen years older than Sorensen, and he was beginning to think it was time for a new phase of his career, perhaps in private practice. He asked for some time to think about it. "I went home, talked to my wife," Feldman recalled, "and she said that if I didn't take the job, I may regret it the rest of my life. So I went to work for him."

In Kennedy's Senate office, Feldman had taken on the work of managing Kennedy's relations with the Jewish community, which meant shaping the senator's bona fides on immigration. In 1957 the Anti-Defamation League (ADL) approached Kennedy about writing a pamphlet about immigration history, part of a series called One Nation Library funded by Jacob Kaplan, a Massachusetts philanthropist who had built his wealth running the Welch's grape juice company. Feldman helped to shape the idea into *A Nation of Immigrants*, a text that would in time become a famous declaration of American values by an American president—but that started out as a slim, stapled-together pamphlet just shy of forty pages aimed at high-school seniors and newly naturalized Americans. With Kennedy barely involved in the project, Feldman attended to every detail. In February 1959 ADL administrative director Oscar Cohen sent an early copy to Feldman, who offered minor critiques that the senator's photo should be shown, and that his name should have his title in front of it. Cohen demurred. "We have every confidence that *A Nation of Immigrants* is going to be a smashing success and will endure for years which is the reason we didn't use the Senator's title," wrote Cohen in response, adding, correctly, "After all it could change."

The pamphlet was rudimentary compared to Kennedy's book *Profiles in Courage*, which had won him a Pulitzer Prize the year before, even though in that case, too, Kennedy had left a substantial part of the writing to his aides. "There is no part of America that has not been touched by our immigrant background," stated the pamphlet, which described various waves of immigrants and celebrated their contributions. But the most noteworthy section of the work came at the end, where Kennedy called for a change to the country's national origins quotas, saying "the most serious defect in the present law is not that it is restrictive but that many of the restrictions are based on false or unjust premises." Kennedy wasn't calling for anything radical, arguing only that "a new, enlightened policy of immigration need not provide for unlimited immigration but simply for so much immigration as our country could absorb and which would be in the national interest." A new law, he explained, should allow the country to "turn to the world with clean hands and a clear conscience." Still, he was attaching his prominent name to a cause that had languished in the political margins for decades.

But by the time Kennedy entered the White House, there was more support than there had ever been for at least revisiting the country's immigration quotas. The work of scholars including Handlin was creating a new nationalist narrative in which immigrants were no longer a scourge but a source of the country's strength. At the same time, the language of the civil rights movement was seeping into the discussion of who should be allowed to enter the country. During the 1960 presidential race, both political parties, in need of votes from states with large immigrant populations such as New York, ramped up their criticism of the national origins quota system. The Democratic platform called the system "a policy of deliberate discrimination" that was "inconsistent with our beliefs in the rights of man." The Republicans said the volume of immigration had fallen so low that it harmed the country's economy, and that the formulae for calculating the quotas—pegged to the country's ethnic makeup in 1890—were "obsolete." The GOP argued that the quotas should be set to the 1960 population, and that the overall number of immigrants admitted to the country should be at least doubled.

Kennedy's election only stoked expectations for immigration reform even higher, given his promises on the campaign trail and his carefully cultivated image as a politician who identified with newer Americans and their children. On February 5, 1961, Lehman spoke of his confidence in Kennedy at an annual meeting of the United HIAS Service, a refugee aid group, at the Hotel Roosevelt in New York: "I am deeply convinced that President Kennedy intends to perform on his promises in regard to immigration and citizenship." But even Lehman, after the torrent of defeats during the 1950s, acknowledged that it was perhaps time to compromise, and that he would not blame Kennedy for settling for less than the abolition of ethnic quotas. "In legislative matters he is, above all, a practical-minded man. He knows the legislative process and the compromises which are entailed. He is inclined to go along with a solution that is less than ideal, if it represents some forward progress." Lehman added, "Speaking for myself, I am ready to accept and embrace any hope for substantial progress on this front, and to acclaim any real progress which is actually made." Five days later Hyman Bookbinder, a lobbyist for the AFL-CIO who would soon join the Kennedy administration, sent a copy of Lehman's speech to Feldman, saying he was delighted to see it. "This is the first real break from the dogmatic position held for years by the Lehman-Celler immigration forces."

But within months of taking office, other matters immediately took precedence. In his first State of the Union speech, Kennedy did not even mention immigration, instead running through a long list of other concerns: that the American economy was "in trouble" because of an incomplete recovery from a recession in 1958; that the country's supply of clean water was dwindling; that colleges were ill prepared for all the baby boomer high-school graduates; and most of all, that the threat of Communism persisted. "Each day the crises multiply," Kennedy warned. "Each day their solution grows more difficult. Each day we draw nearer the hour of maximum danger, as weapons spread and hostile forces grow stronger." One day after Feldman presented Kennedy with his first executive order, the CIA was already briefing the president on Cuba's Communist leader Fidel Castro, who had overthrown President Fulgencio Batista two years earlier. On April 17 the Bay of Pigs invasion ordered by Kennedy turned disastrous, as the U.S.-backed Cuban exiles proved no match against Castro's forces. "Every president needs about twelve months to get his executive team organized, to feel his way into the vast and dangerous machinery of the bureaucracy," wrote John Fischer for *Harper's Magazine*. "While [Kennedy] was still trying to move in the furniture, in effect, he found the roof falling in and the doors blowing off."

After the euphoria of winning the presidency, Kennedy's White House immediately entered into some of its darkest days. Julius Edelstein, a former aide to Lehman who remained active in pressing for immigration reform, mentioned to Feldman in an April 21 letter that over the phone, "you sounded rather frayed." Edelstein, who was eager to strategize on immigration reform, told Feldman that he had been in Washington the past weekend, right before the Bay of Pigs invasion, but "I wouldn't have dreamt of intruding upon you, in the midst of what I am sure is your total preoccupation with the Cuban situation. . . . Take it easy and save yourself: tomorrow's problems are going to seem bigger than today's."

Aides detected correctly that Kennedy's appetite for domestic issues was far smaller than his interest in foreign affairs, an arena in which he had more power and where Americans' greatest fears resided. "It really is true that foreign affairs is the only important issue for a President to handle, isn't it?" Kennedy asked Nixon in a phone call soon after the Bay of Pigs disaster. "I mean, who gives a shit if the minimum wage is $1.15 or $1.25, in comparison to something like this?"

Even though Kennedy would remain preoccupied with overseas events, his administration would initiate the most aggressive effort by any president to abolish the national origins quotas once and for all—and replace them with an entirely new system.

—

IT WASN'T THE NONSTOP MARCH of foreign crises alone that prevented Kennedy from making progress on immigration. As Lehman had observed, the president was a practical man, and he had quickly assessed that the math on Capitol Hill for a Democratic president did not add up.

On the same night that Kennedy celebrated his election, the Democratic Party lost twenty seats in the House and one in the Senate. The party still retained large majorities, but a bloc of southern Democrats voting with the Republican Party had gained power. Conservative southerners dominated powerful committees like the House Rules Committee and the Senate Judiciary, blocking bills that exuded even a whiff of liberalism from ever reaching the floor.

At first Kennedy tried to overcome these obstacles through sheer charm. During his first State of the Union, he addressed the members of Congress as "among my oldest friends in Washington." To the men assembled that night, this sentiment rang a bit false. Kennedy had always seemed to think he was too good for them and their byzantine parliamentary rules, spending just enough time in the House and the Senate to springboard to the next job, rather than waiting patiently for leadership roles. "Congressmen liked Kennedy, but they did not feel close—or personally obligated—to him," commented Kennedy historian James Giglio.

The chief trait that Joe Kennedy, Sr., had cultivated in his sons was competitiveness, and when it became clear that Congress was not going to be a willing partner, Kennedy held back from proposing bold legislation: "Why fight if you are not sure to win?" To the dismay of liberals, he avoided putting a major civil rights bill before Congress in his first year. Even efforts on far less controversial issues seemed to fail on the Hill. Kennedy rallied support for legislation providing medical insurance for the elderly, but the votes fell just short in the Senate. An effort to win federal aid for elementary and secondary education never made it out of congressional committees. The bills he *was* passing were negligible: winning approval for a new assistant secretary of labor, for instance, or extending the Sugar Act of 1948.

On immigration, one man in the House stood squarely in the way of reform. As head of the House subcommittee on immigration, Francis Walter wielded enormous power, and for a decade had resisted any efforts to change the massive immigration bill bearing his and McCarran's name. "The man in charge of immigration in this country is, and has been for some time, Francis E. Walter," wrote a young Meg Greenfield, then beginning what would be a long, storied career, in *The Reporter* in October 1961. Walter had the "two most effective weapons—superior knowledge of the technicalities of the law and an unparalleled canniness in parliamentary maneuver. . . . Half of the time, it is safe to say, his colleagues are not quite sure what it is Walter is introducing or repealing or amending." Walter was so effective that he was considered, at one point, a potential successor to Sam Rayburn as Speaker of the House. But the politics of the Cold War would ultimately consume him personally and destroy his career.

The ugly 1952 fight over the McCarran-Walter Act embittered the Pennsylvania congressman for the rest of his life. Walter, who had worked to help refugees after World War II, was never as conservative as McCarran; he had softened some of the law's most restrictive aspects. But when opponents attacked the law as discriminatory, they did not distinguish between the two men whose names were on the bill. Feeling personally attacked as a racist, the congressman lashed back at his critics, calling them "out and out Reds" and demagogues who inflamed the debate around race to earn minority votes.

Those who questioned Walter's immigration bill faced his wrath at its fullest. In 1953 President Eisenhower had signed a modest refugee law that was supposed to admit more than 200,000 immigrants outside the country's quotas. Unfortunately, the man placed in charge of the effort had been Robert W. Scott McLeod, one of the most divisive figures in State Department history. A former FBI agent tasked with overseeing security at the State Department, McLeod worshipped J. Edgar Hoover and relished hunting down and firing homosexuals because he considered them security threats and moral deviants. And he had no interest in admitting more immigrants, given that his "first impulse upon seeing huddled masses was to search them." Under McLeod's watch, so few immigrants were admitted that Secretary of State Dulles appointed Edward Corsi, a Republican former immigration commissioner, to accelerate the effort. An immigrant himself who had come from Italy as a child, Corsi was a prominent New York figure who had run unsuccessfully for mayor in 1950. He had also been publicly critical of the McCarran-Walter Act by stating to the Truman-appointed commission that the law should be "junked entirely."

When Corsi was named to his new job, Walter went to war, sending a letter to Dulles denouncing Corsi for "poor judgment, loose treatment of the truth and scorn for the law." Walter's main concern revolved not around Corsi's potential handling of the refugee law but around his past criticism of the McCarran-Walter Act. "I am quite certain that if for nothing else but for having called American legislators in effect 'Nazis' and candidates for an insane asylum, Mr. Corsi would never have been confirmed by the Senate," said Walter, who was wrong on both counts. Corsi, whose job did not in fact require Senate confirmation, had never said anything to that effect. Walter also falsely alleged that Corsi had ties to Communist groups.

But under pressure from Walter, the State Department fired Corsi, setting off a full-blown scandal that dominated newspaper front pages for weeks in the spring of 1955. Lehman called Corsi's firing "a shameless surrender to the opponents of immigration and citizenship law reform." Celler accused Dulles of "cowardly buckling up." Corsi was furious that after uprooting his life in New York and signing a six-month lease in Arlington, he had been so quickly dismissed under pressure by an oversensitive congressman. "I symbolize the liberal opposition to the McCarran-Walter Act with its un-American and discriminating features, to which the President himself has objected. . . . I think Mr. Walter takes personally any attack on the law. He resents deeply any attack on it."

Walter's sense of betrayal would fuel his work on the House Un-American Activities Committee (HUAC). The panel had been established in 1938 to root out subversive Americans and eventually became a symbol of the worst excesses of McCarthyism. Walter had been first appointed as a member in 1949 in order to tone down the committee and bring to it a higher level of professionalism and competence; later, in 1955, he had been named chairman. But his own anger over his treatment by pro-immigration liberals led him to continue HUAC's pattern of launching showy hearings targeting innocent Americans with flimsy evidence, dragging before the committee such figures as the musician Pete Seeger and playwright Arthur Miller. After a 1960 HUAC hearing in San Francisco set off massive student protests, the committee produced a propaganda film, with Walter narrating, called *Operation Abolition*, falsely claiming that the students had rioted at the direction of Communist leaders. In fact, eyewitnesses saw San Francisco police hurling students down staircases. All the characteristics Walter had despised in his predecessors at HUAC "reappeared during his chairmanship: malice, vindictiveness, irresponsibility, inanity," according to one contemporary account. The work of being chairman made Walter miserable. "I'm just doing a job. And it's a stinking job, one I don't relish. But one of the things that makes it more difficult is the opposition of those who have more at stake in this fight than anyone else."

With Kennedy in office, Walter continued to rage against those who dared to cross him. In the summer of 1961 he was furious about two recent Kennedy appointments, Salvatore Bontempo and Michael Cieplinski. The two men had been tapped to run the State Department's Bureau of Security and Consular Affairs, which oversaw the system for granting visas and passports. Walter claimed that Bontempo was "totally unqualified" for the job, which was not an unreasonable assessment. Bontempo, described by *The Washington Post* as a "jovial but determined man of 52, noted in Washington as an excellent cook," had little experience in immigration; his previous job had been commissioner of New Jersey's Department of Conservation and Economic Development. Ralph Dungan, an aide to Kennedy who acted as a talent scout, had recommended him as a way to appease the Italian-American groups that had been pressuring the president for high-level appointments to reflect their interests, particularly on immigration.

The selection of Bontempo infuriated Walter, who engaged for months in "bureaucratic guerilla warfare" to destroy the appointee, at one point obtaining the transcript of a secret recording of a conversation between Bontempo and a shady New Jersey political figure who had hidden the recording device in his wooden leg, which Walter said was proof that Bontempo was involved in Democratic Party corruption. On June 28, 1961, Mike Feldman heard about an angry phone call from Walter to Roger W. Jones, a top official at the State Department. "I just want you to know that I think you and the Department of State are fools," Walter told Jones, while threatening to hold up the administration's legislation on foreign aid and refugees. "If you want Cieplinski and Bontempo to bring your legislation down here . . . don't let them come near me. Don't you come near me either. If you think your Foreign Aid Bill is going anywhere, think again. I will show you that I am not a damned fool," Walter said, then hung up the phone.

Jones told Feldman that in order to salvage the foreign aid bill, there was always the option of asking the president to call Walter, but they decided against it. Walter was clearly unafraid of the White House, and "we would run the great risk of subjecting the President to abuse."

In the Senate, however, Kennedy was about to gain the truest ally imaginable.

—

THE YOUNGEST OF THE NINE Kennedy children and fifteen years younger than the president, Ted Kennedy had grown up worshipping Jack and Joe Jr. They, in turn, had treated their baby brother more like a child to be watched over than a peer, teaching him how to sail, swim, and ride a bike. When Ted was born, Jack had been away in high school at Choate Rosemary Hall and wrote his mother asking if he could be godfather to the new baby. Ted followed in his brothers' footsteps to Harvard, where he was a mediocre student who was expelled at one point for cheating on a Spanish exam. When it came time for him to figure out what to do with his life, his mind automatically turned to politics. His brothers had already achieved so much in public life, and as he wrote in his memoir years later, "It sometimes has occurred to me that my entire life has been a constant state of catching up." His father had also made clear to him that there was only one way to get his attention. "You can have a serious life or a nonserious life, Teddy. I'll still love you whichever choice you make. . . . But if you decide to have a nonserious life, I won't have much time for you. You make up your mind. There are too many children here who are doing things that are interesting for me to do much with you."

In 1962, when Ted ran for Jack's old Senate seat in Massachusetts, he did not have the thickest résumé; his only political experience had been helping his brother's campaigns in 1958 and 1960. Indeed, he was so young that he had to wait until he turned thirty to run for the Senate seat in order to fulfill the minimum age requirement for the upper chamber. When asked why he wanted to become a senator, Ted told a reporter, "Listen, this thing is up for grabs, and the guy who gets it is the one who scrambles for it and I think I can scramble for it harder than the next guy."

Compared to the pummeling the president's party typically receives in the midterm elections, the Democrats did relatively well in the fall of 1962, gaining three seats in the Senate and losing only four in the House. Among the bright spots was Ted's sizable win over Republican George Cabot Lodge, son of Henry Cabot Lodge, Jr., in yet another match-up between the Kennedy and Lodge families. But the southern Democrats remained a powerful bloc uninterested in liberal reforms. The president surveyed the scene and concluded, "We'll probably be in a position somewhat comparable to what we were in for the last two years."

Among the still-powerful southern Democrats was James Eastland of Mississippi, the gruff chairman of the Senate Judiciary Committee, who had learned at the feet of the late Pat McCarran. In 1953, when Eastland had considered retiring from politics, McCarran urged him to stay, pointing out that he and Harley Kilgore, the two Democrats senior to Eastland on the Senate Judiciary Committee, were both old and not in good health. "You're a young man, and I'm an old man," McCarran told Eastland. "You're going to be chairman of the committee." Sure enough, McCarran died just a year later, followed by Kilgore in 1956.

Johnson, then the Senate majority leader, handed the committee to East-land, over the objections of liberals such as Lehman and groups including the NAACP, which argued his racist views made him "an accessory to murder and treason." Arthur Schlesinger, Jr., hardly a fan, described him years later as "a combination of Mississippi demagogue and Washington cynic." In addition to opposing Communism and immigration, Eastland had steadily built a reputation as one of the Senate's staunchest defenders of segregation in the South. Following the *Brown v. Board of Education* ruling, Eastland praised African-Americans for their "great contribution" to the South but insisted segregation was necessary because America's greatness "depended upon racial purity and the maintenance of Anglo-Saxon institutions." At other times, he would defend the South by accusing northerners of hypocrisy on civil rights, given the level of segregation in New York City schools. When Hawaii's statehood was under consideration in the 1950s, Eastland feared that such an admission would set a precedent that would allow territories with large nonwhite populations, such as Puerto Rico, to join soon after.

Eastland, who was rarely seen without a cigar in his mouth, was not a man of many words. He chose them well; unlike McCarran, as he grew older, he became more careful not to antagonize his Democratic colleagues. By 1960, he and the other southern Democrats had realized that if they were to retain their committee leadership roles and protect the interests of southern whites, they would need to cooperate occasionally with the rest of the party. Eastland also developed a genuine fondness for the Kennedy brothers. During the 1960 presidential convention, he had pledged to support the Kennedy-Johnson ticket, while most of the Mississippi delegation, led by the state's governor Ross Barnett, opposed it on the grounds that the two would integrate schools. On Kennedy's inauguration day, several Mississippi Democrats hatched a plan to cover the official Mississippi car in the parade with stickers for Barnett. Eastland refused to have anything to do with the prank, and when one member of the group joked that Eastland could have ridden with them in the car, Eastland told him to "go to hell."

As head of the Senate Judiciary Committee, Eastland had power over key Kennedy nominations, starting with the brazen bid for Bobby Kennedy's confirmation as attorney general. Aside from being the president's brother, thirty-five-year-old Bobby was unusually young for the job; the last attorney general who had been close to that age was a thirty-three-year-old Richard Rush, picked by James Madison in 1814. Several newspapers, including *The New York Times*, pointed out Kennedy's lack of qualifications. "If Robert Kennedy were one of the outstanding lawyers of the country, a pre-eminent legal philosopher, a noted prosecutor or legal officer at Federal or state level, the situation would be different," wrote the *Times* editorial board. "But his experience . . . is surely insufficient to warrant his present appointment." Given that Kennedy had never tried a suit before a judge or jury, written a trial brief, or negotiated a settlement, critical questions about his lack of experience were expected at his Senate Judiciary hearing. But with Eastland in charge of the proceedings, nothing of the sort happened. Instead, the hearing was filled with overwhelming praise for the nominee and almost no discussion of his shortcomings. Referencing Bobby Kennedy's work as counsel on two Senate select committees, including once for Joseph McCarthy, Eastland said to him, "I think you have had considerable legal experience." After a hearing of just two hours, the Senate Judiciary Committee unanimously approved Kennedy's nomination. Eastland went on to handle with equal ease President Kennedy's Supreme Court nominees Byron R. White and Arthur J. Goldberg.

When Ted Kennedy arrived in the Senate, Eastland practically adopted him, inculcating in the young man the arcane ways of the Senate. For years Kennedy enjoyed regaling people with the story of his first extended encounter with Eastland, complete with the Mississippi senator's drawl. Soon after arriving in Washington, Kennedy went to Eastland's office seeking committee assignments and was told to take the weekend to figure out what he wanted to do. The next Tuesday morning Kennedy's telephone rang. It was Eastland's office, telling him to meet with the chairman now. When Kennedy arrived, Eastland immediately asked whether he drank bourbon or scotch. Stunned, Kennedy blurted out, "Scotch," and an Eastland aide poured the young senator a glass of Chivas Regal, of which, like the cigars, Eastland kept a seemingly endless supply in his office. Ted eyed the glass nervously, noticing that it was a generous pour for a morning meeting. "Now, I think I know what you want," Eastland said, as he leaned back in his chair and swirled his drink. "Let me see if I'm right. You've got a lot of Eye-talians up there in Boston, don't you?" Before Kennedy could answer, Eastland went on, "You've got a lot of Eye-talians. Now, the Kennedys are always talking about immigration and always talking about Eye-talians and this kind of thing. You drink that drink there, and you're on the immigration committee." Kennedy surmised that the drink "had the power to curl my hair," and so when Eastland got up from his desk and turned away to walk to another part of the office, Kennedy dumped half of it into some nearby potted plants. When Eastland turned back around, he poured Kennedy another glass of scotch. "Now you have to decide that second committee."

Nearly two hours later, Kennedy's committee assignments were settled. And, he recalled, "Both the plants and I were well lubricated."

—

By the end of his second year in office, the only substantive immigration reform President Kennedy could claim credit for was a 1962 bill authorizing special assistance to Cuban refugees fleeing the Castro regime. The Migration and Refugee Assistance Act was the first refugee law that did not require renewal, unlike the various laws signed by Truman and Eisenhower. It gave the president broad executive powers over refugee policy, a reflection of its importance to the White House's foreign policy aims. But on the issue of the national origins quota system, the administration had yet to even draft a proposal.

On January 24, 1963, President Kennedy strode confidently to the front of the State Department's well-appointed auditorium, renovated just a few years earlier. Three hundred fifty-nine reporters sat before him in rows of orange-and-black-upholstered seats, arrayed in ascending tiers. It was Kennedy's forty-seventh live televised press conference, and he was a master of the form.

Many of his aides had initially been terrified of the idea; no president had tried it before. But Kennedy's quick wit and easy manner made the events a hit with reporters and the public. Kennedy was able to communicate directly with Americans, who could see for themselves that the country was in the able hands of its tanned, relaxed leader. "We couldn't survive without TV," Kennedy remarked once while watching a rebroadcast of one of his conferences.

On this January day, Kennedy started with a brief opening statement on the need to work with Europe to defeat Communism. Then he turned to questions, which at first touched on fears about a military buildup in Cuba, then on congressional term limits. Then a woman reporter, a rarity in the press conferences, asked Kennedy about immigration. "Mr. President, when you were Senator, you were very active in efforts to liberalize our immigration laws. Have you any plans to advance this ambition of yours now?"

It was a fair question, given how long it had been since Kennedy had so much as mentioned the immigration overhaul he had championed as a presidential candidate. The subject had not come up in any of his three State of the Union addresses, one of which he had given just ten days earlier. When he was asked about it at the press conference, Kennedy said the White House was going to "make some proposals in regards to redistributing—particularly the unused quotas." When pressed for more details, Kennedy said he had none.

After two years of lackluster legislative achievements, the Kennedy White House was growing anxious about the prospect of running for reelection in 1964 practically empty-handed on domestic issues. Kennedy himself was enormously popular: a Gallup poll in March showed him with around a 70 percent approval rating, and most Americans expected he would be reelected. But Kennedy knew that political fortunes could turn at any moment, and the midterm races had brought some troubling news about the base that had helped vault him to the White House. Among Catholic and Jewish voters, there was "big Democratic slippage over 1960," according to Kennedy's highly paid pollster Lou Harris. This alarmed Kennedy, who knew these voters formed the core of his support.

If Kennedy wanted to lock up ethnic votes, the surest way to do so would be to fire up his support for immigration reform. With time running out, it was finally time to propose a serious reworking of the country's immigration system.

———

THERE WAS JUST ONE PROBLEM. Even though immigration reform was a subject the president and others had been discussing for years, no one had come close to assembling a viable legislative template that the Kennedy administration could work from.

"It was really astonishing, in view of the fact that people had been complaining about the immigration law for forty years, how utterly useless all the bills were that had been introduced to take its place," remembered Norbert Schlei, an assistant attorney general, who began working on a proposal out of the Justice Department. "So it became apparent that one of the great problems of getting a bill passed that would abolish the national origins quota system was to think up some system that would not produce chaos to take its place."

Schlei recruited Justice Department lawyers Leon Ulman and Adam Walinsky to hammer out the details. While Ulman was a veteran at Justice, Walinsky was a young graduate of Yale Law School who had recently moved to Washington to work under Bobby Kennedy for a simple reason. "That's just where the best lawyering in the country was going on," he recalled years later. Walinsky would go on to become one of Bobby Kennedy's closest and most talented aides in the Senate. At Justice, Walinsky thrived in a competitive environment with people floating from one special assignment to another with little regard for staff hierarchy. "They took a ball and they threw it to somebody and they said, 'Run.'" For

Walinsky, that project was now an immigration bill the Kennedy White House could propose that would end the national origins quota system.

While Walinsky, Ulman, and Schlei worked on the proposal at Justice, officials at the State Department assembled their own plan. Leading the effort there was Abba Schwartz, a Baltimore-born bon vivant who had only recently joined the government. Schwartz frequently hosted powerful friends at his glamorous Georgetown townhouse, which was complete with a private swimming pool and "one of the best small groups of modern art in Washington," according to one local critic. His new government salary, at $20,000 a year, would not be enough to cover such fineries as the Wassily Kandinsky paintings he favored, but he hadn't pursued the job for the money. He was the new head of the State Department's Bureau of Security and Consular Affairs, after Francis Walter pushed out Salvatore Bontempo in January. (During Christmas 1961, Bontempo told his staff he was going home for the holidays and would be back after New Year's. He never returned.) Schwartz's new post overseeing the issuance of visas and passports, had become "the State Department's hottest political seat," according to *The Washington Post*. After Bontempo's ignominious departure, Bobby Kennedy suggested appointing a young assistant U.S. attorney named James T. Devine from the Justice Department's internal security division. Yet again Walter was displeased with the choice, and late on the Saturday night before Devine was to be sworn in the following Monday, the White House pulled Devine's name. By this point, the job had been vacant for more than six months. Finally, Walter and the Kennedy White House came to an agreement, according to Allen B. Moreland, a liaison to Congress for the State Department. The administration needed a conservative congressman to support a foreign aid program that included assistance to Yugoslavia, and so Walter agreed to give a speech supporting the aid bill if the Kennedy administration appointed Schwartz, whom Walter had met in the late 1940s, when both men worked on solving the refugee problem in Europe.

A *New York Times* reporter wrote that when Schwartz was appointed, critics said he would be "Walter's boy in the State Department," to which a friend of Schwartz's replied, "It would be more accurate to say that he is—almost by adoption—Mrs. Roosevelt's boy." Schwartz was indeed among Eleanor Roosevelt's closest friends, traveling with the former first lady and advising her on politics until the end of her life. The two had met through a shared interest in saving refugees during World War II, when Schwartz was studying at Harvard Law School and Jim Landis, the dean of the school, introduced him to Franklin and Eleanor, who was far more engaged with the refugee issue than her husband. (Schwartz remembered Roosevelt cordially meeting him and then telling him, "This is something for the missus.") Roosevelt encouraged Schwartz to join the Justice Department and work with Earl Harrison, then the immigration commissioner and later the man who wrote the report on Jewish refugees that moved Truman to action. Schwartz declined but remained so close with Eleanor that Schwartz tried to delay his swearing-in ceremony at the State Department in 1962 so that the former first lady, who was seriously ill, could come to Washington to attend. Her last letter to him told him to stop waiting, since she was unable to travel. She died a month later.

Even with all his powerful connections in Washington, Schwartz faced significant challenges in his new role at the State Department. "I knew that I was taking over direction of a Bureau that had often been compared to a viper's nest." For more than a decade, the unit had exuded a distinctly McCarthyist air, as officials exploited their broad discretion over who posed a threat to America's national security to deny travel documents to liberals and Jews, often citing vague or outlandish rationales. In 1950 the State Department asked civil rights activist and performer Paul Robeson to surrender his passport because "any trip abroad that Robeson would make would not be in the interest of the United States," according to a State Department spokesperson. When Robeson refused, the government invalidated his passport, and immigration and FBI officials were ordered to stop Robeson if he tried to leave the country. An eight-year legal battle followed, and it was not until 1958 that Robeson's passport was restored.

Such conflicts continued under the Kennedy administration because the chief instigators were career public officials who stayed on from one president to the next. In the State Department, the most powerful of them all was Frances Knight, who headed the passport division and had amassed political influence in Congress by being extraordinarily efficient with lawmakers' requests for expedited travel documents. "It would take a cannon to blast her out of her job," Senator Karl Mundt told *Life* magazine in 1966. Knight, who often bemoaned the country's declining patriotism, considered J. Edgar Hoover one of her closest allies, going so far as to have a phone in her office that dialed directly to Hoover's. Schwartz accidentally discovered the line one day and immediately had it disconnected.

Like others in the Kennedy administration, Schwartz supported eliminating the national origins quotas. But knowing Walter well, he believed that no serious effort to undo the congressman's 1952 law would ever succeed. Walter remained as stubborn as ever about changing his namesake bill, even though he, too, was feeling pressure to act. On April 13, 1961, he said he was ready to loosen up the national origins quota system by redistributing unused slots to the relatives of American citizens and lawfully resident aliens who were in countries with long waiting lists, such as Italy. The plan went nowhere. On the tenth anniversary of the McCarran-Walter Act, Walter promised that the House immigration subcommittee would produce a comprehensive report on the country's immigration system; the report never materialized.

In memos to Feldman, Schwartz proposed pooling unused quota numbers and redistributing them to countries with greater demand, citing Kennedy's comments at his January press conference as evidence for why the White House should not do more. But others balked at Schwartz's timidity. Celler wrote to Kennedy, "I do not see why you should not submit a bold proposal for a basic change and a complete and definite departure from an antiquated principle." At Justice, Schlei and Walinsky supported a more aggressive approach that would diminish the number of quotas every year with the ultimate aim of abolishing the system altogether. Schlei insisted that the administration fight now, even if Congress remained relatively conservative on immigration. In a memo to Schwartz, he argued:

> The overwhelming reason why the Justice bill is preferable is that it makes a start toward eliminating the national origins system. This system, which is inherently discriminatory, has been condemned repeatedly by the President and by the platforms of both major parties. If it were applied in any field other than immigration . . . it would be patently unconstitutional. Certainly the system is in conflict with everything this Administration is now doing in the field of civil rights.

While Kennedy officials debated what to do, a potential opening for action emerged. On January 21, 1963, just days after beginning his sixteenth consecutive term in office, Walter was admitted to Georgetown Hospital for what was said to be respiratory trouble. For months Walter grew weaker. Finally in May, his doctor gave the congressman a diagnosis: he had leukemia. Five days after his sixty-ninth birthday, on May 31, Walter died. Kennedy, who had known Walter since their days together in the House, released a statement that said he was saddened by the news. "When I saw him on my recent visit to the hospital he was facing the future with the same faith and courage he had shown throughout his life."

Walter's death raised hopes among liberal immigration advocates that the greatest barrier to altering the McCarran-Walter Act was now gone. A month later, during a meeting between Feldman, Schwartz, and deputy attorney general Nicholas Katzenbach, the Kennedy administration at last settled on its immigration bill. They would go with the more daring proposal from the Justice Department—the one that finally aimed to eliminate the national origins quotas.

On July 23 Kennedy sent a message to Congress outlining his ambition. The existing quotas would be cut by 20 percent every year and assigned to a new general pool until they disappeared altogether within five years. The Asia-Pacific Triangle, restricting immigration from that continent, would be abolished. The new system would cap overall immigration at about 165,000 per year. Rather than select people based on country of origin, Kennedy's plan would prioritize those "with the greatest ability to add to the national welfare," most likely referencing engineers, doctors, teachers, and scientists. The next highest priority would go to those reuniting with family, including unmarried adult children of parents already living in the country. No country would receive more than 10 percent of the total number of immigrants allowed under the overall cap. And, in a clear break from the eugenics era, those with mental illnesses or epilepsy would no longer be barred.

Philip Hart of Michigan quickly introduced a bill to mirror the White House's proposal in the Senate, and Celler did the same in the House. Newspaper editorial boards raved about the plan. *The Washington Post* called it "the best immigration law within living memory to bear a White House endorsement." *The New York Times* said that if Congress were to adopt the recommendations, it "would be an act of justice and wisdom, as well as evidence that we fully understand the true nature of the changed world—now grown so small—in which all humanity lives." The *St. Paul Pioneer Press* found just one area to critique: "Possibly the only negative feature of the administration's new immigration plan is the five years it proposes to take in implementing it. The present system is so archaic and inflexible as to deserve speedier abandonment."

The White House was so eager to sell the legislation that work began to resurrect Kennedy's pamphlet, *A Nation of Immigrants*, in a publishing deal with Harper & Row, as a new and enlarged edition that would be double the length of the original. The process would be quick—Harper & Row planned to deliver finished books within a month of receiving a final manuscript. The book version would require even less of Kennedy's participation than the pamphlet. Again, Feldman would be deeply involved, with assistance from staff at the ADL and Edward Sammis, a special projects writer for Harper & Row. The added pages would come from many more photographs, an expanded section paying tribute to immigrants who had enriched American life, and a longer chapter on the country's current law, with some of Kennedy's recent message to Congress integrated into the book.

But even with Walter gone, Democrats in the House could not agree about what to do on immigration. Celler made a play to become the new chair of the immigration subcommittee, after feeling thwarted for years on reform. He also tried to expand the subcommittee from five to seven members to bring in more liberal congressmen. But his colleagues on the Judiciary Committee rebelled, and instead Walter's replacement was Michael Feighan, a tall, dour congressman from Ohio who seemed to always carry a worried look on his face. Feighan had grown up wealthy as the son of John T. Feighan, former owner of the Cleveland Indians baseball team and co-founder of the successful Standard Brewing Co. After attending Princeton University and Harvard Law School, he had joined a law firm with his four brothers called, accurately, Feighan, Feighan, Feighan, Feighan and Feighan. A *New York Times* reporter noted in 1965 that Feighan had given up golf five years earlier and no longer seemed to have any hobbies or interests outside politics. In a word, he was dull.

There were a number of reasons to believe that Feighan might be amenable to the Kennedy proposal. In his first election to Congress in 1942, he defeated a right-wing isolationist named Martin Sweeney, positioning himself as a liberal alternative to his opponent. His district included the west side of Cleveland, home to many Polish, Hungarian, and Slovak immigrants. And in 1958 he had sponsored a bill to add Hungarian refugees. But Feighan was erratic and petty, and his career in the House, which lasted nearly three decades, was "marked chiefly by his ability to get himself re-elected," as a journalist from *Life* put it. During a rare interview, Feighan had demanded to see all the questions in advance and spent the meeting "reading from a prepared paper, tracing each line with his index finger." Anytime he seemed to stumble, his aide, Edward

O'Connor, would answer for him, while Feighan "stared out the window." More than perhaps anyone else, Celler was suspicious of Feighan's politics, and the two men grew to hate one another. "What can I do about Feighan?" Celler once pleaded to a colleague. "He's driving me crazy." The congressman replied, "Live, Manny [*sic*]. You've got to keep living."

Despite hopes that Feighan would prove to be more liberal than Walter, the Ohio congressman was frequently motivated by conservative impulses. In early 1964 he became infamous for trying to revoke a visa for the Welsh actor Richard Burton, because Feighan thought his romance with Elizabeth Taylor, his co-star in the blockbuster *Cleopatra*, was "a public outrage"; because the two actors were still married to other people, Burton's presence in the country would be "detrimental to the morals of the youth of the nation."

When Kennedy aides went to the Hill to begin building support for the immigration bill, they received a cool reception from Feighan. Norbert Schlei later said he suspected that Feighan felt slighted that the White House had not spoken to him enough in the bill's early stages; he appeared to be unhappy that the White House had gone first to Celler— though it had been a reasonable thing to do, given Celler's position as head of the House Judiciary Committee rather than a smaller subcommittee. "He made us absolutely no promises about whether he would support it or whether he was sympathetic," Schlei recalled.

It looked as though the immigration bill would join the graveyard of other failed legislative efforts by the Kennedy White House. In August *The Washington Post* noted that congressional approval of Kennedy's legislative requests was at an all-time low of 5 percent, while the number of requests was at an all-time high. Out of 403 requests, only 19 were given final approval. By comparison, during Eisenhower's third year in office, Congress approved 14 percent of the president's requests.

That summer the country was consumed by growing unrest over civil rights. On June 12, just hours after Kennedy delivered a televised message to the country appealing for an end to racial discrimination, Mississippi civil rights leader Medgar Evers was shot and killed in front of his home. On August 28 the March on Washington for Jobs and Freedom drew more than 200,000 people to the National Mall to hear Martin Luther King, Jr., deliver remarks capped by his now-famous "I Have a Dream" speech.

In early November, the effort to reform the country's immigration laws—which only a few months earlier had seemed to be gaining momentum—now appeared to be unraveling. Schwartz wrote to Sorensen that Feighan and his counterpart Senator Eastland were planning to hold hearings under the guise of a joint committee that had been dormant since the 1952 debate. The joint committee on immigration had no legislative power, so the hearings would be effectively useless for pushing forward any bill. "If Feighan succeeds in this maneuver, the legislation could be tied up for a long time with no chance of hearings before the proper legislative committees," Schwartz lamented. He reported that Celler "was helpless in this situation" and was urging the White House to help.

Still, Feldman pressed forward with the *Nation of Immigrants* book, soliciting advice on the manuscript from Arthur Schlesinger, Jr. But on November 4 the historian blasted the draft, saying it was "not ready for publication as a book for adults" and in its present form "would do damage to the President's reputation as an historian." Schlesinger said he spent a few hours working on the text but that it "requires a hell of a lot more work." The historian advised either turning the project into a children's book or bringing in an outside historian to fix it. Two days later Feldman asked Julius Edelstein, Herbert Lehman's former Senate aide and an immigration policy expert, to help draft a final chapter on "Where We Stand" that would point the way forward on immigration policy: "I hate to give generous volunteers deadlines but, I must have the material before I leave for Japan and I am leaving for Japan on November 21."

Kennedy had asked Feldman to go to Tokyo as part of a large American delegation, including six cabinet secretaries, to discuss trade issues with Japan's prime minister and other top officials. The president himself was unavailable: a trip to Dallas had long been planned, primarily for Kennedy to shore up support ahead of his reelection campaign and to raise money for local Democratic politicians who could sense their fortunes slipping as voters left the party over its support for civil rights. Lyndon Johnson, whose grasp of Texas politics was keener than anyone's, doubted that a trip to Dallas would improve matters, but he was loyal to Kennedy and had little else to occupy his time.

The vice presidency is a perpetually ill-defined office that can leave its occupants unsure of what to do with themselves. But for Johnson, already plagued by considerable insecurities, the job was torture. "Every time I came into John Kennedy's presence," he remembered years later, "I felt like a goddamn raven hovering over his shoulder. Away from the Oval Office, it was even worse. The Vice-Presidency is filled with trips around the world, chauffeurs, men saluting, people clapping, chairmanships of councils, but in the end, it is nothing. I detested every minute of it." In Texas, at least Johnson would be in familiar territory. After swinging through Dallas with Kennedy, he and Lady Bird planned to entertain the president and the first lady at their ranch in Hill Country outside Austin. They were ready to be consummate hosts, having selected the president's favorite scotch and prepared a special bed for him that would support his troubled back.

On November 22 Feldman and more than half the administration's cabinet secretaries were flying on a special air force jet bound for Japan when a message came over a teletype machine on the plane that the president had been shot. Dean Rusk was the first to see it; he called the others to the front of the plane. "Well that doesn't mean anything," Feldman remembered saying to everyone else. "He's been shot, but so has Orville," referring to Orville Freeman, the agriculture secretary, standing near him on the plane, who had survived a bullet passing through his chin and his skull during the Battle of Guadalcanal during World War II. Moments later, though, another message came. Hope gave way to stunned silence, grief, and fear. As the plane turned back to Honolulu to refuel before heading back to Washington, Feldman remembered looking outside and seeing military planes surrounding them. When the plane stopped in Hawaii, an air force doctor came on board to deliver tranquilizers to some passengers too upset to bear the news. On the journey home, as everyone sat in silence, lost in thought, Feldman resolved to resign from his job. He bore no personal animus toward Johnson; he simply could not imagine remaining in the White House with Kennedy gone. After the plane landed in Washington at two a.m., he went to the Oval Office to leave a letter of resignation on the president's desk. When he walked in, he nearly fainted. The room he had come to know so well had a rug with a new color—a deep red, compared to the green from before, ordered by Jackie Kennedy before the trip to Texas. Thinking at first that he had hallucinated, Feldman quickly dropped off his letter and walked out, imagining he would never set foot in the room again.

Earlier that day Senator Eastland and his wife had been driving through Virginia on the senator's annual long drive home to Mississippi so that he could use his car over the Christmas holidays. At midafternoon they reached U.S. 11 in the Shenandoah Valley, when they noticed flags flying at half-mast. Turning on the radio, they learned that Kennedy had died. "Good God, Lyndon's President," said Eastland, who knew immediately that while Kennedy could be stopped on Capitol Hill, his successor would not. "He's gonna pass a lot of this damn fool stuff."

NINE

A MARTYR'S CAUSE

———————

For years Lyndon Johnson had harbored dreams of becoming president and addressing his former colleagues from the rostrum of the House as president of the United States. But not like this.

Five days after Kennedy's death, Johnson appeared before both chambers of Congress in a somber dark suit and tie. After more than two decades on the Hill as a congressman and then a senator, Johnson had developed a reputation as a bombastic, unsubtle man. On this evening, as he delivered a speech to a country still in shock, he showed a different side—a level of naked vulnerability that stunned the legislators and Supreme Court justices before him. "All I have I would have given gladly not to be standing here today," he said so softly that those in the back of the chamber could barely hear. But as he spoke of the future, Johnson's voice gathered force. He urged lawmakers to pass the civil rights legislation supported by his predecessor, because "no memorial oration or eulogy could more eloquently honor President Kennedy's memory," and added that there was also a tax bill awaiting action and foreign policy to be continued. "In short, this is no time for delay. It is a time for action."

The address brought everyone in the room to their feet, and impressed

.Washington observers who took note of Johnson's "quiet confidence," as *The New York Times* put it. The emotional attunement with the country that Johnson displayed that evening would allow him to help heal a grieving country while simultaneously galvanizing it to action. He would be consoler-in-chief, but he would also assert control and legitimacy. Most of all, he would appoint himself executor of Kennedy's legislative will. "Everything I had ever learned in the history books taught me that martyrs have to die for causes," Johnson recalled years later. "John Kennedy had died. But his 'cause' was not really clear. That was my job. I had to take the dead man's program and turn it into a martyr's cause. That way Kennedy would live on forever and so would I."

If Johnson hoped to complete Kennedy's unfinished business, he would first need to enlist the help of Kennedy's men, many of whom were torn over whether to stay. "I know how much *he* needed you," he told them. "But it *must* make sense to you that if he needed you I need you that much more. And so does our country." Secretary of State Dean Rusk and Agriculture Secretary Orville Freeman decided to remain until the end of Johnson's presidency in January 1969. After seeing Mike Feldman's resignation letter, Johnson called Feldman and invited him for a swim at the White House pool—"the greatest honor you can get in the White House," Feldman recalled—and persuaded him to remain in his job for another several months. Not everyone heeded Johnson's pleas—Sorensen quickly exited, and Bobby Kennedy, falling into a deep depression, rarely showed up to work. But those who stayed witnessed something extraordinary. The same legislative agenda, including the long-shot immigration bill, that had stalled out time and again under Kennedy was about to come to life.

—

LARRY O'BRIEN, a brilliant son of Irish immigrants who had helped to engineer Kennedy's rise in Massachusetts politics, noticed the difference immediately. As the designated liaison to Congress in the Kennedy White House, O'Brien had given the president efficient updates on legislation. Conversations had passed quickly and stayed focused. With Johnson, there was no sense trying to hold back details. The president wanted to know everything. O'Brien remembered losing a tussle on the Hill that had gone into the early hours of the morning. On his way home, depressed, he stopped at a sandwich shop for food he did not even want to eat. He waited a few more hours until six-thirty, when he knew the president would be awake, to call and fill him in. "When did this happen?" Johnson asked. "It was the early hours of the morning," O'Brien explained. "Why didn't you call me?" Johnson admonished him. "You should have called me and told me about it. You know, when you're up there bleeding, I want to bleed with you. We have to share these things."

At the president's weekly Tuesday breakfast meetings with congressional leaders, O'Brien soon found himself presenting elaborate flow charts showing how various priorities were faring on the Hill, something he would not have dared to attempt with Kennedy. Johnson loved the charts, which would sit on an easel in the corner of the room and show the exact status of every bill Johnson wanted passed. He and O'Brien enjoyed talking strategy so much—their conversations going down endless tangents—that Lady Bird would sometimes gently interrupt them at night to tell her husband that he needed to get some dinner.

Johnson knew of no other way to conduct business. As vice president, he had grown frustrated watching Kennedy's priorities founder on the Hill. He had thought the president was too passive, that he did not lean on his vice president's considerable knowledge of congressional procedure and temperament nearly enough. Now that he was president, Johnson understood that his success depended entirely on how well the White House managed the inner workings and large egos on the other end of Pennsylvania Avenue. "The most important people you will talk to are senators and congressmen," Johnson instructed his aide Jack Valenti. "You treat them as if they were president. Answer their calls immediately. Give them respect. They deserve it." Under Kennedy, an aide would ask the president to make a special phone call to a lawmaker only when all other avenues had been exhausted. Johnson, by contrast, worked the phones constantly. Every morning he woke up to fresh clips and summaries of the *Congressional Record*. Every night before bed, he reviewed staff memos with the latest updates.

His first major tests were a foreign aid bill and a tax cut that had cleared the House under Kennedy only to be trapped in the Senate. He dispatched with both within months of taking office. "There is but one way for a President to deal with the Congress, and that is continuously, incessantly, and without interruption," Johnson reflected years later. "If it's really going to work, the relationship between the President and the Congress has got to be almost incestuous. He's got to know them even better than they know themselves. And then, on the basis of this knowledge, he's got to build a system that stretches from the cradle to the grave, from the moment a bill is introduced to the moment it is officially enrolled as the law of the land."

On February 11, 1964, Johnson called Mannie Celler, chair of the House Judiciary Committee, to congratulate him: Celler had helped shepherd Johnson's sweeping civil rights bill through the House, winning passage the night before. "I'm mighty proud of you," Johnson said, before turning immediately to his next priority. "I hope you get my immigration bill out now." Celler responded with some anxiety. "I'm having some trouble with it . . . I'll get to work on it."

It was not obvious, at first, that immigration would be one of Johnson's priorities as president. He had made special efforts as a congressman to save refugees from Nazi Germany, but he had also voted for the McCarran-Walter Act in 1952 and had experienced the hurdles of passing immigration reform firsthand when he and Lehman had made a failed attempt in the Senate.

Johnson had grand visions for his presidency—he wanted to surpass his hero, Franklin Roosevelt, by passing as many bills as possible that would improve Americans' lives—and he knew he had limited political capital to spend. Any bill that stalled could sap his momentum. Would immigration reform—which had failed so many times before—be worth the effort?

The key to persuading Johnson to proceed on immigration, as Feld-man and others discovered, was to tie it to the president's other priorities, civil rights and foreign policy, and convince him that the national origins quotas were as discriminatory as the Jim Crow laws. Broad moral argu-ments captivated Johnson, who quickly picked up on the inherent unfair-ness of the quotas and became a harsh critic of them almost overnight once Feldman pressed his case.

On January 7, 1964, Abba Schwartz at the State Department penned a memo for the White House to bring Johnson up to speed on immigration and to make recommendations for what to do next. He suggested that the president's State of the Union speech endorse immi-gration reform—something Kennedy had not done in any of his annual addresses. Schwartz also recommended that Johnson invite leaders of different groups supporting the bill to the White House to ask for their help. By the end of the month, Johnson had done both.

At a televised meeting in January, Johnson invited both reform advo-cates and a few skeptics—Senator Eastland and Congressman Feighan. Johnson wanted to put the screws to immigration opponents, with TV cameras to provide a public record. He began by laying out some straight-forward moral reasoning. "Now I would hope that each of us and all of us are descended from immigrants. I hope we would ask ourselves this question: How would we feel, if we were put in the other fellow's place? Maybe by doing that and engaging in a little introspection for a time we would find it a good feeling to apply the Golden Rule and do unto oth-ers as we would have them do unto us." Then he startled Eastland and Feighan by putting them on the spot, asking them what they planned to do on reform. They both offered vague answers.

In truth, they were in no mood to work with the president. Johnson's immigration proposal was nearly identical to Kennedy's. The bills pro-posed by Philip Hart in the Senate and Celler in the House were simply reintroduced, and they were running into the same dead-ends that had stymied them the year before. Feighan, as chair of the House immi-gration subcommittee, was refusing to hold hearings because he wanted funding for the separate joint committee on the subject. Celler and several Johnson officials believed rightly that a joint committee, with more drawn-out hearings and investigations, would derail immigration reform yet again.

Democrats managed to block funding for Feighan's joint committee. But the Ohio congressman was only growing more difficult to manage. In April the columnist Drew Pearson reported that seven months earlier Feighan had behaved erratically at a two-week conference in Geneva on European migration. He missed most of the sessions, including one honoring his predecessor the late Francis Walter; representatives from twenty-nine countries appeared to memorialize Walter, but Feighan himself was a no-show. He also failed to attend the conference's last two sessions because he was touring Mont Blanc in a limousine, according to Pearson. When he did make appearances, he horrified the other attendees. At one point, in a closed-door session with the other U.S. delegates— plus his son, who was mysteriously also in attendance—he berated the State Department for admitting a few hundred Russian Orthodox refugees from Turkey, among whom, he claimed with no proof, were Russian spies. But his most disturbing behavior during the trip came at a dinner of American and European diplomats: Feighan insulted recently deceased leaders of his own party. He loudly accused Kennedy of being so soft on Communism that he never would have supported him for reelection. He then accused the late Eleanor Roosevelt of "nigger loving activities." His fellow Americans at the dinner, Congressmen Frank Chelf of Kentucky and Arch Moore of West Virginia, were so horrified and embarrassed that they staged a vaudeville routine, complete with funny voices, to drown out their misbehaving colleague.

But with Feighan in control of the immigration bill through his subcommittee, the Johnson White House had no choice but to deal with him. On June 17 White House aide Jack Valenti struck up a conversation with Feighan on *Air Force One*; the president and a number of Ohio lawmakers were headed to Cleveland for a convention of the Communications Workers of America. On the flights there and back, Valenti prodded

Feighan to make a commitment on the immigration bill that session. "In a loud voice I told the President that Congressman Feighan had made an unequivocal commitment," Valenti wrote that day in a memo to O'Brien. "The President thanked Feighan for this." Knowing that Feighan could not be entirely trusted, Valenti followed up on the conversation with a memo noting what they had discussed. "I just want you to know that the President was delighted with your unequivocal commitment today that the immigration bill would definitely become law this session," Valenti wrote. "This is wonderful news and the President is very grateful to you for your efforts."

That month Feighan, who had just barely survived a primary challenge back home in Ohio, finally relented on allowing testimony before the immigration subcommittee, leading to the first hearings in nearly a decade on the national origins quota system. The first person to offer testimony, fittingly, was Celler, who pointed out that it had been forty years "almost to the day" since the 1924 law had been enacted. "I submit that the fears and phobias of four decades ago have no place in our society in 1964."

In an eerie echo of the past, John Trevor's son, John B. Trevor, Jr., returned to testify and defend the quotas scheme hatched by his father. The younger Trevor had picked up a number of his father's causes, becoming a director of the Pioneer Fund, a group founded by his father that supported research into eugenics and gave financial aid to children "descended predominantly from white persons who settled in the original thirteen states prior to the adoption of the Constitution." He also chaired the immigration committee for the American Coalition of Patriotic Societies, another right-wing group started by the elder Trevor, whose greatest cause was "to keep America American" by opposing immigrants and Communism. At the hearing, Trevor Jr. argued that the national origins quotas had "provided a realistic approach to protecting this Nation from the evils of unrestricted immigration," and he said that any effort to rush through "ill-considered immigration legislation for political gain during an election year" was "potentially dangerous."

Over the years, the arguments on both sides of the immigration debate had calcified into broad slogans: one side preached tolerance and equality, and the other warned about the risks to national security and the country's racial homogeneity. Few supporters of reform bothered mastering the details of the policy, which meant that testifying before Congress, in the face of skeptical lawmakers, would serve as the first real test of their knowledge and commitment. General hand-waving about the virtues of immigration would not do.

Secretary of State Dean Rusk realized this only at the last minute, the night before he was due to testify on July 2, and he called Abba Schwartz, the State Department's expert on immigration reform, abruptly at home. "Abba," he said, "I'm not inclined to testify on the immigration bill tomorrow, because I'm a reluctant witness. You don't really think we should let in people like the . . . on a world-wide competitive basis, do you? After all, we are an Anglo-Saxon country."

Schwartz replied that it was pretty late to be withdrawing as a witness, and that Rusk should speak to the president, who had "a strong political commitment" to the bill. Rusk hung up without replying. But within the hour, he phoned again, clearly having read the briefing book prepared for him on the subject. Rusk peppered Schwartz with technical questions and then told him to meet him in his office earlier than usual before going to the hearing.

Despite his last-minute doubts, Rusk proved an effective witness, though his testimony revealed just how little government officials foresaw of the actual effects of abolishing the quotas. Most everyone spoke in the realm of theory, emphasizing the symbolism of the national origins quotas. At the hearing, Rusk told lawmakers that the country's immigration policy was integral to achieving its foreign policy goals, since it sent important signals to other countries about what the United States thought of them. In this regard, the national origins quota system telegraphed to the world that "our standards of judgment are not based on merit" but rather on "bias and prejudice," in particular in Asia, where strict limits still applied. Rusk added that immigration "is not today the

potentially disruptive element . . . that it might have been had it continued at the relative rate at which we were receiving immigrants, say, in
the second half of the nineteenth century. The impact of immigration
in quantity on our society is relatively limited." When asked how many
more immigrants would enter the country if the law were changed, Rusk
guessed "on the order of 14,000 or 15,000," and added, "It is not the
numbers that I am worried about today, sir. It is the symbolic element of
the national origins idea which is used against us in ways that we should
seek to avoid, if possible, in my judgment."

Later that month, when Bobby Kennedy appeared before the subcommittee as attorney general, he, too, focused on the symbolic importance of abolishing the quotas. When asked about the effect of abolishing
the Asia-Pacific Triangle, Kennedy estimated there would be an influx
of about five thousand immigrants in the first year, "after which immigration from that source would virtually disappear." He and the other
officials were basing their figure on the existing number of Asian immigrants waiting for an open slot under the existing quotas, though because
the quotas had been so small for so long, very few Asians had even bothered to apply for visas.

Another familiar face arrived to speak before the subcommittee offering a similar assessment of Asian immigration. Mike Masaoka said that
while the JACL was "proud of its role in securing the enactment of the
1952 [law], we would be the first to concede that the [law], though an
improvement over the then existing laws, is far from perfect legislation."
The Asia-Pacific Triangle, and its severe limits on Asian immigration,
needed to be abolished, argued Masaoka, who reminded lawmakers
again of the sacrifices made by Japanese-American soldiers during World
War II. When asked about how the new law might affect the total number of immigrants, Masaoka predicted that once the existing backlog was
cleared, "the number would be relatively small."

New allies in the fight to overhaul the country's immigration system showed up at the hearings. Labor unions had for years lobbied hard

against any loosening of the immigration standards. The American Federation of Labor (AFL), under the leadership of Samuel Gompers, had viewed immigrants as a threat to workers' wages and collaborated with right-wing groups to pass both the literacy test in 1917 and the law instituting quotas in 1924. The Congress of Industrial Organizations (CIO), by contrast, had thousands of members within its ranks who were immigrants. In 1955 the AFL and CIO merged under a new president, George Meany, a plumber from the Bronx who supported liberalizing immigration laws.

Soon after taking over the AFL-CIO, Meany removed the AFL's legislative affairs director, who opposed immigration, by storming into his office and shouting, "You're out! Get out!" Meany replaced him with Andy Biemiller, a stocky man with a clipped mustache who often wore a fresh rose in his lapel and was impossible to miss in the halls of the Capitol. "When Andy comes lumbering up here, you know they are really serious," one liberal senator, who was too scared to be quoted by name, told *The Washington Post*. The leadership of the AFL-CIO told Biemiller and his team that one of the group's biggest priorities was abolishing the quota system. The decision by organized labor to switch sides on immigration would transform the political calculus for reform and make it much more difficult for the pro-restriction forces to win.

—

ON AUGUST 7, 1964, Kenneth A. Meiklejohn, a member of Biemiller's team, told the immigration subcommittee that the AFL-CIO was a full-throated supporter of abolishing the national origins quotas. "Racial and ethnic bigotry can no more be justified from the standpoint of justice and morality in our treatment of those who seek to come to our shores than it can be in the treatment of our own citizens." Meiklejohn testified that the AFL-CIO was not worried about competition for its members since most of the immigrants arriving in the country were seeking professional-class jobs. And regardless, the bill would only increase by seven thousand the number of immigrants admitted annually.

In fact, all the pro-reform witnesses were careful to claim that the bill's effect on overall immigration numbers would be minimal both because they believed it and because without such assurances, the public was unlikely to support the administration's effort. In a Gallup poll taken in July and August 1965, 51 percent of Americans favored changing the quota system so that people would be admitted based on their occupational skills rather than on their country of origin; 32 percent opposed. But when asked whether immigration should be kept at its present level, increased or decreased, only 8 percent said the number of immigrants should grow; 39 percent said the current level should be maintained, and 33 percent said it should decrease.

Despite this testimony, the Johnson administration found that negotiations with Feighan were again at a standstill. On July 1, 1964, Valenti wrote to Johnson that Feighan had been "rough and mean over the phone" and was still demanding a joint committee on immigration, or there would be no bill. "That is his quid pro quo," wrote Valenti, who explained to Johnson that this was impossible because Celler and other Democrats were "dead set against the Joint Committee" and "sick and tired of Feighan and his tactics." Johnson wrote back that all such calls should be referred to Larry O'Brien, and that phone conversations with Feighan should be recorded.

Later that month Henry H. Wilson, a White House assistant, wrote O'Brien a memo concluding that the chances of getting past Feighan were slim. "As a practical matter I think we have to call it about an impossibility to get this out of subcommittee," he wrote in a memo, adding that chances in the other chamber looked grim as well. "Senate Democrats are pretty well stacked against it."

But like almost everyone else, O'Brien underestimated the influence of another Kennedy who was ready to make his mark on the Senate.

—

TED KENNEDY, THE KID BROTHER who had always been so eager to catch up to his older siblings, was now trying to keep his family from falling apart. On the day of Jack's death, he hurried to Hyannis Port to be with his parents. His mother had heard the news; his father, who had suffered a stroke two years earlier, had not. When Ted arrived at the family's house, he rushed up the stairs to his father's bedroom. Joe Sr.'s eyes were closed, and when Ted saw the television set next to his bed, he lunged at the wires and tore them from the wall. The next morning he told his father that another Kennedy child was gone. Decades later, the memory of the conversation still brought Ted to tears.

Then there was Bobby, whose depression "veered close to being a tragedy within the tragedy," Ted recalled. Rather than dealing with his own grief, Ted kept watch over his family and poured himself into his work, heeding the words of Johnson to honor Jack's memory by passing legislation.

On June 19, 1964, Ted Kennedy cast one of the prevailing seventy-three votes in the Senate to pass the Civil Rights Act. The margin of victory masked the difficulty of the journey, which had required overcoming a fierce filibuster by a wall of southern Democrats. When the bill passed, Mannie Celler, who had tried and failed countless times over his career to pass aggressive civil rights legislation, declared, "I feel like I've climbed Mount Everest."

For Kennedy, it was a welcome moment of joy and relief after months of sorrow. The bill passed exactly a year after his older brother had sent his own civil rights bill to the Hill. That evening, after casting his vote, Kennedy hurried to Washington National Airport to board a private plane to Springfield, Massachusetts, for the state Democratic Party's annual convention, where he was scheduled to be endorsed for his first full term as a senator. He was joined on the plane by his administrative assistant Edward Moss, Senator Birch Bayh of Indiana, who was giving the keynote address at the event, and Bayh's wife, Marvella.

The flight nearly killed them all. As the pilot, Ed Zimny, approached the airport just outside Springfield, Kennedy looked out in front of the plane and saw fog where he expected runway lights, followed by a hill covered with large rocks. As Zimny desperately tried to lift the plane, it skidded over the tops of some trees before slamming into one and then plowing into the earth. While Bayh and his wife crawled out, Moss and Zimny were motionless in the front. Kennedy, whose body was half-way through a window, could not move his legs. But there was no time to spare. Bayh said he smelled fumes and hurried to drag Kennedy out of the plane. The Bayhs then went to a nearby road and flagged down a driver for help.

At the hospital, the doctors said Kennedy would live but his back and several ribs were broken, while one lung had collapsed. The two men who had been in the front of the plane—Zimny and Moss—were dead. Had Kennedy not been wearing a seatbelt, authorities later concluded, he would most certainly have died as well.

At first the doctors suggested back surgery, to which Joe Sr., remembering Jack's medical struggles, furiously shook his head and shouted, "Naaaa, naaaa, naaa!," the stroke having blunted his speaking ability but not his personality. Instead, Ted tried to allow his back to heal naturally by spending the next five months immobilized, lying flat, able only to lift his chin and move his arms and legs. He turned the time into what he called a "postgraduate seminar," demonstrating an academic seriousness that had been wanting when he was at Harvard. Two evenings a week, from 7:30 to 9:30, various teachers came to his hospital room for lessons. John Kenneth Galbraith, Harvard professor and onetime aide to Jack Kennedy, crammed his tall frame into a bedside chair to teach Ted economics. Another noted Harvard scholar, Sam Beer, lectured on political science. Alain Enthoven, the Pentagon's weapons systems expert, flew in from Washington to share his knowledge.

Immigration was never far from Kennedy's mind during this time. He knew that as head of the Senate subcommittee, he needed to be ready for action when he returned to Washington.

From his hospital bed, Ted assisted Mike Feldman in finishing the project of finally publishing Jack's *A Nation of Immigrants*, which had been abruptly aborted after the assassination. All that was missing was an introduction, which everyone involved had settled on Ted to write. After the crash, Feldman and Milt Gwirtzman, one of Ted's Senate aides, helped him finish the piece—Feldman read it aloud to the young Kennedy for his approval.

When the book came out in early October, its first printing quickly sold out. And there was no mistaking its purpose: to fuse John F. Kennedy's legacy to the cause of immigration reform. "I know of no cause which President Kennedy championed more warmly than the improvement of our immigration policies," read the introduction, exaggerating the late president's interest in the issue. "When President Kennedy sent his historic message to Congress calling for a complete revision of the law, he decided it was also time to revise the book, for use as a weapon of enlightenment in the coming legislative battle. He was working on the book at the time of the assassination. This legacy should not be denied those committed to the battle for immigration reform."

Mysteriously, the introduction now carried Bobby's name rather than Ted's.

When the book project was first conceived in 1963, Ted was the family member who had needed more public exposure and gravitas, given his youth and inexperience as a senator. But by the fall of 1964, it was Bobby who required whatever boost the book might offer. His brother's assassination had devastated Bobby, who had built his life around supporting his older brother's political career. Less than two months after testifying before the House immigration subcommittee, Bobby resigned from his post as attorney general. Utterly lost as to what to do next, he briefly flirted with the idea of trying to become Johnson's running mate in the presidential race that fall. But the two men could not stand to be in each other's company. There was no particular slight that anyone could point to as the cause of all the bad blood—in fact, Johnson had established a decent relationship with Jack and enjoyed a friendly one with Ted. Bobby, on the other hand, never trusted Johnson and would always resent him for taking his brother's place. As Johnson would write in his memoir years later, "Too much separated us—too much history, too many differences in temperament."

Both men were wildly ambitious, and Bobby soon settled on what to do next. He would run for one of New York's Senate seats. The upper chamber made sense; he had worked there before, under McCarthy, and had managed Jack's Senate campaign. But claiming ties to New York was a stretch. His only connection to the state was the limited time he had spent in Riverdale and Bronxville as a child. Making things even tougher for Bobby, the fact that he had investigated the mob at the Justice Department meant that Italian-Americans, who represented a substantial voting bloc in the state, looked at him with suspicion. Nor would it be easy for him to win over Jewish voters, who were partial to the state's popular incumbent, Kenneth Keating, a regular at bar mitzvahs and Jewish weddings who had carved out a reliable record of supporting Israel. Bobby, by comparison, showed his clumsiness as a campaigner for Jewish votes by once ordering milk at a kosher deli. Then there were the old suspicions left over from the 1940s and '50s of Joe Sr.'s anti-Semitism.

But by now the Kennedy family knew what to do when ethnic voters viewed them with skepticism: wrap themselves in the flag of immigration reform. Someone—it remains unclear exactly who—swapped out Ted's name for Bobby's on the immigration book, which was to be published in the thick of Bobby's race against Keating. There's not much evidence that the book helped Bobby's campaign; though he won, he captured only 60 percent of the Jewish vote, less than Keating's last opponent had six years earlier.

Becoming a senator would be a strange fit for Bobby, as it had been for Jack. He grew impatient with the limitations of the job almost immediately. Still, it provided him a national platform and a chance for the Kennedy dynasty to live on after so much tragedy. When Bobby and Ted posed together for pictures after their successful campaigns in November, a photographer said to Bobby, "Step back a little, you're casting a shadow on Ted," to which the younger brother joked, "It's going to be the same in Washington."

—

MEANWHILE, THE SHADOW CAST by President Kennedy over his successor's presidency was receding. No event sealed Johnson's legitimacy more than his landslide win in 1964 over Barry Goldwater. Johnson blasted nearly every record for winning the presidency: most popular votes, the largest percentage of the country's votes, and nearly the biggest margin in the Electoral College (surpassed only by Franklin Roosevelt). He basked in the results as he watched them come in at his Texas ranch. "It was a night I shall never forget," he remembered. "Millions upon millions of people, each one marking my name on their ballot, each one wanting me as their President. . . . For the first time in all my life I truly felt loved by the American people."

Further validation arrived in the form of stunning congressional results, as Democrats scored their biggest majority in the House since the high point of the Roosevelt New Deal in 1936. In the House, Democrats would now outnumber Republicans 295 to 140, and in the Senate, 68 to 32. Finally, for the first time in decades, the party had enough numbers to overcome the conservative coalition of Republicans and southern Democrats who had blocked so many presidents before. On the morning after the election, *The New York Times* declared that the "once powerful conservative coalition . . . appeared to have been rendered impotent, or nearly so." The overall results sent a strong signal to those Republicans who had survived the rout: it was time to get on board with the Johnson agenda, or risk losing the next election.

However much Johnson had been able to accomplish during his first year in office, what followed marked one of the most remarkable stretches of legislative achievement in the country's history. A year later he would look back and tell the lawmakers, "This has been the fabulous 89th Congress."

At a meeting in February 1965 to plot out his legislative strategy, Johnson told his staff, "I want you to work for my legislative program and get as much passed in the next 90 days and in 1965 as is humanly possible." After observing presidents falter before him, he knew exactly what to avoid and warned his staff with stories about Wilson and Roosevelt squandering their political advantages. "Look, I've just been elected by an overwhelming vote, but every day that I will be in office, I will be losing some of my ability to convert that victory into legislative reality," he told them. It was time to build what he called the Great Society, a framework that he had conceived while swimming with his aide Richard Goodwin one day and that he had introduced the previous spring at a commencement speech at the University of Michigan. Johnson's vision was pure New Deal liberalism—an effort to combat society's largest problems through powerful government action. As Johnson had explained in his State of the Union speech in January, "We do not intend to live in the midst of abundance, isolated from neighbors and nature, confined by blighted cities and bleak suburbs, stunted by a poverty of learning and an emptiness of leisure. The Great Society asks not how much, but how good; not only how to create wealth but how to use it; not only how fast we are going, but where we are headed." Central to this plan would be efforts to open up opportunities for all Americans. In Johnson's mind, these initiatives were all linked: supporting the elderly with health care and higher Social Security payments; helping the poor; enforcing the right to vote for African-Americans; and passing an immigration law "based on the work a man can do and not where he was born or how he spells his name."

The Washington Post observed in early February that the Congress was "off to the fastest start of any in recent memory," following a pep talk from Johnson to all the committee chairmen. Rather than spending the first month fussing over rules or organizing committees, as they usually did, lawmakers sprang into action. Less than a month into the new term, the Senate passed three bills on water pollution, fighting poverty in Appalachia, and an international coffee agreement. Senate and House committee hearings on health and education were speeding along.

In April, the president signed the Elementary and Secondary Education Act, which provided the largest infusion ever of federal money into local school districts. Another bill created the Head Start program, which offered education and support for preschool-age children living in poverty. In July he established Medicare and Medicaid to administer government health insurance to the poor and the elderly.

Johnson was at first unsure whether to pursue another civil rights bill so soon after the hard-won success of the year before. He believed a law explicitly protecting the right to vote for African-Americans was necessary; he just did not know whether Congress could rise to the occasion yet again. But events in the Deep South gave Johnson and the civil rights activists the momentum they needed. In March police attacked civil rights protesters marching from Selma to Montgomery with clubs, whips, and tear gas. Americans watching the events unfold on their televisions grew outraged. Later that month, to gin up more support from the Hill, Johnson delivered the most moving speech of his career in a joint session of Congress, exhorting the lawmakers to pass a voting rights law and concluding his remarks with words straight from the hymn of the civil rights movement itself: "We shall overcome."

When Johnson had finished speaking, the congressmen and senators sat before him in stunned silence. Then seventy-six-year-old Mannie Celler on the House floor "leaped to his feet," remembered Richard Goodwin, "cheering as wildly as a schoolboy at his first high-school football game." Perhaps no legislator was more thrilled by this resurgence of New Deal liberalism than Celler. Now the most senior member of the House, Celler could tell that as chair of the Judiciary Committee, he was on the cusp of passing the agenda of his dreams. "I have climbed the greasy pole," he boasted to a reporter.

Celler played a pivotal role for Johnson on the Hill, deftly maneuvering the president's priorities through the House Judiciary Committee. In August, Johnson signed the landmark Voting Rights Act, which ended the literacy tests that had blocked African-Americans from registering to vote and forced states with a history of discrimination to submit any changes in their voting laws first to the federal government for approval.

Between this and the previous year's Civil Rights Act, Johnson, son of the South, had done more to advance the rights of African-Americans than any American president since Abraham Lincoln. Everything the president wanted, he seemed to get.

—

IT WAS EARLY EVENING by the time Michael Feighan arrived at the White House on May 7, 1965. The day had already been a busy one for Johnson. There had been a signing ceremony in the East Room for a bill pouring an extra $700 million into the U.S. military's uncertain adventures in Vietnam. That afternoon he had received a leather-bound book of photos from the White House Photographers Association, marking his presidency from its first day in November 1963 through his 1965 inauguration—a memento that surely delighted Johnson, since it documented a stretch of his life that had become the fulfillment of his wildest political fantasies.

His appointment with Feighan was important. For more than a year, seemingly the entire Johnson White House—not least the president himself—had been trying to persuade the Ohio congressman to stop blocking the immigration bill. Feighan, unused to finding himself at the center of any significant legislative push, was flattered by the attention and had begun to crave Johnson's approval, just as the president had hoped. In early January he asked for a one-on-one meeting with Johnson. When he was told the president did not have time but would be meeting with all the congressional committee chairmen, he asked whether subcommittee chairmen handling important legislation could be included— even though the idea of dozens more subcommittee chairmen being included in such a meeting, already packed with people, was preposterous. Johnson's loyal vice president, Hubert Humphrey, buttonholed Feighan at every opportunity, including at a party hosted by Illinois congressman Barratt O'Hara. Humphrey sent Feighan a note after the party, trying again to apply pressure. "As you know, the President has his heart set on passing the immigration bill this year. It means a great deal to him.

I know it also means a great deal to you. Why not surprise the President? Let's pass the bill this year."

All the cajoling seemed finally to be having an effect. Feighan, who had been so stubborn the year before, was now coming to the White House to discuss his intent to abolish the national origins quotas once hearings for the Voting Rights Act were over. What had made him change his mind was not simply the pressure from the White House. It was an unusual view that was beginning to gain traction among right-wing groups: that the national origins quota system was in fact not restrictive enough—or at least not working as designed. They were not wrong.

The 1952 McCarran-Walter Act was supposed to reinforce the framework of the 1924 law, essentially renewing a system based on national origins quotas that was limited to 158,000 slots per year. By 1965, this should have allowed just over 2 million new immigrants since the law's passage. In reality, there had been 3.5 million, according to immigration scholar Roger Daniels. This was because there were more immigrants counted outside the quotas than within them. With one president after another signing special provisions for refugees who could be admitted with no regard to quotas, the number of people exempt from the country's cap had ballooned. Between 1945 and 1965, more than 750,000 refugees had been admitted into the country, as a patchwork of laws had allowed refugees "of Chinese ethnic origin," Palestinians, Hungarians, and many others to seek shelter in the United States. Most alarming to those who favored restrictions, Europeans were making up a declining percentage of the new arrivals. By 1965, 20 percent of immigrants were coming from Asia, roughly double the share of a decade earlier.

In February, at the thirty-sixth annual conference of the right-wing American Coalition of Patriotic Societies, Feighan called the quota system "a myth" and vowed to eliminate it. He cited numbers to prove his point: Greece, which was supposed to have 308 entrants a year, had an average of 2,666. China, with a quota of 100, was sending an annual average of 2,103. Portugal, with a quota of 438, was sending 2,736, thanks in part to Kennedy's legislation to assist those on the Azore Islands displaced by volcanic eruptions and earthquakes. "It is futile to support myths and corruptive of national purposes to hold tightly to theories which have little practical application," Feighan told the audience of anti-Communist and anti-immigrant activists.

Feighan appeared to be edging closer to support for the Johnson administration's basic framework for the bill, but he still had some demands to make. The Johnson bill—like the one proposed by Kennedy—prioritized immigrants with special skills over those trying to reunify with their families. Feighan wanted those preferences swapped, thinking that giving family members a higher preference would help to preserve the country's ethnic status quo. He also wanted assurances that Schwartz would later be pushed out of the State Department—he had unhappily tussled with him over the visa for actor Richard Burton and other security issues. In the end, the White House acceded to both requests. But ahead of Johnson's May meeting with Feighan, Norbert Schlei of the Justice Department warned the president that Feighan had one major request that the administration could not support: the congressman wanted to impose an overall cap on the number of immigrants entering the country from the Western Hemisphere.

This was a radical idea—one that had never been carried out before.

—

GIVEN TODAY'S FIXATION on the U.S.-Mexico border, it's remarkable to think that just over a century ago, the border between the two countries was effectively open. Anyone who could brave the difficult terrain could cross; no one was "illegal." The line between the United States and Mexico felt especially fluid given that in the 1800s, the Mexican government itself had encouraged Americans to colonize the land now known as Texas. After the Americans rebelled and tried to claim the land as their own, the U.S. military trampled Mexican forces and claimed a shockingly large part of its neighbor's territory, including not just Texas but land that is now California, Utah, Nevada, and parts of Arizona, New Mexico, Colorado, and even Wyoming. From the beginning, figuring out who belonged on which side of the border was not easy. In the ensuing confusion of the war, an 1848 treaty allowed more than eighty thousand Mexicans living on land that had, overnight, become part of the United States to either leave or become U.S. citizens.

There had been a brief push to limit Western Hemisphere immigration during the debate over the Johnson-Reed Act in 1921. But those favoring restriction—because they viewed Mexicans and other Latin Americans as racially inferior—did not prevail because of the growing clout of industry in America's West and employers' demand for Mexican labor. The ban on Chinese immigration in 1882 had forced businesses to look increasingly to Mexico as a major source of labor, and by the turn of the twentieth century, Mexicans made up the vast majority of track crews building railroads in the Southwest. Then came an even greater transformation: in 1902 Theodore Roosevelt signed the National Reclamation Act, which created large-scale irrigation projects that would allow farming to flourish where there used to be merely desert. In California, between 1909 and 1929, the amount of irrigated land expanded by more than 2 million acres. Without a large enough local population—and again because of restrictions on Asian immigration—farms became dependent on Mexican workers. A violent revolution in Mexico that began in 1910 made it an especially easy time to recruit.

The line between the two countries continued to feel porous because most Mexicans who worked for American employers cycled back home when their seasonal work was finished, rarely settling down permanently in the United States. Only in 1917, after the passage of an immigration act requiring literacy for all newcomers, did a barrier to movement between the two countries emerge. Even then, concerned about the impact on farms and rail companies, employers demanded an exemption from the rule so they could continue to hire Mexican workers, many of whom were illiterate.

Apart from all of these practical economic considerations, Washington had a basic understanding that the United States should not be trying to cut off immigration from its neighbors, if only as a matter of maintaining good relations. Just as the Japanese had interpreted the ban on immigration in 1924 as an insult, there was a risk that Mexico—which was even more important for the country's security, given its proximity—could be offended.

Adding limits to Western Hemisphere immigration, Schlei explained in his memo to the president, "would disturb our relations with Latin America at a very bad time." Jack Valenti agreed, telling Johnson that Secretary of State Rusk felt that going along with Feighan's plan would "vex and dumbfound our Latin America friends" and would be "too much too quick for them to take."

The timing was especially poor because of a growing crisis in the Dominican Republic, where the U.S. military had hastily intervened in a local power struggle. In 1961 Rafael Trujillo, a ruthless dictator who tortured and killed his political opponents and once ordered the massacre of thousands of Haitians, was assassinated after ruling for more than three decades. His successor, a democratically elected liberal reformer named Juan Bosch, lasted less than a year before being overthrown by the Dominican military in 1963. But two years later, in April 1965, pro-Bosch forces tried to reinstate their leader. Fearing that Bosch was a Communist sympathizer who would turn the Dominican Republic into another Cuba, and convinced that violence against American nationals trapped on the island was imminent, Johnson sent hundreds of Marines to the island. Using the same techniques he had employed to sell the Great Society, Johnson tried to persuade the American public that he had no choice but to act. He claimed that bullets were flying at Americans on the island and that "the lives of thousands, the liberty of a nation, and the principles and the values of all the American Republics" were at stake. When reporters arrived to investigate, they discovered that no Americans had been wounded or killed, and that the situation was nowhere near as dire as Johnson had claimed. When asked for proof that Communists were behind the revolt, the government was unable to. Alongside

Johnson's hyperbolic claims, the push to send troops to the Dominican Republic appeared to be a fiasco in the making. Thankfully for Johnson, the two sides soon signed a cease-fire agreement, though the damage to his credibility would last the rest of his presidency.

Given that relations with Latin America were delicate, it was no time to be imposing immigration limits for the first time. So the administration proposed a compromise to Feighan. Rusk suggested that a line be added to the bill requiring the president to notify Congress and make recommendations if the total number of immigrants in a given year surpassed 350,000. "What this will do is keep non-quota status for Latin America—but allow Feighan to tell his right-wing friends that the Congress and the President will act if immigration looks like it's getting out of hand," Valenti explained in a memo to the president.

The meeting between Feighan and Johnson did not resolve all of the Ohio congressman's concerns, but it kept negotiations moving in the right direction. A week later Valenti had good news to report to Johnson. He had held two long meetings with Feighan in two days, and the Ohio congressman appeared ready to drop the request for a worldwide ceiling on immigration, including the Western Hemisphere, and told Valenti that he would "get a bill the President likes." Valenti was still a bit wary of Feighan, though, "since he is not what I would call a thoroughly reliable fellow."

Indeed, Feighan had still not given up on demanding funds for a joint committee. The year before, a House vote led by Celler had defeated his request; now Feighan asked again for funds at a House Appropriations hearing, which Celler did not attend. This time he received $120,000. During a Senate Appropriations Committee meeting to review the request, Celler showed up and rehashed his argument against the joint committee: it had met once in fifteen years for a session that had lasted four minutes and had never met again. And it was not needed for any action that a regular House or Senate committee could not already do. The senators, who, as *The New York Times* reported, "were impressed with Mr. Celler's thunder," agreed and cut the funds to $24,000. When

Feighan discovered this, he was furious, taking to the House floor multiple times to attack his colleague. He demanded that Celler resign from the joint committee and accused him of "misrepresenting the facts." The *Post* mocked Feighan with the headline, "Feighan Asks Celler to Quit Dutyless Job." Celler, not a man of few words, said icily, "To what the gentleman from Ohio says, I give the thunder of my silence."

The fighting continued on July 21, when Feighan intoned dramatically on the House floor that it was "a black day in the annals of representative government." He explained that he had dropped his demand for a limit on Western Hemisphere immigration only because he had been assured that the joint committee would undertake an "immediate review of the policy implications of nonquota status for natives of the independent countries of the Western Hemisphere. I did not seek immediate repeal of that privileged status because of this firm agreement. With this unexpected and inexplicable turn of events the issue now remains open."

Celler saucily replied, "There is an old saying that when two men ride a horse one man must ride behind. I am going to tell you that nobody is going to ride in front of me when I ride the horse of the Committee on the Judiciary."

The next day, July 22, at three-fifteen p.m., the House immigration subcommittee met to vote on the legislation. The bill was now a compromise between Feighan and the Johnson administration: the national origins formula would be phased out in three years, compared to the five proposed by Johnson. Overall immigration would be capped at 330,000 a year. Unlimited immigration was allowed from the Western Hemisphere, as well as spouses, parents, and minor children of American citizens. Families seeking to reunify would get highest priority, followed by those possessing special skills.

Feighan, angry over his confrontation with Celler, moved to reconsider an amendment from Clark MacGregor, a Minnesota Republican congressman, to add a limit to Western Hemisphere immigration. The proposal was defeated six votes to three, with even Feighan voting against it, apparently giving up his battle for good. With that, Frank Chelf, a

Kentucky Democrat, moved that the subcommittee vote to report H.R. 2580 to the full House Judiciary Committee. The vote was 8 to 0. That evening Valenti wrote a memo to the president laced with palpable relief: "We got it out." Peter Rodino, an unassuming Democrat from New Jersey who had made a last-minute fuss since he wanted his name on the bill, "performed like a soldier after innumerable conversations." And Schlei "shepherded this bill through the entire tangle."

Even though Johnson had driven his staff hard, he knew how to thank them when they had done extraordinary work. On July 26 Johnson wrote to Schlei, "Your unflagging work on the immigration bill did not go unnoticed by me. . . . Your Nation is grateful to you for this task and the hope that an ancient and outworn procedure may now be reconstructed."

—

AFTER THREE YEARS of being trapped in Feighan's subcommittee, the bill was finally ready to reach the House Judiciary Committee. Feighan promised that the bipartisan support for the bill "virtually assures its swift enactment by the House." As the administration looked toward the Senate, Henry Wilson instructed Schwartz that the bill was "not to be changed by one comma," and that any contacts between Schwartz and Congress should be reported back to Wilson.

On July 27, after a committee session on the bill, Celler told Larry O'Brien that "things went awfully well," and that the committee would likely report out the bill two days later. Things did not move quite that quickly. An exhausted Nicholas Katzenbach, another Johnson aide tasked with pushing the immigration bill forward, updated Johnson on the phone on July 30: that day, the committee had run out of time, since the ever-loquacious Celler had spoken for too long and had given the committee only three minutes to vote. "Honest to Pete, there are times I could resign on stupidity," said Katzenbach.

The following week, on August 3, the Judiciary Committee finally reported the bill out by a vote of 27 to 4. The procedure made front-page news, with Johnson congratulating the committee and calling the vote "a breakthrough for reason, a triumph for justice."

Right until the end, Feighan behaved like a petty child. He picked fights with Celler, complaining in a long letter to Jack Valenti that he wanted to manage the bill when it reached the House floor, rather than Celler, who he claimed "played no part whatever" in the bill and was "not intimately informed on its substantive content or the intent" of the legislation. Ever delusional, Feighan said of Celler, "I am not convinced he is in agreement with its purposes." There was no way to respond except in disbelief. O'Brien, upon seeing the letter, sent a note to Valenti: "Congratulations! You have only the finest of pen pals."

On August 25, the full House voted to pass the immigration overhaul 318 to 95, with most Republicans and northern Democrats supporting the bill and, as usual, southern Democrats opposing it. On the floor of the House, Celler was filled with pride and emotion, reflecting on how long it had taken to reach this point. He was the only member of the House who had also been in Congress in 1924 when the original national origins law had passed. "I made a speech then against this theory. I am glad I am living today and have lived to see that my theories have been vindicated, that we are now to obliterate and nullify and cancel out this abomination called the national theory of immigration."

Now it was up to the Senate, "if you'll ever get Teddy Kennedy to catch up with old man Celler," Johnson told his attorney general Katzenbach in a phone call later that month. "Here he is, 70 years old, and he's already got his bill passed."

———

SINCE RETURNING TO THE SENATE after his accident, Ted Kennedy had impressed his colleagues. During the debate over the Voting Rights Act, he had spearheaded an ambitious effort to add a provision that would prohibit states from charging voters or people registering to vote with a poll tax. Marshaling support from colleagues and civil rights groups, Kennedy showed mastery of a complex subject and a talent for parliamentary procedure. The measure lost, 49 to 45, but political journalists took notice. One reporter called Kennedy's effort a "legislative tour de force." Another said Ted "earned the right not to be called 'kid' anymore."

James Eastland, self-appointed mentor to the young Kennedy, was taking note as well. And Eastland could tell that the power of southern Democrats was waning. A genuine admirer of Johnson, Eastland resolved that rather than fight the president on immigration, it was time to extract as much as he could and then get out of the way. In August, Eastland told Johnson aide Mike Manatos that he was putting Ted Kennedy "in charge of immigration," and that it was time to "give in." "I received the definite impression that he will be guided by Ted Kennedy's wishes in the matter," noted Manatos. Eastland's price would be a judge in Mississippi, but otherwise he would not try to stop the bill from exiting the immigration subcommittee or the Judiciary Committee.

There was trouble elsewhere on the Senate Judiciary Committee, however. Sam Ervin of North Carolina, a Democrat who liked to call himself an "old country lawyer" with a primary allegiance to the American Constitution, was not convinced that abolishing the quotas was a good idea. Ervin would be one of the few legislators during the debate in 1965 who correctly predicted that the immigration bill would have dramatic consequences for the country's ethnic makeup. During Senate hearings in February, Ervin testified that the bill was "just one little hole in the dike for unrestricted immigration," and if there were more immigration from Africa and Asia, "the country will be drastically changed."

Ervin told Manatos that he would support the bill on one condition— that there be a cap on immigration from the Western Hemisphere. It was the provision that the Johnson aides had fought so hard to kill in the House. O'Brien concluded that "it is clear some sort of compromise involving a worldwide quota may be necessary to spring a bill from the Judiciary Committee." Ervin wasn't alone; Minority Leader Everett Dirksen also wanted a cap on the Western Hemisphere. Dirksen, like

Ervin, suspected that supporters of the bill were underestimating the potential rise of immigration levels from around the world. He predicted that the population of Latin America, which was 200 million, would grow to 374 million in fifteen years, and that a strong flow of people from Latin America would soon enter the United States if Congress did not act. That week Katzenbach gave Dirksen language regarding the limit that he felt would get the immigration bill out of the committee. He had also received a sign-off from Secretary of State Rusk, who had been so fiercely opposed to a Western Hemisphere cap but was now willing to go along as a last resort. They settled on a ceiling of 120,000 annually, the country's first-ever limit on immigration from the Western Hemisphere. Valenti assured Johnson, though, that they would handle the politics delicately. It was important that "the new language be played as a Committee sponsored thing—not as something the Administration has consented to."

On September 8 the Senate Judiciary Committee reported the bill out on a vote of 14 to 2. Eastland and John McClellan of Arkansas voted against it, asking in their minority view report, "Why is it that of all the nations of the world the United States is the only one that must answer to the rest of the world and be apologetic about its immigration policy? Certainly no other country that we are aware of seems to be concerned about its 'image' in other countries." Kennedy, Philip Hart, and Jacob Javits criticized the new limit on Western Hemisphere immigration: "At no other time in the history of our immigration policy have we disturbed or altered the unique relationship that exists among the nations of the New World."

While Kennedy served as the bill's floor manager, the four days of debate that followed echoed the arguments from decades past, as southern Democrats defended an ethnic nationalist vision. Strom Thurmond of South Carolina argued, "The wish to preserve one's identity and the identity of one's nation requires no justification—and no belief in racial or national superiority—any more than the wish to have one's own children, and to continue one's own family through them, need be justified or rationalized by a belief that they are superior to the children of others." Spessard Holland of Florida asked of his colleagues, "Why for the first time, are the emerging nations of Africa to be placed on the same basis as are our mother countries, Britain, Germany, the Scandinavian nations, France, the Mediterranean nations, and the other nations from which most Americans have come?"

Alarmed by Holland's comments, Ted and Bobby Kennedy together quickly leaped to the bill's defense. "I am very pleased and proud of the fact that our family came from Ireland," Bobby Kennedy said, words that would have mortified his father. "As the Senator from Massachusetts has said, we are past that period in the history of the United States when we judge a person by his last name or his place of birth or where his grandfather or grandmother came from."

But there was no need to debate more, for Holland was well outnumbered. After just four days of deliberation, the Senate overwhelmingly passed the law on September 22, in a vote of 76 to 18.

Because there were differences in the Senate and House versions, the bill headed to a conference between the two chambers to iron out discrepancies. Celler still held out hope that the Western Hemisphere cap could be removed. "I'm going to raise hell," he vowed to Johnson in a phone call. But in the end, the fight was over. The final bill contained an annual limit of 170,000 visas for immigrants from the Eastern Hemisphere, and 120,000 in the Western Hemisphere. No single country could have more than 20,000 slots. Rather than prioritizing highly skilled immigrants, as the McCarran-Walter Act had done, the new law gave far greater preference to families trying to reunite. Three-fourths of the visas would be for those reunifying with family members; spouses, minor children, and parents of U.S. citizens would be exempt from the caps.

On September 30 the House adopted the final version, 320 to 69. An hour later the Senate approved the bill by a voice vote.

Johnson immediately announced that he would sign the immigration bill in three days at the Statue of Liberty. The last president to have visited the statue was his hero, Franklin Roosevelt, in 1936, to mark the fiftieth anniversary of the statue's dedication. "Perhaps Providence did prepare this American continent to be a place of the second chance," Roosevelt had said then as he gazed out at the harbor. "Certainly, millions of men and women have made it that. They adopted this homeland because in this land they found a home in which the things they most desired could be theirs—freedom of opportunity, freedom of thought, freedom to worship God. Here they found life, because here there was freedom to live."

EPILOGUE

—

FERRYBOATS CARRYING HUNDREDS of men in dark suits bobbed toward Liberty Island. The skyscrapers across the water in downtown Manhattan sparkled in the afternoon sunlight, and the wind carried the faintly salty smell of the East River as the boats approached their destination, the green-hued Statue of Liberty.

Finally, the passengers—among them senators and congressmen, TV camera crews and a handful of curious tourists—disembarked to crowd under the shadow of Lady Liberty. A large lectern, a glossy wooden desk, and a chair stood before them. Hearing the choppy thrum of helicopter blades whipping through the air, the assembly looked skyward. It was President Johnson, touching down to join them.

Johnson enjoyed turning signing ceremonies into celebrations. He looked at them as opportunities to thank those who'd been involved in the accomplishments at hand and to broadcast to Americans the significance of his achievements. He had initially wanted Ellis Island for the day's backdrop, but the site there was practically in ruins after decades of disuse; the island would not be restored and reopened to the public until 1990. A congressman had first suggested Liberty Island as a joke, so exaggerated and patriotic was its symbolism, but Lady Bird said of the idea in her diary, "If anybody shouts it's corny, well, make the most of it!"

The president closely controlled the settings and guest lists for such events, savoring the chance to honor particular people. When he signed the law creating Medicare, he had flown all the way to Independence, Missouri, so that Harry Truman, now frail at eighty-one, could attend. Truman, the first president to propose the idea of a public health care system for all Americans, greeted Johnson on the front steps of his presidential library by saying, "Mr. President, I'm glad I lived this long." At the signing of the Elementary and Secondary Education Act, Johnson had called on his childhood schoolteacher, Kate Deadrich Loney, to join him in Johnson City, Texas.

As Johnson sat down at the desk on Liberty Island and took up his pen, Bobby and Ted Kennedy stood behind him, all toothy smiles. Not too far from them was Celler, basking in the moment. There, too, was Mike Masaoka.

But not all who had devoted themselves to the cause of immigration reform were able to attend. Earl Harrison, whose report to Truman had ignited the president to action, had died ten years earlier of a heart attack while on vacation in the Adirondacks at just fifty-five. Also missing was Herbert Lehman, whose wife, Edith, had been invited to the event. Nearly two years earlier Lehman had been felled by a heart attack just as he was leaving his apartment on Park Avenue to travel to Washington to accept the Presidential Medal of Freedom. John F. Kennedy had chosen him for the honor before his assassination. On learning of Lehman's death, Johnson, who had so often envied the New Yorker's reputation for moral righteousness in the Senate, said that perhaps the best words to honor Lehman were from the citation that would have accompanied the award: "Citizen and statesman, he has used wisdom and compassion as the tools of the government and has made politics the highest form of public service."

Deeper in the crowd, standing too far from the signing to see much of anything, was Erich Leinsdorf, the Jewish-Austrian refugee whose life Johnson had saved nearly thirty years earlier. The two men had continued to cross paths on occasion. When Johnson had been vice president and Cold War tensions between Cuba and the United States were running high, Johnson had joked with Leinsdorf about the musician's unusual path to American citizenship. At a party in Georgetown, after hearing Leinsdorf explain to another guest how he'd met Johnson, complete with details of how the U.S. consulate in Havana had come to the rescue, Johnson said to him, "Now Erich, this is a lovely story and I certainly would like to hear it again, but let me ask you something: What kind of town shall we now put in that story to replace Havana?"

Johnson never forgot his friend, who, upon settling in New York, went on to become an accomplished American orchestra conductor. On the day Kennedy was shot in Dallas, Leinsdorf received word of the tragedy just before he was to conduct the Boston Symphony Orchestra at Symphony Hall. He relayed the devastating news to the audience, whose members gasped in shock, then led the orchestra through Beethoven's *Eroica* funeral march. When Johnson was inaugurated in 1965, he invited Leinsdorf to ride with him in a limousine to a State Department reception. During that short drive he asked the conductor about the immigration bill he wanted to introduce, explaining that Leinsdorf's case "had been perhaps the beginning to open his eyes to the difficulty which a man could have [entering the country]."

For Johnson, Leinsdorf symbolized the great promise of the American dream. "Our beautiful America was built by a nation of strangers," Johnson said in front of the Statue of Liberty that day. "From a hundred different places or more they have poured forth into an empty land, joining and blending in one mighty and irresistible tide."

And so Johnson had insisted on having Leinsdorf in the audience on Liberty Island. After the bill was signed, the President hailed his old friend and invited him into the White House helicopter. When they landed in Manhattan, the president implored Leinsdorf to also join him in a packed limousine headed to the Waldorf Astoria hotel for a dinner party. "Everybody was terribly crowded because I was not of the party originally," Leinsdorf remembered, "but he made space."

The group was whisked away, passing thousands of New Yorkers who had gathered in the streets to get a glimpse of the motorcade. From their hotel suite, Lady Bird could see protesters down below marching back and forth, shouting about Vietnam. Johnson couldn't have known that the immigration law he'd just signed would be one of his last and most ambitious achievements before the war would consume his presidency.

—

AT LIBERTY ISLAND, Johnson had assured everyone that the bill he was signing "is not a revolutionary bill. It does not affect the lives of millions. It will not reshape the structure of our daily lives." The president was hardly the type to downplay the importance of his own work. But in this case, neither Johnson nor his allies realized what they had set in motion. The law's transformative impact would take years to reveal itself.

Initially, as reform advocates had intended, the number of immigrants from eastern and southern Europe increased and surpassed the number of arrivals from the rest of the continent. But though writers of the law were committed to ending racial immigration quotas in principle, they had not anticipated that many more immigrants would soon be arriving from Asia, the Middle East, and Central and South America—or that the law's own mechanics would encourage their numbers. A *Washington Post* story on February 8, 1971, buried deep inside the newspaper, hinted at the changes slowly becoming evident under the headline, "1965 Law is Changing Pattern of Immigration in U.S." Observing that more Chinese, Italians, Filipinos, Greeks, and Indians were now arriving, the article introduced readers to Dennis C. Syntilas, a Greek immigrant to New York who had arrived in 1956 under a special provision for refugees fleeing Communism. Since the passage of the 1965 law, and given its priority on reunifying families, Syntilas had sponsored no fewer than twenty-four of his Greek relatives to enter the United States. "I advised them all to start out in pizzas," he told the reporter. Syntilas was in effect describing chain migration, in which one immigrant's arrival makes pos-

sible the entrance of an entire extended family through the system created by the 1965 law.

A man from Taiwan could enter the country for postgraduate studies
in science and obtain a visa based on his specialized skills. Then he could
bring his wife and children, who, under the 1965 law, would be given a
preference over immigrants without family ties. If he were to become a
citizen several years later, he could then sponsor his brother and sister,
each of whom could bring their respective spouses and children. His wife
could become a citizen as well and bring in her siblings and children.
The couple's parents could also be allowed to enter and would not count
toward the overall cap on immigration. And so on.

By 1971, more Asians were entering the country than Europeans,
often relying on exactly such a pattern of migration. The new immigrants
established roots across the country. New York's Chinatown, which had
taken on a moribund air by the mid-1960s, was revived by the rush of
new arrivals. Two more Chinatowns spawned in the city, one in the
Flushing area of Queens and another in Brooklyn's Sunset Park neighborhood. Iranians, many arriving first as students and later claiming asylum after the overthrow of the shah in 1979, settled in California and
Texas. Arab immigrants gravitated to the Detroit area and took jobs in
the American auto industry. Many of the new immigrants entered the
medical profession, as Johnson's work to establish Medicare and Medicaid had stimulated tremendous new demand for health care services.
Between 1965 and 1974, 75,000 foreign physicians entered the country,
many of them Filipino, Iranian, Indian, and Korean. By 1989, the top ten
countries sending immigrants to the United States were all in the third
world. Meanwhile immigration from Europe, which was now enjoying a
much stronger economy, typically accompanied by a robust social safety
net, tapered.

It was not merely the types of immigrants entering the country that
changed. The 1965 law also ushered in a return to mass immigration that
had not been seen since the turn of the twentieth century. The number of immigrants living in the United States has more than quadrupled

since the law's passage, increasing from 9.6 million in 1970 to a record 44.4 million in 2017. Perhaps most striking, the foreign-born population has now reached its highest share since 1910, returning the country to the very state that supporters of the national origins quotas wanted to unwind a century ago.

Given that the creators of the 1965 law were so careful to impose overall caps, how could this have happened? The answer is simple. Many of the new arrivals were immediate family members who did not count toward the worldwide limits. In addition, thousands of refugees from Cuba, Vietnam, and the Dominican Republic were admitted as nonquota immigrants, and they too brought their families. On the same day that Johnson signed the 1965 law, he declared an open door for Cuban refugees, leading to about 368,000 Cubans entering between December 1965 and 1972.

The creators of the 1924 law, who feared a mixing of European nationalities, would be aghast at the fact that the population of the United States now skews more nonwhite every year. In 2015 Pew Research estimated that without post-1965 immigration, the country that year would have been 75 percent white, 14 percent black, 8 percent Hispanic, and less than 1 percent Asian. Instead, it was 62 percent white, 12 percent black, 18 percent Hispanic, and 6 percent Asian—and was on its way to having whites constitute less than half the total population in the coming decades. We are only beginning to see the political ramifications of these demographic changes, especially in America's suburbs. During the 2018 midterm elections, Democrats swept Orange County, onetime bastion of the GOP and home of Richard M. Nixon, now one-fifth Asian and more than one-third Latino. Similar changes have already shifted the state of Virginia to the political left and are potentially under way in Texas, Nevada, Arizona, and Georgia.

At the same time, because the 1965 law imposed the first-ever numerical cap on Western Hemisphere immigration, it also laid the groundwork for our modern illegal immigration crisis. A year before the law, Johnson had ended a system for temporary Mexican labor known as the bracero program, which had been created during World War II to address worker shortages, particularly in farming. As evidence of abuse came to light—with Mexican workers arriving at jobs to find much lower pay and harsher conditions than promised—criticism of the program amplified. But ending the program, which had allowed an average of 200,000 braceros into the country each year, and then restricting immigration across the southern border, did not end the U.S. demand for cheap Mexican labor. On the contrary, in the more than forty years since the 1965 law, the number of deportations has exploded, yet migrants have continued to enter the country, where they are routinely exploited for their willingness to work for little money in an underground economy. Thus a law that was designed to create equality among immigrants unwittingly helped spawn a shockingly unequal system in which some immigrants are counted as desirable, while others are treated as criminals, in a country that depends on their labor but claims not to want them.

—

IMMIGRATION LAW is at root a question about who we want and do not want in this country. For those who believe in a multicultural America, this question can be uncomfortable to confront, because any system short of open borders invariably requires drawing distinctions that declare some people worthy of entry and others unworthy.

All of this has become impossible to ignore during Donald Trump's presidency. Starting immediately after his inauguration, Trump placed immigration policy at the center of the political debate by imposing a travel ban on seven predominantly Muslim countries. The primary weapon used by lawyers who argued that Trump's ban was illegal was the 1965 immigration law, with its clause banning discrimination against immigrants based on race, nationality, or ethnicity.

Because it abolished the national origins quota system—arguably one of the most explicitly racist ideas ever signed into American law—the 1965 Immigration and Nationality Act deserves a place in history alongside this country's most significant civil rights breakthroughs. It is a powerful document that helped define America as a multicultural nation. But because its ultimate effects were barely envisaged by its creators, the principles it is based upon are tremendously fragile.

I have noticed that those who want to restrict immigration are often more literate in this country's immigration history than are many liberals, who see President Trump's anti-immigration platform as a gross aberration from America's consistent identity as "a nation of immigrants." In an October 2015 interview on Breitbart radio, former attorney general and onetime top adviser to the president on immigration, Jeff Sessions, explained that the percentage of foreign-born Americans was now historically high, and he counted this as "a radical change." "When the numbers reached about this high in 1924, the president and congress changed the policy, and it slowed down immigration significantly, we then . . . created really the solid middle class of America, with assimilated immigrants, and it was good for America. We passed a law that went far beyond what anybody realized in 1965." The interview offered a clear window into the Trump administration's thinking and its interpretation of history, in which the 1924 law, with its effort to keep America white, marked a high point for cultural progress, while the 1965 reform spawned a racial downfall. It was no surprise, then, when officials began to talk about ending chain migration: knowing that America had turned back the clock on demographic changes before, they understood that it could be done again.

History shows us that overhauling this country's immigration system has never been easy. Major reform comes but once every two or three decades, and each time it serves as a marker for fundamental questions of American identity: whether we embrace a nationalism centered on a shared set of civic ideals or shared ethnic origins; whether immigrants are here to benefit businesses or to fulfill humanitarian moral obligations; and whether we believe borders take precedence over human rights. The country is now well overdue for another serious look at its immigration system. The last ambitious, large-scale overhaul came in 1986 under President Ronald Reagan and a Democratic Congress. That law gave amnesty to millions of undocumented immigrants while increasing enforcement at U.S. borders and making it unlawful for an employer to "knowingly" hire workers who were in the country illegally. President Reagan predicted that "future generations of Americans will be thankful for our efforts to humanely regain control of our borders and thereby preserve the value of one of the sacred possessions of our people—American citizenship."

Since then, paranoia over illegal immigration has instead intensified, with both Democratic and Republican presidents taking hard-line stances on border security to win over voters, while failing to fix the country's broken system. In 1996, President Bill Clinton signed an immigration bill that fueled a perpetual state of crisis by dramatically expanding the number of people who could be deported, while narrowing the paths to legalization. More recently under President Trump, a "zero tolerance" policy toward migrants forced the separation of thousands of children from their families and created a humanitarian disaster at the border. For those who seek an alternative, it is time to examine the most basic assumptions we bring to our immigration system. Do we want the more open borders we had a century ago? And if not, who exactly should have priority to enter? Will we judge based on need? On ability? On family status? Should we draw such distinctions at all?

The image of the Statue of Liberty, the Emma Lazarus poem at the statue's base, the notion of America as an eternal "nation of immigrants"—these make up an intoxicating part of this country's mythology. Set against all the sins of America's past—from slavery to the removal and genocide of American Indians—the arrival of open-hearted immigrants, grateful for a chance at a new life on our shores, serves as a constant renewal of hope in the American project. If there is salvation for this country, it very well may lie in the undying gratitude of a refugee whose life has been saved by the granting of a visa. But the story we tell ourselves about being a "nation of immigrants" is also self-serving. Could there be any idea more validating to America's sense of superiority than the belief it is *the* place that everyone in the world wants to be a part of? Like any myth, the idea easily goes unexamined—exalted and treated as if it were a divine, immutable basis for this country's existence, when it is the work of human beings, easily erased by other human beings.

The people who fought for the 1965 Immigration and Nationality Act knew what it was like to live in a country that embraced a race-based definition of itself. They watched the grisly consequences during and after World War II, and they recognized that a nation with an immigration system built on racism could not be defended in an ideological war. But they also could not imagine living in a country as thoroughly multiracial as the United States is today. That means that for those Americans who want ethnic pluralism to be a foundational value of their nation, there is unfinished work. The current generation of immigrants and children of immigrants—like those who came before—must articulate a new vision for the current era, one that embraces rather than elides how far America has drifted from its European roots. If they do not, their opponents can simply point to the America of the last fifty years as a demographic aberration. And they would not be wrong.

This task will not be easy. While the Jewish and Italian families who arrived at the turn of the twentieth century eventually blended into white America, it remains to be seen what will come of the post-1965 immigrants from outside Europe and their children. Our generation is still carving out a place for itself in America's racial landscape, one where white has long been pitted against black and where those who fit neither category are frequently conscripted into battle on both sides. Sometimes the post-1965 generation falls under the vague umbrella term *people of color,* in solidarity with black Americans; at others, they seek to bind themselves as closely as possible to white America in order to gain all its attendant advantages. The way forward, if it is to be just, must honor the principle of equality that the proponents of the 1965 law celebrated, even if they did not understand its full demographic consequences.

The fact that many of the people who supported the 1965 law might not have intended to allow my own extended Asian family into this country makes me no less grateful. Instead, it offers me a lesson: that it was never a given that we would be allowed to come here, or to become citizens. We are here because of the political struggle of others. And that goes for all Americans. Not one of us deserves to be here. So what difference is there between us, with our precious papers, and the people we see at our border who are dying to come in? There is none.

ACKNOWLEDGMENTS

THE IDEA FOR THIS BOOK began with a lark in early 2016: with a few hours to kill before a flight out of Austin-Bergstrom International Airport, I looked to see whether the LBJ Presidential Library was close enough for me to make a quick trip. It was, and as I walked through a room devoted to cataloguing Johnson's Great Society accomplishments, I was struck by a law I'd never heard of—one that I suspected was intimately connected with my family. Roughly two years later I was back in the archives of that same library, researching the Immigration and Nationality Act of 1965.

This book would not have been possible without this country's tremendous presidential libraries and the archivists who work at them. The staff at the Truman Library, the JFK Library, and the LBJ Library all gave generously of their time and knowledge and made me feel welcome. These libraries are public treasures—to be relentlessly protected and supported—because they give the American people direct access to their country's history. I was stunned by their openness, pinching myself every minute I was allowed to access box after box of documents. I would also like to thank the librarians at the Columbia University Rare Book & Manuscript Library, the Nevada Historical Society, the University of Nevada-Reno, the United States Holocaust Memorial Museum (USHMM) , and the Library of Congress. Thank you especially to Sam Rushay at the Truman Library and Becky Erbelding and Ron Coleman at the USHMM.

Every work of history rests on the shoulders of writers who have come before. I am particularly indebted to the work of Mae M. Ngai, whose book *Impossible Subjects* remains the most trenchant analysis available of twentieth-century American immigration. John Higham's *Strangers in the Land* is a classic for anyone seeking to understand the history of nativism in this country. And Doris Kearns Goodwin and Robert Dallek are peerless biographers of Johnson and Kennedy.

Jill Rifkin and her husband Dick graciously took me out to lunch and invited me into their home in Albany to share memories of Jill's incredible grandfather, Emanuel Celler. Sue Serphos, another granddaughter of Celler's, spent time on the phone with me also sharing wonderful stories. They helped make their grandfather come alive for me, and I am so grateful they took the time.

Many friends and family members provided untold amounts of love, support, and patience while Zach and I both wrote our books. Some even traveled with us, letting us turn vacations into writing retreats. Ana Muñoz, Justin Steil, Alma Muñoz Steil, and Alvaro and Beatriz Muñoz invited us to join them for a magical week in Menorca. Albert Wu and Michelle Kuo encouraged us over many dinners in Portugal. Thank you especially to Michelle for reading over the manuscript and giving excellent feedback.

Shonu Gandhi and Julio Gonzalez Altamirano hosted and fed me in their home in Austin while I was doing research at the LBJ Library; it was their gorgeous wedding that led me to that city in the first place, where the idea for the book began.

Britt Peterson listened to me talk about this book and asked me brilliant questions on many long walks in Rock Creek Park. Suzy Khimm was a champion from the start and made me believe this book was worth writing, especially for Asian-Americans seeking to understand our political heritage. Jacob Remes generously took the time to read the manuscript at a late stage and gave eagle-eyed feedback.

Thank you to Nate Shockey for inviting me to speak at Bard to a wonderful group of students and professors who gave me an invaluable chance to share some of what I'd learned and hear their smart questions.

I was lucky beyond measure to meet Erin Scharff my freshman year of college. Erin, who also kindly read parts of this manuscript, taught me to treasure my family's immigrant roots. Without her influence, this book would likely not exist.

I want to thank my colleagues at *The New York Times* and *The Washington Post* for their constant inspiration. There is nothing like going through decades of archives of these publications while editing stories for them in the present—a true reminder of the honor and responsibility that comes with being a journalist. When I thought it seemed mad to write a book in the middle of the roiling, all-consuming story of Trump and Russia in 2017, I learned that my unflappable boss at the *Post*, Peter Finn, was writing one too. That gave me hope. Thank you to Marc Lacey for his support and bringing me to the *Times*. Working on this book made me realize how much I wanted to spend my time as an editor thinking about where this country is headed. It's a joy to do so every day alongside so many talented and kind colleagues on the National desk.

Thank you to my agent, Lauren Sharp, for immediately understanding what this project could be, shepherding it with consummate professionalism and cheering me on through the depths of the writing. At Norton, my editor John Glusman saw the possibilities for this book from the beginning; he and his assistant Helen Thomaides gave me sharp edits that improved the manuscript at every turn.

Doug Carter's steadfast love made everything possible. Doug, you reminded us to treasure our marriage every day and to nurture our biggest hopes for the world. We think of you and miss you every day.

My parents, Ed and Mei-Shin, supported us from the very start of the process, interrupting us during a trip to Taiwan only when it was time to go out and eat the world's most delicious beef noodle soup. They taught me to hold close to our family's Chinese roots while embracing the culture and history of their adopted country with endless curiosity and gratitude. They have never made me feel torn between two worlds—only that by having access to more than one culture I was given the rarest of gifts. I owe everything good in my life to their love.

Finally, I want to thank my husband, Zach. When I encouraged him to write a book, he told me I should do the same, and it turned into the shared intellectual adventure of a lifetime. Sitting in the magnificent main reading room of the Library of Congress reading old books next to the love of your life—it simply does not get better than that. You have supported my dreams with your unending care and love. You told me to keep going when I doubted it would ever get done. Someday we will try to explain to our daughter Ming what we were doing in the weeks and days leading up to her arrival.

NOTES

PROLOGUE

1 **Shaughnessy:** "New Entry Plan Leaves Ellis Is. to the Seagulls," *Brooklyn Daily Eagle*, November 12, 1954; "E. J. Shaughnessy, Immigration Aide," *New York Times*, November 5, 1958.

1 **"Business is closed":** "Ellis Island, 62-Year-Entry, Closed," *Washington Post*, November 13, 1954.

2 **"If all the stories":** "Last Man Off Ellis Island," *New York Times*, November 14, 1954.

2 **"that had formed":** Higham, *Strangers*, 330.

2 **The *Atlantic Monthly*:** Simon and Alexander, *Ambivalent Welcome*, 134.

2 **"Some members of this radio":** Herbert Lehman, remarks recorded for Clear Channel Broadcasting Company, April 28, 1952, Edelstein Papers.

2 **More immigrants:** Daniels, *Guarding the Golden Door*, 4.

2 **share of foreign-born:** Ibid., 5.

3 **"The new immigration legislation":** "Conferees Incline to Modify the Ban Against Japanese," *New York Times*, April 28, 1924.

ONE: "GOD'S CRUCIBLE"

7 **On March 2, 1924:** "1,000 at Mass Meeting Condemn Johnson Bill," *Brooklyn Daily Eagle*, March 3, 1924.

7 **"Jerusalem of America":** Abramovitch and Galvin, *Jews of Brooklyn*, 41.

7 **Between 1905 and 1914:** Daniels, *Guarding the Golden Door*, 45.

8 **By 1921:** "Immigrants Diverted to Boston," *New York Times*, February 2, 1921.

8 **"An ostrich could assimilate":** Roberts, *Why Europe Leaves Home*, 5.

9 **Just five-foot-two:** "La Guardia Is Dead," *New York Times*, September 21, 1947.

9 **"It is proper":** "Speakers Attack Alien Quota Bill," *New York Times*, March 3, 1924.

10 **"A freshman congressman":** Celler, *You Never Leave Brooklyn*, 7.

11 **"the stumbling block":** "1,000 at Mass Meeting Condemn Johnson Bill," *Brooklyn Daily Eagle*, March 3, 1924.

11 **According to a favorite family story:** Celler, *You Never Leave Brooklyn*, 26.

11 **the slur "kikes":** Goldstein, *Price of Whiteness*, 127.

12 **Every Friday:** Emanuel Celler, interview by Lawrence Rubin, June 24, 1970, 3–4, in

Association of Former Members of Congress, Oral History Collection, Manuscript Division, Library of Congress.

12 **Mannie, his siblings:** Celler, *You Never Leave Brooklyn*, 32.

12 **to later wonder:** Ibid., 30.

12 **taking some Italian classes:** Ibid., 35.

12 **graduating from Columbia Law School:** Ibid., 25.

12 **remembered his father:** Celler interview, 10–11.

12 **He was shy:** Celler, *You Never Leave Brooklyn*, 30.

13 **"the minstrel campaigner":** "Daring Political Banner Wins Praise and Criticism," *Brooklyn Daily Eagle*, October 29, 1922.

13 **"Eventually why not":** Ibid.

13 **"you'd get up":** "Congressional Bulldog Emanuel Celler," *New York Times*, February 24, 1967.

13 **"There's my district":** "In Washington: Celler's District," *Brooklyn Daily Eagle*, December 6, 1923.

14 **"a most amiable man":** Hoover, *Memoirs*, 101.

14 **"If all the members":** Ibid.

14 **"whether such vast":** "One Hundred Years of Immigration," *New York Times*, February 17, 1924.

14 **"as useless as a candle":** "Interest in Citizenship," *New York Times*, February 20, 1024.

14 **Davis left his hometown:** Quotes in this paragraph are from Davis, *Iron Puddler*, 15, 22–23, 33, 37, 43.

15 **"keeping labor quiet":** Hoover, *Memoirs*, 101.

16 **"We have let":** "Asks to Rid Aliens of Red Propaganda," *New York Times*, June 30, 1921.

16 **"Don't be fooled":** "Celler Scores Davis After His Astor Address," *Brooklyn Daily Eagle*, December 21, 1923.

17 **"America is God's Crucible":** Nahshon, *Ghetto to Melting Pot*, 288.

17 **"appeal to claptrap patriotism":** "A Spread-Eagle Play by Israel Zangwill," *New York Times*, September 12, 1909.

17 **"That's all right!":** "Roosevelt Criticizes Play," *New York Times*, October 10, 1908.

17 **"That particular play":** Nahshon, *Ghetto to Melting Pot*, 242.

18 **"There is no room":** "Roosevelt Bars the Hyphenated," *New York Times*, October 13, 1915.

19 **"second birth":** Antin, *Promised Land*, 3, 6.

19 **The brilliant industrialist:** Higham, *Strangers*, 247–48.

19 **The scholar Horace Kallen:** Quotes in this paragraph are from Kallen, *Culture and Democracy*, xii, xxiii.

20 **"every type of instrument":** Ibid., 116.

20 **"What do Americans":** Ibid., 109.

20 **"Democracy involves":** Ibid., 53.

22 **"What this war":** Ibid., 15.

22 **the automaker magnate:** Higham, *Strangers*, 283.

23 **"We Americans must realize":** Grant, *Passing of Race*, 263.

23 **"The summer hotel":** Karabel, *Chosen*, 88.

23 **roughly 200,000 members:** "Ku Klux Klan: Decline," *Time*, March 1, 1926.

24 **"Jew Movies":** Gordon, *Second Coming*, 50.

24 **By 1915:** Goldstein, *Price of Whiteness*, 36

24 **Mary Phagan:** Olney, *Dead Shall Rise*, 5.

24 **around three-thirty a.m.:** Ibid., 18.

25 **Leo Frank:** Ibid., 10.
25 **Frantic Jewish supporters:** Ibid., 366.
25 **"Knights of Mary Phagan":** Dinnerstein, *Leo Frank Case*, 133, 136.
26 **By 1924:** Harcourt, *Ku Klux Klan*, 5.
26 **as money poured in:** Gordon, *Second Coming*, 66.
26 **At its peak, the Klan:** Ibid., 164.
26 **as a law student:** "Albert Johnson's Mother Expires," *Washington Post*, April 29, 1928.
27 **When he landed:** "District Man in Congress," *Washington Post*, November 9, 1912.
27 **In the fall of 1898:** "Some Reminiscences," *Grays Harbor Washingtonian*, April 29, 1934.
27 **On the night of:** Lee, *Asian America*, 163.
27 **"was engaged on a mission":** "Some Reminiscences," *Grays Harbor Washingtonian*, June 24, 1934.
28 **Johnson led:** Higham, *Strangers*, 177.
28 **"The greatest menace":** Hillier, "Albert Johnson," 199.
28 **he studied the subject:** Ibid., 200.
29 **immigration to the United States:** Daniels, *Guarding the Golden Door*, loc. 951.
29 **"abnormally twisted":** Higham, *Strangers*, 309.
29 **Unlike his charming friend:** Zimmerman, *First Great Triumph*, 186.
30 **"This bill embodies":** Woodrow Wilson, "Veto of Immigration Legislation" (transcript), January 28, 1915, Presidential Speeches, Miller Center of Public Affairs, University of Virginia, https://millercenter.org/the-presidency/presidential-speeches/january-28-1915-veto-immigration-legislation.
30 **"neither skill nor energy":** Vought, "Division and Reunion," 29.
30 **"God sifting the nations":** Ibid., 40.
31 **Between 1880:** Ngai, *Impossible Subjects*, 18.
32 **winning only 49.26 percent:** Cooper, *Woodrow Wilson*, 358.
32 **"The League is now":** Quoted by Tichenor, *Dividing Lines*, 141.
32 **"you can not make":** Hall, "Immigration and World War," 193.

TWO: SLAMMING THE DOOR

33 **high-school principal:** "Dr. Harry Laughlin Returns to Kirksville," *Macon Chronicle-Herald*, January 31, 1940.
33 **"The character of a nation":** House Committee on Immigration and Naturalization, *Biological Aspects of Immigration*, 66th Cong., 2d sess., 1921, 3.
33 **"comes from":** Ibid., 4.
33 **"As good Americans":** Ibid., 7.
34 **"the problem of the moron":** Ibid., 13.
34 **"Our failure to sort":** Ibid., 17.
34 **"printed in such numbers":** Ibid., 23.
34 **"expert eugenics agent":** Kevles, *Name of Eugenics*, 103.
35 **Working at an Augustinian monastery:** Ibid., 41.
35 **"The most progressive":** Ibid., 48.
36 **Amzi Davenport:** Ibid., 49.
36 **"tendency to crimes":** Davenport, *Heredity*, 218.
36 **"intense individualism":** Ibid., 216.
36 **"darker in pigmentation":** Ibid., 219.
36 **The terms *ethnicity*:** Roediger, *Working Toward Whiteness*, 18.
37 **"45 races or peoples":** Jacobson, *Whiteness*, 78.
37 **Two years later:** Cohen, *Imbeciles*, 107.

37 **Laughlin's mother:** Ibid., 104–5.

37 **"a true son":** "Sam Houston," *Eugenical News* 3, no. 1 (January 1918), 2.

38 **trained young men and women:** Kevles, *Name of Eugenics*, 55.

38 **"a sort of inventory":** "The Progress of Eugenics," *Scientific American*, December 13, 1913.

38 **By 1913:** Cohen, *Imbeciles*, 70.

38 **more than seven thousand:** Ibid., 1.

39 **a bill barring immigration:** "Two-year Bar Against Aliens, House Program," *(Baltimore) Sun*, December 3, 1920.

39 **lawmakers rolled back:** Daniels, *Guarding the Golden Door*, Kindle loc. 961.

40 **"There are only":** Quoted in Hillier, "Albert Johnson," 204.

40 **"one of the worst things":** "Immigration Views Explained by Gary," *New York Times*, April 24, 1923.

40 **"The restrictions upon immigration":** "Symposium Assails Immigration Law," *New York Times*, February 5, 1923.

40 **"New York spends millions":** "Against Any Opening for Alien Flood," *Times Herald* (Olean, N.Y.), April 28, 1923.

41 **"not meant to report":** House Committee on Immigration and Naturalization, *Analysis of America's Modern Melting Pot*, 67th Cong., 3d sess., 1922, 757.

41 **"they are both":** Ibid., 731.

41 **"the older immigrant":** Ibid., 755.

41 **"The outstanding conclusion":** Ibid. 755.

41 **"one of the most valuable":** Cohen, *Imbeciles*, 131.

41 **"If the farmer":** Spiro, *Defending*, Kindle loc. 4236.

42 **The number of immigrants:** Daniels, *Guarding the Golden Door*, loc. 1029.

42 **"the first instance":** Divine, *American Immigration*, 16.

42 **"fans the flames":** "20 Representatives Fight Bar on Aliens," *Washington Post*, February 25, 1924.

42 **"want of faith":** House Committee on Immigration and Naturalization, *Restriction of Immigration*, 68th Cong., 1st sess., January 3, 1924, 349.

43 **"largely manufactured":** House Committee on Immigration and Naturalization, *Restriction of Immigration* (to accompany H.R. 7995), 68th Congress, 1st sess., Report No. 350, 16.

43 **"The use of":** Ibid., 16.

44 **an elite New Yorker:** "John Trevor Dies; Urged Alien Law," *New York Times*, February 21, 1956.

44 **The guests:** "J.B. Trevor Weds Miss Wilmerding," *New York Times*, June 26, 1908.

44 **began to monitor:** Fischer, *Spider Web*, 98.

45 **this would allot:** Ngai, *Impossible Subjects*, 22.

45 **David A. Reed:** "Young Man to Fill Senator Knox's Shoes," *New York Times*, May 21, 1922.

45 **Mellon pushed:** Cannadine, *Mellon*, 443.

45 **"to make us":** "300,000 Aliens Yearly Is Senate Bill Limit," *New York Times*, April 4, 1924.

45 **"entirely unfair":** "America of the Melting Pot Comes to End," *New York Times*, April 27, 1924.

46 **The country's first census:** Ngai, *Impossible Subjects*, 25.

47 **In 1890:** Daniels, *Guarding the Golden Door*, loc. 815.

47 **"return home in golden brocades":** Lee, *Asian America*, 112.

47 **On the morning:** "Japanese Petition for Citizenship Is Accepted in Honolulu," *Honolulu Star-Bulletin,* October 16, 1914.

48 **Japanese-Korean Exclusion League:** Lee, *Asian America,* 125.

48 **"Anarchy is a harsh word":** "Social Order at Stake in Unhappy San Francisco," *New York Times,* May 26, 1907.

48 **mobs of white men:** Lee, *Asian America,* 126.

48 **When a delegation:** Fradkin, *Great Earthquake,* 297.

49 **"the deepest offense":** Ibid., 300–1.

49 **"a wonderful and civilized people":** Roosevelt, *Letters: Square Deal,* 1240.

49 **"purely local":** Roosevelt, *Letters: Big Stick,* 473.

50 **"horribly bothered":** Ibid., 475.

50 **"wicked absurdity":** Quoted in Daniels, *Politics of Prejudice,* 38–39.

50 **Born just south of Tokyo:** Ichioka, *Issei,* 219.

51 **In January 1915:** "Decision Held Up in Citizenship for Japanese," *Honolulu Star-Bulletin,* January 30, 1915.

51 **"I do not know":** "Ozawa's Plea for Citizenship Again Deferred," *Honolulu Star-Bulletin,* May 29, 1915.

51 **"In name, General Benedict":** Ichioka, *Issei,* 219.

51 **twenty typewritten pages:** "American at Heart—Ozawa," *Honolulu Star-Bulletin,* September 4, 1915.

52 **"in every way":** Ichioka, *Issei,* 220.

53 **Pacific Coast Japanese:** Ibid., 221–22.

53 **"face of death":** Ibid., 223.

53 **In June 1917:** "Noted Ozawa Case Goes to Supreme Court," *Honolulu Star-Bulletin,* June 1, 1917.

53 **"well qualified":** *Ozawa v. United States,* 260 U.S. 178 (1922).

54 **"The slim hope":** Ichioka, *Issei,* 226.

54 **Congressman Adolph Sabath:** Daniels, *Politics of Prejudice,* 98.

54 **"every worthy man":** House Committee on Immigration and Naturalization, *Restriction of Immigration,* 68th Cong., 1st sess., January 3, 1924, 373–74.

55 **"less assimilable":** Daniels, *Politics of Prejudice,* 99.

55 **"resented by Japan":** "Sees an Insult to Japan," *New York Times,* February 27, 1924.

55 **"I am unable":** "Hughes Would Put Japan on Equality in Immigration," *New York Times,* February 14, 1924.

55 **Wilson typed a secret letter:** Cooper, *Woodrow Wilson,* 356.

56 **"than all the admirals":** Krepon and Caldwell, *Politics of Arms Control Treaty,* 65.

56 **Hiram Johnson:** Daniels, *Politics of Prejudice,* 100.

56 **"It is indeed difficult":** Committee on Immigration, United States Senate, *Japanese Immigration Legislation,* 68th Cong., 1st sess., March 11, 12, 13, and 15, 1924, 169.

57 **"affect the validity":** *Congressional Record* 65, pt. 6, April 12, 1924, H6231.

57 **"what I had said":** Daniels, *Politics of Prejudice,* 102.

58 **President Coolidge:** "Huge Vote for Exclusion," *New York Times,* May 16, 1924.

58 **On May 26:** "Exclusion Law Is Scored," *New York Times,* May 27, 1924.

58 **"In my opinion":** "America of the Melting Pot Comes to End," *New York Times,* April 27, 1924.

58 **"America's second":** Hillier, "Albert Johnson," 208.

58 **The Tokyo press:** Divine, *American Immigration,* 21.

58 **On May 31:** "Japanese Kills Himself Near Tokio Embassy," *New York Times,* June 1, 1924.

59 **"I was never":** "Suicide Stirs Japan to Patriotic Fervor," *New York Times,* June 2, 1924.

59 **On July 1:** "Immigrants Storm Consulate in Paris," *New York Times,* July 2, 1924.

59 **A year after:** "Ellis Island Has Its Easiest July 1," *New York Times,* July 2, 1925.

59 **"You can see":** "Once More the Immigration Issue Rises," *New York Times,* January 16, 1927.

59 **total arrivals:** Ngai, *Impossible Subjects,* 272.

60 **"Today the right":** Whitman, *Hitler's American Model,* 45–46.

60 **Kikuichi Fujita:** FitzGerald and Cook-Martin, *Culling the Masses,* 104.

60 **"long and unhappy story":** Kennan, *American Diplomacy,* 52–53.

61 **In 1926:** "Fabric Store Weathered Changes," *Honolulu Star-Bulletin,* October 25, 2009; "Knowing What You Like to Wear Is Part of Her Job," *Honolulu Star-Bulletin,* June 8, 1962.

61 **On the night:** "Obituaries: Takao Ozawa," *Honolulu Star-Bulletin,* November 17, 1936.

61 **Six months:** "Sgt. G. Y. Ozawa Reportedly Killed in Italy Fighting," *Honolulu Star-Bulletin,* November 13, 1943.

THREE: A "TRAGIC BOTTLENECK"

62 **had insisted:** Goodwin, *Johnson and American Dream,* 80.

62 **As they cruised:** Gillette, *Lady Bird Johnson,* 51.

62 **"I thought that":** Smith, *President's Lady,* 38.

63 **"I just sat":** Gillette, *Lady Bird Johnson,* 51.

63 **Johnson complained:** Lyndon Johnson to Lady Bird Taylor (telegram), September 14, 1934, Courtship Letters, Johnson and Lady Bird Johnson Papers.

63 **"Tomorrow I plan":** Lyndon Johnson to Lady Bird Taylor, September 15, 1934, ibid.

63 **"had no idea":** Lady Bird Taylor to Lyndon Johnson, October 5, 1934, ibid.

63 **"Lyndon, when I":** Lady Bird Taylor to Lyndon Johnson, September 24, 1934?, ibid.

64 **sent her books:** Lyndon Johnson to Lady Bird Taylor, October 3, 1934, ibid.

64 **"thrilled":** Lady Bird Taylor to Lyndon Johnson, October 6, 1934?, ibid.

65 **"To Bird":** Woods, *LBJ,* 99.

65 **His grandfather and his aunt:** Claudia Wilson Anderson, "Congressman Lyndon B. Johnson, Operation Texas, and Jewish Immigration," *Southern Jewish History* 15 (2012): 102.

66 **"go against":** Jessie (Mrs.) Hatcher, interview 1 by Paul Bolton, March 28, 1968, 38, Oral Histories, LBJ Library.

66 **"Kukluxsonofabitch":** Caro, *Path to Power,* Kindle loc. 17879–90.

66 **In 1924:** Goodwin, *Johnson and American Dream,* 43.

66 **"My daddy always":** Ibid., 42.

67 **In 1930:** Breitman and Lichtman, *FDR and Jews,* Kindle loc. 133.

68 **When Johnson decided:** "Lyndon Johnson Was Scheduled to Visit My Austin Shul the Day After Kennedy Died," *Tablet,* November 18, 2013.

68 **"six or eight languages":** Lyndon Johnson, "Remarks in Austin at the Dedication of the Agudas Achim Synagogue," December 30, 1963, in Johnson, *Public Papers 1963–64,* 101.

69 **The law had slashed:** Breitman and Lichtman, *FDR and Jews,* Kindle loc. 507.

69 **By the most generous:** Ngai, *Impossible Subjects,* 235.

69 **"If we had behaved":** Ibid.

70 **reduced the U.S. Army:** Goodwin, *No Ordinary Time,* 23.

70 **In the spring of 1938:** Breitman and Lichtman, *FDR and Jews,* Kindle loc. 2086.

70 **"horror at the":** Ibid., loc. 1010–15.

71 **"I visited the White House":** "Asserts President Supports Protests," *New York Times,* July 31, 1935.

72 **"at last":** Breitman and Lichtman, *FDR and Jews,* Kindle loc. 1168.

72 **The next day:** "U.S. Drafts Reply to Berlin Protest," *New York Times,* August 1, 1935.

72 **"I want to assure you":** Emanuel Celler to Franklin D. Roosevelt, August 1, 1935, President's Personal File, FDR Library.

73 **"It was good of you":** Roosevelt to Celler, August 6, 1935, ibid.

74 **"infested with Jews":** Larson, *Garden of Beasts,* 30.

74 **In fiscal 1936:** Breitman and Lichtman, *FDR and Jews,* Kindle loc. 1737.

74 **On March 24:** "U.S. Asks Powers to Help Refugees Flee Nazis," *New York Times,* March 25, 1938.

75 **"Celler, to our amazement":** Breitman and Kraut, *American Refugee Policy,* 101.

75 **"The news of the past":** "President Says U.S. Is 'Shocked' by War on Jews," *Washington Post,* November 16, 1938.

75 **"to open the doors":** Simon and Alexander, *Ambivalent Welcome,* 31.

76 **One Austin journalist:** Dallek, *Lone Star Rising,* 185.

76 **He had obtained:** Ibid., 171.

76 **"When I thought":** Goodwin, *No Ordinary Time,* 91.

77 **"head like a Roman emperor":** Gillette, *Lady Bird Johnson,* 96.

77 **"a Viking princess":** Dallek, *Lone Star Rising,* 190.

77 **"Alice had a great presence":** Russell, *Lady Bird,* 128.

77 **When Marsh met Glass:** Dallek, *Lone Star Rising,* 189.

77 **briefly crossed paths:** Gillette, *Lady Bird Johnson,* 95–96.

77 **working as a secretary:** Caro, *Path to Power,* 189.

78 **"You have to understand":** Dallek, *Lone Star Rising,* 190–91.

78 **"Do you have a brain":** Woods, *LBJ,* 136.

79 **studied piano:** "Erich Leinsdorf, 81, a Conductor of Intelligence and Utility, Is Dead," *New York Times,* September 12, 1993.

79 **he had hiked:** "Musician of the Year 1963," *Musical America,* December 1963.

79 **He refused to allow:** "Salzburg Festival to Lack Germans," *New York Times,* July 8, 1937.

79 **"glorious":** "Salzburg Ovation Greets Toscanini," *New York Times,* August 3, 1937.

79 **four months:** Erich Leinsdorf, interview by Joe B. Frantz, March 8, 1969, Oral Histories, LBJ Library.

80 **"There was a constant":** Leinsdorf, *Cadenza,* 75-76.

80 **"careful":** "Conductor with Poise," *New York Times,* September 22, 1962.

80 **"You know":** "Portrait of a Moody Maestro and How He Mellowed," *New York Times,* January 2, 1977.

80 **"with a terrific shock":** Leinsdorf, *Cadenza,* 76.

80 **"a man of quick decisions":** Leinsdorf interview.

80 **"a lanky young man":** Leinsdorf, *Cadenza,* 76.

81 **"exerted his pressure":** Ibid., 77.

81 **combined the quota numbers:** Breitman and Lichtman, *FDR and the Jews,* Kindle loc. 1957.

81 **Coert Du Bois:** Anderson, "Congressman," 91.

81 **When Leinsdorf:** Ibid.

82 **"In short":** Ibid.

82 **"I did not know":** Leinsdorf interview.

82 **Gela Nowodworski:** Anderson, "Congressman," 94.

82 **Johnson would later:** A small legend has flourished, almost entirely on the Internet,

that Johnson illegally brought hundreds of Jews to Texas and saved them from the Holocaust. The story originates from a 1989 dissertation called "Operation Texas" written by
Louis Gomolak, a Ph.D. candidate at the University of Texas. Lyndon Johnson Presidential Library archivist Claudia Anderson has been unable to find proof of any such
operation.

82 **Abram Vossen Goodman:** Anderson, "Congressman," 94–95.
83 **Months earlier:** Breitman and Lichtman, *FDR and Jews*, Kindle loc. 2217.
84 **One man:** "Unable to Land in Cuba, Refugee Tries Suicide," *New York Times*, May 31, 1939.
84 **"collective suicide pact":** "Fear Suicide Wave on Refugees' Ship," *New York Times*, June 1, 1939.
84 **More than seven hundred:** Breitman and Lichtman, *FDR and Jews*, Kindle loc. 2616.
84 **an estimated 254:** Ibid., loc. 2678.
85 **"systematically building":** Ibid., loc. 2888.
85 **As a legislator:** Anderson, "Congressman," 98–99.
86 **"One thing is clear":** Goodwin, *No Ordinary Time*, 95.
87 **"We owe it":** "President Urges Congress Repeal Chinese Exclusion Act as War Aid," *New York Times*, October 12, 1943.
87 **"We can delay":** Goodwin, *No Ordinary Time*, 173.
87 **"cold and austere":** Medoff, *Blowing the Whistle*, 23.
88 **"drips with sympathy":** "Jews Debarred, Celler Declares," *New York Times*, December 12, 1943.
88 **"Unless remedial steps":** "Report to the Secretary on the Acquiescence of This Govern-ment in the Murder of the Jews," January 13, 1944, Morgenthau Diaries 693, pp. 212, 229, FDR Library.

FOUR: "A LAND OF GREAT RESPONSIBILITIES"

90 **"In the long cabinet room":** Hamby, *Man of the People*, 293.
90 **"I don't know":** "Congress to Hear Truman Monday," *New York Times*, April 14, 1945.
91 **"just a heartbeat":** McCullough, *Truman*, 308.
91 **"Well, you tell him":** Ferrell, *Truman: A Life*, 170.
91 **"I've never":** Ibid., 171.
91 **John Truman:** Ibid., 6.
91 **a four-volume set:** McCullough, *Truman*, 43.
92 **His aging father:** Ferrell, *Truman: A Life*, 38.
92 **"I have been working":** Harry Truman to Bess Truman, in Ferrell, *Dear Bess*, 88.
92 **"a job somebody":** McCullough, *Truman*, 103.
93 **"I know nothing":** Ferrell, *Truman: A Life*, 198
93 **Truman committed:** Ibid., 199.
93 **"made him sick":** Ferrell, *Truman in the White House*, 72.
94 **"most important":** Beschloss, *Conquerors*, Kindle loc. 849.
94 **"a difficult chap":** Keynes, *Collected Writings*, 87–88.
94 **"You can't be vindictive":** Beschloss, *Conquerors*, Kindle loc. 4147.
94 **"hear from me":** Ibid., loc. 3994.
94 **"likes me":** Diary entry, May 9, 1945, Morgenthau Diaries, 1581, FDR Presidential Library.
95 **more than 7 million:** Dinnerstein, *America and Survivors*, 9.
95 **roughly sixty thousand:** Ibid., 28.
95 **"What good":** Edward D. McKim to Truman, May 28, 1945, Truman Papers.

95 **"I have about"**: Harry Truman to Henry Morgenthau, June 2, 1945, Official File, Truman Papers.

95 **"I wonder"**: Penkower, "Earl Harrison Report," 11.

95 **Earl Harrison**: Stevens, "Life and Character of Harrison," 593.

96 **"It is important"**: Penkower, "Earl Harrison Report," 17–18.

96 **"Seldom have I"**: Earl Harrison diary, entry for July 24, 1945, Harrison Papers.

96 **about thirty camps**: Dinnerstein, *America and Survivors,* 39.

96 **Harrison's full report**: Ibid., 291–94.

97 **"As matters now stand"**: Ibid., 300–1.

97 **"systematic slaughter"**: Cohen, *Truman and Israel,* 36–37.

97 **"For weeks"**: Harry S. Truman, interview in *Motion Picture MP2002-289,* Screen Gems Collection in association with Ben Gradus, ca. 1961–63, Harry S. Truman Library.

98 **"Harry, this is"**: Hamby, *Man of the People,* 22.

98 **"What happened"**: Truman interview.

98 **"highest humanitarian"**: Radosh and Radosh, *Safe Haven,* 94.

98 **"As a general rule"**: Dinnerstein, *America and Survivors,* 13

98 **"believe that the"**: Ibid., 16–17.

99 **"The lowest thing"**: Ibid., 24.

99 **"clean up the conditions"**: Harry S. Truman to Dwight D. Eisenhower, August 31, 1945, Official Files (Truman administration), 1945–1953, National Archives.

99 **"because they realized"**: Dinnerstein, *America and Survivors,* 296.

100 **"help bring about"**: Judis, *Genesis,* 192.

100 **"would do nothing"**: Ibid., 192

101 **Eight days**: Radosh and Radosh, *Safe Haven,* 58.

101 **"although President Roosevelt"**: Joseph Grew to Harry S. Truman, May 1, 1945, President's Secretary's File, Truman Library.

101 **"at all costs"**: Donovan, *Conflict and Crisis,* 313.

101 **"No single matter"**: Radosh and Radosh, *Safe Haven,* 95.

101 **"set aflame"**: Ibid., 100.

102 **"I sincerely wish"**: Daniels, *Immigration and the Legacy of Harry S. Truman,* Kindle loc. 1474–85.

102 **"just another British"**: Radosh and Radosh, *Safe Haven,*115.

103 **At fifty-two**: Beschloss, *Conquerors,* Kindle loc. 829.

103 **"The Nazi terrors"**: Celler, *You Never Leave Brooklyn,* 113.

103 **groups like**: Dinnerstein, *America and Survivors,* 263.

103 **In January 1946**: Simon and Alexander, *Ambivalent Welcome,* 32.

104 **Bess often mailed**: Ferrell, *Dear Bess,* 183.

104 **"This is to buy"**: Fields, *My 21 Years,* 134–36.

104 **"The immensity"**: Truman, *Public Papers,* 1:572.

105 **"May God bless you"**: Graber, *Haven,* 135–36.

105 **"being born again"**: Walter Greenberg, interview (video), August 6, 1994, Oral History, United States Holocaust Memorial Museum, https://collections.ushmm.org/search/catalog/irn512748.

106 **"You're asking"**: Gruber, *Haven,* 250.

106 **"In the circumstances"**: "Truman Statement on Displaced Persons," *New York Times,* December 23, 1945.

106 **On January 17**: Gruber, *Haven,* 279.

106 **only about 13,000**: Dinnerstein, *America and Survivors,* 113.

106 **In the first**: Divine, *American Immigration,* 113.

107 **more than 100,000:** Dinnerstein, *America and Survivors*, 112.

107 **"Jesus Christ":** Radosh and Radosh, *Safe Haven*, 177.

107 **his first extended:** "Truman Will Sail on Yacht Today for 18-Day New England Cruise," *New York Times*, August 16, 1946.

107 **"must assume":** "Mr. Truman on Refugees," *New York Times*, August 17, 1946.

108 **"dangerous precedent":** "Senator Is Against Plan for Refugees," *New York Times*, September 3, 1946.

108 **"result in catastrophe":** Joseph Proskauer to American Jewish Committee, Box 18, Celler Papers, Library of Congress.

109 **Two days later:** "Drive Is Opened to Admit 100,000 Jews into U.S.," *New York Herald Tribune*, October 10, 1946.

109 **"These circumstances":** Ibid.

109 **midterm elections:** Ferrell, *Truman: A Life*, 218; McCullough, *Truman*, 520.

109 **"all good citizens":** McCullough, *Truman*, 529.

109 **"the limitation of":** Truman, *Public Papers*, 3:10, 12.

110 **"We are completing":** Harrison to Celler, Celler Papers, Library of Congress.

110 **million-dollar budget:** Dinnerstein, *America and Survivors*, 126.

110 **William G. Stratton:** "Populist Governor Built State's Highway System," *Chicago Tribune*, March 4, 2001.

110 **"The idea":** Dinnerstein, *America and Survivors*, 132.

110 **"We could solve":** Ibid., 139–40.

111 **"Many of those":** Ibid., 140.

111 **"I have heard":** Ibid., 138.

111 **"now trying":** Frank J. Quin to Emanuel Celler, January 6, 1947, Celler Papers, Library of Congress.

111 **"Just as the human":** Celler to Quin, January 8, 1947, ibid.

112 **"The tasks":** Divine, *American Immigration*, 116.

112 **"our political institutions":** Dinnerstein, *America and Survivors*, 145.

112 **"has become a lawless":** "Would Halt Immigration," *(Baltimore) Sun*, May 23, 1947.

112 **the RKO film:** Dinnerstein, *America and Survivors*, 127.

113 **"it is about time":** "Send Them Here!" *Life*, September 23, 1946, 36.

113 **"a very definite":** "Bill on Displaced Faces Stiff Fight," *New York Times*, May 18, 1947.

114 **"booby trap":** Dinnerstein, *America and Survivors*, 171–72.

114 **"wasn't 'half a loaf'":** Celler, *You Never Leave Brooklyn*, 96.

114 **"the most anti-Semitic":** Dinnerstein, *America and Survivors*, 176.

114 **"would rather":** Ibid., 168.

114 **"with very great reluctance":** Truman, *Public Papers*, 4:382–83.

FIVE: A SON OF NEVADA

116 **"Every citizen":** Hubert Humphrey, address to Democratic National Convention, Philadelphia, July 14, 1948, Speech Text Files, Humphrey Papers.

116 **Truman watched:** Pietrusza, *1948*, 232.

116 **"a lonely figure":** Emanuel Celler, interview by Ronald J. Grele, April 3, 1978, 21, Association of Former Members of Congress, Oral History Collection, Manuscript Division, Library of Congress.

116 **"is no longer":** Fite, *Richard B. Russell*, 240.

116 **"Never have I seen":** M. Truman, *Harry Truman,* Kindle loc. 219.

116 **As the band played:** Pietrusza, *1948*, 233.

117 **"Get those damned":** Ibid., 234.

117 **"lifted the delegates"**: Ferrell, *Truman: A Life*, 270.

118 **"a foregone conclusion"**: "Talk Is Now Turning to the Dewey Cabinet," *New York Times*, October 24, 1948.

118 **"Does he really think"**: Ferrell, *Truman: A Life*, 270.

118 **He spent**: McCullough, *Truman*, 705; Hamby, *Man of the People*, 463.

118 **"Crow Banquet"**: Giangreco and Moore, *Dear Harry*, 171–72.

118 **"As I said en route"**: Ibid.

119 **"If we revise"**: Divine, *American Immigration*, 133.

119 **Standing five-foot-seven**: Ybarra, *Washington Gone Crazy*, 185.

120 **"an earth-shaking force"**: Ibid., 7.

120 **"There is nothing"**: McCarran, television talk on UNESCO, Fall 1952 (transcript), Box 1, Adams Papers.

120 **"an open door"**: Dinnerstein, *America and Survivors*, 218

120 **"There goes"**: Nevins, *Lehman and His Era*, 316.

120 **His parents**: McCarran autobiographical material, Box 3, Adams Papers.

121 **Each day**: Edwards, *Pat McCarran*, 2.

121 **his father promised**: McCarran autobiographical material, Adams Papers.

121 **graduated**: Edwards, *Pat McCarran*, 3.

121 **"McCarran defended"**: Ibid., 14.

122 **"One particular"**: Ibid., 48

122 **"believe they have"**: Ibid., 53.

123 **Even a janitor**: Ibid., 105.

123 **"This is the first"**: *Congressional Record* 81, pt. 6, July 10, 1937, S7022; Edwards, *Pat McCarran*, 78.

124 **"When a mayor"**: McCullough, *Truman*, 589.

124 **"The president's control"**: "Rugged Days for the Majority Leader," *New York Times*, July 3, 1949.

124 **"a taste for snappy"**: "National Affairs: Party Man," *Time*, January 10, 1949.

125 **"His outstanding achievement"**: Marquis Childs, "McCarran's Prize Obstructionism," *Washington Post*, April 16, 1949.

125 **"a despicable charge"**: "Senators Plan to Blast Out DP Measure Unless McCarran Group Acts by Mid-August," *Washington Post*, July 27, 1949.

125 **"no reason"**: "No DP Bills Plans, McCarran Asserts," *Washington Post*, July 28, 1949.

125 **"Senator McCarran happens"**: "German Press," *Washington Post*, July 11, 1949.

125 **"groundswell of public"**: "M'Carran Scorns Celler's DP Plea," *New York Times*, August 19, 1949.

126 **"inefficiency, neglect"**: "To Propose Board to Rule Air Lines," *(Baltimore) Sun*, January 9, 1935.

126 **"There is only"**: "More Power for President Becomes Issue," *(Baltimore) Sun*, May 13, 1938.

127 **"Not only"**: "Senate Accords President Wide Aviation Power," *Washington Post*, May 14, 1938.

127 **McCarran ended up**: "M'Carran Air Bill Passed by Senate," *New York Times*, May 17, 1938.

127 **The Roosevelt White House**: "On Capitol Hill: Senator Lonergan Must Have Swim Despite Campaign; McCarran Completely Ignored," *Washington Post*, July 9, 1938.

127 **"I do not know"**: Edwards, *Pat McCarran*, 85.

127 **"the great gambling"**: Ferrell, *Off the Record*, 317.

127 **"Truman will go"**: Ybarra, *Washington Gone Crazy*, 689.

127 **"might produce"**: Dinnerstein, *America and Survivors*, 229.

128 **"invading"**: "Lucas Pledges Aid to GOP on DP Bill," *Washington Post,* August 11, 1949.

128 **"ordinarily"**: "Lucas Lays Fuse to Blast DP Bill Out," *Washington Post,* August 25, 1949.

128 **"The smallest State"**: "Pooh Bah McCarran," *Washington Post,* August 30, 1949.

129 **"Since I am defending"**: "M'Carran Fears DP Burden Here," *New York Times,* September 15, 1949.

129 **"I wouldn't give"**: Ybarra, *Washington Gone Crazy,* 467.

129 **"serious mistake"**: "M'Carran Charges Fraud in DP Set-Up," *New York Times,* October 8, 1949.

129 **"to tear down"**: Dinnerstein, *America and Survivors,* 231.

130 **His maternal grandfather:** Annis, *Big James Eastland,* 16.

130 **His father:** Zwiers, *Senator Eastland,* Kindle loc. 221–31.

130 **drove a car:** Ibid., loc. 231.

130 **"I hear folks say"**: "The South: The Authentic Voice," *Time,* March 26, 1956, 27.

130 **served as district attorney:** Zwiers, *Senator Eastland,* Kindle loc. 221.

130 **"My father"**: Ibid., loc. 231.

131 **In 1932:** Ibid., loc. 272.

131 **Governor Paul Johnson:** Ibid., loc. 363.

131 **"Colorless, closemouthed"**: "The South: The Authentic Voice," *Time,* March 26, 1956, 28.

131 **"Cotton obsessed"**: Vance, *Human Geography,* 266, 270.

131 **"I call on"**: "Political Notes: Prince of the Peckerwoods," *Time,* July 1, 1946.

132 **"maintain control"**: "The South: The Authentic Voice," *Time,* March 26, 1956, 26.

132 **"would rape"**: Congressional Record 92, pt. 1, January 23, 1946, S253.

132 **"I am not"**: Zwiers, *Senator Eastland,* 67.

133 **"All we have"**: "South Urged to Run Own Candidate," *Washington Post,* February 10, 1948.

133 **The move:** "President Declines Comment on Eastland's Appointment," *Atlanta Daily World,* September 18, 1949.

134 **"It was rough treatment"**: "Committee, 7-3, Reports DP Bill; Filibuster in Prospect for Senate," *New York Times,* October 13, 1949.

134 **"I wish"**: Ybarra, *Washington Gone Crazy,* 471.

134 **"What this comes down to"**: Ibid.

134 **"take a two-week trip"**: "Liberalization of DP Bill Put Off Until 1950 by Senate," *Washington Post,* October 16, 1949.

134 **On the afternoon of:** Ibid.

135 **"no more than burial"**: Ibid.

136 **"My visit with Franco"**: Ybarra, *Washington Gone Crazy,* 473.

136 **When Truman was asked:** "McCarran Acting on Own in Spain, Truman Declares," *Washington Post,* September 16, 1949.

136 **"with a little"**: "McCarran Gives Tips to Franco," *Washington Post,* November 23, 1949.

136 **"far better than"**: "DPs in Europe Living Well, McCarran Says," *Washington Post,* December 8, 1949.

137 **A survey:** Edwards, *Pat McCarran,* 140.

137 **"most expendable"**: "The Senate's Most Expendable," *Time,* March 20, 1950, 20.

137 **"This money"**: "M'Carran Charges D.P. Law Failure," *New York Times,* January 7, 1950.

137 **Richard Arens:** "McCarran and His Man Dekom," *Washington Post,* February 23, 1950.

138 **"That man has"**: "Richard Arens, Ex-House Aide," *New York Times,* October 27, 1969.

138 **"every patriotic American"**: Dinnerstein, *America and Survivors,* 241.

138 **"outside pressure groups"**: Series 1: Senate Office Files, 1922–1960, Box 5, Adams Papers.

138 **"a New York invasion"**: Ibid.,140.

138 **"Jew money"**: McCarran to Petersen, January 19, 1050, Box 2, Petersen Papers.

138 **"any particular element"**: Dinnerstein, *America and Survivors*, 235

139 **popular support**: Ibid., 246.

139 **Whereas the law**: Divine, *American Immigration*, 141.

139 **"with very great"**: Harry Truman, Statement by the President, June 16, 1950, Official File, Truman Papers.

140 **"of Protestant and Orthodox faith"**: Daniels, *Guarding the Golden Door*, Kindle locs. 2151–62, 2176–87, 2202

140 **Zinaida Supe**: "200,000th Displaced Person Honored at City Hall," *New York Times*, December 21, 1950.

140 **"God love America"**: "New Americans One Year Later," *Life*, December 26, 1949.

140 **"You son of a"**: Dinnerstein, *America and Survivors*, 248.

SIX: INTERNAL SECURITY

142 **Herbert Lehman of New York**: Tananbaum, *Lehman*, Kindle loc. 7753.

142 **Just a month**: "Mrs. Rosenberg to Be Named Assistant Defense Secretary," *New York Times*, November 10, 1950.

142 **a petite and charming**: Nelson, "Rosenberg, 'Honorary Man,'" 135–36, 138–39.

143 **"She knows more"**: "Anna Rosenberg Hoffman Dead; Consultant and 50's Defense Aide," *New York Times*, May 10, 1983.

144 **When McCarthy returned**: Nevins, *Lehman and His Era*, 336.

144 **"Nearly all"**: Ibid., 334–35.

144 **"I hope to"**: Nevins, *Lehman and His Era*, 312

144 **"felt a very"**: Ibid.

144 **"If I were"**: Ibid., 317.

145 **"one of the most"**: Tananbaum, *Lehman*, Kindle loc. 7757.

145 **"Jewess"**: Nelson, "Caught in the Web," 179.

145 **"While our boys"**: Ibid, 180.

146 **"He is a liar"**: Ibid., 181

146 **Two weeks after**: "Namesake Is Found in Rosenberg Case," *New York Times*, December 20, 1950.

146 **His father**: Nevins, *Lehman and His Era*, 4-5.

147 **"He is a business"**: Ibid., 10

147 **By the time**: Ibid., 49.

147 **"the poverty"**: Tananbaum, *Lehman*, Kindle loc. 276.

148 **"You know the job"**: Nevins, *Lehman and His Era*, 102–4.

148 **"He refused"**: Ibid., 354.

149 **"I let Herbert"**: Tananbaum, *Lehman*, loc. 1071

149 **"He will think"**: Ibid., loc. 1069.

149 **"Louis Howe"**: Ibid.

149 **The chief feature**: "Internal Security Act," *CQ Almanac 1950*, 6th ed., 390–98. Washington, D.C.: Congressional Quarterly, 1951, http://library.cqpress.com/cqalmanac/cqal50-1378031.

150 **"He'd come into"**: Nevins, *Lehman and His Era*, 323.

150 **"the most dangerous"**: Tananbaum, *Lehman*, loc. 7403–15.

151 **"I am going to vote"**: Ibid., loc. 7465.

151 **"a special accolade"**: "Letters to the Times," *New York Times*, September 18. 1950.

151 **"Even in"**: "Veto Likely for Anti-Red Bill," *New York Times*, September 22, 1950.

151 **"Failure on your part"**: Joseph McCarthy to Truman, February 11, 1950, President's Secretary's Files, Truman Papers.

151 **"Your telegram is"**: Truman to McCarthy (unsent draft), ibid.

152 **"a message"**: Tananbaum, *Lehman*, Kindle loc. 7487.

152 **"about as practical"**: Truman, "Veto of the Internal Security Bill," September 22, 1950, Truman Papers.

152 **"one of the great"**: Tananbaum, *Lehman*, Kindle loc. 7511.

152 **officials at Ellis Island**: "127 Aliens Now Held on Ellis Island for Inquiry Under New Security Act," *New York Times*, October 10, 1950.

153 **Between September**: Loescher and Scanlan, *Calculated Kindness*, 29.

153 **"spending millions"**: Ibid., 36–37.

154 **"many inequities"**: "Celler-McCarran Clash Opens Hearing on Immigration Laws," *Washington Post*, March 7, 1951.

154 **"I believe"**: *Congressional Record* 99, pt. 2, March 2, 1953, S1518.

155 **For two years**: Divine, *American Immigration*, 165–66.

155 **"without giving credence"**: Ibid., 166–67.

156 **"implies the doctrine"**: Bernard, *American Immigration Policy*, 260, 262.

157 **"He was a rough"**: "Francis E. Walter," *Washington Post*, June 2, 1963.

157 **A World War I veteran**: "25 Years After Death, Walter Still Controversial," *Morning Call (Allentown, Pa.)*, February 28, 1988.

157 **In 1944**: "The Washington Merry-Go-Round," *El Paso Times*, June 13, 1944.

157 **befuddling**: "Representative Walter Dies of Leukemia at Age of 69," *(Baltimore) Sun*, June 1, 1963.

157 **Celler was the first**: *Congressional Record* 98, pt. 4, April 23, 1952, H4304–5.

157 **"would have the effect"**: Ibid., H4313.

157 **"It seems"**: Ibid., H4314.

158 **"sub-clause (b)"**: Felix S. Cohen, "The Position of Immigrants Under the McCarran Omnibus Immigration Bill," October 29, 1951, Immigration—Letters and Memoranda, David Lloyd Files, Truman Papers.

159 **"Today . . . as never"**: *Congressional Record* 98, pt. 4, April 23, 1952, S5089.

159 **"xenophobic" and "racist"**: Ibid., S5102.

159 **"an insult"**: Tananbaum, *Lehman*, Kindle loc. 7927.

160 **"apathetic chamber"**: "Alien Bill Passed Intact by Senate; Foes Rely on Veto," *New York Times*, May 23, 1952.

160 **A Gallup poll**: Ferrell, *Off the Record*, 358.

160 **"making his diurnal"**: Ibid., 357–58.

161 **"eight years"**: Hamby, *Man of the People*, 599.

161 **"guffawed"**: "Alien Bill Passed Intact by Senate; Foes Rely on Veto," *New York Times*, May 23, 1952.

161 **On June 20**: William J. Hopkins, June 20, 1952, Immigration Policy: President Truman's Veto of the McCarran-Walter Act, President's Secretary's Files, Truman Library.

161 **Walter Besterman**: Masaoka and Hosokawa, *They Call Me*, 237.

161 **When Masaoka**: Ibid., 222.

161 **one time**: Ibid., 114–15.

163 **Masaoka's father**: Ibid., 24, 27–28.

163 **"When an alien"**: Ibid., 42–43.

163 **The white lawmakers**: Ibid., 87.

164 **"If, in the judgment"**: Ibid., 88.

164 **"There are politicians"**: Hosokawa, *Nisei*, 361.

164 **"never to do":** Ibid., 362.

164 **"In my lifetime":** Masaoka, *They Call Me,* 124–25.

165 **"The principle":** Hosokawa, *Nisei,* 366.

165 **The 442nd regiment:** Lee, *Asian America,* 242.

166 **As a boy:** Edwards, *Missionary for Freedom,* Kindle loc. 355–65.

166 **"welded":** Ibid., loc. 847.

166 **At one point:** Ibid., loc. 1286, 1295.

166 **Over two years:** Ibid., loc. 1392–401.

167 **He would lift:** Ibid., loc. 127.

167 **His pace:** Ibid., loc. 1604.

167 **On the morning:** Ibid., loc. 1614.

167 **He went:** Ibid., loc. 4362.

167 **In the dark:** Ibid., loc. 4394.

167 **"Abraham Lincoln's task":** Ibid., loc. 837.

167 **His first speech:** Ibid., locs. 1783, 1812.

167 **"influence greatly":** Divine, *American Immigration,* 155.

168 **"What then":** Edwards, *Missionary for Freedom,* 3009–19.

168 **Each year thousands:** Jane Hong, "A Cross-Fire Between Minorities," *Pacific Historical Review* 87, no. 4 (Fall 2018): 680.

168 **"House evidently":** Ibid., 683.

169 **"Certainly":** Ibid., 685.

169 **"should have":** Masaoka, *They Call Me,* 221.

169 **"I had learned":** Ibid., 222–23.

170 **"Well, I'm a Republican":** Edwards, *Missionary for Freedom,* Kindle locs. 1841, 1860.

170 **"This is such":** Department of State, Memorandum on H.R. 5678 Immigration and Nationality Bill, ca. May 1952, Immigration—Letters and Memoranda, David Lloyd Files, Truman Papers.

171 **"This McCarran bill":** A. Philip Randolph to President Truman, May 29, 1952, Official File, Truman Papers.

171 **"would be a repudiation":** Harry N. Rosenfield to President Truman (memo with attachment), June 12, 1952, White House Bill File, Truman Papers.

171 **"embedded in a mass":** "Text of Truman's Message to House on Veto of Immigration Bill," *New York Times,* June 26, 1952.

172 **"one of the most":** Tananbaum, *Lehman,* Kindle loc. 7959.

172 **"We know that":** Phyllis Craig to President Truman, June 26, 1952, Official File, Truman Library.

173 **"In God's name":** *Congressional Record* 98, pt. 6, June 25, 1952, S8255.

173 **"If we lost":** Masaoka, *They Call Me,* 232.

173 **"a myth":** *Congressional Record* 98, pt. 6, June 25, 1952, S8256.

173 **"to perpetuate":** Ibid., S8259.

173 **"an insult":** Ibid., S8267.

174 **"the consummation":** "Text of McCarran Statement on New Act," *New York Times,* December 25, 1952.

174 **"a lot less":** "Humphrey Rips Own Party over Alien Bill," *Washington Post,* June 29, 1952.

174 **"I am certainly":** President Truman to Estes Kefauver, June 30, 1952, President's Secretary's Files, Truman Library.

174 **"My ultimate objective":** Emanuel Celler to Herbert Lehman, December 22, 1952, Lehman Papers.

175 **"impossible to compute"**: Committee on Law and Social Action of the American Jewish Congress, "Analysis of House Debate on Walter Omnibus Immigration Bill H.R. 5678," Edelstein Papers.

175 **"I blessed"**: Masaoka, *They Call Me*, 237.

SEVEN: AN IRISH BRAHMIN

176 **"Goddamn it"**: Dallek, *Unfinished Life*, 3.

177 **"shriveling to bits"**: William De Marco, interview by Frank Bucci, April 8, 1964, 1–3, Oral History Collection, JFK Library.

177 **"Honey Fitz"**: Dallek, *Unfinished Life*, 9–10.

177 **"one of the most"**: Goodwin, *Fitzgeralds and Kennedys*, 201.

178 **"Joe used to talk"**: Ibid., 699.

178 **"I'm just filling"**: Dallek, *Unfinished Life*, 123.

179 **During his first week**: Ibid., 5.

179 **Georgetown townhouse**: Ibid., 150.

179 **"I never felt"**: Ibid., 136.

179 **"The point is"**: Ibid., 154.

179 **"I think from the time"**: Ibid., 135.

180 **"It is fashionable"**: Ibid., 102.

181 **who counted Joseph McCarthy**: Nasaw, *Patriarch*, Kindle loc. 11960.

181 **"To Eunice and Bob"**: Reeves, *Life and Times of McCarthy*, 203.

181 **"How dare you"**: Robert Armory, Jr., interview by Joseph E. O'Connor, February 9, 1966, 2–3, Oral History Collection, JFK Library.

181 **"The failure"**: Dallek, *Unfinished Life*, 160.

182 **the sting of social rejection**: Nasaw, *Patriarch*, Kindle loc. 826.

182 **several friends**: Goodwin, *Fitzgeralds and Kennedys*, 473.

182 **"a bunch of ignorant"**: Ibid.

183 **"Anti-Semitism"**: Nasaw, *Patriarch*, 582.

183 **"We were in a real"**: Goodwin, *Fitzgeralds and Kennedys*, 763.

183 **"Remember"**: Ibid.

184 **"Even for the president"**: Harry N. Rosenfield, interview by James R. Fuchs, July 23, 1980, Truman Library.

184 **"contains more inequities"**: John O'Grady, "The McCarran Immigration Bill," *Commonweal*, entered into *Congressional Record* 98, pt. 6, June 27, 1952, S8263.

184 **Weeks before the election**: "Truman Calls Ike Captive of Nazi-Like GOP," *Washington Post*, October 18, 1952.

185 **"second-class citizenship"**: "Charges Nominee Accepts 'Master Race' Theory of New Alien Law," *New York Times*, October 18, 1952.

185 **"disgusting exhibition"**: "Truman Calls Ike Captive of Nazi-Like GOP," *Washington Post*, October 18, 1952.

185 **"un-American"**: John F. Kennedy, "Statement Before Perlman Committee on Immigration and Naturalization," Pre-Presidential Papers, Congressional Campaign Files, 1946–1958, Kennedy Papers.

185 **Perlman thanked him**: Philip B. Perlman to Kennedy, September 11, 1952, Campaign Files, 1952 Campaign, Kennedy Papers.

186 **"Massachusetts needs"**: Press Release, Campaign Files, 1952 Campaign, Box 100, Kennedy Papers.

186 **Impellitteri**: Vincent R. Impellitteri, "Remarks in Behalf of Congressman John F. Kennedy," Boston, October 27, 1952, Campaign Files, 1952 Campaign, Kennedy Papers.

186 "CHAMPION OF HUMAN RIGHTS": Tananbaum, *Lehman*, Kindle loc. 10849.

187 **Among Catholic precincts:** Dallek, *Unfinished Life*, 175.

187 **"I think that you":** Ibid.

187 **"Sometimes in reading":** Nasaw, *Patriarch*, 670.

188 *Oxford English Dictionary:* Roediger, *Working Toward Whiteness*, 21.

188 **"most of the immigrant":** Jacobson, *Whiteness*, 98.

189 **the son of Russian:** Tyler Anbinder, "Boston's Immigrants and the Making of American Immigration History," *Journal of American Ethnic History* 32, no. 3 (Spring 2013): 19–21.

190 **"Once I thought to":** Handlin, *Uprooted*, 3.

190 **"He reoriented":** "Oscar Handlin, Historian Who Chronicled U.S. Immigration, Dies at 95," *New York Times*, September 23, 2011.

191 **"Two wars":** Oscar Handlin, statement to President's Commission on Immigration and Naturalization, Box 8, Presidential Commissions and Boards (RG 220), Truman Library.

191 **the commission's full report:** Commission on Immigration and Naturalization, *Whom We Shall Welcome* (Washington, D.C.: U.S. Government Printing Office, 1953).

192 **"ought to receive":** Harry S. Truman, statement on *Whom We Shall Welcome*, January 5, 1953, Truman Papers.

192 **"does not contain":** "President's Board Favors Rewriting of Immigration Act," *New York Times*, January 2, 1953.

192 **"How do I know":** Edwards, *Missionary for Freedom*, 195–96.

193 **"You know, they're":** Rosenfield interview.

193 **"Every man":** Edwards, *Missionary for Freedom*, 197–98.

193 **"His work":** Ibid., 199.

193 **"He was a giant":** *Congressional Record* 100, pt. 2, November 9, 1954, S15902.

194 **"I moved up":** Nevins, *Lehman and His Era*, 346.

194 **In June 1954:** Tananbaum, *Lehman*, Kindle loc. 8248.

194 **"tended to bring":** "Colleagues Bring Their Judgement on 2 Counts," *Washington Post*, December 3, 1954.

195 **"one of the most poignant":** "Senate Pauses to Honor Johnson," *Washington Post*, July 6, 1955.

195 **"What I wish to":** Caro, *Master of the Senate*, 629–30.

195 **"Seldom in the history":** *Congressional Record* 101, pt. 8, July 5, 1955, S9839–40.

195 **"one of the most important":** Tananbaum, *Lehman*, Kindle loc. 9724.

195 **"speak of it":** Ibid., Kindle loc. 9731.

195 **"Johnson didn't enjoy":** Goodwin, *Fitzgeralds and Kennedys*, 132–33.

196 **"You'll be ignored":** Caro, *Master of the Senate*, 460.

196 **"liberal doer":** Goodwin, *Fitzgeralds and Kennedys*, 132.

196 **"He wouldn't return":** Caro, *Master of the Senate*, 567–68.

197 **He coveted:** Tananbaum, *Lehman*, Kindle loc. 9702.

198 **"any progress":** Ibid., loc. 9901.

198 **"something cooked up":** *Congressional Record* 102, pt. 2, July 27, 1956, S14999.

198 **"designed not only":** Ibid., S15004.

199 **"I know the bill":** Ibid., S15012.

199 **From midafternoon:** "New Alien Law Lost in Rush to Adjourn," *Washington Post*, August 1, 1956.

199 **"particularly disheartened":** Tananbaum, *Lehman*, Kindle loc. 9958

200 **"only token opposition":** "New Alien Law Lost in Rush to Adjourn," *Washington Post*, August 1, 1956.

200 **a cross was burned:** "Cross Is Set Ablaze at Warren's Home," *New York Times,* July 15, 1956.

200 **"A fight is worthwhile":** Tananbaum, *Lehman,* Kindle loc. 14497.

201 **nine months later:** Kennedy to John Foster Dulles, June 28, 1958, Kennedy Papers.

201 **"Everywhere within":** *Congressional Record* 104, pt. 10, June 30, 1958, S12661.

202 **"Jack is the greatest":** Goodwin, *Fitzgeralds and Kennedys,* 792.

EIGHT: A BOLD PROPOSAL

203 **On January 21:** Sorensen, *Kennedy,* 248.

203 **"Do you think":** Ibid., 249.

204 **"the White House's anonymous man":** "Myer Feldman, 92, Adviser to Kennedy, Dies," *New York Times,* March 3, 2007.

204 **"You were far more":** Ted Sorensen to Myer Feldman, January 23, 1965, Feldman Papers.

204 **"Nixopedia":** Sorensen, *Kennedy,* 176.

204 **"Good morning":** "Witness to the New Frontier," *Pennsylvania Law Journal* 40, no. 1 (Spring 2005): 34.

204 **his first executive order:** Executive Order 10914, "Providing for an Expanded Program of Food Distribution to Needy Families," *Federal Register* 26, no. 14 (January 24, 1961), 639, National Archives.

204 **"I understand that":** Frederick G. Dutton to Myer Feldman, January 31, 1961, Box 53, Feldman Papers.

204 **Himself the son:** "Counsel to Kennedy Myer Feldman; Vital to Special Olympics," *Washington Post,* March 3, 2007.

205 **"I went home":** Myer Feldman, interview by Charles T. Morrissey, January 23, 1966, 1–2, Oral History Collection, JFK Library.

205 **"We have every confidence":** Myer Feldman to Oscar Cohen, February 11, 1959; Cohen to Feldman, February 13, 1959, both in Kennedy Papers.

206 **both political parties:** Daniels, *Guarding the Golden Door,* Kindle loc. 2512.

207 **"I am deeply convinced":** Herbert H. Lehman, address to Annual Meeting of United HIAS Service, February 5, 1961, Feldman Papers.

207 **"This is the first":** H. H. Bookbinder to Myer Feldman, February 10, 1961, Feldman Papers.

207 **"Each day the crises":** John F. Kennedy, "Annual Message to the Congress on the State of the Union," January 30, 1961, *American Presidency Project,* https://www.presidency .ucsb.edu/documents/annual-message-the-congress-the-state-the-union-5.

207 **One day after:** Dallek, *Unfinished Life,* 356.

208 **"Every president":** Sorensen, *Kennedy,* 291.

208 **"you sounded":** Julius Edelstein to Myer Feldman, April 21, 1961, Feldman Papers.

208 **"It really is true":** Dallek, *Unfinished Life,* 370.

209 **"Congressmen liked Kennedy":** O'Brien, *Kennedy,* 581.

209 **"Why fight":** Ibid.

209 **"The man in charge":** "The Melting Pot of Francis E. Walter," *Reporter,* October 26, 1961, 24–28.

210 **"first impulse":** Goodman, *Committee,* 370.

211 **"junked entirely":** Edward Corsi, statement to President's Commission on Immigration and Naturalization, Presidential Commissions and Boards (RG 220), Truman Library.

211 **"poor judgment":** "Walter Testifies He Urged Dulles to Dismiss Corsi," *New York Times,* April 16, 1955.

211 **"I am quite certain"**: Ibid.

211 **"a shameless surrender"**: "Corsi Ties Ouster to His Liberalism on Refugee Act," *New York Times*, April 10, 1955.

211 **"I symbolize"**: "Coris Embittered by Dulles Ouster," *New York Times*, April 9, 1955.

212 **1960 HUAC hearing**: "Distortions," *Washington Post*, December 28, 1960.

212 **"reappeared during"**: Goodman, *Committee*, 443.

212 **"I'm just doing"**: "Rep. Francis Walter, 69 Dies; Wrote Immigration Restrictions," *New York Times*, June 1, 1963.

212 **he was furious**: "Walter Scores 2 Security Aides; Would Abolish Office They Head," *New York Times*, July 7, 1961.

212 **"bureaucratic guerrilla warfare"**: Murrey Marder, "State's Insecure Security Boss Resigns," *Washington Post*, December 20, 1961.

213 **"I just want you"**: Roger W. Jones (confidential memo), "Subject: Telephone Conversation with Congressman Walter," June 28, 1961, Feldman Papers.

213 **"we would run"**: Ibid.

213 **"It sometimes has"**: Kennedy, *True Compass*, 22.

214 **"You can have"**: Ibid., 40.

214 **"Listen"**: Clymer, *Edward Kennedy*, 31.

214 **"We'll probably"**: Dallek, *Unfinished Life*, 579.

214 **"You're a young"**: Zwiers, *Senator Eastland*, 140.

215 **"an accessory"**: Annis, *Big James Eastland*, 155.

215 **"a combination"**: Schlesinger, *Robert Kennedy*, 234.

215 **"great contribution"**: Annis, *Big James Eastland*, 122.

215 **"go to hell"**: Ibid., 175.

216 **"If Robert Kennedy"**: "From Treasury Down," *New York Times*, December 17, 1960.

216 **"I think you have"**: "Robert Kennedy Wins Approval of Senate Panel," *New York Times*, January 14, 1961.

217 **"Scotch"**: Kennedy, *True Compass*, 193–95.

218 **"We couldn't survive"**: Sorensen, *Kennedy*, 325.

218 **"Mr. President, when"**: "Transcript of President Kennedy's News Conference," *Washington Post*, January 25, 1963.

218 **70 percent approval**: Andrew Kohut, "JFK's America," Pew Research Center, Nov. 20, 2013; republished July 5, 2019.

219 **"big Democratic slippage"**: Dallek, *Unfinished Life*, 580.

219 **"It was really astonishing"**: Norbert Schlei, interview by John Stewart, February 20–21, 1968, 35, Oral History Collection, JFK Library.

219 **"That's just where"**: Adam Walinsky, interview by Thomas F. Johnston, November 29, 1969, Robert F. Kennedy Oral History Collection, JFK Library.

220 **"one of the best"**: "Rusk's Security Chief: Abba Philip Schwartz," *New York Times*, September 12, 1962.

220 **During Christmas 1961**: Cornelius D. Scully III, interview by William D. Morgan, April 16, 1992, Foreign Affairs Oral History Project, Association for Diplomatic Studies and Training.

220 **"the State Department's"**: "New Occupant for State's Hot Seat Gets 'Reprieved' at the Last Minute," *Washington Post*, June 24, 1962.

220 **Walter and the Kennedy White House**: Allen B. Moreland, interview by Charles Stuart Kennedy, November 8, 1989, 10, Foreign Affairs Oral History Project, Association for Diplomatic Studies and Training.

220 **"Walter's boy"**: "Rusk's Security Chief," *New York Times*, September 12, 1962.

221 **Schwartz tried to delay:** Schwartz, *Open Society*, 28.

221 **"I knew":** Ibid., 31.

221 **"any trip abroad":** "U.S. Cancels Robeson's Passport After He Refuses to Surrender It," *New York Times,* August 4, 1950.

222 **"It would take a cannon":** "Close-Up: Frances Knight, 'Ogress' of the Passport Office," *Life,* July 8, 1966, 31.

222 **phone in her office:** Scully interview, 13.

222 **On April 13:** "Walter Offers Bill for Reserve of Unused Immigration Quotas," *Washington Post,* April 14, 1961.

222 **On the tenth anniversary:** Daniels, *Guarding the Golden Door,* Kindle loc. 2536.

222 **"I do not see why":** Gjelten, *Nation of Nations,* 105.

223 **"The overwhelming reason":** Norbert Schlei to Abba Schwartz, April 10, 1963, Feldman Papers.

223 **On January 21:** "Francis Walter Is Undergoing Leukemia Tests," *Warren Times Mirror,* May 21, 1963.

223 **"When I saw him":** "Rep. Walter Dies, Lauded by Kennedy," *Pottsville Republican,* June 1, 1963.

224 **"with the greatest ability":** "President Urges Repeal of Quotas for Immigration," *New York Times,* July 24, 1963.

224 **"the best immigration law":** "Immigration: A Sea Breeze," *Washington Post,* July 24, 1963.

224 **"would be an act":** "A New Immigration Law," *New York Times,* July 25, 1963.

224 **"Possibly the only negative":** *St. Paul Pioneer Press,* July 26, 1963.

225 **with assistance from staff:** Oscar Cohen to Myer Feldman, August 20, 1963, Feldman Papers.

225 **Celler made a play:** "Kennedy Meets the New Germany," *Washington Post,* June 25, 1963.

225 **the son of John T. Feighan:** "Michael Feighan, 88, Ohio Representative, Dies," *Washington Post,* March 20, 1992.

225 **joined a law firm:** Bernstein, *Guns or Butter,* 253.

225 **given up golf:** "Immigration Reformer," *New York Times,* August 25, 1965.

225 **"marked chiefly by":** "An Obscure Congressman to Keep an Eye On," *Life,* June 4, 1965.

226 **"a public outrage":** "U.S. Finds No Grounds to Bar Burton," *New York Times,* February 14, 1964.

226 **"He made us absolutely":** Schlei interview, 37.

226 **In August:** "Kennedy Scores Low 5% on Requests to Congress," *Washington Post,* August 4, 1963.

227 **"If Feighan succeeds":** Abba P. Schwartz to Ted Sorensen, November 6, 1963, Lee C. White White House Staff Files, Box 6, JFK Library.

227 **"not ready for publication":** Arthur Schlesinger to Myer Feldman, November 4, 1963, Feldman Papers.

227 **"I hate to give":** Myer Feldman to Julius Edelstein, November 6, 1963, Feldman Papers.

228 **"Every time I came":** Goodwin, *Fitzgeralds and Kennedys,* 164.

228 **They were ready:** Dallek, *Flawed Giant,* 47.

228 **"Well that doesn't mean anything":** Myer Feldman, interview by Meredith Coleman, March 12, 2000, 13, Legal Oral History Project, University of Pennsylvania Law School.

228 **When the plane stopped:** "Tokyo-Bound Rusk Plan Turns Back Toward Capital," *(Baltimore) Sun,* November 23, 1963.

229 **"Good God":** Zwiers, *Senator Eastland,* 220; Annis, *Big James Eastland,* 189–90.

NINE: A MARTYR'S CAUSE

230 **"All I have"**: Lyndon Johnson, "Address Before a Joint Session of Congress," November 27, 1963, in Johnson, *Public Papers 1963–64*, 10–11.

231 **"quiet confidence"**: Tom Wicker, "Johnson Bids Congress Enact Civil Rights Bill with Speed," *New York Times*, November 28, 1963.

231 **"Everything I had ever"**: Goodwin, *Johnson and American Dream*, 178.

231 **"I know how much"**: Ibid., 175.

231 **"the greatest honor"**: Myer Feldman, interview by Meredith Coleman, March 12, 2000, 13, Legal Oral History Project, University of Pennsylvania Law School.

232 **"When did this"**: Lawrence F. O'Brien, interview 2 by Michael L. Gillette, October 29, 1985, 10, Oral Histories, LBJ Library.

232 **At the president's weekly:** Lawrence F. O'Brien, interview 1 by Michael L. Gillette, September 18, 1985, 39, ibid.

232 **enjoyed talking strategy:** Lawrence F. O'Brien, interview 6 by Michael L. Gillette, February 11, 1986, 3, ibid..

232 **"The most important people"**: Dallek, *Flawed Giant*, 191.

233 **"There is but one way"**: Goodwin, *Johnson and American Dream*, 226.

233 **"I'm mighty proud of you"**: Emanuel Celler and Lyndon Johnson (phone call, audio), February 11, 1964, Miller Center of Public Affairs, University of Virginia.

234 **penned a memo:** Abba P. Schwartz, "Subject: The Administration's Immigration Proposal," January 7, 1964, LBJ President 1963–1969, Legislation, Box 73, Johnson Papers.

234 **"Now I would hope"**: Lyndon Johnson, "Remarks to Representatives of Organizations Interested in Immigration and Refugee Matters," January 13, 1964, in LBJ President 1963–1969, Immigration—Naturalization, Box 1, Johnson Papers.

235 **"nigger loving"**: Drew Pearson, "Feighan Roasted Kennedy Abroad," *Washington Post*, April 29, 1964.

236 **"In a loud voice"**: Jack Valenti to Larry O'Brien, June 17, 1964, LBJ President 1963–1969, Legislation, Box 73, Johnson Papers.

236 **"I just want you"**: Valenti to Michael Feighan, June 17, 1964, ibid.

236 **"almost to the day"**: House Committee on the Judiciary, Subcommittee on Immigration, hearing, 88th Cong., 2nd sess., 6.

236 **"descended predominantly"**: Fischer, *Spider Web*, Kindle loc. 2886.

236 **"to keep America American"**: Ibid., loc. 2827.

236 **"provided a realistic"**: House Committee on the Judiciary, Subcommittee on Immigration, hearing, 88th Cong., 2nd sess., 785–86 (Statement of John B. Trevor, Jr., Chairman, Immigration Committee, American Coalition of Patriotic Societies, Inc., August 14, 1964).

237 **"I'm not inclined"**: Schwartz, *Open Society*, 119–20.

238 **"proud of its role"**: House Committee on the Judiciary, Subcommittee on Immigration, hearing, 88th Cong., 2nd sess., 878, 909 (Statement of Mike M. Masaoka, Washington Representative, Japanese American Citizens League, September 2, 1964).

239 **"You're out!"**: Tichenor, *Dividing Lines*, 204.

239 **"When Andy comes"**: "Presidents Come and Go, but Labor's Might Stays," *Washington Post*, April 13, 1971.

240 **In a Gallup poll:** Simon and Alexander, *Ambivalent Welcome*, 37.

240 **"rough and mean"**: Jack Valenti to Lyndon Johnson, July 1, 1964, LBJ Handwriting File, May 1964–August 1964, Box 3, Johnson Papers.

240 **"As a practical matter":** Henry H. Wilson, Jr., to Lawrence F. O'Brien, July 11, 1964, LBJ President 1963–1969, Office Files of Henry H. Wilson, Box 3, Johnson Papers.

241 **On the day of Jack's death:** Kennedy, *True Compass,* 209–10.

241 **"veered close":** Ibid., 210.

241 **"I feel like":** "Emanuel Celler, Former Brooklyn Congressman, Dies at 92," *New York Times,* January 16, 1981.

242 **authorities later concluded:** "Fastened Seat Belt Saved Kennedy," *Washington Post,* July 4, 1964.

242 **At first:** Kennedy, *True Compass,* 222.

242 **"postgraduate seminar":** "He Did More Than Just Get Well," *Life,* January 15, 1965; Clymer, *Edward Kennedy,* 61.

242 **From his hospital bed:** Myer Feldman to Ted Kennedy, July 24, 1964, Feldman Papers.

244 **"Too much separated us":** Johnson, *Vantage Point,* 99.

244 **Making things even tougher:** Tye, *Bobby Kennedy,* Kindle loc. 6414.

244 **"Step back a little":** Clymer, *Edward Kennedy,* 63.

245 **"It was a night":** Goodwin, *Johnson and American Dream,* 209.

245 **"once powerful conservative":** "Democrats Score Big Gain in House," *New York Times,* November 5, 1964.

245 **"This has been":** Lyndon Johnson, "Remarks at the President's Salute to Congress," October 7, 1965, in Johnson, *Public Papers 1965,* 2:1059.

245 **"I want you to work":** Zelizer, *Fierce Urgency of Now,* 166.

246 **"We do not intend":** Lyndon Johnson, "Annual Message to Congress on the State of the Union," January 4, 1965, in Johnson, *Public Papers 1965,* 1:4, 6.

246 **"off to the fastest":** "Congress Spurred by Johnson, Runs Fast Race on Bills," *Washington Post,* February 3, 1965.

247 **"leaped to his feet":** Zelizer, *Fierce Urgency of Now,* 214.

247 **"I have climbed":** "Celler Becomes Dean of House, After Climbing 'the Greasy Pole,'" *New York Times,* January 4, 1965.

248 **It was early evening:** Johnson Daily Diary Collection, May 7, 1965, Johnson Papers.

248 **"As you know":** Hubert Humphrey to Michael Feighan, April 30, 1965, LBJ President 1963–1969, Legislation, Box 73, Johnson Papers.

249 **"a myth":** "New Immigration Proposal Is Advanced by Feighan," *(Baltimore) Sun,* February 5, 1965.

250 **overall cap:** Norbert Schlei to President Johnson, "Re: Appointment with Congressman Michael A. Feighan," May 7, 1965, in "President, 1963–1969, Legislation," Box 73, Johnson Papers.

251 **Mexicans made up the vast majority:** Henderson, *Beyond Borders,* 17.

251 **In California:** Ibid., 18.

252 **"would disturb our relations":** Schlei to Johnson, "Re: Appointment with Congressman Michael A. Feighan," May 7, 1965, LBJ President 1963–1969, Legislation, Box 73, Johnson Papers.

252 **"vex and dumbfound":** Valenti to Johnson, May 8, 1965, ibid.

252 **"the lives of thousands":** Dallek, *Flawed Giant,* 265; Randall Woods, "Conflicted Hegemon: LBJ and the Dominican Republic," *Diplomatic History* 32, no. 5 (November 2008).

253 **"What this will do":** Valenti to Johnson, May 8, 1965, LBJ President 1963–1969, Legislation, Box 73, Johnson Papers.

253 **"get a bill":** Valenti to Johnson, May 14, 1965, LBJ Legislative Background, Johnson Papers.

253 **"were impressed":** "Old Feud Erupts on House Floor," *New York Times,* July 10, 1965.

254 **"To what the gentleman"**: "Feighan Asks Celler to Quit Dutyless Job," *Washington Post*, July 10, 1965.

254 **"a black day"**: *Congressional Record* 111, pt. 13, July 21, 1965, H17592–93.

254 **The next day**: "Minutes, Subcommittee No. 1, Committee on the Judiciary, July 22, 1965," LBJ President 1963–1969, Office Files of Henry H. Wilson, Johnson Papers.

254 **The bill was now**: "Immigration Reforms Approved," *Washington Post*, July 23, 1965.

255 **"We got it out"**: Valenti to Johnson, July 22, 1965, LBJ Legislative Background Part II, Johnson Papers.

255 **"Your unflagging work"**: Johnson to Schlei, July 26, 1965, LBJ President 1963–1969, Legislation, Box 73, Johnson Papers

255 **"virtually assures"**: "Immigration Reforms Approved," *Washington Post*, July 23, 1965.

255 **"not to be changed"**: Henry Wilson to Larry O'Brien, July 23, 1965, LBJ President 1963–1969, Office Files of Henry H. Wilson, Box 3, Johnson Papers.

255 **"things went awfully well"**: Larry O'Brien to Johnson, July 27, 1965, LBJ President 1963–1969, Legislation, Box 73, Johnson Papers.

255 **"Honest to Pete"**: Nicholas Katzenbach and Lyndon Johnson (phone call, audio), July 30, 1965, Miller Center of Public Affairs, University of Virginia, https://millercenter.org/the -presidency/secret-white-house-tapes/conversation-nicholas-katzenbach-july-30-1965.

256 **"a breakthrough"**: "House Unit Votes an End to Quotas for Immigration," *New York Times*, August 4, 1965.

256 **"played no part"**: Michael Feighan to Jack Valenti, August 9, 1965, LBJ President 1963– 1969, Legislation, Box 73, Johnson Papers.

256 **"Congratulations!"**: Larry O'Brien to Jack Valenti, August 12, 1965, ibid.

256 **"I made a speech"**: *Congressional Record* 111, pt. 16, August 24, 1965, H21579.

256 **"if you'll ever get"**: Nicholas Katzenbach and Lyndon Johnson (phone call, audio), August 26, 1965, Miller Center of Public Affairs, University of Virginia.

257 **"legislative tour de force"**: Clymer, *Edward Kennedy*, 66.

257 **"in charge of immigration"**: Mike Manatos to Larry O'Brien, August 16, 1965, Office Files of Mike Manatos, Box 8, LBJ President 1963–1969, Johnson Papers.

257 **"just one little hole"**: *CQ Weekly Report* 23, pt. 1, 1965, 361.

257 **Ervin told Manatos**: Mike Manatos to Larry O'Brien, August 20, 1965, LBJ President 1963–1969, Office Files of Mike Manatos, Box 8, Johnson Papers.

257 **"it is clear"**: O'Brien to Johnson, August 24, 1965, LBJ President, 1963–1969, Legislation, Box 73, Johnson Papers.

258 **He predicted**: "Immigration Measure Voted by Senate, 76-18: Immigration Bill Passed by Senate," *Washington Post*, September 23, 1965.

258 **"the new language"**: Valenti to Johnson, August 25, 1965, in "President, 1963–1969, Legislation," Box 73, Johnson Papers.

258 **"Why is it"**: Senate Judiciary Committee, *Amending the Immigration and Nationality Act, and for Other Purposes: Report Together with Minority Additional and Separate Views*, September 15, 1965.

258 **Philip Hart**: While the Senate bill was sponsored by Hart and the final law would bear his name as the Hart-Celler Act, the Michigan senator would play only a marginal role in the law's passage.

258 **"The wish to preserve"**: *Congressional Record* 111, pt. 18, September 17, 1965, S24237.

259 **"Why for the first time"**: Ibid., S24776.

259 **"I am very pleased"**: Ibid., S24778.

259 **"I'm going to raise"**: Emanuel Celler and Lyndon Johnson (phone call, audio), August 26, 1965, Miller Center of Public Affairs, University of Virginia.

259 **Johnson immediately announced:** "Congress Sends Immigration Bill to White House," *New York Times*, October 1, 1965.

260 **"Perhaps Providence did":** "Roosevelt's Address at the Statue of Liberty," *New York Times*, October 29, 1936.

EPILOGUE

262 **"If anybody shouts":** Johnson, *White House Diary*, 321.

262 **"Mr. President":** "Johnson Signs Medicare Bill, Hails Truman's Role," *(Baltimore) Sun*, July 31, 1965.

262 **Earl Harrison:** "Earl G. Harrison, Ex-Law Dean, 55," *New York Times*, July 30, 1955.

262 **Lehman had been felled:** "Herbert Lehman, 85, Dies; Ex-Governor and Senator," *New York Times*, December 6, 1963.

262 **"Citizen and statesman":** Ibid.

263 **"Now Erich":** Erich Leinsdorf, interview by Joe B. Frantz, March 18, 1969, p. 4, Oral History Collection, LBJ Library.

265 **By 1971:** Daniels, *Guarding the Golden Door*, Kindle loc. 2707.

265 **Between 1965 and 1974:** Reimers, *Still the Golden Door*, 100.

265 **By 1989:** Ibid., 93.

265 **The number of immigrants:** Jynnah Radford and Luis Noe-Bustamante, "Facts on U.S. Immigrants, 2017," Pew Research Center, June 3, 2019, https://www.pewhispanic.org/2019/06/03/facts-on-u-s-immigrants/.

266 **foreign-born population:** "U.S. Has Highest Share of Foreign-Born Since 1910, with More Coming from Asia," *New York Times*, September 13, 2018.

266 **On the same day:** Reimers, *Still the Golden Door*, 163.

267 **which had allowed:** Ngai, *Impossible Subjects*, 139.

268 **"a radical change":** Jeff Sessions, interview by Breitbart News Sunday Sirius XM, October 4, 2015, https://soundcloud.com/siriusxm-news-issues/the-american-people-are-angry.

269 **"future generations":** "President Signs Landmark Bill on Immigration," *New York Times*, November 7, 1986.

BIBLIOGRAPHY

Manuscripts and Archives

ADAMS, EVA BERTRAND, Papers, Special Collections Department, University of Nevada, Reno

CELLER, EMANUEL, Papers, Manuscript Division, Library of Congress

EDELSTEIN, JULIUS C. C., Papers, Columbia University Rare Books & Manuscript Library

FELDMAN, MYER, Papers, John F. Kennedy Presidential Library

HARRISON, EARL G., Papers, United States Holocaust Memorial Museum

HUMPHREY, HUBERT, Papers, Minnesota Historical Society

JOHNSON, LADY BIRD, Papers, Lyndon B. Johnson Presidential Library

JOHNSON, LYNDON B., Papers, Lyndon B. Johnson Presidential Library

KENNEDY, JOHN F., Papers, John F. Kennedy Presidential Library

LEHMAN, HERBERT, Papers, Columbia University Rare Books & Manuscripts

PETERSEN, PETER C., Papers, University of Nevada, Reno, Special Collections Department

TRUMAN, HARRY S., Papers, Harry S. Truman Presidential Library

Books

ABRAMOVITCH, ILANA, AND SEÁN GALVIN, EDS. *Jews of Brooklyn.* Hanover, N.H.: University Press of New England, 2002.

ANDERSON, CLAUDIA WILSON. "Congressman Lyndon B. Johnson, Operation Texas, and Jewish Immigration." *Southern Jewish History* 15 (2012).

ANNIS, JR., J. LEE. *Big James Eastland: The Godfather of Mississippi.* Jackson: University Press of Mississippi, 2016.

ANTIN, MARY. *The Promised Land.* Boston: Houghton Mifflin, 1912.

BERNARD, WILLIAM S. *American Immigration Policy: A Reappraisal.* New York: Harper, 1950.

BERNSTEIN, IRVING. *Guns or Butter: The Presidency of Lyndon Johnson.* New York: Oxford University Press, 1996.

BESCHLOSS, MICHAEL. *The Conquerors: Roosevelt, Truman and the Destruction of Hitler's Germany, 1941–1945.* New York: Simon & Schuster, 2002.

BREITMAN, RICHARD AND ALAN M. KRAUT. *American Refugee Policy and European Jewry, 1933–1945.* Bloomington: Indiana University Press, 1988.

BREITMAN, RICHARD, AND ALLAN J. LICHTMAN. *FDR and the Jews.* Cambridge, Mass.: Belknap Press of Harvard University Press, 2013.

BRINKLEY, ALAN. *Voices of Protest: Huey Long, Father Coughlin, and the Great Depression.* New York: Alfred A. Knopf, 1982.

CANNADINE, DAVID. *Mellon: An American Life.* New York: Alfred A. Knopf, 2006.

CANNATO, VINCENT J. *American Passage: The History of Ellis Island.* New York: Harper, 2009.

CARO, ROBERT A. *Master of the Senate.* New York: Vintage, 2003.

———. *The Path to Power.* New York: Alfred A. Knopf, 1982.

CELLER, EMANUEL. *You Never Leave Brooklyn.* New York: John Day, 1953.

CLYMER, ADAM. *Edward M. Kennedy: A Biography.* New York: Morrow, 1999.

COHEN, ADAM. *Imbeciles: The Supreme Court, American Eugenics, and the Sterilization of Carrie Buck.* New York: Penguin, 2016.

COHEN, MICHAEL JOSEPH. *Truman and Israel.* Berkeley: University of California Press, 1990.

COOPER, JOHN MILTON, JR. *Woodrow Wilson: A Biography.* New York: Vintage, 2011.

DALLEK, ROBERT. *Flawed Giant: Lyndon Johnson and His Times, 1961–1973.* New York: Oxford University Press, 1998.

———. *Lone Star Rising: Lyndon Johnson and his Times, 1908–1960.* New York: Oxford University Press, 1991.

———. *An Unfinished Life: John F. Kennedy, 1917–1963.* Boston: Little, Brown, 2003.

DANIELS, ROGER. *Guarding the Golden Door.* New York: Hill & Wang, 2005.

———. *The Politics of Prejudice: The Anti-Japanese Movement in California and the Struggle for Japanese Exclusion.* Berkeley: University of California Press, 1962.

DANIELS, ROGER, ED. *Immigration and the Legacy of Harry S. Truman.* Kirksville, Mo.: Truman State University Press, 2010.

DAVENPORT, CHARLES BENEDICT. *Heredity in Relation to Eugenics.* New York: Holt, 1911.

DAVIS, JAMES J. *The Iron Puddler.* Indianapolis: Bobbs-Merrill, 1922.

DINNERSTEIN, LEONARD. *America and the Survivors of the Holocaust.* New York: Columbia University Press, 1982.

———. *The Leo Frank Case.* Athens: University of Georgia Press, 1999.

DIVINE, ROBERT A. *American Immigration Policy, 1924–1952.* New Haven: Yale University Press, 1957.

DONOVAN, ROBERT J. *Conflict and Crisis: The Presidency of Harry S. Truman, 1945–1948.* New York: W. W. Norton, 1977.

EDWARDS, JEROME E. *Pat McCarran: Political Boss of Nevada.* Reno: University of Nevada Press, 1982.

EDWARDS, LEE. *Missionary for Freedom: The Life and Times of Walter Judd.* St. Paul, Minn.: Paragon House, 1990.

ERBELDING, REBECCA. *Rescue Board: The Untold Story of America's Efforts to Save the Jews of Europe.* New York: Doubleday, 2018.

FERRELL, ROBERT H. *Harry S. Truman: A Life.* Columbia: University of Missouri Press, 1994.

FERRELL, ROBERT H., ED. *Dear Bess: The Letters from Harry Truman to Bess Truman, 1910–1959.* Columbia: University of Missouri Press, 1998.

———. *Off the Record: The Private Papers of Harry S. Truman.* New York: Harper & Row, 1980.

———. *Truman in the White House: The Diary of Eben A. Ayers.* Columbia: University of Missouri Press, 1991.

FIELDS, ALONZO. *My 21 Years in the White House.* New York: Coward-McCann, 1961.

FISCHER, NICK. *Spider Web: The Birth of American Anticommunism.* Urbana: University of Illinois Press, 2016.

FITE, GILBERT C. *Richard B. Russell, Jr., Senator from Georgia.* Chapel Hill: University of North Carolina Press, 1991.

FITZGERALD, DAVID SCOTT, AND DAVID COOK-MARTIN. *Culling the Masses.* Cambridge, Mass.: Harvard University Press, 2014.

FONER, NANCY. *From Ellis Island to JFK: New York's Two Great Waves of Immigration.* New Haven: Yale University Press, 2000.

FRADKIN, PHILIP L. *The Great Earthquake and Firestorms of 1906.* Berkeley: University of California Press, 2005.

GERSTLE, GARY. *American Crucible.* Princeton: Princeton University Press, 2001.

GIANGRECO, D. M. AND KATHRYN MOORE. *Dear Harry . . . Truman's Mailroom, 1945–1953.* Mechanicsburg, Pa.: Stackpole Books, 1999.

GILLETTE, MICHAEL L. *Lady Bird Johnson: An Oral History.* Oxford: Oxford University Press, 2012.

GJELTEN, TOM. *A Nation of Nations: A Great American Immigration Story.* New York: Simon & Schuster, 2015.

GOLDSTEIN, ERIC L. *The Price of Whiteness.* Princeton: Princeton University Press, 2006.

GOODMAN, WALTER. *The Committee: The Extraordinary Career of the House Committee on Un-American Activities.* New York: Farrar, Straus & Giroux, 1968.

GOODWIN, DORIS KEARNS. *The Fitzgeralds and the Kennedys.* New York: St. Martin's Press, 1991.

———. *Lyndon Johnson and the American Dream.* New York: St. Martin's Press, 1976.

———. *No Ordinary Time.* New York: Simon & Schuster, 1994.

GORDON, LINDA. *The Second Coming of the KKK.* New York: Liveright, 2017.

GRABER, RUTH. *Haven: The Dramatic Story of 1,000 World War II Refugees and How They Came to America.* New York: Times Books, 2000.

GRANT, MADISON. *The Passing of the Great Race.* New York: Scribner, 1918.

HALL, PRESCOTT F. "Immigration and the World War." *The Annals of the American Academy of Political and Social Science.* Vol. 93, *Present-Day Immigration with Special Reference to the Japanese,* January 1921.

HAMBY, ALONZO L. *Man of the People: A Life of Harry S. Truman.* New York: Oxford University Press, 1995.

HANDLIN, OSCAR. *The Uprooted: The Epic Story of the Great Migrations that Made the American People.* Boston: Little, Brown, 1951.

HARCOURT, FELIX. *Ku Klux Klan: America and the Klan in the 1920.* Chicago: University of Chicago Press, 2017.

HENDERSON, TIMOTHY J. *Beyond Borders: A History of Mexican Migration to the United States.* Oxford: Wiley-Blackwell, 2011.

HIGHAM, JOHN. *Strangers in the Land.* New Brunswick, N.J.: Rutgers University Press, 1955.

HILLIER, ALBERT J. "Albert Johnson, Congressman." *Pacific Northwest Quarterly* 36, no. 3 (July 1945).

HOOVER, HERBERT. *The Memoirs of Herbert Hoover: The Cabinet and the Presidency, 1920–1933.* New York: Macmillan, 1952.

HOSOKAWA, BILL. *Nisei: The Quiet Americans.* Boulder: University of Press of Colorado, 2002.

ICHIOKA, YUJI. *The Issei: The World of the First Generation Japanese Immigrants, 1885–1924.* New York: Free Press, 1988.

JACOBSON, MATTHEW FRYE. *Whiteness of a Different Color.* Cambridge, Mass.: Harvard University Press, 1998.

JOHNSON, LADY BIRD. *A White House Diary.* Austin: University of Texas Press, 2007.

JOHNSON, LYNDON B. *Public Papers of the Presidents of the United States: Lyndon B. Johnson: 1963–64.* Washington, D.C.: Office of the Federal Register, 1965.

———. *Public Papers of the Presidents of the United States: Lyndon B. Johnson: 1965.* 2 vols. Washington, D.C.: Office of the Federal Register, 1966.

———. *The Vantage Point: Perspectives of the Presidency.* New York: Holt, Rinehart & Winston, 1971.

JUDIS, JOHN B. *Genesis: Truman, American Jews and the Origins of the Arab/Israeli Conflict.* New York: Farrar, Straus & Giroux, 2014.

KALLEN, HORACE. *Culture and Democracy in the United States.* New York: Boni Liveright, 1924.

KARABEL, JEROME. *The Chosen: The Hidden History of Admission and Exclusion at Harvard, Yale, and Princeton.* Boston: Houghton Mifflin, 2005.

KENNAN, GEORGE F. *American Diplomacy, 1900–1950.* Chicago: University of Chicago Press, 1951.

KENNEDY, EDWARD M. *True Compass: A Memoir.* New York: Twelve, 2009.

KENNEDY, JOHN F. *A Nation of Immigrants.* New York: Harper & Row, 1964.

KEVLES, DANIEL J. *In the Name of Eugenics: Genetics and the Uses of Human Heredity.* New York: Alfred A. Knopf, 1985.

KEYNES, JOHN MAYNARD. *The Collected Writings of John Maynard Keynes XXIII: Activities 1940–1943: External War Finance.* Cambridge, U.K.: Cambridge University Press, 1979.

KREPON, MICHAEL AND DAN CALDWELL, EDS. *The Politics of Arms Control Treaty Ratification.* New York: St. Martin's Press, 1991.

LARSON, ERIK. *In the Garden of Beasts: Love, Terror, and an American Family in Hitler's Berlin.* New York: Crown, 2011.

LEE, ERIKA. *The Making of Asian America.* New York: Simon & Schuster, 2016.

LEINSDORF, ERICH. *Cadenza: A Musical Career.* Boston: Houghton Mifflin, 1976.

LOESCHER, GIL, AND JOHN A. SCANLAN. *Calculated Kindness: Refugees and America's Half-Open Door, 1945–Present.* New York: Free Press, 1986.

MASAOKA, MIKE, WITH BILL HOSOKAWA. *They Call Me Moses Masaoka.* New York: Morrow, 1987.

McCULLOUGH, DAVID. *Truman.* New York: Simon & Schuster, 1992.

MEDOFF, RAFAEL, ED. *Blowing the Whistle on Genocide: Josiah E. DuBois and the Struggle for a U.S. Response to the Holocaust.* West Lafayette, Ind.: Purdue University Press, 2008.

MELVILLE, HERMAN. *Redburn.* New York: Modern Library, 2002.

NAHSHON, EDNA, ED. *From the Ghetto to the Melting Pot: Israel Zangwill's Plays.* Detroit: Wayne State University Press, 2006.

NASAW, DAVID. *The Patriarch: The Remarkable Life and Turbulent Times of Joseph P. Kennedy.* New York: Penguin, 2012.

NELSON, ANNA KASTEN. "Anna M. Rosenberg, an 'Honorary Man,'" *Journal of Military History* 68, no. 1 (January 2004).

———. "Caught in the Web of McCarthyism: Anna M. Rosenberg and the Senate Armed Services Committee," *Congress and the Presidency* 30, no. 2 (Autumn 2003).

NEVINS, ALLAN. *Herbert H. Lehman and His Era.* New York: Charles Scribner's Sons, 1963.

NGAI, MAE M. *Impossible Subjects.* Princeton: Princeton University Press, 2004.

O'BRIEN, MICHAEL. *John F. Kennedy: A Biography.* New York: St. Martin's Press, 2005.

OLNEY, STEVE. *And the Dead Shall Rise: The Murder of Mary Phagan and the Lynching of Leo Frank.* New York: Pantheon, 2003.

PAINTER, NELL IRVIN. *The History of White People.* New York: W. W. Norton, 2010.

PENKOWER, MONTY NOAM. "The Earl Harrison Report: Its Genesis and Its Significance." *American Jewish Archives Journal* 68, no. 1 (2016).

PIETRUSZA, DAVID. *1948: Harry Truman's Improbable Victory and the Year That Transformed America.* New York: Diversion Books, 2011.

RADOSH, ALLIS, AND RONALD RADOSH. *A Safe Haven: Harry S. Truman and the Founding of Israel.* New York: HarperPerennial, 2009.

REEVES, THOMAS C. *The Life and Times of Joe McCarthy.* New York: Stein & Day, 1982.

REIMERS, DAVID M. *Still the Golden Door: The Third World Comes to America.* New York: Columbia University Press, 1985.

ROBERTS, KENNETH. *Why Europe Leaves Home.* Indianapolis: Bobbs-Merrill, 1922.

ROEDIGER, DAVID R. *Working Toward Whiteness.* New York: Basic Books, 2005.

ROOSEVELT, THEODORE. *The Letters of Theodore Roosevelt: The Square Deal, 1901–1905.* Edited by Elting Elmore Morison. Cambridge, Mass.: Harvard University Press, 1951.

———. *The Letters of Theodore Roosevelt: The Big Stick, 1905–1909.* Edited by Eltin Emore Morison. Cambridge, Mass.: Harvard University Press, 1952.

RUSSELL, JAN JARBOE. *Lady Bird: A Biography of Mrs. Johnson.* New York: Scribner, 1999.

SCHLESINGER, ARTHUR. *Robert Kennedy and His Times.* Boston: Houghton Mifflin, 1978.

SCHWARTZ, ABBA P. *The Open Society.* New York: Morrow, 1968.

SIMON, RITA J., AND SUSAN H. ALEXANDER. *The Ambivalent Welcome.* Westport, Conn.: Praeger, 1993.

SMITH, MARIE D. *The President's Lady: An Intimate Biography of Mrs. Lyndon B. Johnson.* New York: Random House, 1964.

SORENSEN, TED. *Kennedy: The Classic Biography.* New York: Harper & Row, 1965.

SPIRO, JONATHAN PETER, *Defending the Master Race: Conservation, Eugenics, and the Legacy of Madison Grant.* Burlington: University of Vermont Press, 2008.

STEVENS, LEWIS M. "The Life and Character of Earl G. Harrison." *University of Pennsylvania Law Review* 105, no. 5 (March 1956).

TANANBAUM, DUANE. *Herbert H. Lehman: A Political Biography.* Albany: State University of New York Press, 2016.

TICHENOR, DANIEL J. *Dividing Lines: The Politics of Immigration Control in America.* Princeton: Princeton University Press, 2009.

TRUMAN, HARRY S. *Public Papers of the Presidents of the United States: Harry S. Truman.* Vol. 1, *1945.* Washington, D.C.: U.S. Government Printing Office, 1961.

————. *Public Papers of the Presidents of the United States: Harry S. Truman.* Vol. 3, *1947.* Washington, D.C.: U.S. Government Printing Office, 1961–66.

————. *Public Papers of the Presidents of the United States: Harry S. Truman.* Vol. 4, *1948.* Washington, D.C.: U.S. Government Printing Office., 1961–66.

TRUMAN, MARGARET. *Harry Truman.* New York: Morrow, 1973.

TYE, LARRY. *Bobby Kennedy: The Making of a Liberal Lion.* New York: Random House, 2016.

VANCE, RUPERT. *Human Geography of the South.* Chapel Hill: University of North Carolina Press, 1932.

VOUGHT, HANS. "Division and Reunion: Woodrow Wilson, Immigration, and Myth of American Unity." *Journal of American Ethnic History* 13, no. 3 (Spring 1994).

WATTS, STEVEN. *The People's Tycoon: Henry Ford and the American Century.* New York: Alfred A. Knopf, 2005.

WHITMAN, JAMES Q. *Hitler's American Model.* Princeton: Princeton University Press, 2017.

WOODS, RANDALL. *LBJ: Architect of Ambition.* New York: Free Press, 2006.

YBARRA, MICHAEL J. *Washington Gone Crazy: Senator Pat McCarran and the Great American Communist Hunt.* Hanover, N.H.: Steerforth Press, 2004.

ZELIZER, JULIAN E. *The Fierce Urgency of Now: Lyndon Johnson, Congress, and the Battle for the Great Society.* New York: Penguin, 2015.

ZIMMERMAN, WARREN. *First Great Triumph: How Five Americans Made Their Country a World Power.* New York: Farrar, Straus & Giroux, 2002.

ZOLBERG, ARISTIDE R. *A Nation by Design: Immigration Policy in the Fashioning of America.* New York: Russell Sage Foundation, 2006.

ZWIERS, MAARTEN. *Senator James Eastland: Mississippi's Jim Crow Democrat.* Baton Rouge: Louisiana State University Press, 2015.

INDEX

Acheson, Dean, 136, 151, 170

Adams, Eva, 123, 136

ADL (Anti-Defamation League), 205, 225

AFL (American Federation of Labor), 31, 239

AFL–CIO, 239–40

African Americans, 4, 22–23, 115–16, 131–32, 168, 188–89, 197, 200, 215, 246, 247–48, 266, 270

AJC (American Jewish Committee), 70, 108

alien registration, 16

America First, 39

American Breeders' Association, 37

American Coalition of Patriotic Societies, 112, 236, 249–50

American Eugenics Society, 41–42

American Federation of Labor (AFL), 31, 239

American Immigration Policy: A Reappraisal (Bernard), 155–56

American Jewish Committee (AJC), 70, 108

American Legion, 85, 103

American Protective Association, 24

American Zionist Emergency Council, 101

Anglo-American Committee of Inquiry, 102–3

Anglo-Saxon ideal, 2, 20, 29–30, 43, 46, 67, 132, 159, 215, 237

Anschluss, 81

anti-Communism

  James Eastland and, 132–33

  Internal Security Act, 149–55

  John F. Kennedy and, 181

  Pat McCarran and, 119–20, 125–26, 135–37, 192

  and McCarran–Walter Act, 158–60

  Joseph McCarthy and, 119–20, 143, 151–52, 181, 194

  Anna Rosenberg confirmation battle, 142–46

Anti-Defamation League (ADL), 205, 225

Antin, Mary, 19

anti-Semitism

  Father Coughlin and, 70

  and Displaced Persons Act (1950), 138–39

  Henry Ford and, 22

  Leo Frank case, 24–26

  and Jewish displaced persons crisis after WWII, 98

anti-Semitism (*continued*)
  and Jewish refugee crisis in WWII, 68,
    70, 74, 81, 85, 87
  Joe Kennedy and, 182–83
  Ku Klux Klan and, 24
  Pat McCarran and, 154, 155
  and 1948 refugee bill, 113–14
  George S. Patton and, 98
  Anna Rosenberg confirmation battle,
    145
  in U.S. Army, 98–99
  and Zionism, 99
Arab immigrants, 265
Arens, Richard, 137–39, 199
Army–McCarthy hearings, 194
Asian immigrants, 4, 46–61, 249; *See also*
    specific Asian groups, e.g.: Japanese
    immigrants
  and Chinese Exclusion Act (1882),
    31–32, 47, 86–87, 251
  and McCarran-Walter Act, 162
  since 1965 Immigration Act passage,
    265
Asia-Pacific Triangle, 168, 224, 238
Asiatic Barred Zone, 32, 47
assimilation, 8–9, 18, 19, 190–91; *See also*
    "melting pot"
Atlantic Monthly, 2
Attlee, Clement, 101
Austin, Richmond, 130
Austria, 79, 81, 99, 102, 108, 113
Azore Refugee Act, 201, 250

Balfour Declaration, 100
Barnett, Ross, 215
Baruch, Bernard, 144, 145
Batista, Fulgencio, 207
Bayh, Birch, 241, 242
Bayh, Marvella, 241, 242
Bay of Pigs, 207–8
Beer, Sam, 242
Beethoven, Ludwig van, 263
Bergen-Belsen, 96
Bernard, William S., 140, 156
Besterman, Walter, 161
Biemiller, Andy, 239
Bilbo, Theodore, 130–32

Birth of a Nation, The (film), 24
B'nai B'rith, 70
Bontempo, Salvatore, 212–13, 220
Bookbinder, Hyman, 207
Bosch, Juan, 252
Boston, Massachusetts, 8, 19, 24, 30, 42,
    177–78
Boston's Immigrants (Handlin), 190
Boston Symphony Orchestra, 263
Box, John C., 34
Boyle, William S., 127
bracero program, 266–67
Bremen incident, 72–73
Brooklyn, New York, 12–13, 265
Brooklyn Jewish Center, 7–11
Brownsville (Brooklyn, New York), 7
Brown v. Board of Education, 200, 215
Bryan, William Jennings, 12
Buck, Carrie, 38
Buck v. Bell, 38
Bureau of Security and Consular Affairs,
    212, 220
Burton, Richard, 226
business leaders, opposition to quotas by, 40

CAA (Civil Aeronautics Authority),
    126–27
Cain, Harry P., 134, 173
Caribbean colonies, 168
Castro, Fidel, 207–8
Catholics and Catholicism, 18, 24, 67, 85,
    92, 135–36, 140, 182, 187, 202, 219
Catholic schools, 24
CCDP, *See* Citizens Committee on Dis-
    placed Persons
Celler, Emanuel (Mannie), 10–14
  and alien registration, 16
  Bremen incident, 72–73
  and Civil Rights Act (1964), 233, 241
  on Edward Corsi's firing, 211
  and Displaced Persons Act (1948), 114
  and Displaced Persons Act (1950), 125
  and House Judiciary Committee, 118–19
  and Immigration Act (1924), 42, 57
  and Immigration and Nationality Act
    (1965), 233–36, 240, 241, 247, 253–
    56, 259, 262

and Internal Security Act, 151
and Jewish refugee crisis in WWII, 71–75
and joint committee on immigration, 253–54
and Kennedy-era immigration reform, 222, 224–27
and John F. Kennedy's first Senate race, 186
and Breckenridge Long, 87–88
and McCarran-Walter Act, 153–54, 157, 174
and McCarran–Walter Act amendment proposals, 199
at 1948 Democratic National Convention, 116
and Palestine, 102–3
and refugees, 111
and Voting Rights Act (1965), 247
and Western Hemisphere quotas, 259
Celler, Henry, 12
Celler, Jane, 12
Celler, Josephine, 12
Celler, Judy, 10
Celler, Stella, 10, 12
Central Intelligence Agency (CIA), 153, 207
chain migration, 264–65, 268
Chamberlain, Neville, 182
Chambers, Whittaker, 143
Chelf, Frank, 235, 254–55
Chiang Kai-shek, 167
China, 136, 166–67, 181
Chinatown (New York), 265
Chinese Exclusion Act (1882), 31–32, 47, 87, 251
Chinese immigrants, 31–32, 54, 86–87, 162, 167, 168, 249, 264–65
CIA (Central Intelligence Agency), 153, 207
Cieplinski, Michael, 212, 213
CIO (Congress of Industrial Organizations), 239
Citizens Committee on Displaced Persons (CCDP), 108, 110, 112, 125, 137–38, 140
Civil Aeronautics Authority (CAA), 126–27

civil liberties, 149–50
civil rights, 4, 226–27, 267–68
    as issue at 1948 Democratic National Convention, 115–16
    Lyndon Johnson and, 230, 233, 234, 247–48
    John F. Kennedy and, 209, 223, 226, 230
    Ted Kennedy and, 241, 256–57
    and McCarran–Walter Act, 170–71
    and McCarran–Walter amendment fight, 200
    and Truman's agenda after 1948 election, 124
Civil Rights Act (1964), 233, 241, 247
civil rights subcommittee, 133
Civil War, 97–98, 147
    General Order No. 11, 97–98
Clark, Mark W., 169
Clarke, Edward Young, 26
Clay, Lucius D., 139
Clemons, Charles F., 52
Cleveland, Grover, 30
Clifford, Clark, 116, 117
Clinton, Bill, 269
Cohen, Felix S., 158
Cohen, Oscar, 205
Cold Spring Harbor Laboratory, 33, 35–38
Cold War
    civil rights as issue during, 116
    damage to American efforts caused by Internal Security Act, 153
    and Displaced Persons Act (1950), 119
    internal security, 142–75
    and Johnson's immigration reform initiatives, 237–38
    John F. Kennedy and, 181
    Pat McCarran and, 120
Columbia Law School, 12
Columbus Day, 18
Commission on Immigration and Naturalization, 190–92
Communism, 111, 136, 207–8; *See also* anti-Communism; Cold War
Congress, U.S.
    Emanuel Celler's election to, 12–13
    election of 1948, 118–19
    election of 1964, 245

Congress, U.S. (*continued*)
 Immigration Act (1917), 32
 and Johnson's quota reform initiative,
  248–59
 John F. Kennedy in, 178–82
 and Palestine, 102
Congress of Industrial Organizations
 (CIO), 239
Connally, John, 78
Coolidge, Calvin, 11, 15, 58
Corsi, Edward, 210–11
Coughlin, Father Charles, 70
court-packing, 123
cross-burning, 26
Cuba, 81–84, 207–8
Cuban refugees, 217, 266
Culture and Democracy in the United States
 (Kallen), 20
Cutler, John Wilson, Jr., 139
Cutting, Bronson, 126

Dachau, 82
Daniels, Jonathan, 90
Daniels, Josephus, 83
Daughters of the American Revolution, 58,
 85, 103, 112
Davenport, Amzi, 36
Davenport, Charles, 35–37, 39
Davis, James J., 10–11, 14–16
Dearborn Independent, 22
DeMarco, William, 177
"Democracy Versus the Melting Pot"
 (Kallen), 20
Democratic National Convention (1944),
 90–91
Democratic National Convention (1948),
 115–17
Democratic National Convention (1960), 215
Democratic Party
 Emanuel Celler and, 12
 James Eastland and, 132–33
 election of 1946, 178
 election of 1948, 118–19
 election of 1964, 245
 Immigration Act (1917), 32
 and immigration issue in 1960 election,
  206

Ted Kennedy and, 214
 loss of Congressional seats in 1960
  election, 209
 Pat McCarran and, 122
de Sola, Ralph, 145–46
Devine, James T., 220
Dewey, Thomas, 117–18
Die Meistersinger (Wagner), 79
Dillingham, William, 39
Dillingham Commission, 37
Dirksen, Everett McKinley, 198, 257–58
displaced persons (DPs), 95–98, 104–6,
 152–53
Displaced Persons Act (1948), 110–14,
 117, 185
Displaced Persons Act (1950), 119, 124–
 25, 127–28, 133–35, 137–41
Dixiecrats, 116, 124, 133
Dole, Sanford B., 51, 52
Dominican Republic, 252–53
Douglas, Helen Gahagan, 182
Douglas, Paul, 120, 194
Du Bois, Coert, 81
DuBois, Josiah, 88
Dulles, John Foster, 134–35, 201, 210–11
Dungan, Ralph, 212
Dutton, Frederick G., 204
Dworshak, Henry C., 135

eastern Europe
 and Displaced Persons Act (1950), 140
 immigrants, 8, 11–12, 29, 45
 Jewish refugee crisis in WWII, 69
 persecution of Jews after WWII, 106–7
Eastland, James O., 129–35
 appointment as senator, 131
 and Displaced Persons Act (1950),
  133–35, 138
 early years, 129–31
 and Johnson's immigration proposals, 234
 and Johnson's immigration reform initiatives, 234
 and Kennedy administration, 214–17
 on John F. Kennedy assassination, 229
 Ted Kennedy and, 257
 McCarran–Walter amendment fight,
  198–99

Eastland, Woods, 130, 131
Edelstein, Julius, 160, 196, 208, 227
Edlin, William, 53
Edwards, Jerome, 121, 122
Eisenhower, Dwight D.
  and election of 1948, 115
  and Harrison's displaced persons report, 99
  Henry Cabot Lodge, Jr. and, 180, 186
  and quota reform, 196–97
  refugee law, 210
  Truman and, 185
election of 1946, 109, 178
election of 1948, 115–18
election of 1952, 184–85
election of 1960, 204, 206, 215
election of 1962, 214
election of 1964, 218–19, 245
election of 2018, 266
Elementary and Secondary Education Act, 246–47, 262
Ellis Island, 1–2, 8, 16, 59, 261
Engel, Irving, 114
Enthoven, Alain, 242
Ervin, Sam, 257
espionage, 69, 86, 120, 143, 150
ethnic (term), 188
Eugenical News, 37
Eugenical Sterilization in the United States (Laughlin), 38
eugenics, 33–38
Eugenics Record Office, 37–38
Evans, Tom, 90, 118
Evers, Medgar, 226–27
Executive Order 9066, 162

family separation policy, 269
Fay, Paul, 203
Federal Aviation Administration (FAA), 126
Federal Bureau of Investigation (FBI), 86, 146
Feighan, Michael, 225–26
  and Johnson's immigration reform initiatives, 234–36, 240, 248–50, 255, 256
  and joint committee on immigration, 253–54

and Kennedy's immigration reform initiatives, 225–27
and Western Hemisphere quotas, 250, 252–54
Feldman, Myer "Mike"
  early career, 204–5
  and immigration reform, 207, 222
  importance to Kennedy administration, 202–4
  as member of Johnson administration, 231
  and *A Nation of Immigrants*, 224–25, 227, 242–43
  and persuading Johnson to pursue immigration reform, 234
  resignation of, 229
  Francis Walter and, 213
Fellows, Frank, 113
Fields, Alonzo, 103–4
Fifth Amendment, 153
Fine, Phil, 183
Fischer, John, 208
Fisher, Irving, 35, 42
Fitzgerald, John F. "Honey Fitz," 177, 178, 179–80
forced sterilization laws, 38
Ford, Henry, 19, 22
foreign aid, 233
foreign policy
  and Chinese Exclusion Act, 86–87
  and Japanese immigration, 48–50
  and Johnson's immigration reform initiatives, 237–38
  and McCarran–Walter Act, 171–72
Fortas, Abe, 67
442nd regiment, U.S. Army, 165, 168, 169
Frank, Anne, 81
Frank, Leo, 25–26
Frank, Otto, 81
Frankfurter, Felix, 73–74
Freeman, Orville, 228, 231
Fuchs, Klaus, 143
Fujita, Kikuichi, 60

Galbraith, John Kenneth, 242
Gallup poll
  on Jewish issues in 1930s, 70
  on Jewish refugees, 103

Gallup poll (*continued*)
  Kennedy's approval ratings, 218
  on quota system, 240
  Truman's approval ratings, 160
Galvin, Michael J., 170
Gary, Elbert H., 40
genetics, 35
Gentleman's Agreement (movie), 188
Gentlemen's Agreement, 50, 54, 56, 57
George, Walter, 102
German immigrants, 11, 69, 74, 75, 84, 86, 106
German Jews, 4, 11, 69, 71, 73–75, 84
Glass, Alice, 77–80
Goldberg, Arthur J., 216
Goldman Sachs, 147
Goldwater, Barry, 245
Goodman, Abram Vossen, 82–83
Goodwin, Richard, 246
Gore, Albert, Sr., 195
Grant, Madison, 23, 42, 44
Grays Harbor Washingtonian, 27–28
Great Britain, 56, 72, 75, 84, 99, 100, 101–3, 107, 146, 168, 182–83
Great Depression, 21, 66–69, 72, 73, 76, 122
Great Migration, 188–89
Great Society, 246
Greek immigration, 264–65
Greenberg, Walter, 105
Greenfield, Meg, 210
Grew, Joseph, 101
Griffith, D. W., 24
Griffith, Paul H., 112
Grossman, James, 190
Guernica, 135
Gwirtzman, Milt, 243

Haber, William, 114
Hall, Prescott F., 32
Handlin, Oscar, 189–91
Hanihara, Masanao, 56–57
Harding, Warren G., 15, 39, 55
Harriman, Mary, 35–36
Harrison, Earl, 95–99, 101, 107
  and CCDP, 108, 110
  death of, 262
  and Displaced Persons Act (1950), 125

and immigration reform, 184
National Committee on Immigration
    Policy, 155
and 1948 refugee bill, 114
and Abba Schwartz, 221
Harrison, Pat, 131
Hart, Philip, 224, 234, 258, 299
Hart–Celler Act, 258*n*; *See also* Immigration and Nationality Act (1965)
Harvard University, 20, 23, 29, 30, 49, 143, 177, 180, 181, 182, 189, 204, 221, 225, 242
Haskins, Charles Homer, 189
Hatch, Carl, 111
Hawaii
  Japanese immigrants in 1920s, 47
  Takao Ozawa case, 47–48, 50–54, 61
  US annexation of, 48, 51
Head Start, 247
Henry Street Settlement House, 147
Herblock (Herbert Lawrence Block), 137
Heredity in Relation to Eugenics (Davenport), 36
Hero Tales from American History (Roosevelt and Lodge), 29
Hersey, John, 160
Higham, John, 2
Hill, Herbert W., 190
Hiss, Alger, 143, 181
Hitler, Adolf
  as chancellor of Germany, 69
  and Francisco Franco, 135
  Nuremberg Laws, 74
  reaction to Immigration Act (1924), 60
Hobbs, Samuel, 85
Holland, Spessard, 259
Holmes, Oliver Wendell, 38
Holocaust, 88–89
  and Palestine, 103
  resettlement of displaced persons after
      WWII, 95–114
Hoover, Herbert, 14, 66, 73, 85
Hoover, J. Edgar
  Frances Knight and, 222
  Pat McCarran and, 193
  Robert W. Scott McLeod and, 210
  and "suspected enemy aliens" in WWII, 86
Hoover rule, 73–74

Hopkins, William J., 161
Hoquiam, Washington, 27–28
House Immigration Committee, 26,
    28–29, 33–34, 39, 41, 42, 54
House Judiciary Committee
    Emanuel Celler and, 10, 118–19
    and Johnson's legislative agenda, 247
    and Johnson's quota reform, 255–56
    and McCarran–Walter bill, 154
    resettlement of displaced persons after
        WWII, 109–12
House Un-American Activities Commit-
    tee (HUAC), 157, 211–12
housing shortage, 111
"How Can We Win in the Pacific?" (Judd),
    167
Howe, Louis, 149
Hughes, Charles Evans, 55–57
Humphrey, Hubert, 116, 158–60, 174, 195,
    196, 248
    Lyndon Johnson and, 195
    Lyndon Johnson's warnings about liber-
        als, 196
    and McCarran–Walter Act, 158–60, 174
hyphenated Americans, 18–19

Ibn Saud (founder of Saudi Arabia), 100
"I Have a Dream" (King speech), 227
illegal immigration, 269
Immigration Act of 1917, 32
Immigration Act of 1924 (Johnson-Reed
    Act), 54–60
    and Asian immigrants, 162
    and Caribbean immigrants, 180
    and Jewish refugee crisis in WWII, 69,
        75, 85
    and McCarran-Walter Act, 155, 249
    and Western Hemisphere immigration
        debate, 251
Immigration and Nationality Act (1952),
    See McCarran–Walter Act
Immigration and Nationality Act (1965),
    3–5, 259–64, 267–68, 270–71
immigration patterns, 264–65
Immigration Reform and Control Act of
    1986, 269
Immigration Restriction League (IRL),
    30–32

Impellitteri, Vincent R., 140, 186
Indian immigrants, 27, 162, 264, 265
Industrial Workers of the World (IWW),
    28
Internal Security Act (1950), 149–55, 181
Iranian immigrants, 265
Irish Catholic immigrants, 182, 187, 202
IRL (Immigration Restriction League),
    30–32
Ishii Kikujiro, 53
isolationism, 70, 120
Israel, *See* Palestine
issei, 162
Italian-Americans, 244
IWW (Industrial Workers of the World),
    28

JACL, *See* Japanese American Citizens
    League
Jacobson, Eddie, 107
Japan
    Pearl Harbor attack, 86
    reaction to Immigration Act (1924),
        58–59
    war with China in 1930s, 166
Japanese American Citizens League
    (JACL), 161, 164, 165, 169, 173, 175,
    238
Japanese-American internment, 86,
    162–65
Japanese immigrants
    and exclusion clauses in 1924 Immigra-
        tion Act, 162
    Albert Johnson and, 26, 27
    during 1920s, 47–61
    Takao Ozawa case, 50–52
Japanese–Korean Exclusion League, 48, 49
Javits, Jacob, 258
Jenner, William E., 134
Jewish Joint Distribution Committee, 84
Jewish state, *See* Palestine
Jews and Judaism; *See also* anti-Semitism
    college quotas, 23
    and Displaced Persons Act (1950), 140
    immigration after WWI, 29
    and Immigration and Nationality Act
        (1965), 4
    Lyndon Johnson and, 65–68

Jews and Judaism (*continued*)
  John F. Kennedy and, 205
  and John F. Kennedy's first Senate race,
    187
  Ku Klux Klan and, 24
  in 1920s New York, 7–11
  refugees from Europe during WWII,
    68–89
  resettlement of refugees after WWII,
    93–114, 96–110, 113, 114
  Anna Rosenberg confirmation battle,
    142
  John B. Trevor and, 44
Jim Crow laws, 189
John Reed Club, 145–46
Johnson, Albert, 26–29, 32, 34, 39–46, 54,
  55, 59
Johnson, Edwin C., 129
Johnson, Hiram, 56
Johnson, Lady Bird, 62–65, 77, 195, 232,
  261–62, 264
Johnson, Lyndon, and administration
  assumption of presidency, 230–31
  and bracero program, 266–67
  and Civil Rights Act (1964), 241,
    247–48
  and Dominican crisis, 252–53
  James Eastland and, 214–15
  election of 1964, 245
  Michael Feighan and, 235, 240, 250,
    253, 254
  Alice Glass and, 77–78
  and Great Society, 246
  heart attack, 195
  and Immigration and Nationality Act
    (1965), 3
  immigration record while in Congress,
    233
  and immigration reform, 195–200,
    233–34, 255–60
  and Jewish people, 65–68
  and Jewish refugee crisis in WWII, 76,
    80–83, 85–86, 283–84
  Lady Bird Johnson and, 62–64
  Bobby Kennedy and, 243–44
  legislative achievements in 1965, 245–46
  Herbert Lehman and, 195–96

on Pat McCarran, 120, 193–94
McCarran–Walter amendment fight,
  198–200
management of Congress while president, 232–33
signing of Immigration and Nationality
  Act, 259–64
and vice-presidency, 228
Johnson, Paul, 131
Johnson, Sam, 66
Johnson, Sam Houston, 66
Johnson-Reed Act, *See* Immigration Act
  of 1924
joint committee on immigration, 227, 235,
  240, 247, 253–54
Jones, Roger W., 213
Judd, Walter, 166–70
Justice Department, 17, 170, 219–20,
  222–23, 244

Kallen, Horace, 19–22
Kaneko, Baron Kentaro, 49
Kaplan, Jacob, 205
Katzenbach, Nicholas, 223–27, 255, 256,
  258
Keating, Kenneth B., 199, 244
Kefauver, Estes, 174
Kennan, George F., 60
Kennedy, Edward M. "Ted"
  early years, 213–14
  James Eastland and, 216–17
  and Johnson's quota reform, 258, 259
  and Bobby Kennedy, 244
  and John F. Kennedy's assassination, 241
  and *A Nation of Immigrants*, 242–44
  in Oval Office after John F. Kennedy's
    inauguration, 203
  plane crash, 241–42
  at signing of 1965 immigration bill, 262
  and Voting Rights Act (1965), 256–57
Kennedy, Eunice, 179
Kennedy, Joe, Jr., 178
Kennedy, Joe, Sr.
  as ambassador, 176, 180
  anti-Semitism, 182–83
  and competitiveness, 209
  on JFK's popularity, 202

Joe Kennedy, Jr. and, 178
and John F. Kennedy's assassination, 241
and John F. Kennedy's first Senate race, 187
and Ted Kennedy's plane crash, 242
resistance to Irish immigrant past, 176
Kennedy, John F.
assassination of, 228–29, 263
as congressman, 178–82
Dallas trip, 227–28
early days of presidency, 203–8
early years in politics, 176–79
election to presidency, 202
election to Senate, 187
immigration reform as legacy, 243
Lehman and, 200–201
McCarran–Walter Act, 183–84
and Joe McCarthy, 194
national origins quota reform efforts, 208–27
quota reform, 201–2
and quota reform, 196, 200–202
as Senate candidate, 183–87
Kennedy, Kathleen, 179
Kennedy, Robert F. ("Bobby")
James Eastland and, 216
and immigration cases, 204
immigration reform testimony, 238
Lyndon Johnson and, 231, 243–44
and Johnson's quota reform, 259
and John F. Kennedy's assassination, 241
McCarran–Walter Act amendments, 186
Joe McCarthy and, 181
and *A Nation of Immigrants*, 243
as senator, 244
at signing of 1965 immigration bill, 262
Adam Walinsky and, 219–20
Kennedy, Rose, 177–78
Keynes, John Maynard, 94
Kielce, Poland, 106–7
Kilgore, Harley
and Displaced Persons Act (1950), 133–34
James Eastland and, 214
McCarran–Walter amendment fight, 197–98

King, Martin Luther, Jr., 227
Kirchwey, Freda, 69
Kleberg, Richard, 62, 67, 81
Knight, Frances, 222
Korean immigrants, 162
Korean War, 160
Kristallnacht, 75
Ku Klux Klan, 8, 23–24, 25–26, 66, 130
Kurihara, Joe, 164

Labor Department, 15–16, 170–71
labor unions, *See* organized labor
La Follette, Robert, 38–39
La Guardia, Fiorello H., 9, 142–43
Langer, William, 134
Laughlin, Harry, 33–34, 37–39, 41, 44
Lazarus, Emma, 3, 269
Lehman, Edith, 262
Lehman, Emanuel, 146, 147
Lehman, Henry, 146
Lehman, Herbert
on Edward Corsi's firing, 211
death of, 262
early years, 146–48
end of career, 200–201
entry into politics, 147–48
and immigration as topic in 1952, 2
and Internal Security Act, 150–52
Lyndon Johnson and, 195
on Kennedy and national origins quota reform, 207
and John F. Kennedy's first Senate race, 186
and McCarran–Walter Act, 159, 173, 174
and McCarran–Walter amendment fight, 198–200
Joe McCarthy and, 144, 194
as New York lieutenant governor, 148–49
and quota reform, 196–97
Franklin Roosevelt and, 67
Anna Rosenberg confirmation battle, 142, 144, 145
Lehman, Irving, 71–73
Lehman, Mayer, 146, 147
Lehman Brothers, 147

Lehman–Humphrey bill, 159
Leinsdorf, Erich, 79–82, 262–63
Lewis, Fulton, Jr., 145
Life magazine, 113
Lincoln, Abraham, 167
Lindsay, Ronald, 75
literacy bill, 30–31
literacy tests, 30
Lodge, George Cabot, 214
Lodge, Henry Cabot, Jr., 179, 186, 187
Lodge, Henry Cabot, Sr., 29–32, 57–58,
  179–80
Loney, Kate Deadrich, 262
Long, Breckenridge, 87–88
Los Angeles Times, 169
"Lost Battalion," 165
Love, William L., 12
Lower East Side, 7
Loyal Order of Moose, 15, 16
Lucas, Scott, 124–25, 127–28, 133–34, 144
lynching, 25–26

McCarran, Pat, 119–22
  childhood and early years, 120–22
  decline and death of, 192–94
  and Displaced Persons Act (1950),
    125–28, 134, 135
  James Eastland and, 132–33, 214
  election to Senate, 122–23
  European trip, 128–29, 136–37
  and Francisco Franco, 135–36
  immigration policy report, 155
  and Internal Security Act, 149–55
  law career, 121–22
  Herbert Lehman and, 149
  and McCarran–Walter Act, 156–57,
    159–60
  and McCarran–Walter Act veto, 172
  and passage of Displaced Persons Act
    (1950), 140–41
  and *Whom Shall We Welcome* report, 192
McCarran, Patricia, 193
McCarran–Walter Act (Immigration and
  Nationality Act of 1952), 153–62,
  170–75
  and immigration reform, 184–85
  Lyndon Johnson's support for, 233

Kennedy administration's attempts at
  amending, 210–11, 222–23
John F. Kennedy and, 183–84
and quotas, 249
Walter's resistance to changes in, 209–10
in *Whom Shall We Welcome* report,
  191–92
McCarthy, Joseph, 119–20
  downfall of, 194
  and Franco, 135
  Bobby Kennedy and, 244
  John F. Kennedy and, 181
  Anna Rosenberg confirmation battle,
    145, 146
  and vetting of State Department
    employees, 151–52
  Wheeling, West Virginia, speech, 143
McCarthyism; *See also* House Un-Ameri-
  can Activities Committee (HUAC)
  Herbert Lehman and, 146
  in State Department, 221
  Francis Walter and, 211–12
McClatchy, V. S., 55
Macdonald, Torby, 187
MacGregor, Clark, 254
McKim, Edward D., 95
McKinley, William, 48
McLeod, Robert W. Scott, 210
McMahon, Brien, 144
Manatos, Mike, 257
Manzanar internment camp, 164
Mao Zedong, 136
March on Washington for Jobs and Free-
  dom (1963), 227
Marsh, Charles, 76–80
Marshall, George C., 112, 142
Marshall, Herbert, 128
Marshall, Thurgood, 168
Marshall Plan, 136
Masaoka, Eijiro, 163
Masaoka, Etsu, 169
Masaoka, Mike, 161–66, 169, 173–75, 238,
  262
"Meaning of Americanism, A" (Kallen), 20
Meany, George, 239
Medicaid, 247
Medicare, 247, 262

Meiji government, 48, 49

Meiklejohn, Kenneth A., 239–40

Mein Kampf (Hitler), 60

Mellon, Andrew W., 45

Melting Pot, The (Zangwill), 17–18

"melting pot," 18–22, 32

Mendel, Gregor, 35

Menorah Society, 20

Messersmith, George, 83

Metropolitan Opera, 80

Meuse-Argonne campaign, 92

Mexican immigrants, 4–5, 46, 70, 266–67

Mexico, 83, 250–52

Migration and Refugee Assistance Act, 217

Military Intelligence Division (U.S. Army), 44

Miller, Arthur, 212

Moore, Arch, 235

Moreland, Allen B., 220

Morgenthau, Henry
    and Oswego, New York, displaced
        persons camp, 106
    and Palestine, 103
    Roosevelt and, 88–89
    Truman and, 94–95, 103, 106

Morse, Wayne, 195

Moss, Edward, 241, 242

multiculturalism, 267–68

Mundt, Karl E., 185, 222

Munemori, Sadeo, 168

Nation, The, 20

National Association for the Advancement
    of Colored People (NAACP), 189, 215

National Association of Manufacturers, 40

National Committee on American-Japa-
    nese Relations, 55

National Committee on Immigration Pol-
    icy, 155–56

nationalism
    after WWI, 31
    during Great Depression, 21
    and *The Melting Pot*, 18
    and Zionism, 99

national origins quota system, 39–46; *See
    also specific legislation, e.g.:* Immigra-
    tion Act of 1924

    and displaced persons after WWII,
        106–8
    and evolving concepts of race, 188
    Michael Feighan's view of, 249–50
    as inimical to Cold War policy goals,
        237–38
    and Jewish refugee crisis in WWII, 65,
        68–70, 73–75, 81, 83–85, 89
    and Kennedy administration, 223–27
    and 1960 Democratic platform, 206
    public opinion in 1965, 240
    Truman's view of, 171–72

National Pencil Company, 24–26

National Reclamation Act, 251

National Youth Administration, 67

Nation of Immigrants, A (Kennedy), 205,
    224–25, 227, 242–43

"nation of immigrants," 269–70

nativism, 70

Naval Reserve, 86

Nazi Germany
    and eugenics, 35
    and Jewish refugee crisis, 68–89
    Joe Kennedy and, 182–83
    Spain and, 135

New Deal, 67, 76, 146

New York City, 7–13, 18–19

New York Times
    and Leo Frank case, 25
    immigration survey, 14
    support for 1950 Displaced Persons Act,
        139

Niebuhr, Reinhold, 151

Niles, David, 110

Ninth Circuit Court of Appeals, 52–53

nisei, 162, 164, 169

Nixon, Richard M.
    and election of 1960, 204
    and Internal Security Act, 151
    John F. Kennedy and, 179, 181–82, 208

Nixopedia, 204

Nokrashy, Mahmud Fahmy el-, 101

Nordic race, 32

Novy, Jim, 67–68

Novy, Sam, 82

Nowodworski, Gela, 82

Nuremberg Laws, 74

O'Brien, Larry, 231, 232, 236, 240, 255–57
Ochs, Adolph, 25
O'Connor, Edward, 225–26
Oddie, Tasker, 122
O'Hara, Barratt, 248
Olsen, Ed, 192–93
Oltorf, Frank, 77
One Nation Library, 205
Operation Abolition (film), 212
Orange County, California, 266
organized labor, 15, 26, 146, 238–40
Osborn, Henry Fairfield, 35
Oswego, New York, displaced persons
  camp, 105–6
Ozawa, George, 61
Ozawa, Masako, 61
Ozawa, Takao, 47–48, 50–55, 61

Pacific Coast Japanese Association Delib-
  erative Council, 53
Pacific Northwest, 27–28
Palestine, 99–103, 107, 108
Paplonskis, Vaclovas, 140
Paris, 59, 129
Passing of the Great Race, The (Grant), 23
Passport to Nowhere (movie), 112–13
Pastore, John O., 173, 201
Patton, George S., 98
Paul, Randolph, 88–89
Pearl Harbor, 60, 86
Pearson, Drew, 138, 235
Peck, Gregory, 188
Pehle, John, 88–89
Pendergast, Tom, 92
Perkins, Frances, 74
Perlman, Philip B., 185–86
Petersen, Pete, 123
Peterssen, Arne, 1
Phagan, Mary, 24–26
Philippines, 48
Phillips, William, 74
Picasso, Pablo, 135
Pioneer Fund, 236
Pittman, Key, 122
pluralism, 20–21, 270
Poland, 42, 43, 69, 82, 83, 106–7, 113
Portugal, 201
Powell, Adam Clayton, Jr., 168

Presidential Medal of Freedom, 262
President's Committee on Civil Rights,
  189–92
Profiles in Courage (Kennedy), 200–201
Progressive era, 21
Prohibition, 12, 24
Promised Land, The (Antin), 19
Proskauer, Joseph, 108, 109
Protocols of the Elders of Zion, 22
"public charge," 31, 73, 74, 80, 105
public opinion polls
  on Jewish issues in 1930s, 70
  on Jewish refugees, 75, 103
  Kennedy's approval ratings, 218
  on quota system, 240
  Truman's approval ratings, 160
Pythian Temple protest meeting (1935), 71

Quin, Frank J., 111
quota system, *See* national origins quota
  system

race and racism
  at end of WWII, 115–16
  in eugenics, 36–37
  shifting contours of, 187–89
  Tulsa riots, 22–23
race riots, 22–23
racial homogeneity, 43
Randolph, A. Philip, 170–71
Rankin, John, 145
Rayburn, Sam, 117, 199
Reagan, Ronald, 268–69
"Red Summer" (1919), 23
Reed, David A., 3, 45–46, 54, 58
refugees; *See also specific legislation*
  and exceptions to McCarran-Walter Act
    limitations, 201
  and Internal Security Act (1950), 152–53
  Jewish refugee crisis during WWII, 65,
    68–70, 73–75, 79–85, 89
  Jewish refugee resettlement after WWII,
    93–114
  John F. Kennedy and, 217
"Report to the Secretary on the Acqui-
  escence of this Government in the
  Murder of the Jews" (Treasury report),
  88–89

Republican Party, 26, 109, 186, 196, 206, 209, 245

Revercomb, William Chapman, 110–11, 113

Reynolds, Robert, 85

Roberts, Kenneth, 9

Robeson, Paul, 221

Robison, John, 161

Rockne, Knute, 126

Rodino, Peter, 255

Rogers, Edith, 85

Romania, 69

Roosevelt, Eleanor
and CCDP, 108
and Displaced Persons Act (1950), 139
Walter Judd and, 167
Herbert Lehman and, 149
Abba Schwartz and, 221
and Wagner–Rogers bill, 85

Roosevelt, Franklin Delano, and administration
death of, 89
and Japanese-American internment, 162–63
and Jewish Americans, 67
and Jewish refugee crisis in WWII, 68–75, 81, 83–89
Lyndon Johnson and, 64, 233
Joe Kennedy and, 176
Herbert Lehman and, 147–49
Pat McCarran and, 123, 127, 135
and Palestine, 100
Abba Schwartz and, 221
and Statue of Liberty, 259

Roosevelt, Theodore "Teddy," and administration
and "Americanism," 18–19
and Japanese immigrants, 49–50
Henry Cabot Lodge and, 29
and *The Melting Pot*, 17–18
and National Reclamation Act, 251

Rosenberg, Anna, 142–46

Rosenberg, Julius and Ethel, 143, 145

Rosenfield, Harry N., 153, 171, 184

Rosenfield, Leonora, 193

Rural Electrification Administration, 76

Rusk, Dean
immigration reform testimony, 237–38
as member of Johnson administration, 231
on news of John F. Kennedy's assassination, 228
and Western Hemisphere quotas, 253, 258

Russell, Richard, 107–8

Russian Jews, 17–18

Russo-Japanese War, 49

Sabath, Adolph, 42, 54

St. Louis incident, 84

Salinger, Pierre, 203

Salzburg Festival, 79

Sammis, Edward, 225

Sanders, Everett, 57

San Francisco, California, 48–52

San Francisco earthquake (1906), 48–49

Sanger, Margaret, 35

Sargeant, Howland H., 184–85

Saturday Evening Post, 8–9, 40, 41

Saudi Arabia, 100

Saxons, 29–30

Schacht, Hjalmar, 71–72

Schlei, Norbert, 219, 222–23, 226, 250, 252, 255

Schlesinger, Arthur, Jr., 204, 215, 227

Schlesinger, Arthur, Sr., 189–90

Schmitz, Eugene, 48, 50

Schroeder, Gustav, 84

Schwartz, Abba, 220–23, 227, 234, 237, 250, 255

Seeger, Pete, 212

segregation, 49–50, 132, 133, 215

Senate Armed Services Committee, 142–46

Senate Democratic Policy Committee, 199

Senate Immigration Committee, 43–44, 107

Senate Judiciary Committee
and Displaced Persons Act (1950), 125
James Eastland and, 214–16
and Johnson's quota reform, 257–59
Pat McCarran and, 119–20, 193
and refugee bill, 110–11

"Send Them Here!" (*Life* editorial), 113

Sessions, Jeff, 268

Shaughnessy, Edward J., 1

Shortridge, Samuel, 56

Simmons, William J., 24–26

Slaton, John, 25
Smathers, George, 179
Smith, Al, 148
Smith, Gerald L. K., 145
Sorensen, Ted, 204, 205, 227, 231
South Asian immigrants, 27, 162
southern European immigrants, 8, 9, 28, 30, 42, 44, 45, 59, 67, 132, 185, 197, 264
Southern Manifesto, 200
Southern US
  and civil rights, 241, 247
  and Democratic Party, 124, 132–33, 196, 200, 209, 214–15, 241, 245, 256, 257
  and Ku Klux Klan, 23–24
Soviet refugees, 140
Soviet Union, 107, 111, 113, 143, 151, 153
Spanish–American War, 48
Spellman, Cardinal Francis, 135
sponsorship of refugees, 105
Stalin, Joseph, 107
State Department, U.S.
  Edward Corsi and, 210–11
  and displaced persons, 95
  and Jewish refugee crisis during WWII, 69, 73–75, 82–84, 87–88
  and Kennedy administration's immigration reform, 220–23
  and McCarran–Walter Act, 170
  Joe McCarthy's accusations of Communists in, 143
  and Palestine, 101
  Truman's fight with Joe McCarthy over vetting of employees, 151–52
State of the Union speech (1961), 207, 209
State of the Union speech (1965), 246
States' Rights Democratic Party, 133; *See also* Dixiecrats
Statue of Liberty, 269
Statue of Liberty, signing of Johnson's immigration bill at, 259–64
sterilization laws, 38
Stettinius, Edward R., Jr., 108
Stevenson, Adlai, 184
Stimson, Henry, 165
Stoddard, Lothrop, 188

Stratton, William G., 110–14
Subversive Activities Control Board, 150
Summer Olympics (1936), 71
Supe, Zinaida, 140
Supreme Court, US
  Buck v. Bell, 38
  and Internal Security Act, 153
  Takao Ozawa v. United States, 53–54
  Franklin Roosevelt's attempt at court-packing, 123
Sutherland, George, 53–54
Sutton, Billy, 179
Sweeney, Martin, 225
Swift, Wesley, 145
Syntilas, Dennis C., 264–65

Tacoma News, 27
Taft, Robert A., 134, 186
Taft, William Howard, 15, 30, 53
Takao Ozawa v. United States, 53–54
Takemura, Thomas S., 173
tax cuts, 233
Tayama, Fred, 164
Taylor, Claudia, *See* Johnson, Lady Bird
Taylor, Elizabeth, 226
Texas, 250–51, 265, 266
Thompson, Dorothy, 64
Thompson, J. Wesley, 52
Thurmond, Strom, 116, 124, 133, 258–59
Toscanini, Arturo, 79
Treasury Department, 88–89
Trevor, John B., Jr., 236
Trevor, John B., Sr., 44–45, 112, 236
Trujillo, Rafael, 252
Truman, Bess, 118
Truman, Harry S., and administration, 90–110
  agenda after 1948 election, 124
  assumption of presidency, 90
  and charity at Christmas, 103–4
  and civil rights, 189
  and Committee on Civil Rights, 189
  and Displaced Persons Act (1950), 139–40
  early years, 91–93
  James Eastland and, 133

election of 1948, 115–18
fight with Joe McCarthy over vetting of
   State Department employees, 151–52
Oscar Handlin and, 190
and immigration reform, 184–85
and Internal Security Act, 151
Jewish refugee survey, 93–94
Walter Judd and, 169–70
John F. Kennedy and, 181
Pat McCarran and, 126–27, 136
and McCarran–Walter Act, 160–61,
   171–72, 174
at Medicare Act signing, 262
at 1948 Democratic National convention, 116–17
and 1948 refugee bill, 114
and Oswego, New York, displaced persons camp, 105–6
and Palestine, 99–103, 107
and refugees as Cold War issue, 109–10,
   112
as vice president, 90–91
on *Whom Shall We Welcome* report, 192
Truman, John, 91
Truman, Margaret, 116
Trump, Donald, and administration,
   267–69
Tulsa, Oklahoma, race riots, 22–23
Tyler, Elizabeth, 26

Ulman, Leon, 219
undocumented immigrants, 269
unions, *See* organized labor
United Nations, 120
Uprooted, The (Handlin), 190
U.S. Steel, 40

Vaile, William N., 34
Valenti, Jack, 232, 235–36, 240, 252, 253,
   258
Vance, Rupert, 131
Veterans of Foreign Wars, 103
Vietnam War, 248, 264
Virginia, 266
Volstead Act, 12
Voting Rights Act (1965), 247–48, 256–57

Wagner, Robert, 85, 100
Wagner–Rogers bill, 85
Walinsky, Adam, 219–20, 222–23
Wallace, Henry A., 90, 91
Walter, Bruno, 79
Walter, Francis
   death of, 223
   Michael Feighan and, 235
   and HUAC, 211–12
   and Kennedy administration's attempts
      at immigration reform, 209–13,
      220–23
   and John F. Kennedy appointees,
      212–13
   and McCarran–Walter Act, 156–58
   and McCarran–Walter Act amendment
      fight, 199, 209–11
   opposition to quota reform, 197
War Brides Act (1945), 162
War Refugee Board, 89, 95, 105
Warren, Earl, 200
Washington, D. C., 26
Washington Naval Treaty, 56
Washington Post, The, 27, 118, 139
Watts, T. H., 147
Weisgal, Meyer, 95
Weizmann, Chaim, 95
Welles, Sumner, 75
West Coast, 47
Western Hemisphere, 250–54, 257–58,
   266–67
While England Slept (Kennedy), 180
White, Byron R., 216
white nationalists, 188
whiteness, 23, 36, 53, 188
Whom Shall We Welcome (Commission
   on Immigration and Naturalization
   report), 191–92
Why Europe Leaves Home (Roberts), 9
Wickersham, George W., 53, 55
Wiley, Alexander, 119
Wilson, Henry H., 240, 255
Wilson, Woodrow
   Birth of a Nation screening, 24
   Charles Evans Hughes and, 55
   and Labor Department, 15

Wilson, Woodrow (*continued*)
  literacy bill veto, 30–31
  and WWI, 21
Wingfield, George, 122
Winter, Hermann, 82–83
Wise, Stephen F., 42, 75, 101
Wood, John, 157–58
Woods, Cyrus E., 59
Works Progress Administration (WPA), 76
World War I
  domestic effects, 21–22
  Charles Evans Hughes and, 55–56
  and Labor Department, 15
  Harry Truman and, 91–92, 97–98

World War II
  Japanese-American internment, 86,
    162–65
  Jewish refugee crisis, 68–89
  Spain in, 135–36
  Francis Walter and, 157
WPA (Works Progress Administration),
  76

Zangwill, Israel, 17–18, 43
zero tolerance, 269
Zimny, Ed, 241–42
Zionism, 95, 99–103, 107, 108; *See also*
  Palestine